❡ A work of unquestioned value to those who are seeking an intelligent knowledge of Holy Scripture, by one of the foremost of living expositors. Out of the experience of a full and faithful ministry Dr. Haldeman enlarges on a number of principles which make for a comprehensive and satisfactory study of the Bible. He believes and maintains that the New Testament is a fulfilment of the Old, and that each book of the entire Bible finds place and value by the law of growth—and by a moral and spiritual logic. Special attention is given by Dr. Haldeman to Dispensational Truth, of which he is one of the foremost protagonists of the day.

NEW YORK CITY

PREFACE

This work was originally issued as "Friday Night Papers."

A second edition having been called for, the name was then changed to that of the leading article, "How To Study The Bible." Some two hundred pages were added and the order of contents considerably changed. The original title was due to a series of letters written and sent to the Friday Evening Meetings of the Church during the summer vacation. The last four articles are simply notes of sermons preached in the First Church pulpit. The one on the "Second Coming" was delivered as an address before the Baptist Ministers' Conference. "The Imminent Coming" appeared in the *Examiner*. The other contents are made up of Bible lessons and expositions given from time to time in the course of a rather full ministry.

No attempt has been made at sequence. The papers are just a handful gathered at random and flung like leaves—to be blown about by the winds of God's providence—and with the earnest prayer that, in some measure like the leaves of the Tree of Life, they may be for healing and blessing to the souls of men.

I. M. H.

NEW YORK.

PREFACE

This work was originally issued as "Friday Night Papers."

A second edition having been called for, the name was then changed to that of the leading article, "How To Study The Bible." Some two hundred pages were added and the order of contents considerably changed. The original title was due to a series of letters written and sent to the Friday Evening Meetings of the Church during the summer vacation. The last four articles are simply notes of sermons preached in the First Church pulpit. The one on the "Second Coming," was delivered as an address before the Baptist Ministers' Conference. "The Imminent Coming," appeared in the Examiner. The other contents are made up of Bible lessons and expositions given from time to time in the course of a rather full ministry.

No attempt has been made at sequence. The papers are just a handful gathered at random and flung like leaves—to be blown about by the winds of God's providence—and with the earnest prayer that, in some measure, like the leaves of the Tree of Life, they may be for healing and blessing to the souls of men.

J. M. H.

New York.

CONTENTS.

CONTENTS—Continued.

HOW TO STUDY THE BIBLE.

How to Study the Bible.

"Study to shew thyself approved unto God, a workman that needeth not to be ashamed, rightly dividing the word of truth." —II Tim. ii : 15.

In order to an intelligent and satisfactory study of the Bible there are at least eight principles which must be applied to it.

First, we must recognize that the Bible is written to, or about distinct classes.

Second, we must inquire of each Scripture, whether book, section, or passage, to whom it is written, and righteously give to each the portion belonging to it.

Third, we must know Dispensational Truth.

Fourth, we must put truth in its proper dispensational relation.

Fifth, we must know the distinction between things which appear similar, but are different.

Sixth, we must know the meaning and purport of each book of the Bible.

Seventh, we must know how to divide each book into its component parts.

Eighth, we must recognize that each book finds its place by the law of growth and by moral and spiritual logic; so that it is impossible to take any book out of its place without deranging the whole order of revelation.

Two other observations may be made, namely : that the New Testament is the fulfillment of the Old and therefore many of its books must be, and are, commentaries on the Old; and further, that each book has its own key hung up by the door.

DISTINCT CLASSES.

We must recognize that the Bible is written to, or about distinct classes.

According to the general view everything from Genesis to Revelation is written to, or about the church and Christians.

No greater mistake could be made. The truth is, the church and Christians occupy a very restrained area of the Bible.

If all that is said directly about the church and Christians was printed by itself it would make a very small book.

Not even all of the New Testament is directly written to, or about the church.

In his Epistle to the Corinthians the Apostle speaks of Jew, Gentile, and the Church of God. I Corinthians x: 32.

The Bible is written to, or about one or other of these classes. Sometimes in the same book there are things which belong to all three, or have application to them either as object or subject. Sometimes there are books which belong to one class and rigidly exclude the others either as subject or object. By this is not meant that all Scripture is not profitable for doctrine, reproof, or correction, for we are definitely told that all things which happened to the Children of Israel happened unto them that they might be as types full of instruction to us upon whom the ends of the ages have come, and that the whole Bible from end to end is intended for the profit and furnishing of the man of God unto all good works; it is meant to say, however, that in every Scripture one or other of these classes has priority of claim and that the truth must first be considered in the light of its original relation before its profit can be more extendedly applied. My friend may receive a letter intended exclusively for him; and yet when he hands it to me to read I may discover something quite necessary for me to know, some lessons and truths well enough for me to apply; but even then I would never dream of claiming that the letter was first written to, or about me.

Each class therefore, Jew, Gentile, and Church of God, is the primary subject or object of some particular form or accent of truth; and we must recognize this classification in any endeavor we may make towards the study of Holy Scripture.

TO WHOM IS IT WRITTEN?

We must inquire of each Scripture to whom it is written and give to each class the portion of truth belonging to it.

We have no right to take truth from one class and give it to another: to do so is as much an act of robbery as it would be to go into a man's house, steal his coat, and wear it forth as ours. And yet this robbery has been carried on in the most extensive way by preachers and teachers of the Word.

In no case has this been more marked than in relation to the promises of Israel. Whole sections, chapters, and passages have been taken bodily from the Jew and transferred without compunction to the church and Christians.

It is a common thing to take the sixtieth chapter of Isaiah which speaks of the time when the Jew shall be the head and no longer the tail of nations; when Jerusalem shall be exalted as the capital of the whole earth and the wealth of the Gentiles like a rising tide shall pour into it; it is common to take all this and apply it to the church and Christians.

Again and again it is read in Missionary meetings and preached from as the assurance given by God Himself that the world will be converted by the Gospel and the church exalted to reign in glory over all nations. Mount Zion is made to mean the church. Jews mean Christians, and the Gentiles coming in with their riches the vast multitude of converts yielding to the truth of the Word, the conviction of the Spirit, and the power of missionary zeal.

And for all this not a single ground or warrant. The Jew is never called a Christian any more than he is known as a Gentile, nor has Mount Zion any more reason to be called the church than Bunker Hill to stand for Westminster Abbey. Out of this robbery a whole system of modern theology lives and thrives, finding its only sustenance in the plunder it has obtained by taking from the Jew the promises which God has so solemnly given to him, and to him alone.

When you receive a letter, the first thing to do is to look at its superscription, find out to whom it is addressed, and respect that address by giving it to the owner.

Such a procedure would save from the disastrous results of misplacing truth; and that this misplacement is disastrous is in evidence.

I heard an earnest sermon from the text, "Work out your own salvation with fear and trembling." The preacher with the profoundest conviction that he was doing the will of God echoed the thunders of Sinai and belched its lightnings over the heads of his hearers, insisting that in order to salvation each soul must toil and labor with strong crying and tears to win the Divine favor, and then tremble at the last, lest with all its efforts it should fail to win the salvation it had so

laboriously sought. If the preacher had inquired as to
whom this exhortation was written he would have been
delivered from the misplacement of truth and the dark-
ening of counsel with words without knowledge. The
text in question occurs in an epistle. It is written to
those who are saved, to those whose names are in the
Book of Life. It is written to the church at Philippi
and is an exhortation to those who by the grace of God
already possess salvation to work it out. It is not
an exhortation to work *to* salvation but *from* it. It is
an exhortation to take this salvation and work it out
in our daily lives in such fashion that God may be glorified in us; trembling, that is to say filled with a sense
of carefulness lest in any manner we should obscure the
glory of our salvation, but at the same time fully assured
in our endeavor to live the Christian life by the fact that
in all our *working,* "it is God that worketh in us to
will and do of His own good pleasure."

Take up the Epistle to the Corinthians.

There are many things said in that portion of Scripture which commentators endeavor to explain by local
conditions, such as the order of the ordinances, prayer,
and the public attitude of women in the churches. A
glance at the superscription will demonstrate that the
book is anything but local. The superscription reads:
"to ALL who in EVERY PLACE call upon the name of our
Lord Jesus Christ." So far from being local therefore the
application is as much to Galatia, Rome, or Ephesus. It
is as much for the Twentieth Century as the First, as
much for New York as for Corinth.

In the Epistle of James there are some marked things
about the calling together of the elders and the anoint-
ing with oil. This epistle is written to the TWELVE TRIBES

scattered abroad. A reading of its contents in the light of its superscription might change certain expositions not altogether excuseless for the vagaries of "faith healing."

The Book of the Revelation is not infrequently characterized as dark, difficult to understand and wholly impracticable. And yet the title of the book ought to contradict all such judgment, seeing that it is actually called the *Apokalupsis,* which signifies the UNVEILING, the revealing; while the superscription testifies as to its most practical character not only by the constantly reiterated exhortation, "He that hath an ear to hear, let him hear what the Spirit saith to the churches," but by the superscription itself; for that superscription is "The Revelation of Jesus Christ, which God gave to Him, to show unto His SERVANTS."

His servants are His workmen, working in His Word; and as He through an Apostle exhorts them to so divide that Word that they may not be ashamed before Him but be approved at His coming, it may be said without fear of controversy that He could not send a specially inspired, impracticable, and incomprehensible message to these servants.

The superscription then manifests that the book is for practical purposes and that he who takes it up with the inquiry on his lips, "To whom is this written," will find in the clearness of the answer the justification of the Apostle's exhortation to rightly divide the Word of Truth.

"Study to show thyself approved unto God, a workman that needeth not to be ashamed, rightly dividing the Word of Truth." II Timothy ii; 15.

DISPENSATIONAL TRUTH.

No matter what may be the equipment of the Christian, no matter what intellectual, moral, or spiritual endowment he may have, unless he understands dispensational truth he will never fully lay hold of Bible doctrine; while many of the wondrous testimonies of the Word will be unto him but as the tangled threads in an endless labyrinth.

The warrant for the word "Dispensation" is to be found in Ephesians iii: 2., and Colossians i: 25.

The Greek word for dispensation is *oikonomia,* from which we get our English word economy, system, administration.

Such a word carries with it necessarily the idea of time, a period, an epoch, or age.

From the Bible point of view a dispensation is a definite period or epoch in which God makes manifest some characteristic dealing with man; dealing in one age or epoch distinctly from that of another and with different individuals or classes; revealing in each of these distinct dealings and administrations various and separate principles, various objectives and purposes.

To confound these dispensations, to take the principle of action revealed in one and apply it indiscriminately to another, to ignore the classes of persons and the peculiar aim of each dispensation is to produce confusion, contradiction, and lay the foundation for that disharmony which reigns all too manifestly to-day among Christian expositors.

There are eight dispensations, each having a stated point of departure, and an equally defined place of ending.

THE EDENIC DISPENSATION, beginning at Genesis i:

26, with the creation of man, and ending at Genesis iii: 24, with the expulsion of man.

In this dispensation man is seen as innocent, but untried.

He is at once tested for headship and as the expression of God's governmental authority in the earth. God tests him in His word and declared will. The actual test is whether man will abide by, and rest in what God has said, or lean to his own understanding. Whether he will take the Word of God or the dictates of reason as the standard and rule of his life.

The instrument of the test is necessarily the tree of knowledge; the agent in the test is that Old Serpent which is called Satan and the Devil.

Satan puts the test in the form of a temptation. The temptation is made by *raising a question as to what God has said.*

He does not at first openly deny God's Word, he acts in a very much more modern and hypercritical way; he simply *suggests a doubt as to its authenticity:* "Hath God said?"

That is to say, is this so, is it really after all the Word of God? Then he criticises the unreasonableness of the statement, makes light of its threatenings, swiftly passes on to its open denial and repudiation, and finally declares that man ought to act independently, and for himself.

Man yields to the Devil's subtlety and believes his lie rather than God's truth. He puts sight in the place of faith, exalts his own will instead of the will of God, and by this gets that from which God would have delivered him, the knowledge of sin.

The Edenic dispensation then is man tested and found self-willed rather than God-willed.

THE ANTEDILUVIAN DISPENSATION begins at Genesis iv: 1, with the birth of Cain, and ends at Genesis viii: 3, with the subsidence of the flood.

Man is here without law and under the reign of conscience, conscience coming in not as an original endowment from God, but as an evidence of sin, and as its Nemesis.

There is no restraint put upon the flesh. .The flesh is allowed of God to work itself out. It does work itself out till it becomes a stench in the nostrils of God.

God's testimony in the Edenic dispensation is the tree as seen in Genesis ii: 16, 17. In the Antediluvian dispensation the testimony is the Ark, as indicated in Hebrews xi: 7.

The Antediluvian dispensation gives us man turned over to his own will.

In this dispensation we have a declaration concerning the operation of the Spirit which illustrates the distinctive attitude of God in different dispensations and emphasizes the necessity of knowing dispensational application for truth. In Genesis vi: 3, it is written: "And the Lord said, my Spirit shall not always strive with man."

The text is applied again and again in our times to awaken, to alarm, and to exhort the sluggish sinner to lay hold on the grace of God. And he is assured that if he does not so lay hold the Spirit of God will take his "sad flight" and leave him forever.

Such teaching is in itself absolutely pernicious, opposed to the whole trend of this dispensation, contradictory to the Grace of God; and he who so teaches makes manifest that he is fumbling with instead of expounding the Word of God. An examination of the pas-

sage in question will show that it belongs exclusively to
the Antediluvian dispensation and can belong nowhere
else.   According to Genesis third this striving took place
in the days of Noah.   It was to last One Hundred and
Twenty years.   It was to last till the flood came.

It was to last during the testimony of warning that
God should give the antediluvians, and did so last till
the Antediluvian dispensation itself ended.   The doctrine here taught in general is that the striving of the
Spirit is limited, not individually, but dispensationally,
and that this particular striving concerns the Antediluvian dispensation alone, that it can in no way support
the theory that the Spirit plays fast and loose with the
sinner in this hour of grace.   Own this doctrine of the
striving of the Spirit as belonging to the age of Noah,
keep it there that it may not uselessly invade and spoil
the truth of the Spirit in this age, and in doing that the
order of dispensational distinction will be maintained.

THE PATRIARCHAL DISPENSATION begins at Genesis
viii : 18, with the going-forth of Noah out of the Ark, and
ends at Genesis 1 : 26, with the death of Joseph.

God is now seen dealing with selected families and
ruling for righteousness in the headship thereof, that is
to say through the father, the father being the depository
of revelation, and standing for the family in responsibility to God.   The characteristic principle is election.
God looks upon the world of idolators and alone of His
good pleasure selects Abraham to be the beginning of the
Family of Faith in the earth. (Joshua xxiv : 2, 3.)

This dispensation presents us with four forms of spiritual life as illustrated in the four Patriarchs.

In Abraham you have Faith.

In Isaac, the fruit of faith which is Sonship.

In Jacob, the fruit of sonship which is Service.

In Joseph the fruit of service, that is to say Glory and Rule.

THE MOSAIC DISPENSATION begins at Exodus xiv: 22, with the going-forth of the Children of Israel out of Egypt, and ends at Matthew xi: 13, with the coming of John the Baptist.

As in a previous dispensation God called out and separated unto Himself one family, even as in the dispensation previous to that He had called into view one man, so now He calls out and separates unto Himself one nation. He calls it out to be the memorial of His grace, the witness of His unity, and the inheritor of His unconditional covenant.

The nation despises Grace and puts itself under Law, and henceforth the Law becomes the basis of relationship between Israel and God. The Sabbath is for the first time given as a commandment, and thus both the Law and the Sabbath belong exclusively and dispensationally to Israel.

To take the Law and the Sabbath out of the Mosaic dispensation and enforce them in this age and dispensation of the church and Spirit is as excuseless a bit of confounding as it would be to teach in our public schools that the period of discovery in American history corresponded in all principles and applications with the period of colonization. It would be just as sensible to place the battle of Bunker Hill and the landing of Columbus in the same year as to put Mount Sinai in the same dispensation with Calvary.

THE MESSIANIC DISPENSATION begins at John i: 28, 31, with the Baptism of Jesus, and ends at John xix: 30, with the Cross.

God manifests Himself in the flesh. He comes down in His Son and fulfills the covenant promise made to Israel. (Matthew xv: 24. Romans xv: 8. Galatians iv: 4, 5.)

As a messenger of the covenant Christ comes only to the lost sheep of the house of Israel, characteristically refuses to listen to the Gentile woman when she appeals to Him on Jewish ground, and bids His disciples not to go into the way of, nor to preach the good news of the Messiah to any of the Gentiles.

The Holy Ghost Dispensation begins *secretly,* at John xx: 22, with the breathing on of the Holy Ghost, and thus the coming of the Comforter. It begins *publicly,* at Acts ii: 1-4, with the coming of the Holy Ghost to Israel as the Power promised to them through the prophet Joel. It ends *secretly,* at I Thessalonians v: 2, with the Rapture, or sudden, secret Translation of the church into the air to meet the Parousia of Christ, and ends *publicly,* at Revelation xix: 11-20; xx: 1-2, with the appearing of Christ and the binding of Satan.

God at once begins dealing with man in grace on the basis of the cross as a sacrifice for sin, and invites to faith in a Risen and Ascended Man.

Having concluded the whole world under sin and set aside the Jew nationally, He no longer deals with nations as such, but with individuals, and through the Gospel and the Spirit is calling them out of all nations to form a peculiar body, the Church, the spiritual temple, the habitation and dwelling place of God on earth.

The object of this dispensation is not the conversion of the world but the calling-out of it those who from before its foundation were ordained to eternal life and glory.

To that end the Gospel is to be a proclamation made in all the world, and to every creature.

The dispensation of the Holy Ghost stands over against the Messianic in this that while in the Messianic he is seen walking on the earth in the flesh, in this dispensation He is no longer seen, and yet through the Spirit just as really walks it as though He were flesh clothed before our very eyes. He is on the throne as to body, the Man in the Glory, but by the proxy of the Spirit is in the church, and individually in every person who has been made a partaker of His life.

The question of sin having been settled at the cross according to the demands of Divine righteousness, of which the resurrection of Christ is the infallible witness, it is no longer the Sin question but the Son question which is at issue between God and man. "What think ye of Christ, whose Son is He?" That is the supreme question on the answer of which turns all of heaven or hell.

In this dispensation it is not a question of what you are, but what Christ is. And the Grace of God is so absolute, the power of the Holy Ghost is so imminent that it is written: "If thou shalt confess with thy mouth the Lord Jesus, and believe in thine heart that God hath raised Him from the dead, thou shalt be saved." Romans x: 9.

Under no other dispensation can or will such conditions of salvation prevail.

THE DISPENSATION OF THE TIMES OF RESTITUTION begins with the Appearing of Christ and the Binding of Satan, and ends according to I Corinthians xv: 24, when Christ as the Second Man, the Last Adam, shall deliver up the world restored and regenerated to the Father.

This dispensation has two parts:

1. The Thousand Years, or the Millennium.
2. After the Thousand Years.

The Thousand Years begin with the binding of Satan, at Revelation xx: 1, 2, and end at Revelation xx: 7, with the loosing of Satan.

The Thousand Years is exclusively the Day of Christ, while the whole period of the Times of Restitution inclusive of the Thousand Years is the Day of the Lord, the Last Day.

In the Thousand Years Jerusalem is the Capital of the world, Christ is the King of Israel and the King of nations, and personally and visibly seated in Jerusalem rules through united Israel as the ordained head of the nations over the whole earth.

It is a time not of grace, but righteousness. The Lord rules with a rod of iron and dashes in pieces as a potter's vessel. The people learn righteousness not by the Gospel, but by judgments.

It is the display and administration of a pure government in the hands of a righteous Man. It is the kingdom come upon earth. It is the kingdom whose source of power is heaven, and not earth.

After the Thousand Years, is undefined as to length.

In it Satan is loosed, tests the flesh finally, brings out its failure under any and all circumstances, and himself meets the eternal doom. The fourth and last Judgment, the judgment of the White Throne is set up, there is a great conflagration, the second resurrection, a new Genesis, and then the restored and regenerated earth is handed back to God with more of gain than Adam ever lost, while Christ takes His place as the Father of the Everlasting Age, as that God who is to be All and in All.

The whole period inclusive of the Millennium is a

period of "putting down all rule and authority" under the feet of God and God's Man.

THE ETERNAL STATE, OR DISPENSATION, begins at Revelation xxi : 1, and ends, NEVER.

Christ is God in All, and is characteristically manifested as "The Father of the Everlasting Age." (Isaiah ix : 6.)

Righteousness has at last found a home. In the Millennium righteousness "reigned," but in the Eternal state, under the New Heavens and the New Earth it "dwells." Paradise is no longer a garden spot of earth but the whole shining globe, and the Paradise Lost has been forgotten in the Paradise Regained. Sin and sorrow, sickness and death are forever banished, and God is with men to wipe away the memory of every tear.

God has got His own world again, and no longer merely in the might of that creation over which the morning stars sang together and the sons of God shouted for joy, but in the value of the redeeming blood of His dear Son. Henceforth, He is the unfoldment of the Eternal Father, as the Church is the eternal disclosure of the Son. Israel is the Memorial Nation in eternity, bearing witness of God's covenant faithfulness in time. The nations of them that are saved are transformed into the men with whom God lives, and over all is written that unspeakable decree "that of the Increase of this government of the Father by the Son there shall be NO END."

A perfect world, the witness of God's perfect love and grace, in which the face of Christ with all its measureless glories shall still be the face of Him whom we know as Jesus of Nazareth; a world amid whose splendors the Church shall always be exalted as above things in heaven or things in earth; a world where Christians shall be the trophies of infinite love, the objects of God's eternal kindness through riches of grace in Christ Jesus our Lord; and where with Him we shall shine as the supreme sons of God, the rulers of the universe, the God-men, the aristocrats, the best ones of eternity; where finally, our lives in the full rhythm of God's accomplished purpose concerning us shall constantly utter in every deed, or word, or thought, in every essence of our being, ascriptions of praise and glory to Him who redeemed us by His precious blood and made us to be that New Humanity which is the eternal enthronement of God, the synonym, the symbol of life and joy, of peace and power, absolute, and forever.

One characteristic is common to each time dispensation; each ends in the failure of man under responsibility.

In Eden he fails under responsibility to the Word.

In the Antediluvian dispensation he fails under responsibility to Conscience.

In the Patriarchal, under responsibility to Fatherhood.

In the Mosaic, under responsibility to Law.

In the Messianic, under responsibility to Incarnation.

In the Holy Ghost, to the Gospel.

In the Millennial, to the King of Righteousness.

At the close of each of these dispensations God gives man up to his own way.

In the Edenic, He gave him up to the knowledge of Sin.

In the Antediluvian, He gave him up to the Imaginations of Evil.

In the Patriarchal, He gave him up to the Food of Egypt.

In the Mosaic, He gave him up to Formalism.

In the Messianic, to Judicial Blindness.

In the Holy Ghost, to the Love of the World.

In the Millennial, to the Going after Satan.

At the close of each dispensation God takes off the restraint of evil and allows it to head itself up in some particular form for Judgment.

In the Edenic, it heads itself up in a Fallen Woman.

In the Antediluvian, in Sinful Angels.

In the Patriarchal, in the king who knew not God.

In the Mosaic, in the Hypocrisy of Scribes and Pharisees.

In the Messianic, in Judas.

In the Holy Ghost, in Antichrist.

In the Millennial, in Satan.

Each dispensation ends with a great World Crisis.

In the Edenic, the great world crisis is the Expulsion of Man.

In the Antediluvian, it is the Flood.

In the Patriarchal, it is the Bondage of the Chosen People.

In the Mosaic, it is the Beheading of John the Baptist.

In the Messianic, the Cross of Christ.

In the Holy Ghost, the Rapture of the Church.

In the Millennial, the Binding of Satan.

After the Thousand Years there is the Judgment on Satan, the Great Conflagration, the Second Resurrection, and the Second Death, a Climax of Crises.

It must be evident as already intimated and illustrated that these dispensations include a wide variety of characteristic dealings and principles, and that it is absolutely necessary not only to know the outlines of these dealings and principles, but to be able to classify Truth in its several relations to them. Indeed, the classification of Dispensational Truth affords a distinct subject in itself.

It is sufficient to say that careful examination and prayerful consideration will show whole bodies of truth which belong exclusively to one dispensation and not to another; and that failure to put them in their proper dispensational relation means as great a disaster to that body or bodies of truth as the disarticulation of its members would be to the human body.

CLASSIFICATION OF DISPENSATIONAL TRUTH.

It is not only necessary to know the Dispensations, but eminently important to keep truth in its proper dispensational relation. To put the truth applicable to one dispensation into another is to risk confusion, and not only theological, but spiritual death.

Take, for example, the imprecatory psalms, as indicated in Psalms lviii: 10; cxxxvii: 8, 9.

These Scriptures are full of imprecation and breathe the spirit not of forgiveness but vengeance on the enemy.

This spirit seems such a contradiction to the age in which we live, such a contradiction to the attitude of love grace and forgiveness occupied by the church that many efforts have been made by good Christians to reconcile them with the teachings of Christianity; others finding the attempt useless have been led to expurgate them altogether from their Bibles.

Now it is indisputably true that the spirit of imprecation and vengeance is absolutely contradictory to the present spirit and mission of the church, but it is not contradictory to God's mind nor to His intended dealings. There is a period coming when the Lord will be King over all the earth, when He will rule not in grace, but with a rod of iron, when He will no longer be full of long-suffering and forbearance, but will dash in pieces as a potter's vessel. A time is coming when the people of the earth shall learn righteousness, not by the preaching of the Gospel but by sudden judgments on the guilty. Isaiah xxvi: 9. Revelation ii: 25-29.

At that period the idea will be righteousness and not grace.

Instead of listening to appeals for mercy He will bend His ear to catch the invocations to judgment. It will not be the principle of vengeance but of vindication, not cruelty of feeling but justification of law; a dealing just as much in place then as it would be out of place now.

Apply the imprecatory psalms to this age and there is complete contradiction, put them where they belong in the Millennial era, and there is order, the order of the distinct dealings which God Himself reveals.

In Isaiah lx: 1, 3, 11, 12, we have a passage that is again and again applied to the church, being used to set forth the triumph of the Gospel, and the recompense of missionary zeal. But an examination of the statement in Galatians iii: 27, 28, will show that the passage cannot be related to the church, and does not belong to this dispensation.

Galatians tells us that in Christ there is neither "Jew nor Gentile." That is to say in the church all national distinctions disappear. But in the quotation from Isaiah the distinction of Jew and Gentile is particularly emphasized. The prophet is therefore not speaking of the church but of Israel in the last days after the church has been translated; he is speaking of that time in the Millennial Dispensation when the Jew shall be the head of the

nations and when the Gentiles shall bring in their wealth
to support him.

If you turn to Zechariah xiv: 16-19, 20, 9, 8, 4, 3, you
will find that National Thanksgiving does not belong
to this age but to the Day of Christ. In that day the
nation that does not send its representatives to Jerusalem to pray before the Lord and return thanks for blessings will be smitten in field and harvests.

Dispensational classification gives point and place of
application to the prayer of the Holy Spirit.

In the very nature of the case if the Holy Spirit is in
the church, if He is here as the executive of the Godhead
and the all-potent administrator of the church, the seal
of the individual Christian, then we are not warranted,
but rather forbidden to pray for the coming or outpouring of the Spirit.

And yet we have a Scripture in Luke xi: 13, which
definitely, and by no less an utterance than that of the
Lord Jesus Christ Himself authorizes a prayer for the
Holy Spirit:

"If ye then being evil know how to give good gifts
unto your children; how much more shall your heavenly
Father give the Holy Spirit to them that ask Him."

Is there a contradiction here?

If dispensational classification is not observed there
will be.

Turn to John vii: 37-39. "But this spake He of the
Spirit which they that believe on Him should receive: *for
the Holy Ghost was not yet given;* because that Jesus was
not yet glorified."

Jesus was not yet glorified, that is to say He was not
yet crucified and raised from the dead. He had not yet
ascended into heaven as the Risen Man, of which im-

mense event the descent of the Holy Ghost was to be the
indisputable evidence. The dispensation which gives us
the Holy Ghost as an abiding guest in the hearts of believers had not yet come. The moment in which the Lord
spoke was yet that of the Messianic dispensation, it was
therefore perfectly justifiable to offer the prayer then,
just as it would be thoroughly unjustifiable and contradictory now.

The one settling thing, the one thing that puts an end
to all controversy is in the authoritative phrase: *"The
Holy Ghost was not yet given."*

Dispensational classification explains the place of what
is commonly known as "The Lord's Prayer."

That prayer belongs in the closing hours of this dispensation when the church is gone and when the elect
Remnant among the Jews suffering under the persecution
of the "Wilful" king call on God to deliver them from
the horror of his rule, deliver them from the Great Tribulation and the power of this "Evil One," give them the
daily bread which Antichrist makes it impossible for them
to touch without sin, and bring in the long-promised
kingdom of the Messiah. The prayer belongs essentially in that part of the present dispensation because
grace will be gone and law and righteousness will be in
vogue.

In Matthew xxv: 31-44, there is a picture of the coming of Christ, and the gathering before Him to judgment
of all nations.

This judgment has been expounded as the last judgment and the scene set forth as the resurrection of the
dead.

Not only is there no thought of resurrection in the
passage, but strict examination will show that the Christian does not appear in it at all.

Nations are there, and they are judged, not according to the relation they have held to the Gospel but rather according to the manner in which they have treated the "Brethren of Christ." The brethren of Christ in this case as cognate scriptures demonstrate are the Jews, the elect remnant who escape out of the hands of the Antichrist. As these nations, principally the nations of Europe have treated the Jew, so will they be dealt with and judged in that hour of hours, "before the Son of Man."

The place of this judgment is in order at the commencement of the Millennial dispensation, and at least seven years after the Judgment Seat of Christ before which the church stands after her resurrection and rapture.

Dispensational order is remarkably set before us in Acts xv: 14-18.

"God at the first did visit the Gentiles, to take out of them a people for His name—. After this I Will Return, and will build again the tabernacle of David—."

This is the order as dispensationally indicated by the Spirit:

1. God is now in this dispensation of the Holy Ghost "taking out" a people for His name. It is therefore the dispensation of the Taking Out, the Calling Out, the Called Out Ones, the Church. It is not the time of pell-mell conversion to Christ, but the calling out from among all peoples kindreds and tongues, here and there, an individual to faith and life in Christ.

2. "After this," after the calling out of the church, He will return and build up the house of David. That is to say, He will set up and establish the Jewish economy in the earth.

The church for this dispensation.

The Jew for the next.

That is the Divine Order.

The distinctive value of dispensational truth may be seen by contrasting the dispensation of the Holy Ghost with the Mosaic dispensation.

In the Mosaic dispensation, God dealt nationally.

In the Holy Ghost dispensation, He deals individually.

In the Mosaic dispensation, He dealt with one nation.

In the Holy Ghost dispensation, He deals among all nations.

In the Mosaic dispensation, He brought in the Jew, and shut out the Gentiles.

In the Holy Ghost dispensation, He brings in the Gentiles, and shuts out the Jew.

In the Mosaic dispensation, God dealt according to man's work.

In the Holy Ghost dispensation, He deals according to Christ's work.

In the Mosaic dispensation, God dealt on the basis of Law.

In the Holy Ghost dispensation, He deals on the basis of Grace.

In the Mosaic dispensation, God said: "Do, and live."

In the Holy Ghost dispensation, He says: "Live, and do."

In the Mosaic dispensation, the Law brought a work for man to do.

In the Holy Ghost dispensation, the Gospel brings a Word for man to believe.

In the Mosaic dispensation, all is summed up in a word of two letters. "Do."

In the Holy Ghost dispensation, all is summed up in a word of four letters, "Done."

The attempt to put Christians and Gentiles under the

law of Moses in this dispensation gave this country the witchcraft of Salem, and such modern misnomers as Christian Sabbath, and American Sabbath.

Law is right in its place and for a people on earth in the flesh, *and it is to be remembered that the law is always for the sinful man in the flesh,* but it is out of place and all wrong for a Christian, one who is in Christ and no longer seen of God as in the flesh, but risen, ascended and seated with Christ in heavenly places.

The Priesthood of Christ illustrates dispensational truth and makes manifest that the Christian is not under the Mosaic Law, or dispensation.

In Hebrews viii: 4, it is written: "If He (Jesus) were on earth He should not be a priest."

In Hebrews vii: 12-14, the reason is given: "Our Lord sprang out of Juda: of which tribe Moses spake nothing concerning priesthood."

Priesthood on earth belongs to the tribe of Levi, and is for those who are under the Law.

The Priesthood of Christ belongs in heaven, and is for those only who are joined to Him as the man risen from the dead, ascended and seated in the glory.

The Christian who goes under the law, goes under the Levitical priesthood; as Christ is a priest only for those who are judicially dead, risen and ascended in Him to heavenly places, then the Christian who goes under the law shuts himself out from the priesthood of Christ.

Thus a knowledge of the dispensational place of Christ's Priesthood would settle all controversy as to the Christian's relation to the law.

But more than this, it would settle all controversy about sacerdotalism and make a separate priesthood in the church impossible. And this is self-evident. According to Holy Scripture, *Christ never was a priest on earth.* He could not, He would not be a priest if He were on earth to-day. By what law has any one who wears the name of Christ the right or authority to claim priesthood apart from, or in any other sense than that in which all are spiritual priests.

Accept dispensational distinction and prelacy in the church is at an end.

Dispensational classification can alone save Truth from contradicting itself.

Take for example, Romans xi: 26, and Romans xi: 28, read them in the light of the proposition that there is no such thing as dispensational truth or that both verses belong to the same period, and you have a contradiction that all the ingenuity or piety of men cannot excuse, or minimize, for Romans xi: 26, declares that "All Israel shall be saved," while Romans xi: 28, asserts with equal force that "As concerning the Gospel, they are enemies."

But put verse 28 in this dispensation and all the facts of history and experience will demonstrate its truth. Put verse 26 in the Millennial age, the age that will follow this, and you will see that the nation of Israel is saved, as the Apostle Paul was saved, by the personal Appearing of Jesus Christ in glory.

Thus dispensationally classified the two verses harmonize instead of clashing.

Take Isaiah ii: 1-4, "In the last days—nation shall not lift up sword against nation, neither shall they learn war any more."

Read II Timothy iii: 1, "In the last days perilous times shall come."

Apply these "last days" to the same dispensation and there is a contradiction that cannot be explained away.

Read carefully the passage in Isaiah with the context and you will see that the last days of blessing are introduced by judgments which other scriptures show take place at the coming of Christ. And thus the last days of blessing in the Old Testament actually *follow* the Coming of Christ.

Read the statement in the Epistle to Timothy and you will find that the last days of peril and suffering, of war and apostasy, *precede* the Coming of the Lord.

Put the coming of the Lord between these two classes of last days and they fall naturally into their proper dispensations. This dispensation will end with perilous times in Church and State, a general apostasy and smash-up, at the climax of which the Lord will come and smite the earth for its sin and failure under responsibility to grace. Then when the Lord is come the new dispensation of the Millennium will open in blessing and peace. Thus the passage in Timothy refers to the closing hours of this age.

Dispensationally classified and related, harmony flashes forth from that which otherwise is the centre of discord.

Attention to dispensational order will prevent the excuseless blunder about the church going through the Tribulation.

There are those who teach this to the dishonor of grace and the confusion of the Christian mind.

The Spirit seems to have taken particular care that this blunder should not occur. In Scripture the Tribulation is specially qualified as in relation to God's earthly people the Jews, and not to the church. In Jeremiah xxx: 7, the Tribulation is definitely called "The Day of Jacob's Trouble." Read also Isaiah lxvi: 8. In Matthew xxiv: 16, we are told by our Lord that the scene of the Tribulation will be "In Judea:" verse 20, speaks about flight on "The Sabbath Day;" and all the nomenclature is of a people under the Mosaic law. But Romans vi: 14, positively declares that the church is *not* under the law. This last statement then being so, and those who are to pass through the Tribulation being under the law, under the Sabbath covenant, and unequivocally declared to be Jacob, or the people of Israel, it follows that the church is never referred to in any matter involving the Tribulation.

There are other and direct declarations such as Revelation iii: 10, and the picture of the church in heaven during the whole course of the Tribulation as given in the book of Revelation from the fourth chapter to the nineteenth which settles the question; but the moment the Bible student recognizes that the Law and the Sabbath are not for the church and that the whole earth and not Judea is her arena when in the world, he will see the utter impossibility and absurdity of that doctrine which makes the Christian to go through the Tribulation as a sort of earthly purgatory anticipative to heavenly glory. He will see as in the case of Lot in Sodom that tribulation and judgment will not fall till the church has been clean "taken out" of the world.

The same classification will save from the equally absurd mistake of making the 144,000 of Revelation 14th stand for the church, and on that chapter building certain impossible and confusing doctrines.

The opening verse of the chapter shows this select and numbered company on Mount Zion. To the student of Scripture that word Zion ought to end all controversy. Zion is never the church even by the wildest allowance of imagination or "accommodation," invariably signifies the place itself, and stands only for Jewish thought and dealing. Of course a proper investigation and division of the book of Revelation makes it quite impossible to fall into the error of calling those who are declared in the seventh chapter to be the people of Israel, the church. But independently of all this, dispensational knowledge would save from such a mixture of things in heaven and in earth.

Passage after passage might be further cited to show that classification of truth according to dispensational distinction results in the light of a full dawn upon the divine pages, and touches every chord of revelation into perfect harmony.

Enough, however, has been said to show that knowledge of dispensational truth and ability to relate each truth to its own dispensation is absolutely necessary for him who would lay hold of the treasures of the Word, or reveal them to others.

DISTINCTION BETWEEN THINGS WHICH APPEAR SIMILAR.

We must know and maintain the distinction between things which though apparently similar are quite distinct.

This principle is simply an emphasis of what has been said largely under the head of classification of Dispensational Truth, the classification, however, sometimes falling inside of similar dispensations.

As an example of passages which are quite different although commonly confounded, examine, Luke xxi: 24, and Romans xi: 25. The first reads: "Jerusalem shall be trodden down of the Gentiles, *until the times of the Gentiles be fulfilled.*"

The second reads: "Blindness in part is happened to Israel *until the fulness of the Gentiles be come in."*

"The times of the Gentiles" signify the rule of the Gentile nations. That rule began as owned of God in Nebuchadnezzar, King of Babylon. At that hour God set the Jew aside because of evil and sin against Him and brought in the Gentile governmentally. That rule as owned of God continued on down through the Roman Empire; it continues to-day trampling Jerusalem and the Jew under foot, making the once Holy city the capital of the False prophet, and denying Him who is the King and whose that city is; this rule will continue until the Gentile nations of the old Roman earth under Antichrist shall once more be gathered about Jerusalem; then Christ and His church previously caught up will come to the Mount of Olives to overthrow him, put an end to his confederacy, write finale upon Gentile Times, and bring in "The Times of the Jew."

"Behold the day of the Lord cometh...... for I will gather all nations against Jerusalem to battle...... then shall the Lord go forth, and fight against those nations......and His feet shall stand in that day upon the Mount of Olives......And the Lord shall be King over all the earth......Jerusalem shall be safely inhabited......In those days it shall come to pass, that ten men shall take hold, out of all languages of the nations (the ten nations of Antichrist, of the Roman Earth) even shall take hold of the skirt of him that is a Jew, saying, We will go with you; for we have heard that GOD IS WITH YOU." Zechariah xiv: 1-11, Zechariah viii: 23.

This is the time of the Jew, he is the head and no longer the Tail of the nations. "And the Lord shall make thee the head, and not the tail." Deuteronomy xxviii: 13.

The Times of the Gentiles historically then is the whole period from the reign of Nebuchadnezzar till the Lord shall come again in the clouds of Heaven and set up the Jewish State.

The "Fulness of the Gentile signifies the fulness or filling up of God's purposes in this age to take out from among the Gentiles a people for His name, as it is written: "God at the first did visit the Gentiles, to take out of them a people for His name."

And to this agree the words of the prophet; as it is written: *"After this* (after the people from among the Gentiles are taken out), I will return, and build again the tabernacle (the house, the throne, and kingdom), of David." Acts xv: 14-16.

Our Lord's name is the Christ, those who are taken out now from among the Gentiles unto His name are Christ-ians: this taking out from among the Gentiles began the day Peter preached at the house of Cornelius and the Holy Ghost fell on all those who heard the Word; that taking out is being accomplished by the Holy Spirit and the Gospel as it is preached on the lips of men, and it will go on till the last one who shall constitute the "taking out" is called, then that body of called-out persons will be full, filled to its requisite number; for it must be self-evident that "a taking *out from among* the Gentiles" is not a taking of *all* the Gentiles, it is a taking of *some* Gentiles from among others, and this is election: necessarily in an election there is a definiteness both as to number and time limit; this time limit must be marked by some well-defined point: it is so marked by the Translation of the church, by the resurrection of the dead and the transfiguration of the living into the Lord's presence in the air; an event which will precede the Appearing of

Christ and His church to the Mount of Olives, at least, seven years.

Thus the Times of the Gentiles begin centuries before the birth of Christ and will end only at His Appearing to set up the kingdom of Israel; while the Fulness of the Gentiles begins only after the resurrection of the Lord and may end any moment by the sudden secret translation or rapture of the church into the air to meet Him, when like "the thief in the night" unknown to the world He shall come quietly to snatch away the church as His jewel, His "Pearl of great price." Matthew xiii: 45, 46.

Thus the one truth involves the secret Coming of Christ and the Rapture of the church, the other the public Appearing of Christ and the beginning of that era when the nation of Israel shall be saved unto the glory of coming and millennial days.

The word Gospel is so familiar, its general definition as "good news" so well understood, that its application is supposed to be uniform. When therefore we read of the Gospel of the Kingdom, the Gospel of God, the Gospel of Grace, the Glorious Gospel, and the Everlasting Gospel, it is taken for granted that they all refer to one and the same thing. The similarity is impressed upon the average mind by the word Gospel. But however the word Gospel may make for similarity it is a mistake to imagine that the word covers one subject. On the contrary the several designations of the Gospel are of themselves the indications of marked distinctions which the Spirit impresses on us to observe.

The Gospel of the Kingdom is the good news of the Kingdom to be set up in Israel with Jerusalem as the Capital, when the Lord Jesus shall come the second time as Messiah, as Son of David. It is therefore in the nature of the case a Gospel that cannot be preached until after this particular age or dispensation is passed, not till after the Rapture or Translation of the Church.

The Gospel of God is the good news that God is a Father loving men in spite of their sins and seeking sons who shall worship Him in Spirit and in Truth.

The Gospel of Grace is the good news that Christ died for our sins, and rose again for our justification; this is peculiarly the Gospel that is to be preached in this age.

The Glorious Gospel would be better translated, "The Gospel of the Glory of the blessed (happy) God." Read I Timothy i: 11, II Corinthians iv: 4.

It is the good news that Jesus Christ the crucified and risen man is now exalted to be the happy God. It is the good news of a God-man exalted to Heaven for believing men and their salvation.

The Everlasting Gospel is the good news of that era of time which is called the Age of Ages, the Millennial era; the good news that the King of Righteousness *has* come and is seated *in Jerusalem* as the King of nations, as the Prince of the Kings of the earth.

In recognizing these varied Gospels we get vistas of truth heretofore unopened and behold the keys with which many statements of Scripture otherwise dark are unlocked to our comprehension.

As a simple but striking example of things which seem similar but are absolutely distinct, take Matthew xxv: 34, Ephesians i: 4. The former reads, "The kingdom prepared for you *from* the foundation of the world." The latter reads, "hath chosen us in Him *before* the foundation of the world."

The subject is election in both cases. In Matthew you

have *from* the foundation of the world, in Ephesians you have *before* the foundation of the world. The difference is in the prepositions *before* and *from:* this distinction is rarely if ever seen; and yet the value of the distinction is immense.

From the foundation of the world is a term characterizing the kingdom as relating to earth and time, while before the foundation of the world takes us wholly above the earth and time and projects us into heaven and eternity, both past and future.

A striking illustration of the necessity of maintaining the distinction between things apparently similar may be found in a single passage. In Ephesians iii: 15, it is written: "Of whom the whole family in heaven and earth is named."

Ordinarily this is applied to the same subject, the subject in both members of the verse supposed to be the Church of Christ as the Family of Faith.

The family in heaven is taken to be all those who of the church of Christ have died on through the ages, all who die now and depart to be with Christ in Heaven; the family on earth are supposed, correspondingly, to be those who live in the church on earth to-day; the one is thus the church in heaven, the other the church on earth.

However true it is that those who are in heaven form with those who are really saved on earth the one great spiritual family, it is not true that they are ever known as the family in heaven and the family in earth. The key to the first half of the verse is found in the literal reading, "in the heavens." Now this epistle is the epistle peculiarly of the heavens or the heavenlies. If you take your pencil and mark the word you will find that it is indeed the characteristic of the book, and is intended to set forth the fact that in God's mind the church has already gone home with the ascended Christ, and is seen of God as seated with Him, and in Him, in Heavenly Places, as it is written, "Hath raised us up together, and made us sit together in heavenly places in Christ Jesus." Ephesians ii: 6.

The family in heaven then means the church, the whole church, living or dead, in heaven or on earth. In other words, the church is the *Heavenly Family*.

There is another family, a family that is as much a family of God as the church of Christ, but a family that has to do wholly with the earth. While all the promises to the church are made concerning heavenly things, all the promises made to the other family have to do with the earth, and the earth alone. That family is the nation of Israel, and this is the family of whom we speak as "The Family in Earth." In God's final purpose Israel is to reign on the earth, but the church seated in the Heavenlies with Christ above all principalities and powers is to rule even over all Israel. The object of the Apostle's statement then is to set Jesus Christ as the centre of things in heaven and in earth, both to the church, and also to the Jew.

Fail to recognize the distinction between these two families, allow yourself to be deceived with the idea that both families refer to the same thing and you will miss some of the most wonderful and comforting truths of the Word of God.

Admit the distinction and there will be opened to you whole sweeps of distinct truths which at the last from heaven and from earth gather at His feet to own Him as their objective and glory.

In Ephesians i: 6, it is written: "He hath made us *accepted* in the Beloved."

In II Corinthians v: 9, you read: "We labor......
that we *may be accepted* of Him."

In the one case it is stated that we have been accepted, and in the other we are shown as under obligation to labor and toil in order to be accepted. Is there a contradiction here?

If the things have reference to the same truth there is a contradiction. But do they in spite of their similarity in form apply to distinct things? I answer they do. In Ephesians we are seen as to our standing before God in Christ, and as the rendering might be, "graced in Him."

In Corinthians we are seen as to our state, our daily walk.

Our standing is invariable. It is in Christ and God sees us as perfect as He is. Our state is variable. We do not always live as those who have been accepted as sons of God in the Risen Christ. Because this is so we are exhorted to bring our state up to our standing and seek to live in accord with it, not that we may be accepted as sons of God but that we may live acceptably before Him. A proper rendering of the passage in Corinthians will substantiate this interpretation and will at the same time remove the appearance of similarity.

Instead of accepted read "acceptable." We are to labor then not in order to be accepted as sons of God but to be *acceptable* sons of God. In other words because we are the sons of God accepted in the Beloved, we are to live acceptably, pleasingly before Him.

In the nature of the case, the knowledge of dispensational truth and the principles of strict classification will enable us more and more to distinguish between things which differ.

THE MEANING AND PURPORT OF THE DIF-
FERENT BOOKS OF THE BIBLE.

We must know the meaning and purport of each book of the Bible.

The Bible is made up of separate books, sixty-six in number.

These books are divided into two great parts, the Old and New Testaments, or more correctly, "The Scriptures of Israel," and "The Scriptures of the Church."

The Old Testament, is divided into three great parts: Law, Prophets and Psalms.

This was the division current among the Jews in our Lord's time. He sets His seal to this division: "These are the words which I spake unto you, while I was yet with you, that all things must be fulfilled, which were written in the *Law* of Moses, and in the *Prophets,* and in the *Psalms,* concerning me." Luke xxiv: 44.

The Law is known as the Pentateuch, the latter word signifies the fivefold book, and comes from the Greek, *pente,* five, and *teuchos,* book.

The five books are Genesis, Exodus, Leviticus, Numbers and Deuteronomy.

The Prophets—Twenty-nine books.

This division includes the prophetic and historic books, from Joshua to Malachi.

The Psalms—Five books.

Job, Book of Psalms proper, Proverbs, Ecclesiastes and Song of Solomon.

Thirty-nine books in all in the Scriptures of Israel.

The New Testament is divided into three great parts. Gospels, Acts and Epistles.

Gospels—Four in number. Matthew, Mark, Luke and John.

Three of these Gospels are called the "Synoptics," namely: Matthew, Mark and Luke.

These are called Synoptic from the Greek *sun,* together, and *opsis,* view, things viewed together or a general and uniform view. That is to say, these Gospels seem at first glance to give the same general and sequential view of the history of our Lord, while the Gospel according to John stands out in many and marked contrasts.

The Synoptics may be called the Earthly Gospels. The Fourth, or John's Gospel, the Heavenly Gospel.

The Book of Acts consists of two parts.

In the first part we have the Apostolate of Peter. In the second, that of Paul.

In the first we have the Kingdom presented again to the Jews; and in the second the Gospel given to the Jew first, and then the Gentile, with the gradual unfolding of God's purpose to call out the church from among the Gentiles.

Epistles to the churches—Sixteen in number.

Romans, First and Second Corinthians, Galatians, Ephesians, Philippians, Colossians, First and Second Thessalonians.

These nine epistles are written by Saint Paul.

Seven epistles are written by John: Ephesus, Smyrna, Pergamos, Thyatira, Sardis, Philadelphia, Laodicea.

Paul writes four individual, or personal, epistles:

First and Second Timothy, Titus and Philemon.

He writes one epistle to his nation: The Epistle to the Hebrews; he writes fourteen in all.

John writes two personal epistles: To the Elect Lady and her children, to the well-beloved Gaius.

There are four epistles to the Hebrews:

The Apostle Peter writes two: First and Second Peter. James writes one: The Epistle of James. Paul writes one: The Epistle to the Hebrews, so distinctively called.

There are two general Epistles:

John writes one: The First Epistle of John. Jude writes the other: The Epistle of Jude.

The Epistles of John form the Family Epistles. They consist of letters to little children, fathers, young men, a mother and her children, a beloved brother in the Lord.

The New Testament is composed of twenty-seven books.

In both these testaments we have a marvellous library, a library whose topics range from the creation of the world to the re-creation of a human soul.

The manner in which these books have been written and this library produced is declared by the Apostles Peter and Paul:

"God spake by the prophets." Hebrews i: 1.

"Holy men of God spake as they were moved (carried along) by the Holy Ghost." II Peter i: 21.

"The Spirit of Christ which was in them (the prophets) testified beforehand the sufferings of Christ, and the glory (glories) that should follow." I Peter i: 11.

"All Scripture is given by inspiration of God." II Timothy iii: 16.

Note who some of the authors of these books were, that is to say, those whom God by His Spirit used as His amanuenses:

Kings, such as David and Solomon; *Prime Ministers,* such as Mordecai and Daniel; *Kings' Cup Bearers,* such as Nehemiah.

Prophets, scholars, poets, soldiers, physicians, tax-gatherers, cattle-drivers, shepherds, tent-makers, and il-literate, at least uneducated fishermen.

These are of all sorts; but mainly the weak and those who were not mighty in the world were chosen of God to form His Bible.

And we are told that God makes such choice in order "That no flesh should glory in His presence." I Corinthians i: 29.

The period of time in writing the book was about sixteen hundred years. Think of it! A book taking sixteen centuries to write. What a story its composition would tell of the lands in which written, the circumstances under which written, and the varied emotions in the hearts of those who were privileged to give it forth as the mind and will of God to men.

The Old Testament is written in two languages, the Hebrew and Syriac; the Septuagint, or Greek translation by the Seventy of Alexandria is quoted by our Lord and His Apostles.

The New Testament is wholly Greek.

The supreme object of the Bible from Genesis to Revelation is to set forth the Son of God in His varied relations as Creator, Man, Redeemer, Priest, King and God-man.

The Bible is Christo-centric; without that centre all is chaos; with that the book is order, the expression of infinite intelligence, filled with light, with life and love, and intelligible to the quickened minds of the sons of men.

It is evident that each of these books contributes its part towards the general whole; that each has its special lineament to paint in the common portrait of the King; that each book stands for some definite form of the great revelation, and that necessarily each book has some

special characteristic, some particular purport. This
meaning and purport may sometimes be told in a word or
a phrase. The knowledge of the meaning, the comprehension of the purport will flash light into the mind concerning the truths each book seeks to present.

Let us consider then more particularly the characteristic meaning and purport of the books of the Bible:

Genesis. Book of beginnings. Seed-plot of the Bible.
The germs, the roots of every doctrine afterwards unfolded in the Bible.

The whole doctrine of man, his creation, fall, ruin,
re-creation and glory, may be found in the first chapter.

Exodus. Going out, or book of Redemption.

Redemption by *blood* and Redemption by *power*.

Leviticus. Sacrifice, Priesthood and Worship.

This has been called the Priest's Guide Book.

Numbers. Wilderness Experience.

You have here the suggestions, typically, of the church
in the world, and Christian experience.

Like Israel the church is passing on from the sands
of time to the Promised Land and to the golden floors
of the Temple of God. On the way there are foes to
fight, lessons to learn, and experiences to enjoy in the
manifested grace and forbearance of God.

Deuteronomy. Preparation for the land.

To be read in connection with the Epistle to the
Colossians.

Joshua. Conflict with the enemy in the land.

To be read with Ephesians, the book of the "Heavenlies."

The key, Ephesians vi: 10-17.

Judges. Eye-sight instead of faith-sight.

Key, Judges xxi: 25.

Ruth. Gentile bride for Jewish Lord.

Boaz. Kinsman, Redeemer, Advocate.

Samuel, Kings and *Chronicles,* six books. They set before us the Story of the Kingdom.

I Samuel. King after man's choice, and the King after God's choice.

The king after man's choice, splendid in stature, glorious in beauty, wilful in way.

The King after God's choice, a man of sorrows and acquainted with grief, despised and rejected of men.

II Samuel. The man of sorrows and acquainted with grief exalted to be king over all Israel.

I Kings. The King of Glory.

II Kings. The Great Apostasy.

I Chronicles. God dealing in Grace with the *Ark* as the centre.

II Chronicles. God manifesting Glory with the *Temple* as the centre.

Ezra. Building the Temple.

Nehemiah. Building the City.

Esther. Secret Providence to a Godless people.

Job. Self-righteousness.

Psalms. Christ's Sufferings and Glories.

Proverbs. Rules of Heaven for men on earth.

Ecclesiastes. "Under the sun."

Song of Solomon. The marriage joy of Bride and Bridegroom:

The joy of Christ and the Church in the marriage hour of glory when at last she shall come up out of the wilderness leaning on His arm to enter into the place prepared, where His banner over her shall be love.

Isaiah. The anticipated Gospel, and Israel in "The latter days."

Key chapter, Fifty-third.

Jeremiah. "The day of Jacob's Trouble."

Lamentations. Jerusalem under foot of the Gentiles.

Ezekiel. Visions of God and Latter Day Glory.

Daniel. Hand book of Gentile politics.

Hosea. The wandering nation.

Joel. Day of the Lord.

Amos. Desolation and Restoration.

Obadiah. Judgment on Gentiles.

Jonah. Substitution and Resurrection.

Micah. Bethlehem and the Babe.

Nahum. Gentile Confederacy.

Habakkuk. Messianic Glory.

Zephaniah. Israel the Head, and no longer the Tail.

Zechariah. The Appearing in Glory on the Mount of Olives.

Malachi. The Sun of Righteousness, and the smiting of the earth.

Matthew. The King of the Jews.

Mark. The Servant.

No Genealogy, no record of birth.

Key words of the book, "Immediately," "Straightway."

These words express the servant character of our Lord, as set before us by Mark.

Luke. The Man among men.

John. God the Word who became man and dwelt among us that we might behold the glory of the Divine Fatherhood in the Divine Sonship.

Acts. History of the Holy Spirit acting in the church.

Romans. Justification by Faith.

I Corinthians. Gospel Order.

II Corinthians. Discipline and Benevolence.

Ephesians. The Heavenlies.

Philippians. The mind of Christ.

Colossians. The Deity of Christ.

I Thessalonians. Waiting for the Son of God from Heaven. (Secret.)

II Thessalonians. Appearing of the Son of God from Heaven. (Public.)

Titus. "The Blessed Hope."

Philemon. "Put that on my account."

Hebrews. Shadows and Substance. The Book of Contrasts.

James. Justification by works.

In Romans man is justified by faith in "God's sight."

In James man is justified by works in "Man's sight."

I Peter. Pilgrims and Strangers.

II Peter. The Great Fire, and the Wonderful Reconstruction.

I John. Reading the Title clear, or Written Assurance.

Key text. I John v: 13.

II John. Abiding in the Doctrine, or Christ coming again in the Flesh.

III John. Walking in the Truth.

Jude. The Great Apostasy, and Vengeance Coming.

Revelation. Consummation or the New Genesis taking the place of the Old.

The purport of the book, the purpose for which it was written, forms the point of view from which we must interpret its contents, get the grasp of its intents.

For example, in the Gospel according to Matthew we have no record of the ascension of Christ. Recognize that this book is written to set forth the Lord Jesus

Christ as the Messiah, the King of Israel, and you have the explanation of the omission: as king of Israel His place is not in Heaven but on earth, at Jerusalem the city of "The Great King."

There is no account of the Ascension in the Gospel of John.

Recognize the Lord's own utterance in John iii: 13, that "No man hath ascended up to Heaven, but he that came down from Heaven, even the Son of Man *which is in Heaven,*" and the omission becomes characteristic.

It is just as characteristic that the record of the Ascension should be given in Mark and Luke.

In Mark He is seen ascending as that servant who did the Father's will, and whom the Father would exalt as the witness that "the way to exaltation is in the dust."

He is seen ascending in Luke because as risen from the dead He must take a new, immortal Humanity to heaven, and sit there as "The Man in the Glory," the witness that as man He has met for men in His death perfectly all the demands of God's righteousness against the chief of sinners; He must sit there as the Second Man, the Last Adam, the Head of a new race, the prophecy of what all shall be who believe in Him; the shining glorious proclamation of that hour when the world shall be put not under angels, but redeemed, regenerated, and deathless man.

In Matthew the genealogy of Christ is connected with Abraham and David because as the King of Jews it is necessary that He shall get the Land through Abraham, and the Throne through David.

In Mark there is no genealogy because He is there represented as the Servant, and the servant has no need of ancestry.

In Luke His genealogy is carried back to Adam that He may be presented as the Son of Man and the seed of the woman.

In John we have no genealogy because the purport of that book is to set the Christ before us as the unbegun, eternally begotten Son of God, He who is from everlasting to everlasting.

For a right understanding of the book we read we are under obligation to put ourselves at its point of view and see the truth it presents in the light which that attitude and angle of vision may give.

DIVIDING THE BOOKS INTO THEIR COMPONENT PARTS.

We must know how to divide a Book into its component parts.

A book may be divided into characteristic and constituent parts: for example the Book of Job:

Characteristically, the Book of Job may be divided into five parts:

1. The abode and power of Satan.
2. The manifested folly of human wisdom in its endeavor to explain the providence of God.
3. Thirty chapters of self-righteousness.
4. The need of a Days-man.
5. The vileness of human perfection.

Constituently, the book may also be divided into five parts:

1. God's permitted trial of Job by Satan.
2. The efforts of Job's friends to account for his trial.
3. The address of Elihu.
4. The Lord Himself answering Job.

5. Job coming to a knowledge of his own vileness in the presence of God's Holiness.

On the same principle it is possible to analyze chapters as well as sections.

Take as an illustration the Gospel according to Matthew.

This is the Gospel of the King of the Jews: each chapter sets forth some special action of the King:

1. Generation of the King.
2. Birth of the King.
3. Baptism of the King.
4. Temptation of the King.
5—7. Legislation of the King.
8—9. Manifested power of the King.
10. The King sending out ambassadors.
11. The King reporting Himself through His works to John.
12. The King giving His credentials to His enemies.
13. The King unveiling the mysteries of the Kingdom: or, presenting the Kingdom *in a mystery.*
14. The King acting in compassion.
15. The King acting in grace to Gentiles.
16. The King painting the portrait of His Bride.
17. The King giving a vision of His second Advent.
18. The King pointing out Regeneration as the door into the Kingdom.
19. The King and the Millenium, or the age of the Regeneration.
20. The King seeking laborers.
21. The King presenting Himself to His brethren in the flesh.
22. The King foretelling the destruction of Jerusalem.

23. The King setting aside the Jew as a nation till He comes again.

24. The Great Tribulation, "The day of Jacob's Trouble," before The King comes again.

25. The King coming first as a Bridegroom, and then as a Judge.

26. The King betrayed.

27. The King crucified.

28. The King raised from the dead and made not only the king over all Israel, but the authority over all things in Heaven.

Not only is it possible to take each chapter in some characteristic way, but to take the chapter and find in it an analysis of contents suggestive. Take as an example the Fifth chapter of the Second Epistle to the Corinthians:

1. The location of the Christian between death and resurrection. v, 1.

2. The Christian's perfect body. v, 2.

3. The objective purpose of salvation. v, 4, 5.

4. The Judgment Seat of Christ. v, 10.

5. The true inspiration to service. v, 14.

6. The New Creation. v, 17.

7. The message to the world. v, 20.

8. The supreme argument. v, 21.

In turning a book into its component parts we may inquire *when* it was written, *by whom* it was written, *to whom* it was written, the *circumstances under which* it was written, *why* it was written; these questions will bring the book into its several parts before the student and set its sections, whether of chapter or verse, into clear vision.

EACH BOOK IN ITS ORDAINED PLACE.

There has been as much the manifestation of God's hand in the sequences of the books as in any other part of its creation; necessarily therefore each book is in its ordained place and cannot be taken out of it without the dislocation of the organism.

To illustrate, the Book of Ruth comes in between the Book of Judges on the one side, and the Book of Samuel on the other.

Ruth gives us the Gentile bride of the Jewish Lord and is therefore the type of the Church of Christ. Now the Church of Christ can only come into view after the failure in Israel; only when the marriage in Heaven takes place, or to be precise, when the church is called out, completed, and translated to meet the Lord at His Second Coming can the kingdom of Israel be set up. This is just what the position of the Book of Ruth shows conclusively. Judges gives us failure in Israel, "every man doing that which was right in his own eyes." Samuel gives us the setting-up of the kingdom.

Here then you have the Gentile bride placed in the canon of scripture between the failure of Israel and the coming of the kingdom.

In the Book of Ezra you have the building of the Temple, and in Nehemiah the restoration of the city; it is of little matter what the chronology may be, the moral sequence demands that the dwelling place of God shall be looked at before the dwelling place of man; and examination will show that this sequence is independent of man's ordering.

To see how necessary the Book of Acts is to the place accorded it, it is only required in reading to close the

book at the Gospel of John and open it again at the
Epistle to the Romans. In John you close with Jesus
on the shores of Galilee, but in Romans you find Him
gone from the earth and the Church in His place, but
no account of the origin or constitution of that church.
Without the Book of Acts you cannot assist at the birth
of the Church and the inauguration of the dispensation
of the Holy Ghost.

The Book of the Revelation finds it place by inherent
law.

It is a matter of little import when it was written, there
is but one place which it can logically occupy, that is at
the consummation of the Bible. I recall seeing some
years ago a house in process of building; before the walls
were half way up the carpenters began constructing the
roof, and at a certain stage when the walls were complete, caused that roof to be swung up into its place. No
matter when the roof was constructed there was but one
place for it, and that on top, as the consummation of the
building. No matter at what hour the Revelation was
inspired of God there is but one place it can occupy, and
that is at the close of the canon, resting in its place as the
roof in the palace of Truth.

EACH BOOK IN PLACE BY LAW OF GROWTH.

Each book finds its place therefore by the law of organic growth, each book is a necessity to, and produces
the other, just as each preceding part of a tree is a necessity and inspiration to that which follows.

If Genesis is necessary to bring Israel into Egypt, Exodus is necessary to take them out. If the order of the

New Testament is Gospels, Acts, and Epistles, it is because in the Gospels we get Christ in the flesh, in Acts Christ in the Spirit, and in the Epistles Christ in doctrine; and these are necessary the one to the other as parts of an organic whole.

If each book is thus related to the other it is evident that we may find books acting as divine commentaries, the one upon the other.

Colossians throws light spiritually on Deuteronomy, in that both books are the preparation for the inheritance. Ephesians is a commentary on Joshua, in that both books show conflict in the endeavor to enter into the purchased possession.

Corinthians is a flash light on Judges, the Christians at Corinth being largely in the same attitude as that which characterized Israel in the former book, "every one doing that which seemed right in his own eyes." Hebrews is a key to Leviticus, and the Book of Revelation to the prophecy of Daniel.

From all this it follows that each book being characteristic in itself, *each book* must hang the key up beside its own door.

The key of the Revelation may be found in the nineteenth verse of the first chapter. "The things which thou hast seen, the things which are, and the things which shall be hereafter" (*meta tauta,* after these things) Past, Present, and Future, this is the inspired division of the book. The past things are in the first chapter, the now things are in the second and third chapters, the future things, or things which are after the *now* things, are from the fourth chapter on.

The key of the Book of Ecclesiastes is in the phrase "under the sun." It is the book that looks at the world from that standpoint and sees only vanity and vexation of spirit in the best that can be done there; it stands in contrast to the book of Ephesians where the believer exalted with Christ to the throne of God above the sun sees things from God's point of view, and rejoices in Him as the Author and End of his salvation.

In one of the Cantons of Switzerland whenever the inmates are away the key is placed under the cross at the door. Those who wish to enter the house know where the key is, and always look for it under the figure of the outstretched Christ. The final key that fits every book of the Bible is to be found under the Cross, under the figure of the outstretched Christ.

Take this key which comes from the cross, apply it to any book, open the door and enter in; stand for awhile in listening attitude, and the symphonies of eternal truth shall be heard sounding in Heavenly measures to your soul; stand patiently, and your eyes shall be anointed with eye-salve to behold the face of Him who is Himself, the Face and Likeness of God.

WHAT TO STUDY.

Many persons lose time and wander aimlessly through the Bible because they do not know just what to study. A few suggestions in this respect may be helpful.

1. *We ought to study Topics.* Such topics as Grace, Law, Faith, Hope, Kingdom, Covenants, Sabbath, Second Coming, Inspiration, Angels, Spirits, First and Second Resurrections.

2. *We ought to study the Types.* Types of Persons, Places, Events.

3. *Great Characters.* Such as Abraham, Isaac, Jacob,

Joseph, Moses, David, Saul, Elijah and Elisha of the Old Testament. Paul, Peter, James, John, and scores of others in the New Testament.

4. *Great Chapters.* Genesis xxii, Leviticus xvi, Numbers xxi, Deuteronomy viii, Isaiah liii, Matthew xiii, Luke xv, John iii, Revelation ii and iii.

5. *We ought to study Key Words.* Words and phrases, like Heavenlies, Much-more, Better, Straightway, Overcomes, the Eight Togethers of the New Testament, and the Seven Rests.

6. *The Names of God.* God, Creator absolute; Lord-God, Creator in Covenant relation; Jehovah (Yahveh), He who will be, the Coming One; Almighty God, the God of Providence; the Most-High God, the God of Nations.

7. *The Names of Persons.* Jacob, the Supplanter; Israel, Prince with God; Saul, Destroyer; Paul, the Worker; Simon, man in the flesh; Simon Peter, man in the flesh called by the grace of God into relation with the Son, made a part of the living Rock, and himself a living stone.

8. *Developments of Doctrine.* For example: The Incarnation, seen in Eve's thought about Cain, typified in the supernatural causation of Isaac's birth, fulfilled in Christ, and now expanded in Christians.

In this way we may study, Sacrifice, Atonement, Repentance, Conversion, Regeneration, Justification, Sanctification.

9. *Allusive Utterances.* A striking example of this is to be found in Philippians ii: 6. "Who, being in the form of God, thought it not robbery to be equal with God." That is to say, thought not to snatch at equality with God.)

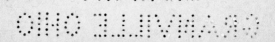

The allusion is evidently to some one who did; one who had the hardihood to think about robbing God of the glory of His supremacy. The very statement of the passage leads to such an inferential conclusion.

It leads to the inquiry as to what Scripture may say about the matter; and Scripture answers that there *was* such a person.

That being was Satan. Isaiah xiv: 12-14, Ezekiel xxviii.

Another example: II Peter iii: 3, 4. In this passage the Apostle warns against a class of scoffers who should arise in the church in the last days, and in the endeavor to justify their worldly lusts would mock and scoff at the thought of the Second Coming. The principle of allusive utterance thus indicates that, in the last days, there will be a *special testimony* in the church to the *imminency* of the Lord's Coming.

Under this head of what to study may be included, also, the Plan of Study.

PLAN OF STUDY.

It is necessary to have some definite plan or method to accomplish any real results.

1. *Compare Scripture with Scripture.*

It is written, that in His light we shall see light.

Illustration (Revelation xix: 15, Ephesians vi: 17). The sword out of His mouth in Revelation is explained by the Ephesians to be the sword of the Spirit, which is the Word of God, and thus the sword out of the mouth is simply the declaration that by the word of His mouth the Lord will arraign the nations at His Coming, and hale them to judgment.

Matthew xxv: 1, is explained by II Corinthians xi: 2,
The virgins of Matthew equalling the assembly of Christ.
presented as a virgin in Corinthians.

2. *Study slowly.*

You cannot "cram" the Bible. You must eat what
you get. Jeremiah xv: 16.

3. *Read carefully.*

Get all the light, examine every word, subject every
part to microscopic investigation; a preposition or an
article makes a difference. Dig into the original if you
can; get helps if you cannot.

4. *Patiently.*

If you do not understand to-day, you may to-morrow.
The *advance* in truth is in exact proportion to the *use* of
truth.

5. *Reverently.*

You are reading God's Word. His breath and presence are in it.

6. *Prayerfully.*

Pray for illumination, for opening "the heart to attend unto the things spoken." (Acts xvi: 14.)

Only when a Risen Saviour opened the understanding
of the Disciples could they understand the Scriptures.
"Then opened He their understanding, that they might
understand the Scriptures." Luke xxiv: 45. How significant that the last act of the Son of God before He
ascended was to open the understanding of His disciples
in relation to the Scriptures; *and how intensely significant that these Scriptures should be none other than the
Scriptures of Israel,* as it is written: "And beginning at
Moses and all the prophets, He expounded unto them in
all the Scriptures the things concerning Himself." Luke
xxiv: 27. And these Scriptures according to verse 44,

are Moses, the Prophets, and the Psalms, or, the Old
Testament from *Genesis to Malachi.*

7. *Read, and study constantly.*

Make it a daily practice to read and always to study
something, no matter how little.

IMPLEMENTS OF STUDY.

1. *The Bagster Bible.*

Always with a broad margin for marking. When you
mark be as systematic as you can. For example: *Black*
lines for Gospel, Historic, or Spiritual, statement. *Blue*
lines for Second Coming, and kindred truths, such as
the Kingdom, etc. *Red* lines for Blood, Sacrifice, the
Cross, and Atonement. *Green,* or violet ink for Holy
Spirit.

If you would make a distinction between the Coming
of Christ *for* His Church, and the Appearing of Christ
with His Church, use a star for the former, and a circle
with rays like a sun for the latter; for in the former He
comes as "The Morning Star" (Revelation xxii: 16),
and in the latter as the Sun of Righteousness. "Unto
you that fear my name shall the Sun of Righteousness
arise with healing in His wings." Malachi iv: 2.

The Bible intelligently marked is a splendid instrument
in the hands of a devoted student.

2. *A Cruden's Concordance.*

3. *A Topical Text Book.*

4. *A copy of the Revised Version* for examining read-
ings and phrase constructions.

Making use of these implements, following these
methods, and applying these principles, you will find:

1. *A splendid style.*

At one moment fresh with Eden blooms, anon hot with Sinai's flames: heaving with prophetic warnings, or jubilant with Messiah's strains: rapt in the glory of Isaiah's vision, or silvery with Bethlehem's natal song: sobbing with Gethsemane's woes, or triumphant with the Resurrection theme: tender with the Gospel call, and pitiful above the contrite heart; sulphurous with curses at the sight of sin, or melting into universal song as the door in Heaven opens, and He is seen, the Living Lord, the Coming King.

Apart from this, the literary value of the English translation is above price; great orators, some of them foreigners, have found in it a classic. Kossuth, the great Hungarian, declared that his pure English came from reading the English Bible.

2. *Supernatural wisdom.*

It tells the story of Light, Sun, Moon, and Stars, of deep Sea, and melted Rock, before Astronomy, or Geology had come to the birth; and waits patiently till Science shall stop its hypotheses, revealing even now to him who loyally reads it that the only opposition ever made from Science was not from Science itself, but from "Science falsely so called." I Timothy vi: 20.

3. *A Royal Dignity.*

Not a silly line in it: filled with the genius of reserve.

4. *Denunciation of Sin.*

5. *The continual cry of "Holy, Holy."*

6. *Unity of Design.*

The first Genesis unfolds in the new, the new Heavens and the new earth answer the old Heavens and the old earth, whilst Christ and His Church point back to the First Man and his bride, and the river under the throne becomes the reality of the river of Eden.

7. *Christ in every line.*

Here is the key that unlocks every mystery.

8. *Your character.*

By transgression and nature, a sinner under the judgment of God; by grace a sinner forgiven, justified, accepted as righteous before God and through regeneration, His deathless child.

9. *Your Future.*

A life of peace and power in the Paradise of God.

BENEFITS OF STUDY.

1. *Faith will be strengthened.* "So then Faith cometh by hearing, and hearing by the Word of God." Romans x: 17.

2. *Joy will be increased.* "I rejoice at thy Word as one that findeth great spoil." Psalm cxix: 162.

3. *Spiritual life nourished.* "Desire the sincere Milk of the Word that ye may grow thereby." I Peter ii: 2.

4. *The Christian thoroughly furnished unto all good works.* "All Scripture is given by inspiration of God, and is profitable for doctrine, for reproof, for correction, for instruction in righteousness; that the man of God may be perfect, *thoroughly furnished* unto all good works." II Timothy iii: 16, 17.

He who studies the Book as thus indicated will find himself able to flash into the darkness and ignorance of infidelic minds the light of the prismatic revelation of the truth of God, meet the difficulties of earnest seekers in the Word, and get for himself an abiding consciousness of its unity.

He will see it rooting there in Genesis, and fruiting here in Revelation.

He will see that the Old Creation begins with the Heavens, comes down to the earth, goes on with man's body and ends with his soul; and that the New Creation begins with man's soul, goes on to a perfect body, a perfect earth, and ends with the new heavens, a fourfold and complete triumph of Regeneration; regenerated soul, regenerated body, regenerated earth, and regenerated Heavens.

He will see that Christ is the centre of Heaven and Earth and Hell; that the whole universe is Christo-centric, and that the centre of the Christo-centric revelation is the immortality of the body as the enthronement and manifestation of God; that from all eternity the thought of God has been to set up a deathless incorruptible man as the image and likeness of Himself, and through him forever make Himself known governmentally and morally to the universe. He who thus studies will see with ever-increasing awe and adoration that God came down to be Man, that man might go up to be God forevermore.

He will get visions of God as by the banks of the river of Chebar; he will see above all the Glory One like unto the Son of Man: and from the throne high and lifted up where the Seraphs sing, he will hear the voices saying, "Behold your God;" and other voices saying, "You shall be like unto Him, for you shall see Him as He is."

AN ADDRESS ON THE SECOND COMING.

An Address on the Second Coming.

Unto them that look for Him shall He appear the Second time.—Hebrews ix: 28.

If the value of a doctrine was to be judged by the frequency of its mention, then easily the Second Coming of our Lord would be the most important doctrine in the Word of God; it will be admitted that the Atonement is the core of the Gospel, the crimson reservoir out of which flow forth the streams of gladness that fill the whole area of the Divine Commission, and yet this sublime word occurs but once in the New Testament, and there when faithfully translated is not atonement at all but reconciliation, something quite different and apart from atonement; on the other hand the doctrine of the Second Coming in this same New Testament is mentioned on an average, at least, once in thirty verses.

When you turn to the Old Testament you find that the seventh man who ever lived on the earth, the seventh man from Adam, even Enoch, spoke of the Second Coming, saying: "Behold the Lord cometh with ten thousands of His saints."

From Genesis to Malachi the book is filled with the doctrine.

It is set forth in type, figure, symbol, parable, story, illustration, and direct statement. The Spirit seems to exhaust human vocabulary in the vain endeavor to proclaim it. The noblest prose and the most exalted poetry the world ever knew break like waves upon the shore and at times seem to turn into mist in utter helplessness to express the coming glory.

The stars of Heaven pale, break loose from their orbits and fall, the waves of the sea roar, the floods lift up their voices, the mountains bow down at His presence, the trees of the wood clap their hands, and every voice in Heaven and earth cries out: "Behold He cometh, He cometh, the King;" and by the time you have reached Malachi and leaned across four centuries of prophetic silence your ears are full of the footsteps of the coming king.

The moment you enter the New Testament John the Baptist is heard speaking not of the First Advent but of the Second; and when the starlight of Bethlehem, the mystery of the manger, and the apprenticeship of thirty years are passed and the Christ sets forth upon His mission His lips are full, not of the First Advent but of the Second. Indeed I do not know that He ever spoke directly of His First Advent, but His lips were continually full of the Second. So filled was He with the thought of it that on one occasion He took His disciples up into the mountain height, and there on the background of the dark and black midnight was transfigured before them till His garments shone whiter than any fuller on earth could whiten them, blazing forth in the beauty of His essential light till they saw Him as their glorious and coming king. And the apostle Peter speaking of that supreme event declares in his epistle that the Lord manifested Himself not only as their king, but set forth in full detail the manner and fashion of the coming kingdom.

When he stood before His judges He was not careful to speak of that marvellous moment when the angels of God saluted Him upon His mother's breast, but lifting up His voice warned them that the hour was at hand when they should see Him coming on the bosom of the clouds in great power and glory.

When for the last time He passed through the Temple He so spoke of coming days that His disciples sought Him out privately and entreated Him that He would explain to them the import of His words; and sitting down there upon the Mount of Olives where the whole city and the vista of the centuried years lay before Him, He unfolded to them event after event with Judea and Jerusalem as the arena and centre of their emphasis until they beheld the climax of His Second Coming.

Just before the solemn Tragedy when He would comfort the hearts of His sorrowing followers, sorrowing because of the shadowing hour of separation, He takes them to the window of the little upper room and bidding them look out on the illimitable sweep of the nightly heavens lifts Himself to the level of Godhead and declares that He is going into that upper country to prepare a place for them; and that when He has completed it He will come again and receive them unto Himself.

After the Tragedy, when He has risen from the dead, lined the grave with the light of His own immortality, and ascended heavenwards, two angels stand by the uplooking disciples and say unto them: "Ye men of Galilee, why stand ye gazing up into heaven? This same Jesus, which is taken up from you into heaven, shall so come in like manner as ye have seen Him go into heaven."

On the day of Pentecost the Apostle Peter preaches to the Jews that this man of Nazareth whom they killed, and whom God had raised from the dead, was none other than their own Messiah; and that if they would repent, confess His death and resurrection in baptism, God would give them the times of refreshing promised in the prophets, and would send Jesus Christ to them a second time.

Throughout the Acts while the Apostles lift up the crucified Lord to the vision of faith they are always careful to declare that God raised Him from the dead and will send Him back.

When you pass into the Epistles you are confronted on the very threshold with the testimony that the Son of God is coming again. The Epistle to the Romans is divided into three sections, doctrinal, dispensational, and hortatory. Each section ends with the declaration that Christ is coming. The eighth chapter is the climax of one of the most stupendous and hopeful lines of argument ever written; and the climax of the eighth chapter is the Second Coming of Christ. The eleventh chapter is the climax of an argument concerning the dispensational distinction between Israel and the church; and the climax of that dispensational argument is the Second Coming of Christ. The sixteenth chapter is the climax of exhortations and regulations concerning the simple details of Christian life and obligation; and the climax of this chapter is the Second Coming of Christ.

The first chapter of the Primary Epistle to the Corinthians tells us that as Christians we come behind in no gift, our spiritual equipment is perfect, therefore we ought to be in the constant attitude of waiting for our Lord as stewards who will not be ashamed to meet Him. The climax of the fifteenth chapter is the argument for the resurrection of the dead; and the initial and climax of that argument is the Coming of Christ. Taking the whole race and sweeping it up into Adam for death, the Apostle declares that the race thus dying and dead shall come forth again in Christ both to salvation and damnation, but every man in his own order, and particularly, as described, they that are Christ's at His Coming; thus declaring that the First Resurrection, the resurrection of the saints of God, will take place at The Coming. In the second epistle to the same church Christ is seen coming to set up that Judgment Seat at which each Christian is to be manifested for reward.

In the Epistle to the Galatians we get no mention of the Second Coming because there the Apostle has us on the cross, crucified with Christ.

We get no mention of this great event in the Epistle to the Ephesians because there we are seen as risen and seated with Christ in Heavenly Places; we are there as those who have already ascended in the anticipation of the Spirit, as that church which He has raised, translated, and presented to Himself without spot or wrinkle, or any such thing.

In the first epistle written to the Gentiles, the Epistle to the Thessalonians, the Apostle Paul testifies that these converts had "turned to God from idols, to serve the living and true God; and to wait for His Son from Heaven, even Jesus, which delivered us from the wrath to come." It is a notorious fact that each chapter of these two epistles to the Thessalonians closes with the declaration that Christ is coming.

In writing to Timothy he laces the two epistles together with the Coming of Christ. In Titus he represents that Coming as the Blessed Hope. The whole aim of the Epistle to the Hebrews is to set up the types, figures, and shadows of truth, and let us see how they all melt into the white light of fulfillment in Christ, as their perfect Antitype, at His Second Coming.

James, with all the conservatism of Jerusalem and the

bondage of the Law upon him lifts up his voice and declares that the Lord is coming.

Peter testifies that the Second Coming of Christ is the one thing that appeals to faith and love, and in his Second Epistle warns the believer that the time will come, if the Lord should tarry, when scoffers will arise in the very midst, and in the name of Christ himself scoff and mock at the doctrine of the Second Coming, saying: "Where is the promise of His Coming?"

In his threefold and family epistle the Apostle John sounds the chord of "Home, sweet Home," in the exalted utterances concerning the Coming of Him whom he lovingly describes, as "The Coming One."

Jude quotes Enoch, and thus binds the New Testament back to the Old, making the whole Bible but one testimony as to the Coming of the King.

The Book of the Revelation is written by the Apostle John. It is called in our Bibles the Revelation of St. John, the Divine. Its proper title is, "The Revelation," that is to say, the Revealing, the Manifestation "of Christ." It might well be called in English, the Book of the Second Advent; its one subject from the first to the last of its chapters is the Second Coming of Christ. The book is like the roof of some mighty cathedral, each of the twenty-two chapters like a panel in the roof, each panel filled with a scenic representation of the Coming Christ.

So important is the doctrine to our Lord Himself that He practically puts His own signature to this book which specially speaks of it, openly and unqualifiedly avouching that He is its cause and inspiration, and attaching to it what He does not do to any other portion of Scripture, namely, a threefold blessing: Blessing to him who reads it, to those who hear it read, and to those who keep its "sayings."

As the book closes the Spirit and the Bride say come; and he who has heard the Lord's declaration that He is coming is commanded to say, "Come;" while the voice of Christ as the last utterance out of Heaven earthward, is heard saying: "Behold, I am Coming Quickly."

Thus from Genesis to Revelation this doctrine of the Second Coming is inwrought with the warp and woof of the inspired Word and lies as thick upon its pages as the autumn leaves which at this hour whirl about Manhattan; and he who keeps his ears alert as he opens its pages may hear the rustling of the footsetps of the Coming King.

From all this it is evident that the Coming of Christ is the predominantly mentioned doctrine in the Word of God.

How is it then that faithful preachers, those who claim to love their Lord, neglect it, make it the "Neglected Theme," send it into the background, and rarely mention it except with an apology as to its uselessness; giving the impression indeed that he who does preach it is guilty of some offense, if not against decency and order, at least, against wisdom and knowledge?

Not only is this doctrine the predominently mentioned one of the Bible, it is, also, the one bound up with every other doctrine of the Word of God; so bound up that it cannot be neglected without disaster to the whole body of truth.

It is bound up with every Fundamental doctrine.

It is bound up with the doctrine of the Resurrection.

Victory over death, the change from corruption to incorruption, from mortality to immortality, the resurrection, transfiguration, and translation of the church, are wholly and alone at the Coming of Christ.

It is bound up with the doctrine of Divine Sonship in believers, even as it is written:

"Beloved, now are we the sons of God, and it doth not yet appear what we shall be: but we know that, when He shall appear, we shall be like Him; for we shall see Him as He is."

It is bound up with the doctrine of the Deliverance of Creation from the Bondage of Corruption.

If you will put your ear to the breast of old mother earth you will hear her travail groans and cries as she seeks to bring forth a world into the light of peace, beyond the agony of human suffering and the stain of sin; if you listen, throughout her borders, in all the operation of her laws, you will hear the protest against that condition of existence where birth is followed by death, where hope is chased by despair, and where defeat, night, and silence, end the scene. The Apostle represents this groaning and protesting creation like one on the "tip-toe of expectation" craning the neck and looking forward to that hour when she shall be delivered from her bondage, and be manifested into the "glorious liberty of the sons of God" at the Coming of our Lord Jesus Christ.

It is bound up with the doctrine of the Deliverance of God and Christ over Satan.

Jesus Christ died that He might destroy "him that hath the power of death, that is, the Devil;" but this consummation devoutly to be wished for cannot take place till the door in Heaven opens, and the Lord Christ with His ascended church shall come forth like an army with banners to lay hold on that old Serpent, which is the Devil, and Satan, and bind him for a thousand years.

It is bound up with the doctrine of the Recognition of the dead, as it is written:

"Then," in the day of the Lord's coming, "we shall know even as we are known." Wherefore the Apostle writes to the Thessalonians that they will be his crown and rejoicing, whether by resurrection or translation, in the Presence of our Lord Jesus Christ at His Coming.

It is bound up with every exhortation to Christian Living.

Would the Apostle exhort Christians to attend on the service of the Lord's Day and not forsake the assembling of themselves together as the manner of some is, he does so by an appeal to the imminency of the Lord's Coming.

Would he exhort to faithfulness in the Breaking of Bread, he does so by saying unto them: "Ye do show the Lord's death *till He come.*" Thus making manifest that this ordinance is to be observed in the light of the Lord's Coming and that each time we gather at The Table whether we know it or not we are proclaiming that the Second Coming of Christ is the *terminus ad quem* of Christian pilgrimage.

Does the Apostle exhort to Christian Liberality, he does so, by the Coming of the Lord.

Would he inspire to Holy Living, he says: "I pray God your whole spirit and soul and body be preserved blameless unto the Coming of our Lord Jesus Christ."

Would he comfort those who mourn above their Christian dead, he does so by the fact of the Second Coming, telling them that, "the Lord HIMSELF, shall descend from heaven with a shout, with the voice of the archangel, and with the trump of God; and the dead in Christ shall rise first: Then we which are alive and remain shall be

CAUGHT UP TOGETHER WITH THEM in the clouds to meet the Lord in the air." And then speaking by inspiration he adds: "Wherefore COMFORT ONE ANOTHER WITH THESE WORDS." That is to say, the blessed words that the Lord is coming to bring the dead and the living saints together in His presence.

Does the Apostle see that "perilous times" are at hand in which there shall be a form of godliness but denying the power thereof, an hour coming when the church will no longer endure sound doctrine but heaping to themselves teachers who shall tickle their ears be turned away from the truth and unto fables; and does he desire to exhort the Christian minister to be faithful among the faithless found, he does so, by the Coming of Christ, saying:

"I charge thee therefore before God, and the Lord Jesus Christ, who shall judge the quick and the dead, *and by* (such is the true rendering) HIS APPEARING and His kingdom; PREACH THE WORD."

Does he see the time approaching when there shall be a great apostasy, a great falling away, and Antichrist seated in the Temple of God showing himself that he is God; and would he comfort the minds of the followers of the truth as against The Lie, he does so by declaring that the Lord is coming in His might and power to destroy with the breath of His lips this last masterpiece of Satan.

Does the Apostle James see that in the closing hours of this dispensation Capital and Labor shall look at each other with scowling faces and clenched hands; does he see that rich men shall heap up treasures for the last days, that there will be an immense accumulation of wealth in the hands of the few, and that the rust of un-

used money shall eat like a gangrene in the hands of
those who hold it; does he see that the lawful wage of
the laborer by unjust combination is kept back from him,
and does he hear the voice of that injustice crying in
the ears of the Lord of Sabaoth; does he see that im-
patience at this injustice is unnerving the hearts of those
who confess the name of Christ, and that the temptation
to take justice in their own hands is gaining ground;
and would he counsel them not to be guilty of such
treason against the profession they have made as the
followers of a rejected Christ, he does so by saying unto
them: "Be patient, therefore, brethren, UNTO THE COM-
ING OF THE LORD." Again: "The Coming of the Lord
draweth nigh." And this climax: "Behold the Judge
STANDETH BEFORE THE DOOR."

Would the Apostle Peter exhort the Christian Pastors
to faithfulness in that most solemn and arduous of tasks,
the shepherding of the flock, he does so by announcing
to them that when Christ "the Chief Shepherd shall
appear, they shall receive a crown of glory that fadeth not
away."

Does the Apostle Jude exhort to stand by the faith
once delivered to the saints, he does so by quoting the
testimony of Enoch the seventh from Adam that the Lord
with ten-thousands of His saints is coming.

Do the prophets of the Old Testament announce in
joyful accents that there shall be a time when the knowledge of the Lord will cover the earth as the waters cover
the face of the deep, they do so by declaring in unbroken
symmetry of speech that this era of righteousness and
splendor will be introduced by the Coming of the Holy
One of Israel, even the Lord Jesus Christ.

Does the Lord Jesus Christ Himself fortell the end

of this age as a terrific crisis in the world's history; does He announce with all the ex-cathedra authority of headquarter's truth, with all the incontrovertible authority of Him who is The Truth and no lie that the end of this age will be in wars, in the multiplication of lawlessness, the mob element rising and falling in its emotions with cries like the roaring of the seas, and men's hearts failing them with fear for looking after the things that are coming on the earth; does He raise the question whether faith, *the* faith, shall abide to the end; and would He give comfort in the darkness which His words seem to inspire, He does so, by assuring us that in the deepest hour of the earth's spiritual midnight He will Himself come as the Light of the world, that light without which the earth must abide in its darkness forever.

In short, the Coming of Christ, considered as a testimony, is so bound up with the varied doctrines of the Word of God that it is impossible to neglect it without producing a fatal lack of emphasis in any doctrine preached.

Let the preacher lose sight of the fact that Christ is coming back to this world as a glorified man, the man who was raised from the dead in the body in which He died, and it will not be long before he will lose sight of the veritable resurrection of Christ; and losing sight of that immortal body on the throne, the transition to the moment when the incarnation is to be seen only as an incident, and not as the perpetual incorporation of the eternal God, will not be long deferred; nor will it be long before such a preacher will find himself upon the threshold of that unecclesiastical but all-pervading Unitarianism which finds no need either of Incarnation or Resurrection.

So bound up with the body of truth is this testimony of the Second Coming that there are doctrines which cannot be fully presented without holding them up in the light of it.

This is illustrated in the doctrine of Atonement, and may be demonstrated by looking at the type in the wilderness.

On the great day of Atonement after he had offered the sacrifice on the altar the high priest went within the veil into the most holy place to make atonement (and let it be remembered that the atonement was not made on the altar but within the veil as the type of Heaven, and that in fulfillment of that type the Lord Jesus Christ did not make atonement on the cross but in Heaven after His resurrection); the high priest let it be repeated went within the veil to make atonement, and not till he came out the second time, and not till the man who had led away the live goat came back in the sight of all the people without that sin offering could it be said that the atonement was complete and justified to the expectation of the people. Now says the Apostle referring to this event as only a shadow, and bringing into the mind of his hearers the substance, "So Christ was once offered to bear the sins of many; and to them that look for Him shall He appear the Second Time without sin (offering) unto salvation." Thus this whole dispensation is ante-typically the Day of Atonement, and its last emphasis will be the Coming of Christ.

You might just as well take the auricle and ventricle out of the heart and expect that it would not affect the circulation of the blood as to imagine for a moment that the doctrine of the Second Coming can be neglected without affecting and deranging the whole body of truth.

In the face of such testimony and demonstration, to neglect the preaching of the Second Coming seems well-nigh criminal; and he who wilfully does it with the light of an open Bible before him is arranging for himself at the Judgment Seat of Christ a moment of shame and sorrow, the shame and sorrow of a workman who has not studied to show himself approved unto God, and who in the hour of his chosen responsibility failed to rightly divide His Word.

From the Scriptural point of view the Coming of Christ is a Second Coming.

It has been presented in such fashion that it might well be described as a many times coming.

It is said that Christ came at the destruction of Jerusalem under the Romans, that He comes in pestilence and plague, whenever the clouds gather, the winds sweep, or the tidal waves rush upon the shore as they did at Galveston; that he comes each time a godly man dies, or a saintly woman goes home to God; and in all reverence it may be said that only God Himself knows or can keep account of the different ways and times in which the Lord is to come as taught by those who have neglected the Scriptural declaration that "He shall appear the Second time."

The statement that the destruction of Jerusalem was the Coming of Christ is one of those statements which has been repeated so often that it has all the sacredness of Holy Writ to a certain class of minds.

The statement, however, is so entirely and excuselessly absurd that it seems scarcely worth the while even to reply to its repetition.

The simple facts concerning the Destruction of Jerusalem and its relation to the Coming of Christ are

these: in the twenty-first of Luke, our Lord says three
things: 1. Jerusalem will be besieged and taken.
2. Jerusalem will be trodden down by the Gentiles. 3.
When the treading down by the Gentiles is fulfilled,
"Then shall they see the Son of Man Coming." The
order given by the Lord therefore is, 1. Jerusalem
taken. 2. Jerusalem trodden down. 3. The appearing
of Christ; thus a *Whole Period,* called the *Treading
Down of the Gentiles,* occurs between the Destruction of
Jerusalem and the Appearing of Christ a Second time.

In the twenty-fourth of Matthew, the Lord declares
that there shall be a Tribulation coming upon Jerusalem
and Judea such as the world has never known nor shall
ever know again.

This terrific Tribulation He declares will be followed
immediately by His Appearing in Glory, as it is
written: "Immediately after the tribulation of those days
shall the sun be darkened, and the moon shall not give
her light, and the stars shall fall from heaven, and the
powers of the heavens shall be shaken; *and then* shall
appear the sign of the Son of Man in heaven: and then
shall all the tribes of the earth (of Judea, according to
the context: v. 16: 'Then let them which be in Judea
flee into the mountains);' then shall all the tribes of the
earth mourn, and they shall SEE the Son of man Coming
in the clouds of heaven with power and great glory."

No such event took place *immediately* after the destruction of Jerusalem by Titus, it never has taken place;
therefore the Tribulation cannot refer to any destruction
of Jerusalem in the past, it is a tribulation in connection
with Jerusalem in the future; and as the Appearing of
Christ is to take place immediately after the tribulation,
then the Second Appearing of Christ is still future:

whatever else may be involved in the Tribulation it
does not, it cannot teach that the destruction of Jerusalem centuries ago was the Coming of Christ. To assume that the agony of Jerusalem in that great siege,
and the Providential visitation of judgment on the
guilty people are equivalent to the Appearing of Christ;
or, to assume that Christ came at all, even invisibly, are
gratuitous suggestions and not exposition.

To say that He who is health and strength, and who
is promised to us in the glory of the Father comes in the
Bubonic plague, in pestilence and famine, are contradictions of terms.

To say that the wild lawless storm is the Coming of
Christ, is to contradict the scene yonder in Galilee, when
arising from the pillow in the hinder part of the ship
where He had been asleep, He looked out upon the black,
raging tempest, said, "Peace, be still," and thus became
the end instead of beginning of the storm.

But of all mistaken expositions is that which seeks
to make death figure forth as the Second Coming
of Christ. If it were not so grave a violation of the
Word of God and every legitimate principle of exegesis
it might well provoke the keenest and most merciless
satire. But to the Word and the Testimony, what saith
it? The answer is that so far from Christ coming to
the believer at death, the believer at death GOES TO BE
WITH CHRIST, even as it is written: "Having a desire to
depart, and be with Christ." And yonder we have a
scenic demonstration of it. Stephen has been condemned to death by the Jewish Sanhedrin. In the council he looks up and sees the heavens open and Jesus
standing at the right hand of God. He sees him standing there just as one might stand at the threshold of his

home if he desired to act the part of a cultured host in receiving his invited guests; thus Jesus seeing the tragedy approaching and the hour of the martyr's death and departure for heaven at hand, rises up in all the courtly love of the perfect host to receive His invited guest; now they have their victim down upon his knees outside the gate, the stones raining upon him, marring his face as his Master's face was marred; and knowing the end is near Stephen lifts up his voice beseechingly, for what? That the Lord may come to him? Nay, he lifts up his voice and says: "Lord Jesus, RECEIVE my spirit." Thus at death Stephen departs to be with his Lord. Wherefore speaking by inspiration the Apostle declares that at death we are "Absent from the body and present with the Lord."

But yonder on the shore of the lake after His resurrection the Lord Himself brings the truth to view in open demonstration. He had just told Peter how he might die, and Peter filled with that unconquerable spirit of the unfitness of things which had so often betrayed him turned to the Lord and demanded of Him what John should do. The Lord rebuked him, declaring that it was a matter that did not concern him, saying: "If I will that he tarry till I come, what is that to thee? Follow thou me." And we are told significantly, "then went this saying abroad among the brethren, that that disciple SHOULD NOT DIE." Now if the Coming of Christ meant death then the disciples ought to have said: "This man will surely die seeing that the Lord comes at death and has fixed the term of this man's service till He come." But just because they knew that the Lord was Life and therefore the enemy of death they said: *"Since John is to wait till the Lord comes back, he will never die."*

It is true that the Lord had not said that John should positively wait until His return; it is true He had only raised the question and drawn Peter's attention to the fact that this issue of waiting was a matter entirely dependent on His will, and that this was a domain into which Peter had no right to intrude; yet, nevertheless, the possibility that John might remain till the Second Coming was *prima facie* evidence to the disciples that John would not die. No more living demonstration could be given of the utter fallacy of the doctrine that the Coming of the Lord of Life means death.

All this is in evidence that the Coming of Christ is not the thousand and one things applied to it as such, but that it is indeed, and in very truth, what the Apostle declares it to be, "A Second Appearing."

According to Scripture the Coming of Christ is a Personal Coming.

It is written: "The Lord HIMSELF shall descend from Heaven."

Concerning this selfhood we are in no doubt. No sooner had He ascended into Heaven than the angels descended to comfort the hearts of the sorrowing disciples with the sublime assurance: "Ye men of Galilee, why stand ye gazing up into Heaven, this SAME Jesus— shall so come in like manner."

The same Jesus, He who walked by blue Galilee, who sat on the well-curb of Sychar with the shadows of noon under His feet, the dust of earth on His garments, the love of God in His heart, the grace of salvation on His lips, and the touch of healing in His hands.

He is coming with the stigmata of the cross, so coming that every eye may see Him, and all they who pierced Him; coming so that repentant Israel may ask, whence are these wounds in Thy hands and hear him answer that these are the wounds which He received in the house of His friends; coming so that we may look at Him not only as He is, but as He was, looking upon Him with our eyes, hearing Him with our ears, and handling Him with our hands; coming in the body which His mother Mary gave him, the dust of earth crystallized with immortality.

The doctrine of Scripture is that the Second Personal Coming of Christ is Imminent.

The Apostles believed that the Lord might come in their day. They believed He might come at any moment, that at any turn of the road He might lay His hand upon them and with the sound of the trumpet shout them up into glory.

So far from telling Christians to prepare for death and Heaven the Apostles exhorted them to be on the constant guard for the Lord's Return, assuring them that "we shall not all sleep (that is to say, die) and that there would be thus a possibility of belonging to that generation to whom the Coming of the Lord *could not* mean death." They took up the exhortation of the Lord Himself: "What I say unto you, I say unto all, Watch."

As already shown they based their exhortations to every precept of Christian living on the imminency of this Coming, and couched these exhortations in such precision of language that there is no other alternative if this Coming is not imminent, but that these Apostles were either deceived or ignorant men, or wholly a set of shameless deceivers.

Either dilemma whether of ignorance or wilful deception is destructive to New Testament authority, vitiates every other doctrine, and rings the knell of their inspiration.

Assuming, however, that the New Testament is the inspired word of God it follows inevitably that there is no warrant for the interposition of times and seasons between us and the Coming of our Lord. Certainly there is no warrant for that colossal heresy, that invented theory of a thousand years of Gospel triumph; no warrant for that rhetorical sophistry that we are to have the "purple and gold of Millennial glory" before He comes.

Those who have the courage to proclaim the Postmillennial coming of the Son of God are forced to do so with the assumption that they possess a knowledge as to the date of that supreme event not only greater than that of any other set of men, greater even than that of the angels of God, but greater than that of the Son of God Himself; for He who is supposed to be the final authority in the matter has said: "Of that day and that hour knoweth no man, no, not the angels which are in heaven, *neither the Son.*"

There is no doubt that in the present state of the church it would be easy in any address to start the issue and the controversy as to the inspiration and infallibility of the Bible.

There is a school of preaching which teaches that the Bible is true only in spots; and that those who would read it must do so by a hop skip and jump method, hopping clear over to the other side of the Hexateuch, skipping Joshua and the Judges, skipping the Synoptics, jumping over a large part of the Johannic gospel, quietly but skilfully leaping over the book of Acts as a gymnast will leap over a patch-work quilt spread beneath him, and at the book of the Revelation not jumping at all, considering that book no more worthy of attention than a wild man's ravings.

No doubt battles can be fought over the question as to whether the Bible is true or false, but there is one fact about which no intelligent well-read man has any right to have a single second's issue, and that is: the New Testament does say in language which it is impossible to mistake, that the Coming of Christ is imminent, that it may take place at any moment.

He, therefore, who places ten days or a thousand years between us and the Coming of the Lord contradicts Him, falsifies Him, and charges Him with fallibility within the sound of His own words: "Watch therefore; for ye know *neither the day nor the hour* wherein the Son of man cometh."

.The Coming of Christ is the one event which in Scripture is always on the horizon and like the sunlight, illuminates all the theologic landscape with its glow and color. So emphasized is this imminency that he who should read the New Testament for the first time would close the book with the involuntary impression that the next thing was the Coming of Christ.

The Coming of Christ, while one grand event, has Two distinct stages, or parts; a Secret, and an Open or Public part.

In the first He comes into the air, in the second to the Mount of Olives; in the first He comes to the church, in the second to Israel; in the first He comes for His Church, in the second with His Church; in the first He comes to a marriage, in the second to a judgment; in the first as a Bridegroom, in the second as the King; in the first to gather the Church and present it to Himself, a holy and acceptable Church, in the second, to establish His kingdom, and with the church in righteousness rule the earth.

The first part is symbolized by the morning star, the second by the rising of the sun; the first by the thief who comes in the night without warning, the second by the lightning that flashes across the sky with accompanying thunder; in the first part the church will be caught away into the air secretly as Enoch was caught away before the flood, as Lot was snatched out of Sodom before the fire, as Elijah was swept up to glory without dying, as Paul was caught up to the third heavens alive, and as the Son of God Himself passed upward into and through the heavens to the throne of God without the knowledge of the world.

This first part in the Greek is called Parousia, and means His Bodily Presence; the second in the same language is called the Epiphaniea, and means the *Manifestation* of His Bodily Presence; the first is called "Our Gathering together *unto* Him," the second "Our Appearing *with* Him in Glory," or the Glorious Appearing; the first is commonly spoken of in Scripture as the "Coming of the Lord," the second is known as "The Day of the Lord."

Between these two parts of the second Advent there are at least seven prophetic years, and these seven years form the burden of the book of Daniel and the book of Revelation.

Between us and the Secret Coming of the Lord, the Parousia, there is not a single predicted event; between us and the second part of this Second Coming there are many predicted events, the universal European war, the restoration of Israel to their own land, the rise of Antichrist, and the final union of all the Eastern nations under Russia as the Gog and Magog of Ezekiel.

The attitude of the church is locally and practically in

relation to the first or secret part of our Lord's Coming, while the attitude of Israel is, and must always be, towards the open, or glorious Coming. Israel's attitude is that of waiting for a sign, the church's attitude is that of waiting for a sound; just as Israel of old were waiting on the hither side of Jordan for the sound of a trump that they might go over and possess the Land, so the church is waiting on the hither side of time for the sound of the trump of God that she may go over and possess in the glory of her promised immortality all the land that lieth beyond the shadow of death.

The Coming of Christ is held out as "The Blessed Hope" of the church. Nowhere are Christians exhorted to prepare for death or hope for Heaven, but always, without a single break in the utterance, to watch, to wait, to hope for the Coming of the Lord.

And well may the church so watch, and wait, and hope; that Coming means the end of her long and weary pilgrimage, it means the putting off the garments of the traveller and putting on the garments of home; it means the triumph over sin, sickness, sorrow and death; it means no longer the world's suppliant, but its ruler; it means the presence of the king, the possession of His likeness, the share of His throne, and the administration of His kingdom; it means everything for which the church has hoped and prayed, all for which she has striven and endured; it means the girding her with final power for the accomplishment of all the purpose for which God determined her from the unbeginning depths of eternity; it means the accomplishment in certitude of that which is now sought with hesitation and uncertain success: the bringing of the whole world at last to the feet of the Crucified, where with unspeakable joy she may hear every tongue confess that Jesus Christ is Lord, to the glory of God the Father; it means the reaching of that moment when there will be no longer the need of intercession for erring saints, seeing that each saint shall be shining in all the glory of the Intercessor: it means no longer the need of the written Word, nor of teachers, seeing that "All shall know the Lord from the least to the greatest," as He says, "I will put my laws into their mind, and write them in their hearts," and shall Himself, *as the source of the written Word,* be the living, present and infallible Revelation of God's mind to men; oh, this Coming of Christ and the Translation of the Church means the fulfillment as human minds have little dreamed of that immense promise that "The knowledge of the Lord shall cover the earth as the waters the face of the deep."

Small wonder is it that the Coming of Christ is called the Blessed Hope to the church when it means her exaltation, the triumph of her Lord, and the salvation of the whole world; but wonder beyond measure it is that in the face of the fact that the beginning of these "days of Heaven on earth" is imminent in the imminent Coming of our Lord, and in the face of the fact that all Scripture proclaims it, that the church in any part of it whether in pulpit or in pew should turn her back upon it; or that any of her accredited ministers should neglect the story of it, seek to hide the beauty of its shining, or rob the sorrowing of the blessedness of its comfort.

The Coming of Christ, and in its last analysis, the appearing of Christ in glory, is the only hope for Israel; and this is concretely illustrated in the story of Paul's conversion: he was never converted by the preaching of the Gospel, but by the appearing of Christ in glory above the Damascus gates.

He tells us that he is as one born out of due time, and therefore set ahead of the time that he might be a prophecy and pledge of the way and manner in which his own nation should afterwards be saved.

Only when Israel shall see their Messiah coming in glory will they believe on Him; then shall they be in mourning for Him as one mourneth for the dead; then shall they take up the fifty-third chapter of Isaiah and chant with lamentation and mingled hope before Him: "We did esteem Him stricken, smitten of God, and afflicted. But He was wounded for our transgressions, He was bruised for our iniquities; the chastisement of our peace was upon Him; and with His stripes we are healed;" then shall a fountain be opened for uncleanness and sin in the City of David, and so, "All Israel shall be saved," in fulfillment of that promise that, "The Deliverer shall come unto Zion and turn away ungodliness from Jacob."

Only when Messiah the Lord shall come in glory can Israel become the "Head and no longer the Tail of nations." Only when Christ the Lord comes to take the throne of His father David will Israel and Judah fully enter into and possess the Covenant land.

The Coming of Christ then is that one event which holds out hope for this people "scattered and peeled."

The Coming of Christ taken in its completed sense is the only hope of the world governmentally.

Over all the vain endeavors at self government, over all the uprise of human plans in governmental schemes, over monarchy and mob, may be heard the voice of God saying: "I will overturn it, I will overturn it till He comes whose right it is to reign; and I will give it Him." Only when the Lord's judgments are in the earth, so it is written, "will the people learn righteousness." Only when government is administered in the hands of a righteous man, God's Man, the Second and Eternal Man, will men beat their swords into ploughshares and their spears into pruning hooks.

In short, only by the Coming of Christ will the failure of the first man be undone, the subtlety of Satan be matched, sin be uprooted, death be abolished, redemption be completed, Paradise be regained, and the whole earth be filled with the glory of God.

Such is this doctrine which in many quarters of the church has practically fallen out of the scheme of preaching.

All the more then because of the neglect of it, it ought to be preached. This is indeed Apostolic principle. Just as soon as the Apostle warns Timothy the young preacher that the time is coming when the church will no longer endure sound doctrine, he urges him by all means to preach it "in season and out of season."

This doctrine of the Second Coming therefore ought to be preached, and insistently and fully preached.

It ought to be preached in order that the church might not get a false concept of her relation to the world in this age, and that she might not continue to think that her only way to Heaven and glory was through the darkness and gloom of the grave. It ought to be preached in order that she might always be on the alert to proclaim the Gospel committed to her charge, lest coming suddenly the Lord should find her asleep on the bosom of a dead world.

It ought to be preached in order that the elect remnant in Israel might as in the days of Pentecost believe and become a part of the church, thus attaining, even, unto more than natural blessing.

It ought to be preached that the men of the world might see that there is something more imminent than death, and that at any moment the Master might rise up and shut to the door of grace.

It ought to be preached by the preacher for his own benefit, in order that he might see the stately march of all the doctrines of the Word of God as they move forward in serried rank and cast their trophies at the feet of the Coming King, saluting Him as the inspiration and objective of them all.

The doctrine cannot be preached too much.

No more gratuitous libel was ever circulated than the assertion that the preaching of it has in it a tendency to lead the preacher to ride it as a hobby. Let any man try to ride it as a hobby and he will find instead that he is riding in the chariot car of God's glory, and that every spoke in every wheel is flashing forth every other doctrine, testifying that every doctrine consummates itself in this Doctrine of doctrines; and that this identical doctrine is being born swiftly and triumphantly forward because it rests on the revolution of all other doctrines.

No man can faithfully preach the Second Coming and neglect any doctrine of the Word. No man who believes in the imminent Coming of the Lord and knows how to preach it will ever be guilty of denying the inspiration of that Word, the resurrection of the body, or the glory and necessity of Atonement. If any of the fundamental doctrines are neglected, as it is charged in "Modern Preaching," the neglect will not be found crouching at the door of him who preaches the Coming of his Lord.

* * * * * * * * *

Nay, let any one take up this doctrine and preach it, it

will make the Risen and Ascended Lord the most real thing in all the universe of God to him; it will keep the door in Heaven open and let the light from the land of the living fall across the land of the dying; it will keep the ear open and alert to hear the sound of His voice; it will sweep through the soul like a purifying breath from the lips of the King, leading that soul to purify itself, as it is written, "He that hath this Hope on Him, purifieth himself, even as He is pure;" it will make the written Word to shine as a burnished mirror, reflecting the glory of God; it will gird him who believes and preaches it, in the face of any pain or disaster, with all the strength of one who sore beleaguered hears the sound of delivering footsteps; or, as of one who in the dark and black night feels the gleam of coming day upon his brow.

If to-day Jesus Christ is the supreme actuality of my life; if to-day this written Word is to me the symphony of Heaven and of earth; if to-day my faith is stronger and my hope brighter; if to-day in face of the world's deepening pessimism, its weakness, weariness and woe, I find myself filled with an unconquerable optimism, with an unhesitating faith in God's ultimate and infinite triumph, it is because I believe that at any moment I may hear a voice like the voice of a trumpet talking with me and saying, "Come up hither;" and that in an instant, in the twinkling of an eye, I may be in His presence, not to lay the armor down and be at rest, but to come forth clad in the Master's likeness, and with Him descend as He goes forth to take His own world again, taking it as He will, by creation's undisputed right, by blood redemption and kingly conquest.

*   *   *   *   *   *   *   *   *

Let no man fear that in preaching the Second Coming he is committed to the minimizing of the cross.

Nay, rather, let us hold up the cross till men shall see it as the very heart throb of God, the mighty manifestation of His measureless love; let us hold it up till it shall be seen that all the claims of Divine righteousness have been fully and finally met there; let us hold it up till men shall see that it is no longer the Sin question but the Son question; let us hold it up till men shall see the crown of thorns stabbing His brow and marring His face as no face of man was ever marred; but let us hold it up so that men may see that this marred and crucified One is also the risen and glorified One; yea, let us so hold it up that men may see that this risen and glorified One, this "Man in Glory," is coming back in the body in which he was crucified, "This same Jesus:" yea and amen, let us hold it up for every eye like that of the serpent-bitten Israelite to see; but let us hold it up in the light of that Second Coming, till as men cast their gaze upon it they shall behold the crown of thorns slowly but surely transforming into the crown of Glory on the radiant head of your Coming King and mine.

AN ADDRESS ON THE
HOLY SPIRIT.

An Address on the Holy Spirit.

The Holy Ghost which is in you.—I Cor. vi: 19.

THE TWOFOLD OFFICE.

In the New Testament the Holy Spirit is presented to us as filling two distinct offices. In the one He is the Comforter, in the other He is the Enduer. As Comforter He operates in the Church, as Enduer He operates through the Church. As Comforter He hides Himself, as Enduer He reveals Himself. In the one He is a revelator, in the other an administrator. As Comforter He is the promise of the Son, as Enduer He is the promise of the Father. As the Comforter His coming has to do exclusively with the Church, as Enduer His coming had to do primarily with Israel.

The Holy Spirit, as Comforter, is given by the risen Son of God; the Holy Spirit, as Enduer, is sent by the exalted Lord and Christ. The gift of the Comforter is based on the prayer of Christ, the gift of the Enduer is based on the words of a prophet. The Comforter announces the beginning of the Church, the Enduer announces the opening of the Kingdom of Heaven. The objective work of the Comforter is consolation to troubled disciples, the objective work of the Enduer is aggressive power to waiting witnesses. The Comforter links us to Christ, the Enduer links us to one another in Christ.

Thus the office of the Holy Spirit is twofold and distinct; so is His inauguration into those two offices.

The Holy Spirit, as Comforter, did not come on the

Day of Pentecost. Pentecost is in no sense the coming of the Comforter. At Pentecost there is no thought of consolation for sorrowing orphans, but demonstration of power to helpless messengers. The Comforter as promised in John xiv, was to make manifest the presence of Christ; the coming of the Holy Spirit, as recorded at Pentecost, made evident the absence of Christ. The Comforter was to make known the presence of Christ down here; Pentecost made it clear that the presence was up there. The Comforter was to make known that Christ *is* here to the end of the age; Pentecost proclaimed that Christ *cannot* be here till the end of the age.

The coming of the Holy Spirit at Pentecost was not altogether a new thing; the coming of the Comforter, as promised, was something entirely new: this promise was that the Holy Spirit should be a permanent abiding presence, in the bodies of men. Such an indwelling of the Spirit had never taken place. The Holy Spirit never dwelt as an abiding presence in any man, not in Adam, or Abraham, or Moses, or John the Baptist. He had moved men; He had filled them, filled them from their birth, but He had never stayed in men continuously. David could pray, "Take not Thy Holy Spirit from me." No man who has the Spirit of God can offer that prayer to-day without being guilty of excuseless ignorance, because the Holy Spirit, as an abiding presence in any man, is there as a seal, "sealing him unto the day of redemption."

Men could ask the Father, in the days of Christ, to send them the Holy Spirit. In this day no child of God can offer that prayer without confessing ignorance of the Word of God, because when the Spirit comes to take up His abode in the body, that body becomes the temple of the Holy Spirit, which Spirit, saith an apostle, "is *in* you, which ye *have* of God."

The Comforter, as the promised continual indwelling of the Spirit, was thus something new, and as the coming of the Spirit at Pentecost was not wholly new, then Pentecost was not the coming of the Comforter.

The Comforter as an indwelling presence was promised directly to all believers, but on the day of Pentecost the Holy Spirit came directly only on the original disciples. To all others He was communicated, not when they believed, but after they believed; not by the Spirit Himself, but by the laying-on of the hands of the Apostles. As the Comforter was to be the heritage of all believers, and the manifestation of Pentecost was only upon the Apostles, it is evident that Pentecost is not the inauguration of the Comforter.

At Pentecost the Holy Spirit came audibly and visibly, as a rushing, mighty wind, as flaming tongues of fire, and His presence was made known to all in Jerusalem. But the Son of God declared that when the Comforter should come the world would not see Him, the world would not know Him. The coming of the Holy Spirit at Pentecost therefore stands in direct contrast and contradiction to the manner in which the Comforter was promised to come by the Son of God Himself. Nay, more! The Apostle Peter in his sermon on the day of Pentecost declares that Pentecost and the coming of the Comforter cannot be one and the same thing. Saint Peter declares that Pentecost is the begun fulfillment of the prophecy of Joel. This prophecy is the promise of the Father. The promise of the Father was to restore the kingdom in Israel. Pentecost is therefore the answer of Jesus Christ from heaven to the question of

His disciples as recorded in the first chapter of the Acts. "Wilt thou," they said, "at this time restore the kingdom to Israel?" When our Lord promised the Comforter, none of the disciples thought of asking Him about the kingdom, but the moment, yonder at Bethany, that He spoke of the outpouring of the Spirit as the promise of the Father immediately they said unto Him, "Wilt thou, at this time," that is to say, at the outpouring, "restore the kingdom to Israel?"

Between the promise and the question there is the link of eternal logic, for that promise of God written here in the Prophet Joel, had been made in connection with the announcement of the day of the Lord, and the setting-up of Israel, as the head and no longer the tail of the nations. And thus Pentecost is the affirmative answer to the question. By that mighty outpouring, by that tongue of fire, by that prophetic voice, He says unto them: "Yea and amen, as Jehovah of Israel, as the Wonderful, the Counsellor, the Mighty God, the Everlasting Father, the Prince of Peace, I will restore the kingdom unto Israel now, if Israel will receive Me as the King." And turning to them Peter says: "Repent and convert, that your sins may be blotted out, so that the times of refreshing (the outpouring of the Spirit), may come from the presence of the Lord, and He will send Jesus Christ, who before was preached unto you 'as your King.'"

Thus, according to Saint Peter, Pentecost is the begun fulfillment of a promise which antedates the promise of a Comforter eight hundred years. Now the promise made eight hundred years before Christ, and in connection with the kingdom in Israel, cannot be the promise which Christ gives eight hundred years after, solely in relation to the church in the world.

But if it be still held that Pentecost is the fulfillment of the promise of the Comforter, then it must be said that not only does the day of Pentecost fail to show a single line or characteristic of that promise, not only does it contradict everything that is said of the Comforter, but it goes further, it absolutely ignores the most stupendous event in the history of the Holy Spirit in His relation to men.

That event is recorded in the Gospel according to Saint John xx: 22. On the evening of the day on which our Lord rises from the dead, He meets His disciples, breathes upon them and says: "Receive ye the Holy Ghost." This is fifty days before Pentecost, almost two months. If Pentecost is the fulfillment of the promised Comforter, then this supreme moment, this first act of the risen Son of God must be ignored and set aside. It has been ignored and set aside in theology altogether. But you cannot ignore it with impunity. It is there; you must account for it. It is an actual coming of the Holy Spirit. He comes from Christ. Christ gives Him. Christ sends Him. He says to His disciples: "Receive ye the Holy Ghost." It is an utterly inadmissable exegesis which teaches that Christ leaves it to the will and option of the disciples whether they will receive the Spirit. That declaration "Receive ye," is neither an invitation nor a command. It is an explanation. He breathes on them before He says a word about the Holy Spirit. He breathes on them, He communicates His breath to them, He sends it into them, and then He says: "Receive ye the Holy Ghost." By these words He declares to all time that the disciples had received the Holy Spirit in receiving His breath. He had sent them the Holy Spirit; He had sent Him two months before Pentecost.

And now, mark the manner in which the Holy Spirit comes here, no rushing mighty sound, no whirling wind from heaven, no fire of flaming tongues, nothing the world saw or heard, but, secretly, quietly.

Mark, I pray you, the meaning of that coming. It is emphasized in one word, "Peace." There is no thought of energy here, no thought of aggression, or objective action, or power. It is comfort, it is consolation.

Mark the attitude of Jesus, in this case, as contrasted with His attitude at Pentecost. At Pentecost He is the exalted Lord and Christ; here He is the risen Son of God not yet exalted. There He sends the Holy Spirit as the executive of His will and power; here He gives the Holy Spirit as another friend and companion. There as the head of Israel, here as the head of a new race. There he lifts the sceptre, here He communicates life and peace, His own very presence. At Pentecost He says: "Behold, I send you the promise of the Father;" here, upon the edge of the open grave, on the resurrection side of it, with His feet upon the threshold of heaven, He says: "I fulfill my promise, I give myself, my life, my love, all I am, to be in you and with you."

Here, fifty days before Pentecost, you have every characteristic of John xiv, every characteristic of the promised Comforter. Here is a scene and circumstance which present themselves as the fitting inauguration of the Spirit into the sublime office of the Comforter, just as fittingly as at Pentecost when He was more openly and with greater accessories inaugurated into the equally sublime office of the Enduer.

This twofold office of the Holy Spirit, and the lapse of time between their initial moments, are not intended to exalt the one, or ignore the other; but to set before us the beauty, the blessedness, and the distinctive values in the operation of the one only and eternal Spirit of our God.

THE WORK OF THE COMFORTER.

The work of the Comforter is clear and simple. He begins the church. He begins Christianity as a vital force in the believer's soul. He links him in organic union with a living, risen Head. He forms within Him the Christ, the hope of glory. He testifies of Christ. He glorifies Christ. He brings to remembrance the words of Christ. He feeds the soul with the truth of Christ. He guides us into all the truth of Christ. He shows us the things of Christ. He so subordinates Himself to the will and personality of Christ that He becomes the other very self of Christ. But he goes above and beyond all this: not only does He come to put a new nature in the soul, He comes to manifest the very presence of Christ in the soul; to make Christ dwell in His personality in the soul; so that Christ shall be up yonder in His glorified body as He was in vision above the ladder which Jacob saw, and yet here in the soul, an invisible presence, as Jacob felt and found Him by Bethel's stony pillow. Yea, His work in us is to make Christ as real to us as though He walked flesh-veiled by our side. To so continue His presence to us that the gap may be filled between the open grave and the exalted throne; between the risen Master and the man in the glory. To so continue that presence that Christ Himself shall minister to our need, as though we looked Him in the face, felt the sympathy of His shining tears, and caught the touch of His guiding hand. To so continue Christ in us that Christ shall give us His faith, His peace, His joy, His hope, His power: until when we walk, we may walk by His faith, be calm in His peace, be glad in His joy, be encouraged in His hope, and strong in His power. For, if we will be obedient, the Comforter will give us the very power of Christ, power for the mind; so that we may see the wondrous things which Christ Himself has inspired in the matchless Book. He will give us power, power for our bodies, so that we may not faint, nor grow weary in His service. If we will let Him, the Comforter will so keep the communication unbroken with yonder heaven that Jesus Himself shall come down invisibly and walk with us the weary way; and we shall feel no pain or sorrow or weakness where He leads.

Oh! the wonder, the joy of it, and the unspeakable glory! The Holy Spirit here! here to continue the presence of Christ to us, to make us conscious of Him, to fill us with Him till our hearts shall be as a Holy of Holies; so that we may enter in, even here, into the secret of His presence, and be glad with a great gladness.

Thus the work of the Comforter in relation to us is subjective, in us and for us. We occupy the attitude of recipients, not of those who act, but of those who are acted upon. The Comforter will bring us into the place of power, no doubt, but power is not the objective of His work; it is peace, joy, companionship, increasing companionship. It is Jesus Himself with us, all the centuries blotted out, all the past history gone between Judea and this hour. Jesus with us, talking with us, feeding us, and every day revealing Himself to us.

Such, indeed, is the work of the Comforter, that Comforter who comes as the breath of the risen Christ into every heart that belives on Him; and at the moment, the instant of belief.

A person filled with the breath of Christ! What a definition that is for a Christian; and what a suggestion of infinite comfort, of abiding peace.

THE WORK OF THE ENDUER.

The work of the Holy Spirit as Enduer, is equally clear. On the day of Pentecost He opened the Kingdom of Heaven to the Jew, but, according to the seventh chapter of the Book of Acts, the Jews rose up and shut the door in the Spirit's face, martyred Stephen, and piled the stones above him as a witness that they rejected a risen Lord, even as they had crucified a seeking King. At once the Spirit postponed the kingdom in Israel, turned to the Gentiles, opened to them the kingdom spiritually, set aside Peter, called Paul, through him revealed the doctrine of the church; and from henceforth began to work, not to extend the kingdom in the world, but to withdraw men from the world into the kingdom; to build up the Church of Christ, not as a kingdom, but as the temple of God for a coming kingdom. To call out the church as the body of Christ, as the royal family, as the aristocrats, the choice ones, who should reign and rule in the kingdom and glory yet to come.

At Pentecost the Spirit became the environment into which the Jewish nucleus of the church was baptized into a supernatural body. At Cæsarea, at the house of Cornelius, the act of baptism was performed by the Son of God for the last time, when the Gentile incomers were baptized with the Jewish nucleus into one body, into that body where there is neither Jew nor Gentile.

The baptism in the Holy Spirit being completed, and the church as a spiritual body being set in the Holy Spirit as the divine environment, from that time to this, the Spirit has been in the church, corporately and individually, both as Comforter and Enduer; as Enduer more particularly in relation to the church corporately. As the Enduer and Administrator from on high, He is here in the church, to appoint the officers, to call and ordain pastors, to call, ordain and send forth evangelists; to raise the money needed by the Son of God; to direct its service, its singing, its praying and preaching. To make the church so divine, so supernatural, that unbelief shall go out of it, and doubt shall not dare to enter it. He is here to make the church repulsive as well as attractive. Repulsive to all who are not called of God. He is here as the presiding presence, the Vicar of Christ, as His agent, as the true Pope, to do what Christ would do if present, personally, in His very body. He is here to carry the church forward as a force for God, as an impingement on the lives of men, till the last one foreknown of God shall be added to the Lord and the hour of the kingdom shall sound. He is here with all the power necessary to carry on the church in any age, and under any condition. All the gifts which He brought at Pentecost are in His possession to-day; and He is ready to distribute them according to faith and the special need of the hour. He is ready to work in us and through us, so that we may go forth to the world as very Jesus Christ, risen, glorified and multiplied a millionfold, so that the incarnate Christ shall be no longer local, but omnipresent, opening through us the eyes of the blind, giving strength to the lame, giving speech to the dumb, and hearing to the deaf; making the lame man to leap as the hart, and raising the dead to the new life in God, working through us with the measureless power with which He wrought us in Christ, in every land and among all people.

Thus the twofold work of the Spirit, as Comforter and Enduer, finds its ultimate unity in the purpose to make the church in her journey through the age, divinely glad and divinely strong. He is here as divine comfort and infinite might; and thus equipped, the church needs nothing more. She need raise no prayer to yonder throne or cry aloud to heaven for added means, for the Lord her God, in the midst of her, is mighty. All power in heaven and earth is given to Him, and in giving Himself to her to be with her and in her, He has given to her all power.

WHY WE FAIL.

Why, then, do we fail? Why do the ruins of our failure strew our path? Why, above these ruins, do we cry and plead and fret those heavens as though God Himself were unwilling or unable to meet our need?

Alas! The question is all too easily answered. We fail because we grieve the Holy Spirit who dwells within us; we grieve Him by ignoring His presence. Day after day we cry and beseech our God that He will pour out His Holy Spirit; and lo! He is here. We seek to invent schemes and plans which shall give us power; and lo! He is in us, the very energy of God. We grieve Him by setting aside His methods. We go forth to cleanse Sodom, and He bids us come out of it. We speak to men of reformation, He bids us talk of regeneration. We seek to christianize the world, and He tells us to gospelize it. We try to take the kingdoms of time with the sceptre of the Gospel, and He tells us that Christ alone can take them with a rod of iron. We try to legislate evil out of the earth, and He has said I will overturn it, overturn it, till He comes whose right it is to reign. We talk to men of the purple and the gold of coming days, when the church shall enthrone herself upon the hearts of men, and He tells us that, in the end of this Gospel age, Antichrist shall sit in the Temple of God. We congratulate the listening throng with the pleasant tale that the world is growing better and marching on to millennial peace, and he tells us, and draws our attention to it expressly, that in the last days, perilous times shall come; and thus we grieve Him by contradicting Him and denying His testimony at every turn.

We grieve Him again and again, by making secondary the only tongue by which He can speak to us, the only tongue by which He can fling the fire and the flame of truth into the inmost soul, this written Word. We allow men to hold it up and tell us that it is full of errors, that it is a composite of divine foolishness and human credulity. And we sit at the feet of such men and exalt them into the place of honor and call them the teachers of the truth, the wise men of the church.

We grieve Him by setting aside the first century for the nineteenth, this century of rationalism, materialism, and insane optimism. We preach the Gospel, and we think we must do it in the pride of human learning and the vanity of human understanding. We grieve Him in the administration of the church. He is the President and Vicar, and we seek vicars and presidents among men. He has the power and authority to appoint the officers of the church, and we take it in our own hands to appoint them. He gives the endowment of service through faith, and we seek to get it through sight. He has made the church with as little machinery as possible, and we seek to fill it with as much as we can. He appeals continually to the sense of the uncommon in us, and we appeal to the common sense in us. His way is to add to the Lord and multiply the church through addition, our way is to multiply the church and fail in the divine addition. His way is to bring out sin to the light and judge it, our way is to cover it up and forget it. In short, He is here to sit in the seat of Jesus Christ and be His other self, and to guide the church with His awful presence; and we talk of Him as of a thing impersonal, an abstraction, thin as air. Doctrinally, He has fallen out of practice, until to-day, He is almost unknown as a personal factor in the church; so that it might be said with truth of many churches, as of old the Ephesians said of themselves, "that they had not so much as heard whether there be a Holy Ghost."

We grieve Him in our personal lives. We are full of worry and fret—and carefulness and pride, unworthy ambition and lustful emulation. We regulate our lives, not by the cloudy, fiery pillar of the divine presence, but by our hopes and fears! and then we go out to men and talk to them, and wonder why they do not see God and turn unto Him. We preach to men that Christ offered Himself without spot to God through the eternal Spirit, and then refuse to offer ourselves without spot to God through the same Spirit.

Look yonder, I pray you, at that scene on Mount Carmel's top. Elijah declared that the God who answereth by fire is the only God. He built the altar, laid the wood, dug the trench, drew the water and poured it forth, but there was no fire. Then He took a bullock, slew it, cut it in pieces and laid it on the altar as a whole burnt offering, and waiting till the hour of the evening sacrifice, cried aloud unto God. In giving God the whole burnt offering, he gave Him all, he kept nothing back; and the fire came, the God who answereth by fire answered him. Ah, my brethren, we have built the altar, laid the wood, dug the trench, brought the water and poured it forth, but there has been no fire. There has been no fire, because there has been no burnt offering; and the burnt offering means, everything given to God, nothing kept back, God getting all, getting ourselves; and, alas, some of us, in these years past have been giving God everything else but that, everything else but—ourselves.

If we would have the fire we must go back to that sacrificial hour, yonder, in the evening of the days, to the cross of Christ, and cry aloud to God, and say to Him: "Oh, God! I give Thee not what I *have,* but what I *am,* my own dear self. I nail myself to that altar-cross, and I say unto Thee, 'I die.' I crucify, by faith, everything which does not find its root in Thee!" And the fire will come, not from above, but from within, where it has been almost quenched, the Spirit of the living God, a leaping, flowing, cleansing fire. It will turn into ashes our human will and pride, our vanity and conceit; and we shall die, slain by the gleaming Spirit, as a thing devoted unto God, and made holy to His use for evermore.

May God help us to climb the Carmel heights and lay ourselves on that dear altar of our Master's cross, and die in Him, die to every claim of self; and rise with Him, and with Him go forth in the tireless Spirit of the living God, to speak the word of cheer, to sound the word of hope, and give the touch of help and life to lost and dying men.   Go forth, glad in the divine gladness, strong in the divine strength, filled with peace and endued with power.

and with Him go forth in the tireless Spirit of the living
God, to speak the word of cheer, to sound the word of
hope, and give the touch of help and lift, to lost and
dying men. Go forth, glad in the divine gladness, strong
in the divine strength, filled with peace and endued with
power.

THE TWO NATURES.

The Two Natures.

*The flesh lusteth against the spirit, and
the spirit against the flesh: these are
contrary the one to the other.—Galatians v: 17.*

Every Christian has a conscious *experience* of the Two
Natures.

Few Christians know anything of the *doctrine* of the
Two Natures. Having the experience and not able to
account for it there is much sorrow and discouragement.
For example, the young convert is rejoicing in his new-
found relation to Christ; he has turned his back on the
world, the flesh, and the Devil; he is seeking to cultivate
the spiritual inclinations that have now seemingly taken
possession of his life and made the world, a new world
to him; he is full of exultation and delight that the old
way of sin is gone forever, that henceforth the pathway
to the City of God will be a pathway of perfect peace,
when, suddenly, he is confronted with the stubborn fact
that the old forces of sin and fleshly inclinations are in
him quite as strong if not stronger than ever; he finds
a sudden paralysis in his spiritual tendencies and as a
consequence is amazed, distressed and discouraged. Indeed, it is here that the departure of multitudes of Christians begins into that half-and-half life for Christ, the
going off more and more from Him and the profession
they made of His name, and justifying themselves in
the fact that they have found that they are still in the old
bonds, have been tempted and fallen, and therefore have
no longer any sense of confidence or hope in the Christian
career; justifying themselves still further perhaps with

the conclusion that it was all a mistake, that no doubt they never *were* converted, if, really, there be such a thing *as* conversion.

Now, if they had been taught at the outset that the moment they were brought to know the Lord Jesus Christ a new, distinct spiritual nature was communicated to them, and that the old nature of the flesh remained waiting for its occasion under the suggestion of the Devil to throw itself in their pathway, tempt them, and cast them down; if they had known that while it is not possible to get rid of this "old man" till death or the Coming of the Lord, yet that it is possible to starve the flesh, keep it under and fight the good fight of faith to a finish of victory for God and man; if they had known that this uprising of the flesh is in the very nature of regeneration, that the coming in of Christ into the soul stirs up sooner or later all the enmity of the flesh and that it does not take God unawares; if they had known that the manifestation of the old nature in them was not a witness that they had never been made partakers of Christ but, on the contrary, was an evidence that this new nature of Christ was there, and like Christ Himself in the wilderness was now to be put to the proof by the Devil through the weakness of the flesh; if they had known all this and had been clearly taught how to deal with this dual condition in them, how to starve the old nature and feed the new and thus come forth a triumphant son of God; I repeat that if they had known all this they would have been spared the disappointment and humiliation of their Christian profession.

There can be no question that if Christians to-day comprehended the fact and truth about the existence and interplay of the nature bequeathed to them by Adam hrough generation, and the nature bequeathed to them by the Son of God through regeneration, we should find less numerous that class of religious persons known as "back-sliders," and see a more intelligent and stalwart following of the Christ of God.

It is of the last importance then that the Christian should know the doctrine of the heretofore inexplicable facts in him.

It is to that end this Bible lesson is given.

The teaching of the Scriptures is clear and unmistakable.

1. There is a nature of the flesh.

"Among whom also we all had our conversation in times past in the lusts of our flesh, fulfilling the desires of the flesh and of the mind; and were by nature (this nature of the flesh) the children of wrath, even as others." Ephesians ii: 3.

2. This nature comes in by birth.

"That which is born of the flesh is flesh." John iii: 6; Ephesians iv: 22.

This is the nature originally born in us, or rather this is the nature of our first birth.

3. This nature is called the "Old man." Romans vi: 6; Ephesians iv: 22.

4. Called "The Natural man." "But the natural man receiveth not the things of the Spirit of God." I Corinthians ii: 14.

5. It is enmity against God. "Because the carnal mind (the nature of the flesh) is enmity against God." Romans viii: 7.

6. There is no good thing in it. "For I know that in me (that is, in my flesh,) dwelleth no good thing." Romans vii: 18.

"The heart (that is the nature of the flesh) is deceitful above all things, and desperately wicked; who can know it?" Jeremiah xvii: 9.

And the conclusion is, that God only has fathomed its depths.

"For out of the heart (nature of flesh) proceed evil thoughts, murders, adulteries, fornications, thefts, false witness, blasphemies." Matthew xv: 19.

"What the law could not do, in that it was weak through the flesh." Romans viii: 3.

That is to say, not that the law in itself was weak, for the law is holy and good, but that the flesh is weak; it has no strength to meet the demands of the law for righteousness.

7. The nature of the flesh cannot be changed.

"It is not subject to the law of God, neither indeed can be." Romans viii: 7.

"Can the Ethiopian change his skin, or the leopard his spots? Then may ye also do good, that are accustomed to do evil." Jeremiah xiii: 23.

8. God has pronounced sentence of death against it.

"And God said unto Noah, the end of all flesh is come before me." Genesis vi: 13.

"In Adam all die." I Cor. xv: 22.

"By nature (this nature of flesh) the children of wrath." Ephesians ii: 3.

9. There is a nature of Spirit.

"That which is born of the Spirit is Spirit." John iii: 6.

As that which is born is a nature of things, so that which is born *ek tou pneumatos,* out of the Spirit, is a nature of spirit.

10. This nature of Spirit is called "Christ in you."

"To whom God would make known what is the riches of the glory of this mystery among the Gentiles; which is CHRIST IN YOU, the hope of glory." Colossians, 1 : 27.

11. This nature is called "Life."

"He that hath the Son (Christ in you) hath Life." I John v: 11, 12.

12. This nature of Spirit is received by and through faith in the promises, the written promises of God.

"Whereby are given unto us exceeding great and precious promises: that by these ye might be partakers of the divine nature (the nature of the Spirit) having escaped the corruption that is in the world through lust." II Peter i: 3, 4.

13. This divine nature, this Christ nature, this nature of Spirit, is wrought in the believer through the Holy Spirit and the written Word.

The Holy Spirit is the Divine Agent and Infinite Efficiency.

The written Word is the Perfect Instrument in the hands of the Spirit.

"Except a man be born of water and of the Spirit, he cannot enter into the kingdom of God." John iii: 5.

We have a direct Scripture in which water is set forth as the symbol of the Word. Ephesians v: 26. "The washing of water by the Word." In John xv: 3, our Lord says: "Ye are clean through the Word which I have spoken unto you." In Proverbs xxv: 25, it is written: "As cold waters to a thirsty soul, so is Good News (The Gospel, the Word of God) from a far country (from Heaven, the source of the Word)."

Whenever the Spirit is mentioned in connection with water it signifies the Spirit in operation with the Word; it signifies the Word used by the Spirit as His Instrument.

To be born therefore of water and Spirit, literally out of water and out of Spirit, is the New Testament way of saying that the Spirit is the Agent, and the Word the Instrument in this new birth of a human soul.

"Not by works of righteousness which we have done, but according to his mercy He saved us, by the washing of regeneration (by the washing of the Word) and renewing of the Holy Ghost." Titus iii: 5.

"Seeing ye have purified your souls in obeying the TRUTH THROUGH THE SPIRIT." "Being born again, not of corruptible seed, but of incorruptible, by the Word of God." I Peter i: 22, 23.

"It is the Spirit that quickeneth: the flesh profiteth nothing; the words I speak unto you, they are Spirit, and they are Life." John vi: 63.

Here, then, from headquarters we have the statement that His Words are very spirit and life; that His Word and Spirit are Instrument and Agent in the immense work of creating a new nature for the believer.

14. These two natures of flesh and Spirit dwell side by side in each believer.

"He that soweth to his flesh shall of the flesh reap corruption; but he that soweth to the Spirit shall of the Spirit reap life everlasting." Galatians vi: 7, 8.

The man whom the Apostle is here addressing is a Christian man; and in thus suggesting to him that he may sow either to flesh or Spirit, and as the sowing must necessarily be to himself, the Apostle demonstrates that this Christian man possesses in himself, and side by side, the two natures of flesh and Spirit.

15. The flesh is constantly fighting against the Spirit.

"For I know that in me (that is in my flesh,) dwelleth no good thing: for to will is present with me; but how to perform that which is good I find not."

"For the good that I would, I do not: but the evil which I would not, that I do."

"Now, if I do that I would not, it is no more I that do it, but sin that dwelleth in me."

"I find then a law, that, when I would do good, evil is present with me."

"For I delight in the law of God after the inward man."

"But I see another law in my members, warring against the law of my mind, and bringing me into captivity to the law of sin which is in my members." Romans vii: 18-23.

In this remarkable passage the Apostle speaks of the "inward man" who delights in the law of God, and of the flesh which delights in sin and the violation of the law.

This inward man is none other than that new nature born of the Spirit; and the wretchedness which leads the Apostle to cry out in v: 24, "O, wretched man that I am," is the result of an unceasing assault against every endeavor of the new man to live in the way of righteousness and truth.

In other words, the Apostle represents himself as one who at one moment is led by a power to seek after God and all His ways, and at another is carried off his feet by the sweep of a power for evil that he is just beginning to comprehend as having its headquarters and resource in himself.

His experience is that in varying degree of the average Christian, sinning and repenting; anxious to do the will of God, and in a measure doing it till, alas, in an unexpected moment some sudden surge of that old nature of sin proves stronger in its impetus than all the desires of the Spirit; and the end of his good resolves finds him going, like the dumb beast driven, after all the ways of evil.

And it is here that the discouragement and often the disaster of Christian lives begin, this first awakening to the fact that in spite of regeneration, in spite of the new creation of the Spirit, in spite of the fact of Christ in them the hope of glory, and the promised strength of God, they are still sinful, still pervaded by sinful impulses; and worse than all, that this inclination to sin seems all the stronger for even the slight endeavor to do the will of God and Christ.

Sad and bitter as may be the awakening to the fact, it is a fact; it is a fact that the old nature of sin abides, and has not been changed. Nay, it is all the more virulent because the coming-in of the Christ nature is the challenge to it. Not until we are regenerated, not until the breath of Heaven comes into our souls and we get the light of the revelation of the Divine will do we begin to know the depths of the flesh and its power for sin.

There are Christians who have been dumbfounded to discover in themselves tendencies which they never knew till they had turned unto the Lord.

It ought not to be a surprise. Until that moment when the new nature comes in the body has been the stronghold of sin.

Now there is a new tenant in the soul, none other than the heaven-born sonship of God; and this new life stirs and inspires all the bitterness of the old.

Nor need there be any illusion, the old nature will never cease in its assaults on the child of God thus committed to the soul. Just as all the forces of earth and hell began moving against the first Son of God so soon as He came into the world and continued their assaults to the end, so now that He is wrought once more in earth, but this time in the soul of him who believes, these same earth and hell forces will arise with renewed endeavor to slay and kill, and so continue that endeavor to the end.

16. If the flesh is against the Spirit, the Spirit is equally against the flesh.

And in this is the Christian's light and hope.

"For the flesh lusteth against the Spirit, and the Spirit against the flesh; and these are CONTRARY the one to the other; so that ye cannot do the thing that ye would." Galatians v: 17.

Instead of "ye cannot do the things ye would," the better rendering is, "ye *may not* do the things ye would."

That is to say, the Spirit is here shown to be on the aggressive, and resisting the power of inbred sin delivers the Christian from the surrender to its claims.

But this deliverance requires the active participation of the believer himself. In the seventh of Romans we behold the Christian under the domination of the flesh, sentimentally in favor of the good, but actually the yielding bond slave of the evil: so far as the good goes only "wretched" in his helplessness to get beyond anything better than mere sentiment. But in the fifth of Galatians the Apostle recognizes that the new man has asserted his claims to the Christian and is holding back the motions of the flesh as an invitation to that Christian to be encouraged and walk in the Spirit in surrender to Him, with the assurance that in so yielding the Spirit will bring him victory.

Evidently then there is an instruction needed as to the believer's relation to this new life in him. He needs to know how to deal with it, how to take care of it, and so set it in the line of its ordination that it may be the reinforcement of Heaven to the believing soul.

Just as the natural man is sustained by the food that is given to him, and the individual is responsible to see that the food is given, so is it true that the new nature must be fed and sustained by the food proper to its nourishment.

This leads to note, then, that:

17. The new nature, when it first comes into the believer, is only as a babe.

"Wherefore, laying aside all malice, and all guile and hypocrisies and envies, and all evil speakings, as new-born babes, desire the sincere milk of the Word." I Peter ii: 1, 2.

The Christian is here at the beginning of his profession of Christ to take the attitude of a new-born babe; and that is simply saying that the new nature of Spirit in him is as a babe; it is a new life, and, relatively to the old life, as a weak infant needing nourishment.

Christ the Lord came into the world and lay upon a human breast as an infant, so is it true that He comes now at the outset to lay as an infant in the breasts of those who claim His name. Let no Christian be surprised, then, nor imagine that there is any failure in the relation of God to his soul if at the outset he discovers that the old nature seems the stronger in him. It is so in this, that it is identified with his very body, and with a world which is under the rule of sin; while the new nature, like Christ, finds the body as an inn filled and crowded with the clients of the flesh. Only by the miracle of God was Christ introduced into the world; by a miracle is Christ wrought in any man to-day; and as first He seemed to be the revelation of goodness, but of weakness, so is it now. Christ the Lord must needs grow in stature, wisdom and favor with men, and He must grow in the soul that receives Him.

Thus it is true that at the beginning of the Christian's heavenward life the Christ nature in him is as a babe.

18. This new nature can be sustained and made to grow in us only by feeding on the Word of God.

"As new-born babes desire the sincere milk of the Word, that ye may grow thereby." I Peter ii: 1, 3.

"Thy words were found, and I did eat them; and thy word was unto me the joy and rejoicing of mine heart." Jeremiah xv: 16.

The best merely human literature that was ever written will not feed the new nature. You may bring the noblest thoughts which ever sprung from a human mind, you may couch them in the most fragrant rhetoric that ever distilled the perfume of literature in the book lover's nostrils and you will not quicken a single pulse in the new and spiritual life of the soul. Shakespeare may analyze, Milton soar, Bacon lead us step by step up the royal stairway of induction to the throne of logic, yet not a gleam of light or pulse of strength will be added to the Christ within.

There is only one food for the Son of God, and that is the Word. It is the declaration of the supreme Son of God, "Man shall not live by bread alone, but by every word that proceedeth out of the mouth of God;" and in this He was Himself but quoting from the Word of God in Deuteronomy viii: 3.

How did this son of God conduct Himself in that moment of moments when on the mount of temptation He was assaulted by Satan? The answer is that He continually responded to every subtlety of the Adversary by, "It is written."

He refused to take Himself out of the hands of His Father, and made the Word of His God His meat and drink day and night; indeed, if it be examined it will be found that all His speech, all His discourses on earth were simply the quotation or amplification of the words of the Old Testament, and that His last words in the hour of His agony were the words long ago written of God in the Psalms.

In His prayer, He said to the Father concerning His disciples, "I have given unto them the words which Thou gavest me." John xvii: 8.

It is the Word that reveals the mind and will of God to the sons of God, gives them light and furnishes them with the strength needed by the way. He therefore who would be filled with the will of God, walk in the light, and have strength to meet the assaults of Satan, must be filled with the Word.

You would not expect to have strength to meet the duties of daily life, naturally speaking, if you did not regularly feed and sustain the body; no more can you expect that the spiritual nature in you will have strength to meet its opportunities and responsibilities if you do not sustain it with the food needed by it.

Nor will it do to feed this new nature irregularly and at haphazard. It must be fed just as regularly and carefully as one would feed his natural life.

And here may be found the secret why multitudes of Christians have no power to overcome temptation, no power to walk on in the way of their professed discipleship. They do not give the spiritual life in them any food; they starve it; many of them are living on past experiences, on remembered emotions when they were first brought to know the Lord. They would deem themselves guilty of unpardonable folly if they neglected day after day to sit down at the well-spread board and there sought to meet nature's demands; and yet, there are Christians who scarcely ever pretend to look at the Word of God. The newspaper with its daily record of the flesh, and fleshly suggestions; the light and unreal story, or some speculation of limited reason concerning the contradictions of things in the Word of God; some so-called liberal novel glorifying unbelief and selling by thousands because it writes on the epitaph of its hero the declaration that he is going somewhere and he does not know where, whether North, South, East or West, and is not afraid. Is it any wonder that with the spiritual nature thus starved, cut off from its only nourishment and support that it should seem to be weak, or that the Christian should not have a very lusty concept of his sonship with God, or his responsibility as such to the world about him?

Let it be remembered then that the written Word is the only food by which the new nature can be nourished and made strong to do the will of God in the Christian.

19. While these two natures, the Flesh and the Spirit, are in the Believer, the Believer himself has but one responsibility; he is but one and the same person.

"For the good that I would, I do not; but the evil which I would not, that I do." Romans vii: 19.

Here you have the same personality whether for good or for evil; the one responsibility whether for sin or for righteousness.

"That ye put off concerning the former conversation the old man, which is corrupt according to the deceitful lusts:

And be ye renewed in the spirit of your mind:

And that ye put on the new man, which after God is created in righteousness and true holiness." Ephesians iv: 22, 24.

The Apostle recognizes the "Old Man," and "The New Man," but admits only one responsibility. It is the responsibility of the regenerated man to "put off" and "put on."

While the Word makes clear enough the existence of two distinct natures in the Christian it allows him no opportunity to throw the failure of his life on the possession of a nature adverse to the new. Wherefore says the Apostle: "Let not sin reign in your mortal body, that ye should obey it in the lusts thereof. Neither yield ye your members as instruments of unrighteousness unto sin; but yield yourselves unto God as those who are alive from the dead, and your members as instruments of righteousness unto God." Romans vi: 13.

The divine law is: "To whom ye yield yourselves servants to obey, his servants ye are to whom ye obey." Romans vi: 16.

20. The responsibility of the believer in relation to the flesh is five-fold.

1. He must never attempt to improve, or make a fair show of it. "For I know that in me (that is, in my flesh,) dwelleth no good thing." Romans vii: 18.

Paul's conflict in the seventh of the Romans comes from the fact, not that he sought to turn his back on sin and iniquity but rather *because he sought to lift up the flesh and force it to meet the demands of God's righteous law;* he had not seen the depths of the flesh; in spite of the fact that he was a regenerated man he still had hopes of it.

There are many Christians who are priding themselves on their native honor and integrity; no doubt many Christians serve the Lord in the pride and confidence of their flesh, but the word of God testifies that "all our righteousnesses are as filthy rags.' Isaiah lxiv: 6. We are therefore to turn away from the natural good in us as well as the evil.

We are to take God's estimate of it, believe with the Son of God that "it profiteth nothing," and own that our only confidence is Christ ("in us the hope of glory").

2. We are to starve the flesh.

"Make not provision for the flesh, to fulfill the lusts thereof." Romans xiii: 14.

Do not seek some dainty bit to spice the appetite of the flesh; do not deceive yourself into the folly that if you can only get something refined and cultured, something that appeals to the best in you you can still feed the flesh and do no harm to your spiritual nature; that you can ameliorate and soften the old nature so that it will not assault the new.

The story of the tiger is the illustration of that fallacy. So long as the tiger was nearly starved to death, so long as it caught no smell, or sight, or taste of blood, it seemed very feeble and sufficiently docile; but that fatal day when it got but for a moment the taste of blood as it abraided with its tongue the master's hand while fawning upon him, that instant all the jungle nature was aroused, inflamed; the sudden blazing of the eyes, the quick switching of the tail, the curved back, and the gathering together for a spring at the very object upon which but a moment before it had fawned, told the story of the unchangeableness of the tiger nature; we know the sequel, only when the master recognized that the tiger was tiger still did he escape from its treachery and assault.

You may starve your old nature and reduce it to a minimum of manifestation, but the fatal moment you attempt to feed it, to pamper it, give it the blood taste of the world, no matter how blue or refined that blood is, no matter though it come from the hand of æstheticism itself, it will be alive and crouching, tiger-like, for a spring against the upper and spiritual life in your soul.

Do not cheat yourself with the idea that because you are a Christian and have been linked up with the Risen Man and have been living with Him in heavenly places far above the cries and claims of the flesh, that it has no longer the same tastes, the same cravings; nay, there have been Christians who have lived the most consecrated of lives, have seemed to be above all power of the flesh, and have so said and testified, believing it themselves with all sincerity who in an unguarded moment have yielded to some apparently harmless appetite of the old nature; and lo, desires which they believed forever dead have come upon them with all the rush of a flood against which they had no ready power of resistance.

There is only one way to get rid of the old nature, and that is, to starve it; you cannot kill it (actually), but you can starve it; you can never make it live in heavenly places, but you can live in heavenly places above it.

3. We are to own it as dead (judicially).

"Knowing this that our old man is crucified with Him that the body of sin might be destroyed, that henceforth we should not serve sin." Romans vi: 6.

The moment of faith in Christ as our sacrifice He is accepted as our substitute and God looks upon us just as though we actually had been crucified with Him; wherefore, says the Apostle: "I am (Greek, I was) crucified with Christ." Galatians ii: 20.

Thus in God's sight we are indeed judicially dead. He sees us crucified in the old nature and dead to our creation standing in the old man, the old Adam.

It is for us then to put God's estimate upon ourselves, see ourselves judged and dead in relation to the old nature, and *own* it as such before God.

But we are to own it dead for the good as well as bad.

A dead man is as inactive for good as for evil. Hence we are not even to cultivate the good in our old nature, we are not to rely upon any native righteousness in it, but own it as belonging to the dead in God's sight, and own ourselves as alive only in Christ; own that our only hope of life before God is in the new nature in us, and walk in that new nature in the power and energy of the Holy Spirit, through faith. In other words, be done with all expectation of the flesh, as you would be done with all expectation of a dead man buried out of your sight.

4. We are to mortify the flesh.

"Mortify, therefore, your members which are upon the earth." Colossians iii: 5.

Mortify, that is put to death the members that serve the nature of the flesh. This is simply saying that we are to treat this body as dead to the service of the old nature.

Just as you would recognize that the body of the dead man could no longer serve his will, his desires, so recognize that the membership of our body which has been under the domination of the flesh can no longer yield itself to the old nature. God looks upon that old nature as dead. Let us therefore show that we have made God's estimate practical in its application by our faith; that henceforth the membership of our body considered in relation to the old nature is as though it were also dead. And this is the logic of our standing before God. Says the Apostle: "How shall we that are dead to sin (remember, he does not say that sin is dead in us) live any longer therein?" Romans vi: 2. As he shows in the following verses of the same chapter Believers' baptism is a protest against any such endeavor. In the fourth verse he tells us that "we are buried with Him by baptism into death; that like as Christ was raised up from the dead by the glory of the Father, even so we also should walk in the newness (literally, the new species,) of life." Romans vi: 4.

The first thing to do with the dead is to bury them; hence baptism is a confession that just as we are buried beneath the water, so are we dead and buried in relation to that flesh which is here styled sin. If then, we have made this profession how can we in anywise attempt to serve that old nature?

Nay, in all the future history of our earthly lives we are to keep it in the place of death.

Only in proportion as we thus practically own it dead shall we be delivered from it.

5. We are to put it off.

"That ye put off concerning the former conversation the old man, which is corrupt according to the deceitful lusts." Ephesians iv: 22.

The old nature is considered as a garment to be laid aside, a habit to be put off. You have the same word "put off," rendered "laid down," in Acts vii: 58, where at the stoning of Stephen, "the witnesses laid down their clothes at a young man's feet, whose name was Saul." Put off, laid down, renounced as clothes we no longer intend to wear, a cast-off garment, that is the light in which we are to consider the old nature.

21. Our responsibility to the Spirit nature in us is five-fold:

1. We are to own ourselves as alive in the Spirit.

"If we live in the Spirit, let us also walk in the Spirit." Galatians v: 25. "Likewise reckon ye also yourselves to be dead indeed unto sin, but alive unto God through Jesus Christ our Lord." Romans vi: 11.

Not "through," but "in" Christ. Just as much as we own ourselves by faith to have been in Christ for death on the cross, we are to own ourselves as in Christ risen from the dead for life. This is our very standing before God. He "hath raised us up together (with Christ), and made us sit together in heavenly places in Christ Jesus." Ephesians ii: 6. Wherefore says the Apostle: "If ye then be risen with Christ, seek those things which are above, where Christ sitteth on the right hand of God. For ye are dead (died), and your *life is hid with Christ* in God." Colossians iii: 1, 3.

By faith, in the energy of the Holy Spirit, we are to live as those who have been linked up to "the Man in glory."

We are to live as though we had no other source of life than His; as though in Him we had actually been translated to heaven in our glorified bodies, finding therefore in Heaven and Heavenly things our only joy, our only environment.

2. We are to put on the new man.

"Put on the new man, which after God is created in righteousness and true holiness." Ephesians iv: 24.

Correspondingly as we put off the old man, we are to put on the new; we are put on Christ Himself as a new garment, as a robe of righteousness and truth. "Put ye on the Lord Jesus Christ, and make not provision for the flesh, to fulfill the lusts thereof." Romans xiii: 14.

3. Walk in the new nature of the Spirit.

"Let us also walk in the Spirit." Galatians v: 25.

4. Feed it with the Word of God.

"As new-born babes, desire the sincere milk of the Word." I Peter ii: 2.

5. Depend on the energy of the indwelling Holy Spirit.

"Now unto Him that is able to do exceeding abundantly above all that we ask or think, according to the power that worketh in us." Ephesians iii: 20.

The Holy Spirit is in the believer the all-sufficient power on which to rely for a heavenward walk in the new nature.

If the Christian walk was conditioned upon our individual strength it is evident that we might be hopeless, even with the communicated nature of Christ to suggest the way; but the Holy Spirit has come to take up His abode in us in order that we may be fully equipped. The measure of our responsibility is in relation to the operation of the Spirit in us. The Spirit is here to enable us to receive all that God would do for us and to furnish us with all the strength and power required, but He cannot work if we are determined to resist Him; there is nothing in all the universe so sensitive as the Spirit; He can be grieved by the slightest disobedience or resistance. Let it be stamped deep then in the Christian consciousness that as Christians we are fully equipped to live the Christian life in all its fairest outlines, but that the value of the equipment depends upon the use we make of it.

A man may have a hundred thousand dollars at his command, but if he uses only a thousand he is no better off as to the value of the money than if he had but the thousand.

The Holy Ghost is in us with all the equipment of power and gifts necessary to enable us to walk the noblest and most Son-like life with God; we have all the resources necessary to the most imperial of victories; we have all the wealth of spiritual inheritance to make us richer than those who have the gold of kings, but if with all this Divine endowment we do not use it, how are we better off in all the practical values of life than those who do not possess the Spirit?

The whole issue of our triumph or defeat then turns on the relation we sustain to the Spirit indwelling us. He will work according to our surrender to Him.

22. There are six things to be remembered about the Two Natures:

1. We will not get rid of the nature of the flesh till death, or the Coming of Christ.

Make no mistake upon this point; allow no false concept that by cultivating the Old Nature you can get rid of it, or that by seeking to give it right food you can nourish it in such fashion that it will in the long run turn into Spirit. Let the affirmation of the Son of God ring in your ears: "That which is born of the flesh, is flesh; and that which is born of the Spirit, is Spirit.

2. The food that sustains one nature will starve the other.

Shakespeare and Shelley will not feed the new nature, nor will the Old and the New Testament feed the flesh. The Spirit would starve on Shakespeare, and the flesh would grow very faint on the Old Testament. Mere literature for the flesh, the pure Word for the Spirit.

3. You cannot feed both natures at the same time.

The mind is the channel by which the food is to be taken, and the mind can receive only one class of thought food at a time; the truth is that it is impossible to be taken up with flesh and Spirit at the same moment. One or the other must have the precedence; hence, it is impossible to feed both at the same time.

4. Dead as the flesh is judicially, and dead as you may have kept it practically, you can always quicken it into activity by putting yourself under the law.

The law is meant for a man in the flesh and never for a man in Christ, never for the one who is seated with Christ in Heavenly places. Consequently, the moment a Christian comes down from those exalted heights where we walk in grace and faith to the low level of sight and merit, he stirs up the flesh to all its baleful activity whether of self-righteousness or concupiscence.

Never be absurd enough to come down from the resurrection heights and the intercession of the priest after the order of Melchizedek, to the level of natural life and the priesthood of Aaron; to do so is, as the Apostle clearly shows, to "fall from grace." "Christ is become of no effect unto you, whosoever of you are justified by the law; ye are fallen from grace." Galatians v: 4.

5. You can always sow to the flesh even as others who have not the Spirit and like them you can reap corruption. Galatians vi: 7, 8.

6. There is a definite way in which to deal with the old nature, the flesh.

Deny its claims for life; deny its claims for righteousness as well as unrighteousness; yield to the Holy Spirit; feed the new nature and walk in entire and dependent faith on that God who has saved us and called us with an holy calling.

THE SO-CALLED LORD'S PRAYER.

The So=called " Lord's Prayer."

One of His disciples said unto Him, Lord, teach us to pray, as John also taught his disciples.—Luke xi: 1.

In Matthew vi: 9-13, the following prayer is recorded: "Our Father which art in heaven, hallowed be Thy name.

Thy kingdom come. Thy will be done in earth, as it is in heaven.

Give us this day our daily bread.

And forgive us our debts, as we forgive our debtors.

And lead us not into temptation, but deliver us from evil: For thine is the kingdom, and the power, and the glory, forever. Amen."

This prayer is popularly known as the Lord's Prayer. Like many other popular views of Scripture it is wrong. The Lord's prayer correctly speaking is the great prayer which the Lord Himself offers, as found in John xvii.

The prayer noted above is the disciples' prayer. The prayer which the Lord upon the insistence of the disciples taught them to pray.

This prayer is so wrought into the general service of the Christian church, so made use of on public and private occasions, and thought to be so pre-eminently an expression of Christian faith and devotion, that it is impossible to touch it or put it out of its accepted place without offending the common consensus concerning it: and yet it does not belong to the church, it is not for the Christian at all; and the reasons ought to be self-evident.

1. The prayer for the kingdom is not the prayer, and

does not express the attitude of the church. The prayer of the church in unison with that of the Spirit is set forth in Revelation xxii: 17, "And the Spirit and the *Bride* say, *Come.*"

The prayer of the church is not for the coming of the kingdom, but for the coming of the Bridegroom, that the marriage may take place and the Queen be ready to accompany the King when He shall descend in the splendor of the kingdom.

The attitude of the church is not looking for the King but waiting for the Son : not looking for signs but listening for sounds, the sounds of His voice and the trump which shall summon her to meet Him; not crying out for the manifestation on earth, but yearning to be caught up into the air; not clamoring for revealed power but pleading for ascension into the banqueting house, and over her His banner of love.

2. The ground of the prayer is Law, and not Grace.

Nothing could be more legal than this:

"And forgive us our debts as we forgive our debtors.

For if ye forgive men their trespasses, your heavenly Father will also forgive you.

But if ye forgive not men their trespasses, neither will your Father forgive your trespasses." vv: 12, 14, 15.

According to Romans vi: 14, and in the very nature of the case, the Christian is not under law; to put himself even in the atmosphere of legality is to deny grace and to fall from it.

The assertion that the Father makes forgiveness for ourselves dependent upon our forgiveness of others is, if accepted, working for absolution and under constraint of rule, authority, law. Whether therefore from Sinai or the mount of Beatitudes it is law, and the ground is the very opposite of grace, the opposite of all that constitutes essential Christian characteristic.

So long as grace and legalism are distinct and opposed to each other the Christian cannot consistently offer this prayer.

3. If this prayer is admitted by the Christian, it is equivalent to saying that his standing before God depends not on his relation to Christ but on his relation to his fellow-men, and that a failure to be perfect in these relations will make him imperfect before God.

For the Christian to present this prayer is to take himself off the ground of the immutable covenant of grace, and put himself on the shifting sand of his own weak, vacillating temperament.

To offer this prayer is to deny both the ground and the certainty of his standing.

4. The Christian is not called upon to pray for forgiveness.

There is no warrant in Scripture for the Christian to take such a position. If a Christian sin, and sin is trespass, there is one clear and definite thing for him to do, and that is, go to confession. Go to his Father in heaven and confess it; and the moment he confesses it Jesus Christ as his High Priestly Advocate will sustain his confession and advocate his forgiveness and cleansing by bringing before the Father the memorial of the cross and its sacrificial blood, and testifying to the Father that when He shed that blood He had anticipated this very failure and sin; and on the ground of that perfect sacrifice, the Father, because He is faithful and just, will forgive his erring, but repentant child. I John ii: 1. I John 1: 9.

As Christians, if the Spirit of Christ is in us, we will

forgive those who have sinned against us; it should go without saying that the Christian who is in the plenitude of the Spirit will not do otherwise; nevertheless, whatever else may be the consequences there can be no such thing as that he will remain unforgiven of God on the ground of his failure towards men; the immense issues of the Father's mercy cannot rest on such varying foundation as that for the church.

5. This prayer belongs to a time when the church will be gone from the earth and when Antichrist is in power.

It will be the prayer of the elect Jewish remnant in the day of the Great Tribulation. Here is the explanation of v: 10.

"Thy kingdom come."

At the moment of this utterance the kingdom of Antichrist or the man known in Scripture as "The Wild Beast" will be over all Europe and in Palestine; and these Jews called out after the Translation of the church by the gospel of the kingdom will lift up their voices and pray that the kingdom of the Father, which is the kingdom of the Messiah, may come and deliver them from the tribulation and woe that will then be rampant.

According to Daniel xi: 36, and II Thessalonians ii: 3, 4, this "Man of the earth" is known as "The Wilful King," the king whose will is absolute law; hence, the remnant lift up their voices and cry, "*Thy* kingdom come, *Thy* will be done on earth." They pray that the earth may become a province of heaven and of God and no longer the arena for the sin and wilfulness of this "Man of Sin."

In verse 11 we read:

"Give us this day our daily bread."

It is beautiful to be dependent on God for the very bread we eat, but beautiful as it is we are also expected to earn it in the sweat of our brow. In the time, however, to which this prayer refers, to earn bread or even buy it will be a dangerous thing; for in that day everything, bread as well, will be made and sold only with the mark of Antichrist upon it. Not a loaf of bread not an article of food can be got in the shops or made or found in the houses without this name, as it is written:

"And no man might buy or sell save he that had the mark, or the name of the beast, or the number of his name." Revelation xiii: 17.

Now, the man who refuses to receive or own the mark of the beast will be slain by him, but he who does accept the mark of the beast will be cast into the lake of fire.

It will be death at the hands of Antichrist to take any food without his mark on it. It will be the lake of fire to those who seek to save their lives by taking it. On the one side is violent death, on the other is a burning hell.

What can the disciples of Christ do?

It is in this hour of perplexity that the prophetic remnant lift up the prayer: "Give us this day our daily bread."

God must step in and by His Providence sustain them as He sustained Elijah in the days of Ahab, both being respectively the types of the Remnant and the Antichrist.

"Lead us not into temptation, but deliver us from evil." v: 13.

The word "Temptation" is the same word used in Revelation iii: 10, "I will keep thee from (out of) the hour of temptation, which shall come upon all the world to try them."

This latter passage has reference to The Great Tribulation of which our Lord speaks in Matthew 24, and which Jeremiah the prophet calls the "Day of Jacob's Trouble." The word "Temptation" in the prayer therefore refers to that moment, and the petition in the prayer is the pleading of the disciples that the Lord will not allow them to pass through this terrible and awful time, but afford them a way of escape.

Our Lord Himself declares in advance that this prayer in measure shall be heard, and for the elect's sake these monstrous days will be shortened. Matthew xxiv: 22.

The word translated "Evil" should be rendered with the article, "The Evil One," and signifies him of whom the Apostle Paul speaks as "The Wicked One," he who is the Antichrist.

The disciples therefore are praying that the Lord will surely and finally deliver them from the hands of this man who maketh the earth to tremble and who draweth the trail of the Serpent after him whithersoever he goes.

Such is the full and prophetic meaning of this prayer.

A prayer that has no more place in the Christian church than the thunders of Sinai, or the offerings of Leviticus.

SPIRITUAL GROWTH.

Spiritual Growth.

Mark iv: 26-32.

The seed is a grain of corn.

The first grain of corn is the Lord Jesus Christ.

The sowing in the earth is the death and burial of the Lord as He says: "Except a corn of wheat fall into the ground and die, it abideth alone."

The blade that rises from the seed is the Lord Himself rising from the dead.

The ear of corn is the church made up of grains that have sprung out of the death of the Lord Jesus.

The grains of corn in the ear are the individual Christians, each one of them a multiplication and a duplication of the Lord Jesus Christ, the First Grain.

The full corn in the ear is the hour of ripening, the hour when the church shall be complete.

The harvest is the end of the age, the end of this dispensation.

The man with the sickle is the Lord Jesus Christ coming again into the field of the world.

The reaping with the sickle is the gathering the church out of the earth to meet Him in the air.

The grain of mustard seed represents the church in the beginning.

In the beginning the church seemed like a very little, a very insignificant thing.

The growing up of the little seed into a great herb, a mighty tree, is the sudden increase of the church in numbers and power.

The branches spreading out in every direction, the expansion of the church in all the world.

The fowls that find shelter and shade in the branches are Satan and his agents according to the declaration of headquarters in Matthew xiii: 4, 19. "Some seeds fell by the way-side, and the fowls came and devoured them up. When any one heareth the word of the kingdom, and understandeth it not, then cometh the wicked one, and catcheth away that which was sown in his heart."

THE TWO SEEDS.

These two seeds represent the church in its inward and true character, and in its outward and professing character.

Both represent growth, but one is the growth of the church spiritually, the other is the growth of the church in worldliness.

The two seeds, then, represent spiritual growth and worldly growth.

The mustard tree represents the growth of the church, and the profession of Christ in worldliness. The more a tree grows the more it takes root in the ground. Its expansion outward is in exact proportion to its root downward.

There is a profession of Christ both in individuals and churches which becomes worldly in the exact ratio of its growth.

Some churches are full of growth, crowded, prosperous; but when they are examined it will be found that they are rooted in the world and draw all their inspiration and power from worldly things. They are nothing more nor less than natural organizations with here and there a modicum of spirituality; their growth is in worldly things, worldly methods and principles. They are worldly churches, religious, but not spiritual.

There are individual professors of Christ of whom this

is also true. They make a profession of Christ, but they find their root and fatness in the world, and when left to themselves or given full sweep, will bring the world into the church even as the "mixed multitude" brought Egypt and Egypt's ways among the children of Israel. The profession of Christ that grows into the world and expands in its strength affords sooner or later a shelter and vantage ground for Satan and those who are his, as every page of church history shows.

The outward expansion of a church then, and the mere religiousness of a professor of Christ, do not indicate spiritual growth.

If the mustard tree stands for natural and worldly growth, the grain of corn in its development stands for just the opposite.

The more a mustard tree grows upward the more it tightens its grasp on the earth; the more a stalk of corn grows upward the more it loosens its hold on the earth. The law is that *as it ripens towards heaven it loosens towards earth.*

The mustard tree needs no care but the corn must be constantly cultivated, you cannot neglect it. You must keep the hoe going all the time. If you are going to grow corn *you must be the man or woman with a hoe.* You must keep out the weeds. You must keep the earth loose about the roots. The mustard tree is a natural growth, it grows wild, it needs no care. The corn is not a natural growth. There is no such thing as wild corn. It is purely and simply the gift of God and must be so dealt with.

The analogy is self-evident. The Christian is not the development of the natural life, he is the gift of God. He does not belong in the earth, and as he grows and ripens he will loosen his hold on it and grow and ripen in heavenly things. The world and worldly things will have less and less claim upon him, heaven and spiritual things will more and more attract him.

But great care will be required for this heavenly and spiritual growth. If you would thrive you must keep the hoe going, loosen the earth about you, cast out the weeds, and in patience wait on the rain the dew and sunshine of heavenly grace. And as you grow you will find your place as a perfect grain in the divine ear. As you grow no fowls wil find a resting place in you or a church composed of those like unto you. They may peck at, and fly over you, but they cannot find shelter with you, and you will ripen, not in the SUN, but in the SON, towards the harvest hour and the sickle's swing in the Master's hand.

Certain definite lessons are taught here:

1. Spiritual growth is necessary, as all growth is necessary, for evidence of life, evidence to ourselves and, particularly, evidence to others.

2. Spiritual growth can be maintained only by and through the Word of God.

The Word is the germ power. It is the seed of spiritual things. Our Lord Himself declares that the words He spake were "spirit and life." (John vi: 63.) Wherefore the Apostle Peter says: "Precious promises; that by these ye might be partakers of the divine nature." (II Peter i: 4.) Thus the apostle Paul also exhorts: "Let the Word of Christ dwell in us richly." (Col. iii: 16.) You may read study and fill your mind with the best natural literature in the world it will not stir a single atom of spiritual life, or growth; the growth can come only from the divine seed, the Word of the Living God; and it must indeed be in our hearts.

3. Spiritual growth will be in proportion to the attitude we hold in relation to the Word of God.

In verse 24 the Lord says very significantly, "Take heed *what* ye hear." That is to say also, *how* ye hear. Socrates has said there is an eloquence of the lip, and an eloquence of the ear. It is the eloquence of the ear that is needed, giving attention to what God says, that His Word may enter deeply and germinatingly into the heart. But it must be a hearing that is prompted and inspired by faith. All the failure of Israel was due to the fact that "the Word preached unto them did not profit, not being mixed with faith in them that heard it." (Hebrews iv: 2.)

4. In spiritual growth there is to be no toiling, no labor, or effort.

When a child grows it does not labor, it just grows. This is what our Lord taught in the parable of the lilies. He bids us consider the lilies, how they toil not neither do they spin; He does not draw our attention to their beauty so much, although Solomon in all his glory was not clothed like unto them, but to the great fact that they grow without toiling; they rest where they find themselves, and quietly and gladly receive; receive air and light, dew and rain, sun and heat; and then just grow heavenward in their royal beauty. So we are to rest where God has planted us, and receive; drink in the truth and blessing that heaven pours upon us in the Word, and grow as perfect grains in the golden ear of corn.

A forest of mustard trees, every branch filled with fowls of the air, would not attract you, no matter how strong and lusty the growth of the tree and branch. But a field of corn would attract and inspire you.

I remember riding in the West by a field of thousands

of acres of corn. At one moment the field seemed like an army, rank on rank, each several stalk an upright soldier standing in the sun. At another like a vast and mighty sea of life, swelling, rising, and moving on with lifted waves to the infinite horizon. As I looked I saw the yellow corn bursting in its golden beauty from the emerald folds about it, and I knew that it meant bread and life, strength and hope, to multitudes of the sons of men. As I listened I heard the wind sighing and singing through the vast and ordered way, until the tassels, fine as feathers, rose and fell like martial plumes; and the sight and sounds were as a blessing and a benediction to my soul; for I saw and heard the parable of my Master. I saw the Christian Church as an army with banners. I saw it also as a wide sea of perfect and heavenly life, rising and swelling towards the infinite glory, bearing on every wave hope and blessing to the souls of men. I heard it in the soft tender music of the Spirit Divine breathing across each individual and spiritual soul and making praises unto Him who gave His life for us, and gave it unto us that we might also bring forth abundant fruit of life divine.

Oh, may we in the church be as a field of ripening corn, growing as perfect grains in the swelling ear, growing as individual Christians in the Master's likeness. Let us remember too that corn as it grows in all its yellow beauty in the field is but another name for *stored-up sunshine;* and may we grow until we shall become indeed ourselves the stored-up shining of God's eternal Son; growing so that we may be the S. O. N.-Shine, the SON-LIGHT of God, giving light and hope, joy and blessing, to the troubled hearts of the sons of men.

A FRIEND IN NEED.

A Friend in Need.

Luke x : 26-35.

The certain man in the story who goes down from Jerusalem to Jericho, is the sinner.

The going *down* from Jerusalem is the Fall of man, going down from heavenly and spiritual heights to earthly and sinful depths.

The thieves who stripped him wounded him and left him half dead, are the sins and passions of human nature.

Half dead is the condition of every natural man; dead on the side of heaven and spiritual things and alive on the side of the earth and earthly things; and that is saying that he is, really, only half alive.

The priest who saw him and passed by on the other side is the Law. It has no fellowship with the sinner, cannot help him; when it comes near can do nothing but condemn him, and pass by on the other side of righteousness, the side that bids the sinner be left alone to helplessness and death.

The Levite who acted like the priest represents the good works which the law demands and cannot obtain from man because he is wounded and helpless in sin, and must thus pass him by on the same side of righteousness with the law.

The Samaritan who came where he was is the Lord Jesus Christ who does not wait for the sinner to come to him, but comes down to where the sinner is, to his state of sin and woe.

The oil and wine poured into the traveller's wounds, the spirit and joy which the Lord Jesus gives to the sinner whom He saves on the highway-side of time. The

Samaritan giving the wounded man his own beast is the Lord Jesus giving to the sinner His own power of loco-motion. It is the power of Christ given to the powerless sinner. The Inn is the church, a stopping-place for travellers, for those who can tarry but a night, the night of time.

The host in whose care the wounded man is left is the Holy Ghost, seen not as an influence, but as a living person, the Care-taker, the Paraclete, the Comforter.

He is in the church corporately, and in us as indi-viduals to take care of us and comfort us while the Lord is away.

The money left by the Samaritan in the hands of the host to be credited to and expended for the traveller are the gifts which the Holy Ghost has in charge, in store, for the church of Christ and every Christian.

The responsibility of the host to take care of the cer-tain man while the Samaritan was away is the responsi-bility and office-work of the Holy Ghost in the church during the absence of the Lord; and as the host in the story was an inn-keeper so, in all reverence be it said, the Holy Ghost is the Inn-keeper, the Inn-keeper in the loftiest sense, for only by and through Him can the Christian be *kept in,* and housed and held, while the good Samaritan is away.

The promise of the Samaritan to come again is the last promise which Christ gave to His church: "Behold, I come quickly."

The hope which both the traveller and the host had that the Samaritan would return is the Hope of the church now, and her true attitude is to be like that of the traveller, expecting Him, waiting for Him.

This is the typical and doctrinal side of the parable.

It teaches, however, many and suggestive lessons.

Among others we get here a rebuke to the Jews who professed to be followers of God, the true exponents of the law, and despised the Samaritans as godless and hopeless sinners.

In the face of this pretension the Lord shows the Jews, in the persons of the priest and Levite failing to meet the law on its lower and easier side, the side which required that they should love their neighbor as themselves; and then pictures to them this despised Samaritan, fully and completely carrying out all that the law demanded in taking care so unselfishly of the wounded man.

By this he would show them that religious profession without practice is mere hypocrisy, and that he who does not make a profession but practices what God requires, is the true and real professor, the real confessor of God and His ways.

It is also a prophetic forecast that God would find His true witnesses in this age, not among the Jews but outside of that nation altogether, and among the Gentiles.

I pass by these suggestions, however, and draw your attention to three practical lessons:

1. The answer to the question, "Who is my neighbor?"

My neighbor is everyone who is wounded of Satan and sin; everyone half-dead with his assaults whom I meet in the journey of time. We meet him at every turn, sick, sore troubled unto death, stripped, without Christ, without hope, and without God in the world: this is your neighbor and mine.

2. Our responsibility to our neighbor.

"Go, and do thou likewise."

That means go, not sit still, but go. All the commissions of Christ have "go" in them, and if we would fulfill the mission of Christ there must be "go" in us. Go, go where the sinner is, do not wait for him to come to us, do not wait for him to hunt us up, but go where he is. Go hunt him up, go to him. Go, and bring him into contact with the beast of the Samaritan, that is, into contact with the power of Christ. That is all they did at the grave of Lazarus. They rolled away the stone and brought the dead face to face with the Living Christ and in contact with His power.

This is what you are to do, what I am to do.

We are to bring our neighbor to the Inn, bring him to the church. Never stop till you get him in the church and a part of it. What a mistake the Samaritan would have made if after giving him attention in a degree he had left the wounded man by the wayside. That is the mistake with some kinds of Christian work to-day. It gets the half-dead man aroused and then leaves him outside the church. Nay, bring your neighbor into the Inn, get him into the church without fail.

We must bring our neighbor to the Host and to his care.

Hand him over to the blessed Care-taker, the Holy Ghost; hand him over by means of faith and prayer.

Do not make any mistake about this.

Going and doing as the Samaritan did does not mean going down to Tenth Avenue or the slums, giving soup, clothes and medicine, to the hungry, naked and sick; all that is right and must not be left undone, but this parable means a very much larger thing than that; it means bringing men to the salvation of Jesus Christ. That is what we are to do with our neighbor.

It is the commission of the church and of each individual in the church. It is individual; listen, "go *thou.*" That hits it, hits you every time, hits me every time.

We are to go, each one of us, to the half-dead souls, our neighbors, and bring them to Christ, and to His church.

3. Our responsibility to the Lord Himself, the true Samaritan. He says, "Go." It is His command, a command as loud as Sinai. We cannot escape from it. We must answer the demand at the Judgment Seat of Christ. We will be asked there questions concerning our neighbor. We will be asked whether we did use all our efforts to bring him to the Inn, the church, and the care of the Holy Spirit.

How will we answer then?

How are we answering now; what are we doing?

Here are our neighbors, a great crowd of them, stripped, half-dead; some of them very beautiful, gracious lives, full of life towards the earth, and earthly things, but wholly dead towards God, and with no robe of righteousness to make them acceptable in His sight. We meet them every day. We know that they are wounded, suffering. We know that unless we step in and seek to save them they are woefully lost.

What are we doing?

Are we meeting our robbed and half-dead neighbor, laughing, talking, jesting about many things, but never once warning him of his eternal danger; never once seeking to bind up his wounds, or bring him to the Inn for rest and care in Christ? Are we evading our Lord's solemn command, every day, every hour of His wondrous grace? Are we, like the priest and the Levite, making a mere profession of religion, denying its practical obligations, and passing by on the other side?

Oh, I am sure we are not, nor do we wish, I am equally sure, that this shall be true in any measure of us. Nevertheless, let us arouse; let us pray the Lord to anoint our eyes with eye-salve that we may see clearly who is our neighbor, and that we may have grace to go and seek him in his need and bring him to a Saviour's hands to heal.

And as we search out these neighbors fallen by the way, and in His name bring them one after another to the Inn, we shall be, each of us in spirit a good Samaritan, that "Friend in Need," who is a friend, indeed.

UNHESITATING CONFIDENCE.

Unhesitating Confidence.

II Timothy i: 12.

"I know whom I have believed, and am persuaded that He is able to keep that which I have committed unto Him against that day."

This text is an outburst of confidence. The occasion of it is Paul's reference to his afflictions. In the preceding verses he declares that he suffers affliction because he is a preacher to the Gentiles. As a preacher to the Gentiles he suffers on the one side from Jewish hatred, on the other from Gentile mockery. Both combine to make his afflictions many and his sufferings intense. The record of them is extraordinary. He has been an inmate of prisons. He has been publicly flogged. He has received one hundred and ninety-five stripes on the back. He has been three times beaten with rods. He has been stoned and left for dead. He has been betrayed by Jew and assaulted by Gentile. He has been naked, cold and hungry. He has been houseless and homeless. The Jews hated him because he declared that a Jew crucified on a Roman cross was their Messiah. He was mocked by the Gentiles because he taught that the Jew whom they crucified had risen from the dead, sat on the right hand of God, and was now the alone Saviour of the world.

To continue this preaching meant only to multiply afflictions and emphasize sufferings. At every step there would be a prison door, the lifted hand of violence, or the darkling shadow of death. In every voice there would be a threat, in every look a scowl, on every brow a wrinkle of hate, and on every lip a smile of contempt.

But none of these things move him; on the contrary, as he contemplates his sufferings, knows that he is looked upon as the offscouring of the world, and that should he be put to death it would be with ignominy and shame, cries out in a voice that has in it a trumpet's ring. "Nevertheless I am *not* ashamed;" and sets himself at once to exhort Timothy to steadfastness, to faith, and thus proclaims himself in word as he does in deed, the very incarnation of dauntless courage and unhesitating confidence.

The source of this confidence is three-fold:

1. He knows whom he has believed.

He knows that the Person whom he has believed is the image of the invisible God, the express image of His person, and the brightness of His glory. He knows that He is the Creator of heaven and earth, He by whom all things were made, by whom all things consist, and the supreme centre about whom all things move. He knows that He is the Son of God, yet God the Son, He who came to be man, died for men, rose again, sits at the right hand of God, and is the man in whom dwelleth all the fullness of the Godhead bodily—even Jesus of Nazareth, the Christ of God. He knows Him as his Sacrifice for sin, his Substitute, his Redeemer, his Lord and Master, his precious Saviour. He knew that this Saviour loved him and gave Himself for him. He knew all this because Jesus Christ had appeared to him above the Damascus gates in glory, and had there revealed Himself brighter than the mid-day sun. He knew these things because when he took the life which this glorified man had lived on earth and put it side by side with the Holy Scriptures which he had studied from his youth up, he saw that these Scriptures and the Man fitted each other as the hand and the glove fit each other; and thus he knew that Jesus of Nazareth was none other than He of whom Moses and the prophets did write. He knew all this and he knew Him in all these things; and yet knew Him in a still deeper and fuller way.

He knew Him as the One who makes a constant revelation of Himself to those who love and serve Him. He had met Him in prison, on the decks of sinking ships, had talked with Him, and felt the touch of His love, His grace and power.

In a word, Paul had experienced Christ in his daily life; he knew Him not only in His outward glory, but by the Spirit's power in his own soul; so that he could say as no other man has ever surpassed him in saying it, "Christ in us, the hope of glory;" he knew for himself and not another.

There might be doubt, uncertainty about everything else in the universe, there could be no doubt about Jesus Christ.

He knew Him, felt Him, had Him not only on the throne up there, but here under his breast, in every beat of his heart; so much a part of himself that he could say, "He that is joined to the Lord is one Spirit."

And thus Paul's confidence was born of that kind of knowledge which in the last analysis we call consciousness.

He had the consciousness of Christ, and could therefore say in the profoundest sense of the phrase, "I know Him."

2. He was persuaded that Christ would keep that which he had committed to Him.

Paul *had* committed something to Christ. He had committed his spirit, his body, himself: all he was in his daily life, his thought, his word, deeds, every circumstance and condition.

Paul had made his committal to Christ.

But the text may be translated so that it will read that Christ had committed something to Paul. And He had. He had committed to him His own very nature; He had committed to him the Holy Spirit, yea He had committed Himself through that Spirit, so that Paul could say, "It is no longer I, but Christ that liveth in me." And Paul was assured that Christ would keep this double committal, keep Paul, and keep what He Himself had given to Paul. He is *persuaded* that Christ will do the keeping. That word "persuaded" means convince. He is convinced. No thought, no question about it arises. He is convinced by all that Christ is, by all that Christ has done, and by all that profound consciousness of Christ which nothing can disturb. Christ is his keeper, walling him about with His omnipotent and loving Providence, standing guard over all his circumstances. He is himself so one with Christ that any blow on him must be a blow on Christ.

What matter then whether a dungeon or a palace, a desert or a town, hunger or nakedness, death or life. Christ was on guard: Christ would keep watch through the midnight till the morn.

The keeping power of Christ, this was another of Paul's sources of confidence.

3. He is persuaded that Christ will keep him till that day.

In the text he calls it *that* day. In other writings he speaks of it as the Day of Christ. That day is coming. The day when Christ shall rule unhinderedly over the earth. The day when sin, sickness, sorrow and death shall flee away; and when life shall be as it ought to be, a poem, a psalm of praise, a perfect delight, a victory for God. Paul knows that the Day of Christ will be the Day of the Christian; that in that day the Christian will be transfigured, glorified, immortal, shining in the image of the resplendent Christ, and filled with the unspeakable felicity of God. He knows that Christ will keep him till that day, and for that day.

He knows that the whole object of his redemption, Paul's redemption, has been that he might be brought into that day and set forth as the trophy of God's grace, as the subject of God's kindness through the ages to come.

He is fully persuaded.

The blood of Christ, the Spirit of Christ, the Word of Christ, the past faithfulness of Christ, the inner consciousness of Christ, all proclaim the fact that Christ will keep him to, and for, that day.

He knows that in that day he will find compensation for all his losses, honor for all his shame, wealth for all his poverty, healing for every stripe, balm for every wound, a crown for every robbery, and God's honor and glory for every contempt of man; and above all, that he shall see Christ as He is, and hear Him say: "Well done, thou good and faithful servant;" and thus in the eyes of all who smote him, and in the eyes of all the universe, be justified as the preacher to the Gentiles, the witness of the Gospel of the grace of God.

Paul knows that Christ is coming to inaugurate that Day.

He may come sooner or He may come later. No matter. Say that He should not come for weary centuries; say that Paul should die, and his body turn to dust; say that no man should know his sepulchre and all men should forget him, that even his name should be lost to memory; no matter, Paul knew that He who made Orion and the Seven Stars, who lay a babe in Mary's breast, who hung a victim on the cruel cross, who lay a dead body in a borrowed grave, who was sitting yonder in heaven, the "Man in Glory," who held Paul's heart to His own by the indwelling Spirit and the very throbs of the Divine nature, who had pledged blood and honor, and the very word that upheld the universe, would watch over his dust, would receive his spirit, and when the morning came "without clouds" would bring him forth as a shining jewel from the dusty jewel-case of the grave, and flash him out as a matchless brilliant in the glory-crown.

And Paul was at ease. Paul was content. Paul was confident, with a confidence that never faltered, a confidence that carried him to the sword of death, and made him, as he thought on the eve of his execution, write that sublime sentence: "I have fought a good fight, I have finished my course, I have kept the faith; henceforth there is laid up for me a crown of righteousness, which the Lord, the Righteous Judge, shall give me at that day."

The view of Christ in all His glory as revealed by Paul in the written word, the experience of Christ in the heart as ministered by the spirit and the word, these are the sources of confidence for those who profess His name.

These are the sources of, and inspiration for, service and steadfastness in the face of any trouble, on the brink of any woe.

This is the hour when confidence is lacking. It is the time when doubt, uncertainty and spiritual ignorance are universal. It is the time, therefore, that needs the tonic of spiritual assurance. The Christian who is confident in Christ, the church that is full of confident Christians, Christians who believe, who know, who are persuaded, and who experience the changeless Christ in their hearts, are the Christians and the church that shall move the world, win souls, establish the faith, and glorify God.

universal. It is the time, therefore, that needs the tonic of spiritual assurance. The Christian who is confident in Christ, the church that is full of confident Christians, Christians who believe, who know, who are persuaded, and who experience the changeless Christ in their hearts, are the Christians and the church that shall move the world, win souls, establish the faith, and glorify God.

A NEW NAME.

A New Name.

II Timothy ii : 19.

"Nevertheless the foundation of God standeth sure, having this seal, the Lord knoweth them that are his. And let everyone that nameth the name of Christ depart from iniquity."

To name the name of Christ is to profess the name of Christ.

To profess the name of Christ is to call oneself by the name of Christ. To call oneself by the name of Christ is to call oneself a Christian. To call oneself a Christian is to call oneself by a new name. No matter by what name or names one may have called oneself before, there is one name by which God has known and called that person, and that name is Sinner. That was the old name. But the moment the sinner professes the name of Christ he is called of God by a new name, and that new name is Christian.

That this new name is Christian is the declaration of Holy Scripture. In the book of Acts, xi: 26, it is written: "The disciples were called Christians first at Antioch." It is popularly supposed that this title was given as a nickname by the light and frivolous populace of Antioch.

But such conclusion is a grave and unwarrantable mistake.

The Greek verb to call employed here is never used except when the person speaking or calling is God. When therefore it is said that the disciples were called Christians first at Antioch, it is simply saying that God calls those who name the name of Christ, Christians; and that he did so for the first time officially at Antioch. That this is the official name of those who name the name of Christ is corroborated on the one hand by the exhortation of the Apostle Peter, who declares that if any man suffer as a "Christian" he need not be ashamed, and on the other hand by that pathetic wailing cry of king Agrippa when he says in response to the inspired pleading of the Apostle Paul, "Almost thou persuadest me to be a Christian." Thus by the act of the individual, the logic of nomenclature, and the declared will of God, those who name the name of Christ are called Christians; and therefore Christian is both a new and divinely given name.

In the verses which precede the text the Apostle is exhorting Timothy to give correct teaching to Christians under his charge; to rightly divide the Word of Truth. There were those who did not rightly divide it. Two of them, Hymeneus and Philetus, taught that the resurrection of Christians was already past, and thereby overthrew the faith of some.

"Nevertheless," says the Apostle, "the foundation of God standeth sure, having this seal." By this he would say that in spite of such overthrow there were those who were genuine Christians, who, no matter what the teaching or circumstances, could not be cast down either in faith or character; that they were God's work, God's building, God's founding. And just as in those days, and sometimes in ours, the contractor and builder puts his seal in the foundation to indicate his responsibility for, and his confidence in, his work, so God has put his seal upon those who are really and truly Christians.

This seal the Apostle asserts is double, it has two sides, it has two inscriptions.

On the one side the seal reads:

"The Lord knoweth them that are his." That is Divine Assurance.

The other side of the seal reads:

"And let everyone that nameth the name of Christ depart from iniquity." That is the Manifested Characteristic of those who are the Lord's.

Each genuine Christian bears these two marks of the seal.

One mark towards God assuring him, bearing witness to, and justifying him.

The other mark towards the Christian and the world at large, bearing witness to the consciousness of the one, and the observation of the other.

Let us consider the seal on the side towards God, the Lord.

1. "The Lord knoweth them that are his."

He, himself, made this statement when on the earth. He declared that he knew those who were his, and that he knew them by name. He knew them before they were born into the world.

He knew them before the world itself was born, or ever the stars were made. He knew them from all eternity. From its unbeginning depths their names both as sinners and Christians were engraven on his heart. When therefore he reaches down and by his Spirit through the Gospel calls one here and another there to name his name, to profess him, to follow him, to be his disciple, to become a Christian, he makes no mistake, he cannot be deceived. Men may deceive one another, men may deceive themselves, they cannot deceive him. He knows them that are his. Knows where they are born, under what circumstances they have lived, what is their past in all its details, so that nothing is hidden from his view. Knows just where and what they are at this hour, and all things that may pass. Knows all their ways in the coming days of time, and sees them on even into the midst of the farthest reach of their sure and shining glory. Every failure, every tear, every trouble, every struggle of theirs is known; and he knows, come what may, even though for a time they seem cast down, that they will rise above all circumstances and conditions, victors at the last. In his mind they are as eternal as the ages, as sure as his throne, as certain as his own pledged word and covenant. They are his work, his building, his foundation, the foundation that shall outlast the wreck of time itself. So sure and certified are they before him that no place ever once ordained for the Christian, the true Christian, in the glory, shall ever be vacant, no seat at the Father's table shall ever be empty, nor any Christian ear ever miss the music of the welcome home.

They are as much his as his own heart, and he is content: he knoweth them that are his. He has put his own private mark on them, and he can point them out with confidence to the onlookers of heaven, saying of them now up there, as he said down here, "I know them that are mine."

In a word then, the mark, the seal, the evidence to the Lord that such and such a professed Christian is his, is the consciousness which he has of them. He is conscious of them because the true Christian impresses himself on that consciousness, and thus in the profoundest sense of the word it may be said, "the Lord knoweth them that are his."

Consider the other side of the seal, the Manifested Characteristic of the genuine Christian.

2. "And let everyone that nameth the name of Christ depart from iniquity."

Departure from iniquity is the characteristic of everyone who is the Lord's.

The law of this departure is in the name of Christ.

The name of Christ stands for the power of departure from iniquity. It stands for righteousness, holiness, and truth, for the communication of these qualities to a human soul.

It stands for resurrection life and its impartation, for the communication and indwelling of the Holy Spirit, for vital union with humanity; in short, for reincarnation and enthronement of God in a human life. And he who professes the name of Christ, professes the realization of all these conditions and forces in his own experience. To profess the name of Christ then and continue to live in sin is, on the one hand, to deny the name of Christ, to contradict it for all it stands, to make of it a scandal and a shame; and on the other hand to confess oneself a stranger to all the power of departure from iniquity which that name and its profession demands.

And that name does demand it. It is as much a demand upon the one who professes it as the beating of the heart, the respiration of the lungs, or the circulation of the blood, are the demand of the natural life. And just as the absence of these conditions witnesses the absence of life, or at least the consciousness of its power, and raises a suspicion as to life altogether, so the failure on the part of a professed Christian to depart from iniquity, bears witness that he is unconscious of the power of Christ, and raises a suspicion of his relation to Him either as his life or his Lord.

Departure from iniquity is therefore absolutely necessary as a characteristic demonstration that he who professes the name of Christ is in truth the Lord's.

This departure is to be open and unqualified, a new departure in life. Not only a departure from the old ways of sin and iniquity, from old methods and principles, but a departure into the new ways of righteousness and truth.

The point of departure is the naming of the name of Christ, and therefore, the claiming and professing the name of Christian.

And this departure must be from the very moment that the name of Christ is named. From that moment it must be as clear and distinct a departure, as when a man turns his back on the point towards which he has been travelling, and departs in the opposite direction. It must be a departure as sharply defined as when the train departs from the station, and with each revolving wheel leaves the point of departure farther and farther behind. It must be as marked as when the ship departs from the shore, and puts leagues on leagues of rolling water as a distinct element between it and the land, its point of departure. The one who names the name of Christ must turn his back on the point of sin towards which he was travelling, and depart in the opposite direction of Holiness, with each succeeding step leaving the old way of sin farther and farther behind him, putting the measureless depths of a new and spiritual existence between him and the old life. A departure so supreme, that he who wears the new name of Christian, fits it with the new departure in his life; so it, that the life flowing out of that departure is as new as the name.

Such a departure is a witness to the individual that he is the Lord's; for he knows that of himself he has no power to overcome the inertia of sin, or make any departure in Holiness.

It is a witness to the world; for men of the world know their own helplessness, and the spectacle of a natural sinful human being, departing into a life that bears all the characteristics of the life of Christ, is a witness to them of an intimate and complete relation between the Christian and Christ.

Nor is this the only testimony such a departure bears; nay, it testifies of the truth of Christ, the truth of all that is claimed for him, not only that he lived, but that he is alive now upon the throne of God, and is there, and from thence, the supreme power of God in the human life that owns him.

No greater witness to the resurrection and sonship of Christ can be given, than this spectacle of one who has lived a life of sin, naming the name of Christ, from that moment departing from sin and iniquity, living a life of Holiness, and making Christ every day the law and mastery of his being.

Such an experience as that, is, beyond all argument of speech, beyond all logic and rhetoric, a demonstration that Christ is alive. No dead cause can produce living effects; since therefore the naming of Christ, and the claiming of Christ, produce living effects, then Christ is the cause, and Christ is alive from the dead, the ascended, exalted Lord.

Thus the new name of Christian becomes the translucent name through which shines forth the deeper name of Christ, and the glory of his unspeakable Lordship, while, at the same time, it reveals the Christian's relation to him, and stamps that Christian as the Lord's.

Departure from iniquity then, is the indisputable seal

that the professor of Christ, is the possessor of Christ, and is possessed by him, and is, indeed, the Lord's.

Are we giving this mark of genuine Christianity to men, are we stampng it on our own consciousness, and thus justifying our claim to a new name, this new name Christian? The word of command is, the law absolute is, "Let everyone that nameth the name of Christ depart from iniquity."

Who then can measure the importance, the obligation, the irrevocable necessity on the part of everyone who names the name of Christ, to depart from iniquity?

THE INDWELLING PRESENCE.

The Indwelling Presence.

Galatians ii : 20.
Colossians i : 21-29.

The Indwelling Presence is the Risen Christ.

In Galatians ii: 20, it is "Christ liveth in me."

In Colossians i: 27, it is "Christ in you, the Hope of Glory."

In Galatians, we have the great fact.

In Colossians, we have the Hope which this great fact brings.

Let us consider,

1. The Fact.

"Christ liveth in me."

The stupendous thought presented is The Reincarnation of Christ. The risen Christ dwelling in the flesh. Christ dwelling in the earth, ministering in, and through a human body, just as he did in the days when he was known only in the body of Jesus of Nazareth.

And this is the sum total of Christianity.

This is its highest definition.

Christ in Christians, by and through them multiplied, and become the omnipresent, as he is the omnipotent man, manifesting God in life and blessing to men.

Not only dwelling in the church and Christianity in general, but in the individual and particular Christian, so that each Christian may say, "Christ liveth in me."

Christ lives in each Christian in a two-fold way.

He lives in him by,

His communicated Nature.

When the individual believes on the Lord Jesus Christ, owns him as his Saviour and Lord, the very essence of

Christ as the Risen, Divine Man, is communicated to him. He is made a partaker of the Divine nature, he is made a partaker of Christ. It is this which makes a Christian, the nature of Christ added to the nature of Adam in the believer. The nature of the Second man coming in and dwelling by the side of the First man. It is a new generation. It is regeneration.

By giving his nature, his mind, his desires, Christ essentially lives in the Christian.

There is also another way by which he lives in him.

He lives in him by,

The Holy Spirit.

It is true he lives in him by the Holy Spirit when he makes him a partaker of his nature, for it is by the Spirit through the Word that nature is communicated, but he lives in him in a still deeper and more wonderful way by the Spirit.

That is to say, after the resurrection and ascension of Christ in his glorified body to the throne of God, the Holy Spirit came down to take up his abode in the believer's body, to act in it in the name of Christ, and as his proxy, manifest him personally to the believer; so that while upon the throne yonder in his actual body, he might be manifest in his personality down here, and dwell in, live in, the believer's body through the Spirit, as though it were indeed his own very body. Just as personally dwell in the believer as he does upon the throne.

This is the two-fold way then in which Christ dwells in the believer, by his nature, and the Holy Spirit.

And this indwelling takes place on one ground alone. It takes place on the alone ground of the believer's co-crucifixion and death with Christ.

When Christ died, in God's sight, every believer died. In God's sight every believer is judicially at an end before him now, considered as a member of the old creation, as one in the flesh; and because he is so considered at an end in the old life, Christ comes by the Spirit to dwell in him, and in the midst of this scene of nature's death, bring forth the new life of a son of God.

In the passage before us, it is the personality of Christ rather than the nature of Christ which is looked at. It is Christ himself personally who liveth in the Apostle.

Now while it is true that the measure of Christ's nature in each believer is the same, that is to say regeneration has no degrees and is as perfect in one as another, it is also true that the measure of Christ's personal life depends wholly upon the believer himself, and therefore the degree in which Christ lives in a Christian may vary.

Christ may be personally alive in him and yet so feebly alive that the believer may be scarcely conscious of that indwelling presence, and the world not at all.

Two things are required for the manifestations of the indwelling presence:

First, the believer must own himself as crucified with Christ, and dead. At an end before God for all things in his old life, not only sins and vices, but virtues and righteousnesses.

Henceforth he must no longer count upon the truth and honor that are in him naturally, to aid and sustain him in his Christian life. When a man is dead and buried, his virtues as well as his vices are dead and buried with him. So, on the cross of Christ, all the good in nature as well as the bad was crucified; on the cross the whole man is dead. There is no more hope in him, or of him, than the man in the grave.

In order that Christ may fully and personally live in him, the believer must appropriate this crucifixion with Christ, enter into it, and own himself as wholly dead in the flesh before God.

Second, as one who is dead and therefore has no longer any power over his body, he must yield himself up to the personal, indwelling Christ.

It is well known that certain minds and temperaments can be so acted upon by another that they will think the thoughts and act out the suggestions of that other; so that their bodies may, in a sense, be said to be indwelt and possessed by that other. We call the law of this condition hypnotism, and we say that the person so acted upon is hypnotized.

In a far higher, nobler, and thoroughly reverential sense, it may be suggested that it is the privilege of each Christian to be hypnotized by the indwelling Christ. So submitting ourselves to him that our minds, our wills, shall be his; that we shall think his thoughts and act out his suggestions, until he shall possess our bodies, and by and through his Spirit use them as his own.

And when it is remembered that he does actually live in us both by nature and Spirit, it ought to be with perfect ease and full delight that we own ourselves as dead, yield ourselves entirely up to him, and with the Apostle in thankful tones cry out: "I no longer live, but Christ liveth in me."

The moment this apprehension of death, and this complete surrender of self, is attained by the believer, Christ begins to live in him just as he lived when in his flesh on the earth. That is, by faith. Adam always walks by sight. Christ always walks by faith, and the moment we give him the right of way in us, he begins to live and walk in us by faith.

Now, when this happens a strange thing takes place. The believer himself begins to live, and he begins to live by the very faith of the Son of God. Not by *his* faith in the Son of God, but by the faith of the Son of God operating in him. The Son of God in him furnishes him faith, and through that faith enables him to live and act as a Son of God.

When he is weak, when he would faint by the way, Christ living in him furnishes him with his own faith, meets him at every point with that faith, and through it pours forth his own life into every atom of his being, until the delighted believer is led to cry out with the Apostle: "The life which I now live in the flesh I live by the faith of the Son of God."

It is a wonderful, unspeakable fact, Christ living and dwelling in the believer's body, exercising his own faith, and seeking through the exercise of it to make the believer live in all the joy and power of the Divine sonship.

And the splendor and power of this fact will be in exact proportion as the believer sees that he is crucified with Christ, that he no longer lives, that Christ is his life from the dead, and yields himself completely to him. This is the great fact: The Indwelling Presence— "Christ liveth in me."

Consider,

2. The hope which this great fact brings.

"Christ in you, the Hope of Glory." Colossians i: 27. The glory held out in Scripture is immortality at the Coming of Christ, either by the resurrection of the dead, or the transfiguration of the living. The glory of a perfect body, a body that shall be like unto his own glorious body.

Our Lord Jesus Christ was patient in all things, but he was not content that the body in which he dwelt should remain mortal; hence he carried it into death and the grave, triumphed over them in it, made it immortal, took it up to the throne of God, dwells in it there, and shall dwell in it forever, forever manifesting to the universe the wonder of a shining, glorified, immortal, human body.

If he was not content with his own body as a dwelling place till he had made it immortal, will He be perfectly content till he has made our bodies as his dwelling places also immortal? Sooner or later if he tarries they must die and fall into decay, and thus the body that has been the temple of the Holy Ghost, the dwelling place of the eternal life, shall at the last be vanquished by him who has the power of death, that is the Devil; and over that which had once been a witness to the glory of Christ shall be written that victory of Satan which would be the shame of Christ.

Such a consummation would be indeed a scandal to the Son of God, a fearful commentary on his own immortality, and a grave question as to the permanency of his relation to those whom he calls his own.

In the very nature of the case it is impossible that the body in which Christ has ever dwelt shall finally be destroyed. In the very nature of the case he must make it immortal to justify his own indwelling, and the immortality which he himself achieved. Wherefore it is written:

"But if the Spirit of him that raised up Jesus from the dead dwell in you, he that raised up Christ from the dead shall also quicken your mortal bodies by his Spirit that dwelleth in you."

To say that the Father will quicken the bodies by his Spirit, is to say that the Son in the name of the Father will quicken them by the Spirit; and because the Spirit dwelling in them is in the name of the Son, it is the Son dwelling in them who will quicken them by the Spirit.

Thus Christ living in the believer is the pledge and guaranty of immortality; and therefore Christ in the believer is the sure, the definite hope of glory. The hope that shall never be deferred, or make the heart sick.

In carrying the Living Christ within, the believer carries the hope that casts its light onward to the glory hour, and illuminates all the way between. Just as the Pillar of Cloud and Fire went with the children of Israel by day and by night, assuring them that they were being guided, and guided home, so this Indwelling Presence picturing to us each day the Morning hour and the Morning land, is a constant witness that we are being guided, and that we are being guided home.

What a pledge of grace, of certitude, and love.

Well may the Apostle exclaim, speaking of this inliving Christ: "Who loved me and gave himself for me."

The indwelling of this Presence brings with it a double obligation:

An obligation to the world; an obligation to the Indwelling Christ himself.

As Christians, we are under obligation to the world to let Christ live in us so freely, so fully, that men may see and know Him who is the Way, the Truth, and the Life.

We are under obligation to the Indwelling Christ to let Him so live in us, that he may manifest himself to the world.

It is his desire. This is why he ascended to the throne and sent down the Spirit in his name.

He yearns to-day to use your lips and mine, our hands and feet.

Yonder is one in sorest trouble. The blessed Christ

would speak and comfort him. He can only speak by your lips and mine. There is a hand that is trembling. He would like to take it and hold it in his own and give it the clasp of assurance and perfect love. He can only do so with your hands and mine. Up yonder flight of stairs, in yonder dingy room, is one sick and nigh to death. He would climb those stairs, kneel by the bedside of the sick, and touch the fevered brow. But he can only climb those stairs with your feet and mine; he can only kneel with your knees and mine; only with our hands can he touch the fevered brow; only with our voices utter the message of love; only through our bodies manifest himself to a sad and dying world.

Shall we deny him this?

Shall we deny him our feet to climb those stairs; shall we keep back those hands that he would use; and shall we seal the lips by which he would speak the tender message to the dying soul?

Nay, rather, shall we not say:

> "Take my feet, and let them be
> Swift and beautiful for thee.
> Take my lips and let them be
> Filled with messages from thee.
>
> "Take my hands, and let them move
> At the impulse of thy love.
> Take my voice, and let me sing
> Always, only, for my King."

And by every movement of our bodies say to men as we pass on our pilgrim way: "I no longer live, but Christ liveth in me." So live that our lives shall be a demonstration that "Christ in us, the hope of glory," is the Indwelling Presence that guides us in that way.

ABIDING IN CHRIST.

Abiding in Christ.

John xv : 1-10.

The key words of the passage are:

"I am the true vine, and my Father is the husband-man."

"I am the vine, ye are the branches."

"Abide in me."

"The branch cannot bear fruit of itself except it abide in the vine; no more can ye except ye abide in me."

"Without me ye can do nothing."

In the preceding article in the passages, Galatians ii : 20, and Colossians i : 21-29, we had the dwelling of Christ in the Christian.

In the above passage we have the dwelling of the Christian in Christ.

In the former, it was the union of Christ with the believer. Now, it is the union of the believer with Christ.

The vine and the branches are used to set forth this union.

Nothing could be more familiar to the disciples than the vine and the branches considered as a fact; nothing could have been more suggestive to them considered as a figure.

Every day they saw the vine clambering on the hill-sides and spreading its branches. In the Temple where they had gone from childhood, and where they had recently been with Jesus in all his Passover discourses, they saw a golden vine with golden branches, golden leaves, and great clusters of golden grapes, hanging over its portal, set there as the symbol of that Israel whom

God had planted among the nations of the earth. They knew that the Psalmist testified that Israel was a "vine out of Egypt," and that speaking to Israel by the mouth of the prophet Jeremiah, Jehovah had said: "I planted thee a noble vine," and then declared that this same favored Israel had become unto him "the degenerate plant of a strange vine."

When therefore in the last supper hour the Master turned to them and said: "I am the true vine," they knew, even though they knew it dimly, that he had reference not merely to the vine that grew each day before their faces, but to that golden symbol above the Temple door; and that by this he would declare that so far from being a branch, an individual member of Israel, he was himself the true vine, the very source of Israel's hope and spiritual life; that he was the true plant which God had now set in the earth to bring forth the fruit which Israel had failed to give. When again therefore, he turned to his disciples and said: "Ye are the branches," they saw that Israel as a nation had been put aside, and that in Israel's place they were to be brought into union with him to form that new and vital planting, that new and mysterious system which should bring forth fruit to God, to the glory of his name, even that mystery, the Church of Christ.

Simple as the figure is, nothing could more fitly set forth the truth.

At the beginning, it is the definite declaration that the relation between Christ and those who are his is real and vital. Just as the life of the vine pours into each branch and manifests its identity in each, so the life of Christ by the communication of his nature and Spirit pours into each believer, and stamps itself as the same in each. Just as the branch is the duplicate and multiplication of the vine, so each believer is the duplicate and multiplication of Christ, his very expression; so much so, that each true Christian is in measure the Christ of God abroad in earth again. Just as the branch originates in the vine, draws all its life and substance from the vine, so the Christian originates in Christ, draws all his life from Christ, and in him as his environment, finds all the substance and the sustenance of his spiritual life.

The object of the vine in creating the branch, the purpose of the union between them, is not for a moment to make a passing show of summer beauty, filling the branches with wealth of foliage and fragrant flower; it is true you get wide and verdant leaves, but while these express in all their profusion the surplus vigor of the vine, they do not stand for its beauty, nor proclaim its intent, and if there was nothing more than leaves, wonderful as they are when well examined, no passer-by would stop to note the vine.

Nay, the beauty and the glory of the vine is fruit; purple clusters of gleaming grapes hanging in the sun, each several grape a purple vase filled with the essence of the vine, that distillation of the juice of its root intended of God to fill the heart of man with joy, and make his face to shine.

Nor is the relation between Christ and the Christian intended for mere profession, theologic terms, or homiletic discussion, but for the bringing forth of fruit, royal clustered fruit, each several element of that fruit like each several grape, filled with the essence of Christ, the distillation of his strength, that strength which alone can fill the heart of man with joy, and make his face to shine. Fruit whose every part is named, as the Apostle names them when he writes: "The fruit of the Spirit," and mark you, it is not "fruits," but "fruit," each several part being required to make the whole, to make the perfect fruit; the "fruit of the Spirit" (and therefore the fruit of Christ in us) "is love, joy, peace, long suffering, gentleness, goodness, faith, meekness, temperance."

The branches bringing forth abundant fruit glorified the husbandman, in that they responded to his desires, and were a compensation for all the watch-care and labor he had bestowed upon them. The Christian bringing forth abundant fruit in character and service glorifies the Father, in that he thus responds to the Father's desire for fruitful children, and compensates him as the heavenly husbandman for all the labor, grace, and providence he has bestowed upon them.

The branch as it put forth its characteristic fruit bore witness not only to the vitality of the vine, but that it was following and fulfilling the law of that vine, meeting its every demand. The Christian who brings forth the fruit of Christ in his daily life, proves not only that he is a Christian, but a disciple of Christ, one who owns the law of the indwelling Christ, who seeks to follow him in all his ways and will; and thus fruitfulness both glorifies God, the Father, and demonstrates the discipleship of those who make the claim of Christian.

The husbandman who seeks the fruit from off the vine is not content with little; on the contrary he not only wants fruit, but much. To that end he seeks to keep the branches clean, drive away the little foxes that spoil the tender shoots, remove the insects that endeavor to find a lodgment there, cut all excrescences and prune to suit his will; and does all this that each year he may have fruit, and have it more abundantly.

No less does God demand fruit from those who profess to be his children in union with his risen Son. He wants fruit, not less and less as the days go on, but more and more.

As years add to the fruitfulness of the vine, so each succeeding year should add to the fruitfulness of Christ in Christians, not only in the display of the subjective characteristics of Christ, but in the objective value of his life in us as manifested in work and service in his name. To bring about this multiplied and abundant fruitfulness he will by every means endeavor to cleanse us and cast out the sins that seek to find a lodgment in our lives. He will not hesitate to break off a leaf here, a twig there, or cut away what we may deem of vital importance to ourselves, but what he sees to be an excrescence upon, and a hindrance to, our spiritual development. He will not hesitate to purge us, make us suffer loss or pain, if, thereby happily, he may free us from every obstacle to our spiritual growth; he will do anything if, by this, he may bring forth the fruit for which he so manifestly yearns.

It is clear enough that without the vine the branch can do nothing. Take the branch away from the vine, it is utterly helpless and undone. Nor is the helplessness of the Christian apart from Christ less manifest. Without Christ, without conscious vital union with Christ, the Christian can do nothing either in bringing forth the fruit of the Spirit in his life, or the works and service which his profession demands.

In order that the branch may bring forth fruit it must abide in the vine. But it must be evident that in relation to the vine the branch has no volition either about its origin or continuance. It is the vine that creates it.

It is the vine that holds it, and there is no power in itself considered, by which it may reject the vine or separate itself therefrom. If, however, there should any uncleanness come upon the branch, that uncleanness would act as an obstacle to the life in the vine. The vine is sensitive. It will not flow into or over that which is unclean, it will withhold itself. As a consequence, the branch withers, shrivels, becomes dry, and although it may remain outwardly in the vine, will show no vitality and bring forth no fruit in evidence of its claimed relation.

No more than the branch in the vine is the Christian his own creation; on the contrary, he is the creation of God in Christ of whom that vine is the symbol, as it is written: "If any man be in Christ he is a new creation;" and again: "We are his workmanship, created in Christ Jesus." It is equally true that as the branch cannot separate itself from the vine, neither can the Christian cut himself off from vital relation to Christ; nor yet, and let it be said with reverence but firmness absolute, can God himself so separate him as to vital union, inasmuch as it is written: "He that is joined unto the Lord is one Spirit;" and it is evident that in such a relation there can be no final cleavage; for there could be no point of incision where the knife would not touch the very existence of God himself.

In order then to get the full application of the truth, and not fall into error through a false apprehension of the figure, it must be recognized that the actual relation between Christ and those who are his stands higher than the one which the vine and the branches show; that the vine and the branches show only the relation between Christ and those who are his *while on the earth;* that the essential relation lies higher than any figure or symbol of nature can represent, a relation in which the believer is seen risen, ascended, and seated with Christ in heavenly places in him, on the very throne of God; planted not in earth as the vine is planted, but in heaven itself, rooted in the throne and purpose of God, above the vacillation of earth and time. Recognizing all this, recognizing that there is a side in which it is impossible for one who has ever really been joined to Christ to be separated from him as to eternity and the world to come, either by his own volition or the will of God, yet it must be just as clearly recognized that there is also a side, the side of the earthly, outward walk, in which the believer may so separate himself from the vital power of Christ, that he shall bring forth no fruit, and his life as a professed Christian, be withered, shriveled, dead; an outward profession in which he shall have no more consciousness of Christ, and, in the eyes of the world, no more life than the withered juiceless fruitless branches which the husbandman takes away and men gather up and burn in fire; a profession in which it will be found that God had just as much cut him off and separated him from this actual consciousness, as when the husbandman takes away each branch that beareth not fruit; taking him away and separating him from the fellowship and power of Christ because he brought forth no fruit in his name.

And this condition arises because of some uncleanness of sin. It may be but a very small uncleanness, a deed. a word, a habit, a thought. These are sufficient to grieve the Spirit, and hinder his inflow through the Christian life.

Abiding in Christ then means dwelling in Christ, resting in Christ, making him the source and the environment of our daily lives. And the method for this abiding requires for its complement that the words of Christ shall dwell in us. That is to say, all that the words of Christ express, his mind, his thoughts, his desires, his will; that we shall make these words of Christ, all he says to us, the supreme, the final authority in our lives; making them the rule of our faith and conduct, guiding ourselves, justifying ourselves, and therefore illuminating ourselves always, with a "thus saith the Lord."

And as we thus abide in him and his words abide in us, we shall bring forth fruit, bring it forth abundantly to the demonstration of the indwelling Christ, and the glory of God, the Father.

In the nature of the case withered branches, fruitless branches, are an encumbrance to the vine, a scandal to it, and in the eyes of men fit only for the fire. Nor can it be doubted that the Christian whose profession is a withered, shriveled profession, a profession that is conspicuous by the absence of all that should characterize a Christian, is a scandal to Christ, to the church, to God, and, in the eyes of men, is as fully fit for the fire as the ungodly and the sinner; and if "men," as suggested in the text, were made the *judges, they would,* no doubt, gather them as withered branches, and cast therein.

In view of all this there are some soul searching questions which we may each of us well ask ourselves:

Am I abiding in Christ? Am I dwelling in him by faith? Am I resting in him as my life, my motive and my strength? Am I keeping myself in the sphere of his influence and love? Am I depending wholly on him for all I have and am? Are his words abiding in me as the law of my life, the rule of my conduct, the definition of my duty, and the regulation of my desires? Am I showing forth the fruit of the Spirit? Am I making the hearts of men to rejoice and their faces to shine because of the union between Christ and myself? Am I demonstrating without controversy that I am a true disciple of Christ, and thus each day glorifying God; or, am I a dry, withered, fruitless branch, bearing witness of nothing so much as that I am not abiding in Christ, nor his words abiding in me?

hearts of men to rejoice and their faces to shine because of the union between Christ and myself? Am I demonstrating without controversy that I am a true disciple of Christ, and thus endlessly glorifying God; or, am I a dry, withered, fruitless branch, bearing witness of nothing so much as that I am not abiding in Christ, nor his words abiding in me?

CONSECRATION OF ABILITY.

Consecration of Ability.

Colossians iii : 23, 24.

"Whatsoever ye do, do it heartily, as to the Lord, and not unto men; knowing that of the Lord ye shall receive the reward of the inheritance: for ye serve the Lord Christ."

The emphasized word of the text is, "do." "Whatsoever ye *do, do* it heartily, as to the Lord."

In order to be saved the sinner has *nothing* to "do," but once that he is saved he is *always* to "do." "Doing" is the intent and purpose of salvation. The character of this doing is set forth in the declaration: "Ye serve the Lord Christ." Service of Christ means doing things in the name of Christ and for him; so doing that his name may be glorified and himself exalted both as Saviour and Lord. Any doing, no matter how good, that does not bring in the crucified and risen Christ before men as the personal Saviour of the soul and Lord over the ways of the individual life, is not the doing for which the Christian has been redeemed and saved.

The Christian has been equipped for this characteristic doing. He has been equipped by the impartation of the nature of Christ, the indwelling of the Holy Ghost, the gifts he brings, and that Providence which opens the ways, and creates the opportunities for the doing required. As Christians we are under obligation to be doing, not only by reason of this equipment, but because we are no longer our own.

We have been bought with a price, a price paid by the Lord himself, told out and paid in good round drops of reddest blood in the agony of his cross; a price paid

and purchased claimed, which God the Father has owned
in the triple fact that He raised him from the dead,
seated him at his right hand, and sent down the Holy
Ghost in His name to dwell in the bodies purchased by
his blood; a purchase that thus sealed makes us before
God and man, body, soul and spirit, his, his property,
his slaves, and therefore under obligation to be doing in
his name.

Nor does the objective of the Christian service vary.
It must be always, as to the Lord. Not unto self, self
has no place in the vision of a slave; nor yet, unto men,
a slave must know only one man, one person, his master
and Lord.

"As to the Lord," that is the watchword, that must be
the objective; and this objective kept before the mind of
the servant will clear the sky of every doubt and take
away the conflicting concepts of duty that so often per-
plex the path. "As to the Lord," stamped upon any
work however small however simple will exalt it, dig-
nify it, and make it a part of the throne and purpose of
God.

The value of service depends upon its mode or manner,
as well as objective. All Christian service must be not
only unto the Lord but heartily unto him, even as it is
written: "Whatsoever ye do, do it *heartily,* as to the
Lord." Heartily, that is the centre and core of exhorted
Christian doing.

Doing all we do in his name, and for him, so that we
shall do nothing but what is done for him, but doing all
this heartily. There is no other way in which to do any
service.

Be the service what it may, failure is written in large
letters over every attempt that is not inspired by a whole

heart. To say that a man lacks heart in his work is to say that his work is doomed. A man's heart is himself; he who would accomplish anything must put his heart into it, so that every beat of that heart shall be like the stroke of a hammer, driving the purpose deeper and deeper into the work.

The men who have achieved anything in the world are the men who have put their heart into their work, given themselves up to it, so that each time they did a thing it was felt that the beat of their heart was in it. The Greek used here lets in light, the word rendered "heartily" is "soul," so that the exhortation is, really, to do all that is done "from the soul." The men who have succeeded have done so, because they did their work from the core and centre of their being. They took the concept of it past all the outer lines of selfhood, deep down into the very citadel of self, down into the very soul, showed it to the soul, got its approval, stamped soul on it, and henceforth put soul into the work; so that the work in the end became the concrete of their soul, the epitome of their life; in other words, the work stood forth as the expression of their heart and all that was in them.

Nor can service for Christ, service that means anything, be done in any other way. Says the Apostle: "This one thing I do." It is the key thought of his life matched by that other imperial phrase: "For me to live is Christ;" and the life he lived, the service he gave, the work he accomplished, all respond to, and justify his wholeheartedness. To serve Christ with less than a whole heart, with less than full purpose, with any measure of reservation of self, is not only to contradict the power of service in us and shamefully deny the redemption price paid, but also to commit spiritual suicide. The Christian who does not give himself up wholly to serve Christ does not get the benefit of the divine power in his own soul, does not reap the satisfaction of self-respect for honest work, and fails to reach the heights of intimate fellowship with him in whose name he serves.

Who is it that draws nigh to the Master, looks him in the face, suns himself in his smile, and is assured of his love?

Is it that servant who does his work half-heartedly, or he who serves wholeheartedly out of the depths of the soul? Who is the Christian conscious of blessing and the joy of salvation? Is it that Christian who gives himself up, body, soul, and spirit, or that Christian who holds back, divides his duty, and gives *a service made of fractions?*

There is no need to ask, and certainly there is no need to answer the question. The truth is self-evident. The half-hearted Christian is as a stranger before the Lord, and walks in vain show, carrying the name and burden of a profession without an inspiration. Nor is this all: for, in the prophet Jeremiah xlviii: 10, it is written: "Cursed be everyone who doeth the work of the Lord deceitfully." The margin renders it, "negligently," that is to say, half-heartedly.

The sound of a curse lingers in the shadow of half-heartedness. And Moses, the great law-giver, adds to the warning in Numbers xxxii: 23: "Be sure your sin will find you out." He is speaking to the children of the tribes of Reuben and Gad.

By this he would say that if they did not give themselves up wholly and full-heartedly to the work of the Lord to which he had called them in the Promised

Land, their half-heartedness would be a sin against the Lord, would find them out and betray them at the last.

"Be sure your sin will find you out," is what the Lord is saying to every Christian now who does not give himself up with a whole heart to his service.

It will find him out here in the darkness and blundering in his spiritual life, and in all the suffering of soul that comes to a Christian not in the fullness of communion with Christ; in all the weakness, failure and shame, that attend upon the pathway of one not walking in the power of the indwelling Spirit, betraying him to himself, to the bitterness of his own conscience, and the merciless judgment of others; and it will betray him at the Judgment Seat of Christ in that hour when he shall see himself missing the crown he might have had, and that crown going to another, not because that other was better equipped, but because he gave himself up to do as unto the Lord, and to do it heartily: he consecrated his ability.

Consecrated ability.

That is the thing to which we are called, not the consecration of *our* ability but, rather, the consecration of ourselves to the divine ability in us, giving ourselves up to be possessed and used by the power which the Lord has so freely put within us.

Who can measure the result of such a consecration? Some one has said: "The world yet waits to see what a man or woman fully given up to God can do." The answer is simple enough.

Such an one could do all that God required of him; and if each Christian did the same, the glory of God would break out in the earth and illumine it to the farthest stars.

Such service has its reward.

Reward here in the unspeakable experience of Christ in the soul. Reward yonder at the Judgment Seat of Christ where the consecrated Christian shall receive the crown that fadeth not away, hear the welcome words "Well done," be invited to a special reception in the palace of the King, and enter into the "Joy of the Lord."

The guaranty of the reward both as to the giving and the quality of it is revealed in the simple but sublime phrase: "Ye serve the Lord Christ." When you have taken these two names, Lord, Christ, set them before you as a title and have recognized that this title signifies that all the fullness of the Godhead bodily dwells in him whom we serve, you get indeed the guaranty of the reward, and the assurance that its worth and splendor shall be equal to the glory of the giver.

The blessedness of the reward lies in the tender fact that it will be given by the Lord himself, by his own dear hands.

Behold him yonder on the exalted throne, "The Man in The Glory," the Alpha and Omega, the All in All, his face shining in love, his hands outstretched and full of gifts.

Behold him, and while you gaze at the gifts in his hand, let your eyes take in the vision of the nail prints there, nails by which the handwriting of sin, of Satan and death against us, was cancelled, and say in the light of this wonder of grace and love *what* you will do, and *how* you will do it, while the voice of the Apostle is heard ringing this exhortation in your ears: "Whatsoever ye do, do it heartily, as to the Lord, and not unto men; knowing that of the Lord ye shall receive the reward of the inheritance: for ye serve the Lord Christ."

What shall it be, whole-hearted, or half-hearted service for Christ?

THE SABBATH.

The Sabbath.

1. *The original Sabbath was not given as a command.* Reasons:

a. Because, considered as a day of *rest,* the Sabbath is for those who have labored.

Up to that time man had not labored.

He had no need of rest, nor of a rest day.

If he had not sinned, he never would have labored.

The Sabbath therefore, originally, had no place for man as a command.

b. Because, the only person who rested on the first Sabbath was God himself.

God did not rest in the day because he had need of recuperation from toil.

If God rested in the day at all, it was a moral and declarative rest.

But God did not rest in the day, as a day; he rested in the man whom he had created.

We always rest in the last thing we do; the last thing we do, is the place both of outward and inward rest, rest of mind and body.

The last thing God made was man.

In man God rested, on the seventh day.

The seventh day has the sacramental number seven to qualify it; seven is the number of completion; man was the completion, the completion of creation; in the man, on that day, God rested.

The first Sabbath therefore has nothing to do with the rest of man, but, of God.

The first Sabbath, by so much, cannot be a command to the man.

c. Because, after man sinned God could not rest in man.

He could not rest in any mere day out of man; for, God's rest was not a rest from weariness but a moral rest.

As God could not rest in any mere day after man's sin, He could not command man to rest in any day; He could not command him to rest where all was the unrest of sin.

Thus the Sabbath was not a command either before or after the Fall.

d. Because, God could not rest in a creation marred by sin.

God cannot command man to rest where he cannot rest.

Hence, even, if the first Sabbath had been a command before the Fall, it could not be a command after the Fall.

To sum up the reasons why the first Sabbath was not given as a command:

Before the Fall man had no need of physical rest.

After the Fall he had no place of moral rest; and God cannot give a command that has in it no moral significance.

Man's sin broke up both the moral rest of God and man.

Sin set both God and man to work.

"In the sweat of thy face shalt thou eat bread." Genesis iii: 19.

"My father worketh hitherto, and I work." John v: 17.

Thus the First Sabbath looked at in any wise has no place as a command to man.

It was simply a declaration of God's moral rest in man.

It was God's creation rest in man.

2. *The Sabbath was first given as a command nearly two thousand years later to the children of Israel; and only given to them after the Exodus.*

"Wherefore I caused them to go forth out of the land of Egypt, and brought them into the wilderness:

Moreover also, I GAVE THEM MY SABBATHS, to be a sign BETWEEN ME AND THEM. Ezekiel xx: 10, 12.

3. *The Sabbath was given to the children of Israel as a memorial of creation, that the children of Israel might know that their Redeemer was also the Creator and Ruler of the universe.*

4. *The Sabbath was given only after the blood of the passover lamb had been shed, and the people by an outstretched hand of power had been typically brought into the place of resurrection on the other side of the Red Sea.* By this God would teach that he could not find creation rest in this world; that his rest in relation to this earth henceforth must be on the basis of sacrifice; that he could rest only in a man who should shed his blood and rise from the dead. That henceforth his rest must be Redemption Rest. And therefore, and never forget it, he gives the first command to keep the Sabbath, AFTER THE BLOOD.

THE SABBATH AFTER THE BLOOD; that is the Sabbath that was given as a command. That first Sabbath rest of God after the Fall was the Rest of Redemption, redemption by blood.

5. *The Sabbath was given to Israel as a covenant between them and God, that they might know he was the Lord.*

"A sign between me and them, that they might know that I am the Lord." Ezekiel xx: 12.

6.   *Those who violated the Sabbath were under the penalty of death.*

A man who gathered sticks was stoned to death. Numbers xv: 32-41.

In this incident there is, in passing, a profound spiritual lesson.

Gathering sticks is manifesting works.

Works can bring in death only to the imperfect man.

Life is to be found without works by RESTING WHERE GOD RESTS, IN THE BLOOD OF REDEMPTION, IN THE MAN WHO HAS BROUGHT IN REDEMPTION THROUGH BLOOD.

7.   *The Sabbath was never given to any other nation but Israel.*

"Speak thou also unto the children of Israel, saying, verily my Sabbaths shall ye keep: for it is a sign between ME AND YOU throughout your generations.

A sign between ME and THE CHILDREN OF ISRAEL FOR-EVER." Exodus xxxi: 13-16.

8.   *The Sabbath was never given to the Gentile world.*

The world never has been, and is not now, commanded to keep the Sabbath day.

And this ought to be self evident.

The Sabbath was only for a people separated from the world and brought nigh to God.

It was not for a world far off in sin, a world that knew not God, nor his statutes.

It is as absurd and spiritually illogical to ask a world dead in trespass and in sin to keep the Sabbath, as it would be to exhort a dead man to bring forth the evidences of life; or to ask an unregenerated man to bring forth the fruit of the Spirit.

9.   *The Church of Christ is not commanded to keep the Sabbath.*

The fact that the Sabbath has been given exclusively to Israel would be reason and argument enough; but there are many, and cogent reasons.

a. Because, the Sabbath is a part of the Law.

To be under the Sabbath is to be under the Law.

But the Church is positively *not* under the Law.

"For ye are not under the law." Romans vi: 14.

b. Because, the Sabbath is the day of A DEAD CHRIST.

It was on the Sabbath that Jesus lay dead in the tomb.

To keep the Sabbath is to memorialize his silence, and his dead body, still in the tomb.

The Church does not stand for a dead Christ.

The Church stands for a Christ risen from the dead.

To keep the Sabbath is to join hands with the unbelieving Jew, and seek, with the seals of Rome, to keep the Saviour of the world in the cerements of the grave.

c. Because, the Sabbath was a memorial of the old creation under doom.

But the Church stands for a New Creation freed from doom.

d. Because, Christ did not rise from the dead on the Sabbath.

To keep the Sabbath is to deny the resurrection of Christ.

Those who keep the Sabbath are saying every moment by their attitude: "He is here(here in the tomb), he is *not* risen."

e. Because, the Sabbath has to do with the ceremonial law, with Aaron and all earthly priesthood.

But the Church of Christ has nothing to do with the Aaronic, or Levitical priesthood; the Church has to do alone with the Melchizedeck priesthood of Christ in heaven.

f. Because, the Sabbath has to do with the man on the earth, and not with the man in heaven.

But the Church is linked up with the man in heaven, and not with the man on earth; the Church is called, not to dwell in earthly places, but with the risen One in heavenly places.

g. Because, the Sabbath is made for a man in the flesh.

But the standing of the Church and every Christian, is not in the flesh at all, but in the Spirit.

h. Because, the Sabbath has to do with the First man, Adam.

But the Church has to do exclusively with the Second man, Christ.

For these reasons, and the principles they include, the Church is never commanded to keep the Sabbath.

10. *After his Resurrection, Christ and his disciples never met on the Sabbath.*

If the Sabbath had been intended for the Church, the Church would have met on that day.

11. *The Church met to worship, to break bread, on the First day of the week.*

"And upon the first day of the week, when the disciples came together to break bread." Acts xx: 7.

Each time therefore that the Church met under Apostolic ordination it denied the Sabbath as the day of the Church; and it denied it too, not after the Roman heresy had come in, but long before, centuries before, and under Apostolic authority.

12. *So far from keeping the Sabbath, Christians are directly commanded not to keep it.*

"Let no man therefore judge (rule, command, authorize) you in respect of the Sabbath." Colossians ii: 16.

Read the context and you will see that these are ordinances in relation to the earth and to an earthly people; but the Christian has passed through the judgment with Christ, he has been baptized into his death, he has taken part with him in the resurrection; yea, he has ascended with him into heavenly places above the law and ordinances of the earth; and therefore, in the next chapter, in the opening verse, he is exhorted to seek the things that are above, to recognize himself as in the heavens with the risen Christ.

To such a person the keeping of the Sabbath would indeed be a coming down to the earth and the plane of the flesh; it would be selling the birthright of a Son of God for a mess of pottage.

Raised up with Christ, and in Him taken to the heavenly places outside the realm of the law, the Christian in the very nature of the case has nothing to do with the Sabbath.

But further, the context shows that the system of law and ordinances of which the Sabbath was a part were against us, and that Christ has blotted out their handwriting and nailed them to the cross.

As it is written:

"Blotting out the handwriting of ordinances that was against us, which was contrary to us, and TOOK IT OUT OF THE WAY, NAILING IT TO HIS CROSS." v. 14.

In the far East when a mortgage is to be cancelled, it is taken and nailed up over the door of the house and then blotted out, made illegible; so that every passer-by may know that it no longer has any claim on the inmate.

Precisely so, in that far day on the cross, the Son of God for us men and our salvation, took this law and all its ordinances of condemnation and restriction, and nailed them to his cross, blotting them out in the blood which, answering to every demand of justice against us, cries, "It is finished."

That old law and that old Sabbath are crucified to every Christian, and buried in the grave of Jesus Christ, from whence we have risen with him in the liberty of the Spirit and of life, above all ordinances for the flesh.

Looking at that law, looking at that Sabbath ordinance which was a part of it, seeing them nailed together on the cross of Christ and marred, blotted by his streaming blood, we cry:

"Cancelled, cancelled by the blood."

To those who have been immersed in the name of Christ there ought to be no possibility of misapprehension.

"Buried with him in baptism, wherein also ye are risen with him." v. 12.

Dead.

Buried.

Risen.

Ascended.

Seated with Christ in heavenly places.

To keep the Sabbath is to deny all this; to deny that we are risen with Christ; to affirm that we are under the ministration and bond of death.

13. *The Sabbath is the Seventh day, not the First.*

Nothing can be more unscriptural, and nothing can be more dishonoring to the Word in nomenclature, than to speak of the Sabbath under such titles as "The European Sabbath," "The American Sabbath," "The New Testament Sabbath."

14. *The Sabbath was never changed from the Seventh day to the First.*

In the nature of the case there is no such record in the word of God.

15. *The Children of Israel will yet keep the Sabbath in their own land.*

"And they shall hallow my Sabbaths." Ezekiel xliv: 24.

"There remaineth therefore a rest" (margin: *Sabbath keeping*) "to the people of God" (Hebrews, to whom this epistle is written). Hebrews iv: 9.

16. *The First day of the week is the day to be observed by the Church.*

The proof has already been seen in the fact that the Apostolic Church met on the First day of the week to "break bread."

17. *The First day of the week is called the Lord's day.*
A day made and set apart by the Lord for himself.

"The Lord's Day." Revelation i: 10.

"This is the day the Lord hath made; we will rejoice and be glad in it." Ps. cxviii: 24.

Beginning at the twenty-second verse the Psalm reads: "The stone which the builders refused is become the headstone of the corner."

"This is the Lord's doing; it is marvellous in our eyes." The stone is Christ.

The builders are the Jews.

The stone refused, is Christ rejected by the Jews.

Become the headstone of the corner, is Christ raised from the dead after his rejection.

The Lord's doing so marvellous in their eyes, rather, marvellous in the eyes of the prophetic remnant that is seen in this Psalm, is the mighty act of God whereby he raised his son from the dead.

This day is the day of the "marvellous" doing.

That marvellous doing is the lifting of the rejected stone into the place of the corner in the building of God; and as that is resurrection, then the day is the day of resurrection; as the resurrection day was the First day of the week, then this day the Lord hath "made," "the day of his marvellous doing," is the First day of the week; and as the Lord hath made the day; as the Psalmist distinctly states that the Lord made it; and as whatever the Lord makes is his, then this day, this day of the raising up of the stone (for it had to be raised up before it could become the headstone of the corner), this day is the Lord's day; and as the First day of the week and the day of the raising up of the stone are identical, and this identical day is the First day of the week, then the First day of the week is THE LORD'S DAY; and as the Psalmist speaking by the Spirit commands those who love the Lord to rejoice and be glad in it; and as a command to rejoice and be glad in that day is the recognition of the day above all other days, then as the Christian Church stands for love to the Lord, it follows that the Church, every Christian, is commanded to keep the First day of the week as the Lord's day.

The First day of the week is anticipated in the Old Testament as the "EIGHTH DAY;" as the day "AFTER THE SABBATH."

"Ye shall bring a sheaf of the FIRST FRUITS of your harvest unto the priest; And he shall wave the sheaf before the Lord, to be accepted for you: on the MORROW AFTER THE SABBATH the priest shall wave it." Leviticus xxiii: 10, 11.

Let it be remembered that when the priest "waved" the sheaf he lifted it from the ground where it had been lying and *raised it up before God.*

In the light of this read I Corinthians xv: 20.

"Now is Christ risen from the dead, and become THE FIRST FRUITS."

And when did Christ rise from the dead and become the first fruits but on "THE MORROW AFTER THE SABBATH?"

"In the END OF THE SABBATH, as it began to dawn toward the First day of the week. Matthew xxviii: 1.

Thus in the book of Leviticus, in the book of the Psalms, the resurrection of Christ is anticipated and the day of the resurrection declared as plainly as language can declare it, to be the First day of the week, the Lord's Day.

18. *The First day of the week is a witness to the Church of the resurrection of Christ and Christians.*

19. *The First day of the week is the witness of Redemption achieved.*

20. *The First day of the week is the memorial of the beginning of a New Creation of God.*

The Sabbath stood for the completion and, at the same time, for the END of the OLD creation; the First day of the week stands for the BEGINNING of a NEW Creation and, at the same time, for the consummation, the completion, and the glory of the New.

21. *The First day of the week links the Christian to* THE MAN IN THE GLORY and to the INHERITANCE IN THE HEAVENLY PLACES."

22. *The First day of the week links him to the unfailing intercession of the* HEAVENLY PRIESTHOOD.

And now mark the contrast between the Sabbath and the Lord's Day.

The Sabbath stands for,

The Earth.

Flesh.

Man in sin.

Man under Law.

Man under doom.

Man under sentence of death.

Man, the sentenced criminal, bound up with the old creation on which is the curse of God.

A dead Christ.

Death; nothing but death. *Aye! the penalty for its violation has never for a moment been suspended.*

But look at the Lord's Day

It stands for,

Heaven.

Spirit.

Man in Christ.

Man above Law.

Man in Grace.

Man in Life.

Man in the New Creation.

Glory.

Eternity of Blessing.

Put the two days side by side and lo! THE GRAVE OF CHRIST IS BETWEEN THEM.

The Sabbath is on THIS SIDE OF THE GRAVE.

The Lord's Day is on THE OTHER SIDE OF THE GRAVE.

The Sabbath is on this side of the grave and KNOWS NOTHING OF THE RESURRECTION.

The Lord's Day is on the other side of the grave and, thank God! KNOWS THAT IT IS EMPTY, AND THAT THE MAN WHO LAY IN IT ON THE SABBATH DAY HAS RISEN OUT OF IT.

Ah! the one day, the Sabbath, is as MIDNIGHT.

The other day, the Lord's Day, is as MID-NOON.

Those who teach the Sabbath substitute Law for Grace, Moses for Christ, works for Faith, Earth for Heaven, the Old Creation for the New, a Dead Christ for a Living Christ.

To teach the Sabbath as obligatory either to the Church or the world, is to be guilty of perverting the Word of God; and in the light of that Word, proving a blindness and spiritual darkness without excuse.

Let us turn then to the First Day of the week and prize it as never before, saying with the inspired Psalmist:

This is the day which the Lord hath made; we will rejoice and be glad in it."

Those who teach the Sabbath substitute Law for Grace, Moses for Christ, works for Faith, Earth for Heaven, the Old Creation for the New, a Dead Christ for a Living Christ.

To teach the Sabbath as obligatory either to the Church or the world, is to be guilty of perverting the Word of God; and in the light of that Word, proving a blindness and spiritual darkness without excuse.

Let us turn then to the First Day of the week and prize it as never before, saying with the inspired Psalmist:

This is the day which the Lord hath made; we will rejoice and be glad in it."

GENESIS: FOURTH AND FIFTH.

GENESIS: FOURTH AND FIFTH

Genesis: Fourth and Fifth.

In the beginning.
—*Gen. i: 1.*

GENESIS FOURTH.

While this chapter sets forth the way of Cain and the way of Abel, it might properly be called the "Way of Cain, or the Fruit of the Flesh."

The chapter is introduced by Eve's mistake.

In the first verse we find she bears a son, and when he is born says: "I have gotten a man from the Lord." Properly rendered, she would say: "I have gotten a man, EVEN the Lord."

This shows that:

1. Eve understood the seed promised in the third chapter to mean a divine son.

2. She believed Cain to be that divine son.

3. She believed that through him she would gain the victory over Satan in this world.

4. We thus learn that the promised seed in its full import meant a son whose father is God, and whose mother is a woman; hence, a divine-human son, Son of Man and Son of God. In this suggestion we catch the first gleams of the Star of Bethlehem and the outlines of the Virgin Mother.

This is properly the Introduction to the chapter.

In verse third we have:

Cain's Offering.

In making this offering note:

1. That Cain denied any difference between himself and God.

2. Denied that death as a judgment and sentence of God was upon him.

3. Denied that death must be met and cancelled before he could be accepted of God.

4. Denied that he was a fallen man needing to be reconciled to God by the death of a substitute.

5. Repudiated the idea that the ground was cursed.

6. Testified, on the contrary, that the ground was good, that the fruit of that ground was acceptable unto God.

Now there are those who teach that:

1. There is no distance, morally, between the natural man and God.

They deny that man has ever been driven out of God's presence, or that he is a fallen being.

2. Deny that death is a penal infliction, the witness of God's judgment against man.

3. Do not believe death's claim must be met before God by the death of a victim, a substitute.

4. Deny that human nature is under the curse.

5. On the contrary, they teach that human nature is inherently good, and that by culture, man can bring out of it fruit acceptable unto God.

6. They offer this fruit unto God in the form of good works, good character.

It is the way of Cain.

There are some facts in this story which are indisputable.

1. The ground out of which Cain took his offering had been judged and cursed of God.

2. In offering the fruit of the ground Cain offered that which God had judged and condemned.

3. In offering that which God had condemned Cain denied the word of God and trampled under foot His testimony.

CAIN'S OPPORTUNITY.

From this text as it appears in the Version some have imagined the doctrine clearly taught that to do well is all God requires of any man; but a right rendering of the verse takes away all shadow of ground for such error.

According to a strict translation the passage would read: "If thou offerest well, shalt thou not be accepted?" Proof of this as the right rendering is to be found in Hebrews xi: 4. Cain's offering was not acceptable. God says to him: "Your offering is not right, make it right and you shall be accepted."

Now note the expression: "Sin lieth at the door." In the Hebrew, the word for sin—is "sin-offering," and lieth is, "crouching;" wherefore the Lord says: "Flocks of sheep and goats are crouching at the tent door; go get one of these and bring and offer it for a sin-offering as Abel did and, like him, be accepted."

Thus, God, the Lord, preaches the Gospel to him; He says: "Behold the sin-offering, that is what I want, not your flowers and fruit. I want the sin-offering, and it is right there, right at your very door easy to obtain; it is already crouching at your hand, take it and offer it to me, and I will accept you even as I have accepted Abel."

This was Cain's opportunity; if he had seized it what a different epilogue might have been written upon his life.

This is the opportunity to-day. God says to man: "I do not want your flowers and fruit. I do not want the works of your flesh, no matter how good, I want the sin-offering; bring me that and I will accept you. And you need have no trouble to get it, behold it is at the door, yea it is nigh thee, in thy mouth, the word of faith which we preach; that is, Jesus is the sin-offering provided by my grace, offer Him unto me by faith—and I will accept you; confess Him crucified and risen from the dead for you, and you shall be saved." (See Romans x, 6-10.)

And this is the issue of the hour. God is calling upon all men everywhere to submit to His righteousness, by offering up the Divine Sin-offering.

In verse eight, we have:

CAIN'S CRIME: MURDER.

In the United States alone, in four years, there were 40,000 murders.

Think of it.

But in this crime of Cain, we have a type of the crime of the Jew against his Lord.

Cain is the type of the Jew, Abel, of Jesus. Proof of this may be found by reading Hebrews xii: 24.

Here the blood of Jesus is contrasted to that of Abel; the blood of Abel cried aloud from the ground for judgment. The blood of Jesus speaks from the Mercy-seat in Heaven for better things, for grace towards the sinner.

Now the point common to Jesus and Abel is the fact that both were slain, and their deaths the results of fratricidal blows: this commonalty is the basis of the type.

Abel slain by his brother after the flesh, is a type of Jesus slain by His brother after the flesh, that is by the Jew. And that the Jew is intended in this contrast is evident from the fact that it occurs in the Epistle to the

Hebrews, an epistle written especially to the Jews; it sets forth the idea that although the blood of Christ was upon the people even as they invoked it according to Matthew xxvii: 25, it was not upon them for judgment but for grace.

Thus in Cain killing his brother Abel, you have a picture of the Jew killing his divinely-sent Brother, Jesus.

In verses 11-15, you have:

CAIN'S PUNISHMENT.

The story of Cain's punishment confirms the thought that Cain is a type of the Jew. Note:

1. He was driven from his home.

2. He could get nothing from tilling the ground.

3. He was to be a wanderer on the face of the earth.

4. A mark was to be put upon him by the Lord, that all the world might know him.

5. All hands were to be against him.

6. Although punished of God, God would punish those who killed him.

See how wonderfully these characteristics have been fulfilled in the Jew.

1. Forty years after the crucifixion the Jew is driven out of his own land.

2. He has never succeeded in tilling the ground, he has never succeeded as a farmer.

3. For twenty centuries he has been a wanderer on the face of the earth.

4. For twenty centuries he has been so marked by the hand of God, that no matter among what nation he

may dwell, he cannot hide himself, a Jew is known on sight everywhere.

5. All hands were to be against him.

Deuteronomy xxviii: 64-66; Leviticus xxvi: 36-39; Deuteronomy xxviii: 27-37; Jeremiah xxiv: 9.

6. While God punishes him, He will punish all who maltreat him.

Jeremiah xxx: 11; Zechariah ii: 8.

All history is in evidence of this. Nations persecuting him have passed away, he remains.

A fearful retribution yet awaits European nations on account of him. (See Matthew xxv: 31, 32, 40.)

In verses 16-24, we have:

CAIN'S CIVILIZATION.

1. He called the land into which he was banished the land of Nod; he simply called it after himself; that is to say, Nod signifies a "Vagabond;" this is what he now was before God, a wanderer, a vagabond; hence, in calling the land, the land of Nod, he was calling it after himself, *i. e.*, the land of THE VAGABOND.

2. He founded a city and called it after the name of his son, and thus set up his own name in him. He was seeking to perpetuate his name and establish himself in a world where God had condemned him to be a wanderer.

Through his family he set up music, art, industry.

With his civilization came polygamy, murder, and violence.

Thus the civilization which Cain established was composed of:

A city,
A society,

Music,
Art,
Manufactures,
Polygamy, and
Murder.

And mark you, this civilization, this culture of the world, this filling it with music, art and beauty, as well as with industry, this embellishing the world and making it a place to live in, this civilization, originated with a MURDERER, and was set up by him only after he had been banished from the Presence of God.

Is not all this a vivid picture of man turning his back on God and seeking to make a place for himself in a world where God has condemned him to be but a passing shadow?

Is it not true that to-day his is a civilization that is formed wholly outside of God, independently of him?

And now notice a deep moral meaning in the significant expression of the twelfth verse:

"When thou tillest the ground it shall not, henceforth, yield unto thee her strength."

Considered morally, the earth represents human nature, and no matter how much man might build cities, and establish luxury, or fine arts, he would never succeed in establishing a perfect society. Just as the earth would fail and come short of full fruitage, so society would fail to reach the place of perfect strength.

Statesmen have labored, patriots have died, but man has not yet attained a stable society. Look at the 40,000 murders in four years in this country, and 25,000 divorces in one year.

Think of the corruption that walks abroad in the daylight, then think of the sin out of sight that beggars description. Remember that the whole earth is one vast military camp, and that in this city alone 10,000 men day and night are patrolling our streets lest violence break out among us as a fire, an earthquake, or a wild beast.

Note all this, and you will see that the tillage of the earth has not brought forth the harvest of a perfect, nor even satisfying civilization.

Note the final contrast between Cain and Abel.

Cain founds a city and gathers to himself all the comforts of the world. Abel is seen to the last as a worshipper of God, and taken up with the care of sheep.

Are not these contrasts suggestive of the worldling and the follower of God, the man in the flesh and the man in the Spirit?

The man in the flesh lives in the world and for it, the follower of God worships God. God is the End and Object of his way, he is occupied with the sheep of the Lord's flock. He finds fellowship not in the society which is built and embellished by a Cain, but with those who are the Lord's. His inheritance and abiding are not here, he is a pilgrim and a stranger, looking for a city which has foundations, whose maker and builder is God.

In verse 25, you have:

ANOTHER SEED.

Seth is appointed ostensibly in the place of Abel. He is really appointed as a seed in the place of Cain: that is to say, Cain is set aside as being in the image of fallen man, his father, in order that he may give way to another appointed of the Lord.

In this appointment of the second man you have anticipatively the law which Paul lays down in I Corinthians xv: 46. First the natural and *then* the *Spiritual.* First the man in the flesh and then the man from Heaven.

In verse 26 you have:

THE BEGINNING OF PRAYER.

"Then began man to call upon the name of the Lord." The newly appointed seed is a spiritual seed. Prayer is the first evidence of it. You have the same principle revealed in the New Testament, in the case of Paul's conversion: "Behold he prayeth." (See Acts ix: 11.)

Nowhere do you find that the First Adam prayed, but of the Second Adam, it is written: "He continued all night in prayer." Luke vi: 12.

This passage may be rendered, "Then began men to call themselves by the name of the Lord." That is they owned the name, claim, and authority of the Lord upon them.

While Cain and his seed are seen turning their backs upon the Lord, the appointed seed own the Lord and His way; and thus this chapter shows us the flesh going out from God's presence, beautifying the earth, endeavoring to make it a home without God, a world of the flesh, of the beautiful and the Godless; while God's seed are seen as pilgrims and strangers on the earth, going Heavenward in close companionship and fellowship with Him.

GENESIS FIFTH.

CONTENTS.

1. The New Generation.
2. Death Bells.
3. Walking with God.
4. The Great Exception.
5. Theology in Names.

THE NEW GENERATION.

At the outset of this chapter you have the generations of Adam. Cain was his first born, but neither Cain, nor Abel, nor their posterity are mentioned. The reason for the omission is clear to spiritual apprehension. Seth has been appointed as the new seed. The generation through Cain is not to be counted at all. We get an entirely new generation; and as in this new generation men call upon the name of the Lord, or call themselves by the name of the Lord, and men only call themselves by the name of the Lord when they are regenerated, this new generation of Adam stands typically for Regeneration; and as in Seth and his posterity the history of God in man commences, it may be said that a good definition of Regeneration would be, *"The History of God in Man."*

You will notice that this new generation comes in after the blood of Abel's lamb, and as that sets forth Atonement, you have indicated the divine and actual order: Atonement, Regeneration; that is to say, death claims met, and new life communicated.

DEATH BELLS.

(Verses: 5-31.)

There is but one refrain in these verses, "And he died."

No matter how assured of life a man might seem there came sooner or later a moment when the death bell tolled, "and he died," rang over him.

Methuselah the son of Enoch seemed to defy death. Nine hundred years passed and he still lived; he passed the half century mark on the way to a thousand; he added nineteen years, only thirty-one to make the thousand; when suddenly, alas! the death bell rang, "and he died."

What a change since then. Instead of ringing at intervals of centuries the death bells are appointed to ring at the limit of seventy years; and man was warned that if the ringing of the bells was delayed ten years it would be with the added note of sorrow and pain. (Psalms xc: 10.)

Since then the interval of the death bells has been made still narrower; now they ring on an average every thirty-three years.

In view of this, how startlingly true seems the word of the Apostle, "What is your life? It is even a vapour that appeareth for a little season, and then vanisheth away." James iv: 14.

How the old sentence rings anew, "Dying, thou shalt die."

WALKING WITH GOD.

(Verse 24.)

What an expression that: "Enoch walked with God."
Walking with God signifies:

1. Going in God's direction.
2. Keeping step with God.
3. Talking with God.
4. At ease in God's presence.
5. Perfect confidence in God.
6. Pleasing God. (Hebrews xi: 5.)
7. No separation from God.

THE GREAT EXCEPTION.
(Verse 24.)

"And was not." This curious phrase is explained by Hebrews xii: 5, "God took him." That is to say, he was translated, he did not die, he went alive into God's Heavens.

In later years another was so taken: Elijah.

But there is a Translation coming of which this is only a type. In I Corinthians xv: 51, it is written, "We shall not all sleep (that is, die), but we shall all be changed in a moment, in the twinkling of an eye."

Changed and taken alive into heaven. (I Thessalonians iv: 15-17.)

A generation of Christians alive at the Coming of the Lord Jesus Christ!

Enoch taken to heaven without dying is a picture of this generation.

But Enoch is taken away before the flood-judgment falls, and thus Enoch becomes a type of that generation known as the church who shall be taken away before the Tribulation and threatened judgments fall upon the earth.

That the church will be taken away before the Tribulation is the promise of Scripture. "I will keep thee out" of that hour. (Revelation iii: 10.)

Enoch was taken away before the flood, but Noah goes through it in the ark. Noah is a type of the Elect Remnant in Israel who will go through the Tribulation.

The church *never* goes through the Tribulation; it is Israel and the Gentiles associated with Israel in the last times.

The teaching of Scripture is plain enough.

1. The church is kept out of it. (Revelation iii: 10.)

2. Israel is so identified with it as in contradistinction to the church, that the Tribulation itself is called, "The Day of *Jacob's Trouble.*" (Jeremiah xxx: 7.)

3. God puts his seal on the Elect Remnant, or number in *Israel* as a proof that they do go through the Tribulation. (Revelation vii: 1-4.)

4. In the closing portion of Revelation seventh, a view is given of the *Gentiles* who go through this epoch with Israel.

5. The fourth and fifth chapters of the Revelation show that the *Church is in Heaven,* whither she is caught up at the sound of a voice like a trumpet at the opening of the fourth chapter, while the elect in Israel and the Gentiles are going through the Tribulation.

6. From the fifth chapter till the nineteenth of Revelation the church is not seen at all; *and this disappearance of the church corresponds exactly with the period of the Tribulation.*

7. The disappearance of the church in the Revelation from the scene of Tribulation is in fulfillment of the promise in Revelation iii: 10, "I will keep thee from, (out of,) the hour of temptation, (Tribulation,) which shall come upon all the world to try them that dwell upon the earth."

THE THEOLOGY OF NAMES.

In this chapter we have ten men whose names taken in their moral order and according to their meanings, give the whole story of man's ruin and redemption.

Adam—Out of the earth.

Seth—Second man.

Enos—Fallen man.

Canaan—Worker.

Mahalaleel—Splendor of God.

Jared—One who descends to rule.

Enoch—Teacher, Devoted One.

Methuselah—Offering the death.

Lamech—Victory.

Noah—Rest.

Reading these names as suggested we find that:

In Adam man is taken out of the earth; in Enos becomes a fallen man; in Canaan endeavors to build himself up by his own works. In Seth a Second Man is revealed; like Mahalaleel He is full of the splendor of God; in Jared He descends to rule as King; in Enoch walks the earth as Teacher and Devoted One; in Methuselah offers up His death for Enos the fallen man; in Lamech gains for Him the victory over sin and death; in Noah, as the result of that victory, takes him into the Rest of God.

THE STORY OF ELIEZER AND
THE BRIDE.

The Story of Eliezer and the Bride.

Genesis xxiv.

In this chapter we have one of those marvellous type-stories which bear witness to the inspiration and infallibility of the Bible; and bear it in such fashion that it leaves no room for argument or dispute.

It is the story of Eliezer's search after a Bride for Abraham's son Isaac.

Let us note some of the salient facts of this story and the doctrinal and spiritual correspondences.

1. *Abraham is presented as old and full of years.*

"Abraham was old and well stricken in age." Genesis xxiv: 1.

There is a direct Scripture which declares that Abraham is a type of God, the Father.

"(As it is written, I have made thee a father of many nations) before him whom he believed, even God." Romans iv: 17.

On the margin we read instead of "before," "like unto."

The sentence then would read:

"I have made thee a father of many nations, LIKE UNTO HIM whom he believed, EVEN GOD."

Abraham therefore is a type of God, the Father.

To be old or "full of years" in such a connection is equivalent to eternity.

"The years of the right hand of the Most High." Ps. lxxvii: 10.

"Thy years are throughout all generations." Ps. cii: 24.

"Thy years shall not fail." Hebrews i: 12.

"The Ancient of days." Daniel vii: 9.

The old age of Abraham carries us back typically into the far eternity of God, the Father.

2. *Abraham has in his house an eldest servant who is the Administrator of all that he has.*

"His eldest servant of his house, that ruled over all that he had." Genesis xxiv: 2.

The name of this servant is Eliezer.

"The steward of my house is this Eliezer of Damascus." Genesis xv: 2.

Eliezer signifies "the help of the Lord."

As Abraham's "help," he was Abraham's energy and manifested power.

The Help, the energy, the executive power of Godhead is the Holy Spirit.

The Holy Spirit is the Steward, the Administrator of all that God has.

"But all these worketh (*energei,* energizes) that one and the self-same Spirit." I Corinthians xii: 11.

Eliezer is strictly a type of the Holy Spirit.

3. *Abraham as "the Ancient of days" enters into solemn covenant with Eliezer.*

"And Abraham said unto his eldest servant, * * * Put, I pray thee, thy hand under my thigh;

And I will make thee swear by the Lord, the God of heaven, and the God of earth." Genesis xxiv: 2, 3.

This is covenant.

As Abraham and Eliezer set forth the Father and the Spirit, it is a type of a covenant between the Father and Spirit in the realm and region of Godhead.

The first notes of a covenant in Godhead are recorded in Genesis i: 26.

"God said, let us make man."

The persons of the Godhead here propose something which they agree among themselves to accomplish.

This is covenant in Godhead.

As the Spirit is one of the persons of the Godhead, and the executive energy and administrator of the same, then it is true that the Spirit does enter into covenant relation.

Abraham and Eliezer entering into covenant relation is typically the covenant between God the Father, and God the Spirit.

4. *Eliezer covenants to go forth and seek a wife for the Father's son.*

"And the servant put his hand under the thigh of Abraham his master, and sware to him concerning that matter." Genesis xxiv: 9.

The Spirit as one of the divine persons in the bond of the everlasting covenant has agreed to come forth and seek a bride for the eternal Son of God.

5. *The servant Eliezer proceeds forth from Abraham the father in the name of the son.*

Scripture teaches us that this procession of Eliezer from the father and the son, is precisely the procession of the Holy Spirit from the Eternal Father and the Eternal Son.

"The Spirit which proceedeth from the Father." John xv: 26.

"The Holy Ghost whom the Father will send in my name." John xiv: 26.

6. *Eliezer goes forth to seek a bride for the son only after that son has been typically offered up on Mount Moriah, and received again typically from the dead.*

The twenty-second chapter gives us a view of these typical events; then in the twenty-fourth we have the going out after a bride for this typically risen son.

Not until Our Lord has been offered up as the Son of the Father; not till he has been received again from the dead does the Spirit come forth.

7. *Eliezer goes at once to a people chosen and designated of Abraham beforehand.*

The Spirit comes to the twelve, and to-day, to those who have been known and chosen of God beforehand.

"Chosen in him before the foundation of the world." Ephesians i: 4.

8. *He meets the young woman ordained to be the bride of the son at a well of water.*

"And he made his camels to kneel down without the city (Nahor in Mesopotamia), by a well of water, at the time of the evening, even the time that women go out to draw water." Genesis xxiv: 11.

It was here that he met Rebekah.

The well in Scripture is a type of the Gospel.

"Therefore with joy shall ye draw water out of the wells of salvation." Isaiah xii: 3.

It is by and through the Gospel that the Spirit discovers all those who are to form the bride of Christ.

9. *The servant goes with Rebekah into her brother Laban's house and dwells there for a season.*

Laban signifies "the fleshly man."

Thus the Holy Spirit enters into the fleshly human life of the called of God, and takes up his abode for a season.

Read Matthew xxviii: 20.

"To the end of the world."

"To the end of the age" is the proper rendering.

An age is a season.

This age is the season in which the Holy Spirit takes up his abode in the flesh of those who constitute the

Church of Christ; even with all those who believe in his name.

10. *As soon as the servant is inside the house he takes out a pack of precious things, precious gifts sent from the Father in the name of the Son.*

He discloses these precious things to wondering eyes; he distributes to each severally as he wills.

"Precious things." Genesis xxiv: 53.

This is the work of the Holy Spirit.

He is here in the Church.

He is here to distribute spiritual gifts.

"The self-same Spirit dividing to every man severally as he will." I Corinthians xii: 11.

He takes the things sent from the Father in the name of the Son and shows them to the children of God.

"He shall take of mine and show it unto you." John xvi: 14.

"As it is written, Eye hath not seen, nor ear heard, neither have entered into the heart of man, the things which God hath prepared for them that love him."

BUT God hath REVEALED them unto us BY HIS SPIRIT. for the Spirit searcheth all things, yea, the deep things of God." I Corinthians ii: 9, 10.

"Now we have received, not the spirit of the world, but the Spirit which is of God; that we might know the things that are freely given to us of God." I Corinthians ii: 12.

He brings forth the "precious things."

Note some of them:

Precious Faith. I Peter i: 7. II Peter i: 1.

Precious Blood. I Peter i: 19.

Precious Stone. I Peter ii: 4.

Precious Promises. II Peter i: 4.

11. *Eliezer invites Rebekah to go with him and become the bride of the son.* Genesis xxiv: 48, 49, 58.

Not only is the Church in all its individual membership called out by the Gospel, but also by the convicting power of the Spirit.

"For our gospel came not unto you in word only, but also in power, and in the Holy Ghost." I Thessalonians i: 5.

12. *She willingly consents.*

"And they called Rebekah, and said unto her, Wilt thou go with this man? And she said, I will go." verse 58.

Those who are in the covenant bonds respond willingly when they hear the call.

"Thy people shall be willing in the day of thy power." Ps. cx: 3.

13. *The servant leads Rebekah forth to meet the Son.*

"And the servant took Rebekah, and went his way." Genesis xxiv: 61.

This is the work of the Spirit to-day, to guide the Church in the way until Bridegroom and Bride shall meet.

As he went along the journey the servant would speak to Rebekah about the son, tell her of his looks, his beauty, his possessions; he would tell her of the home that was being prepared for her.

Concerning the Spirit it is said:

"He will guide you into all truth: for he shall not speak of himself; but whatsoever he shall hear, that shall he speak; and he will show you things to come.

He shall GLORIFY ME: for he shall receive of mine and shall show it unto you." John xvi: 13, 14.

If we let the Spirit alone, if we do not grieve, or quench him, he will set the absent Lord before us in all his attractive beauty and tell us of his glory, of the things in store for us, and of the home he has gone to prepare; if we yield to him as Rebekah did he will guide us as the members of his body and the members of his bride.

14. *While the affianced Bride was traveling on the pilgrim way, suddenly the Son came forth to meet her.*

"She said, * * * What man is this that walketh in the field to MEET US." Genesis xxiv: 65.

This is the hope held out to the Church.

The hope that at any moment the Son may come forth to meet her.

This is always the "next thing" in her economy.

"Looking for that blessed hope, and the glorious appearing of our great God and Saviour, Jesus Christ." Titus ii: 13.

15. *Rebekah and Isaac meet in the open field; they met at the* EVENTIDE.

"And Isaac went out to meditate in the field at the eventide." Genesis xxiv: 63.

That is, they met at close of day, and outside the dwelling of man.

Christ and the Church will meet at the close of this day of grace, and in the open field of the air.

1. Thessalonians iv: 14-16.

16. *Isaac the Son receives Rebekah unto himself.*

"And Rebekah lifted up her eyes, and when she saw Isaac, she lighted off the camel.

For she had said unto the servant, "What man is this that walketh in the field to meet us?" Genesis xxiv: 64, 65.

"And Isaac brought her into his mother Sarah's tent, and took Rebekah, and she became his wife." verse 67.

So will Christ present his Church unto himself. "That he might present it to himself a glorious church." Ephesians v: 27.

17. *The marriage took place in the far country, away from the natural home of the bride.*

The marriage of Christ and the Church will take place in that far country called heaven. Revelation xix: 1-7.

18. *The work of Eliezer was not complete till he had brought the bride home and presented her to the bridegroom.*

Nor did he fail; that good work which he began he carried out.

The work of the Spirit will not be complete till he has brought the Church home and presented her to the Bridegroom: nor will the Spirit fail with the Church. He will guide her on till the hour ordained of God arrives. He will bring each individual member of that bride to the palace of the king, to the "place prepared."

Such is the story as it is told in the twenty-fourth chapter of Genesis.

It is well to see these three chapters in their marvellous relation.

The Twenty-first, Twenty-second, and the Twenty-fourth.

In the twenty-first chapter you have a son brought in by the power of God after nature has failed.

In Isaac you have the son given to the woman by the special exercise of the power of God.

Isaac is a son, in reality, above nature.

He is typically, the supernatural son.

In the twenty-second chapter you get that son in whom are all the promises and the hopes, laid on the altar, and so far as the intention and will of Abraham are concerned, offered up to God as a sacrifice.

In the twenty-second chapter you have this son received again from the dead "in figure, in a type," as we
are told distinctly in Hebrews xi: 19.

"Accounting that God was able to raise him up, even
from the dead; from whence also HE RECEIVED HIM IN A
FIGURE." Literally, in a parable. That is to say, his
being raised from the altar was a comparison, an illustration, of the resurrection from the dead.

In the twenty-first chapter you get Incarnation.

In the twenty-second chapter you get death and resurrection.

In the twenty-third chapter Isaac disappears from
view.

He does not come into view till the close of the twenty-
fourth chapter.

He does not come into view after his typical resurrection till Eliezer has brought out the bride.

Now put the four chapters together in their sequences.

Chapter 21. *The Incarnation.*

Chapter 22. *Death and Resurrection of the Son.*

Chapter 23. *The disappearance and absence of the Son
from the view of earth.*

Chapter 24. *The Calling out of the Bride.*

Chapter 24. *The coming of the Bridegroom to take
his Bride to himself into the place prepared.*

On what other ground can you account for the absolute accuracy of these types than on that of divine inspiration?

How can you account for the story of Christ's birth,
death, resurrection, the coming of the Holy Spirit, the
present calling out of the church, the promise of the
Coming and the marriage in heaven, fitting into these
types and becoming absolutely antitypical, correlative

and corresponding, unless, on the one hand, these Genesis stories are the prophecies in picture given by the Spirit of God; and, on the other hand, that Jesus Christ was the Son whom God fore-saw to be born of a woman through his power, who should be offered up as a sacrifice, be raised from the dead on the "third day" as that very day was designated on Mount Moriah, disappear from the earth during the preaching of the gospel, and when the Spirit should have accomplished his work, come forth to receive his church and take her into the place prepared?

The type and Antitype fit each other like hand and glove.

No better nor more conclusive evidence of the inspiration and inerrancy of the Bible as the Word of God could be found; the evidence is conclusive.

THE STORY OF JOSEPH.

The Story of Joseph.

THE STORY OF JOSEPH.

Joseph is the one and only character presented to us in the Bible without a flaw.

As such he is a perfect type of our Lord Jesus Christ, the sinless man.

A study of the story will reveal the completeness of the type.

The correspondence between type and Antitype not only verifies Jesus as the Christ thus anticipated, but demonstrates that the book of Genesis has been inspired of God.

Joseph was the son of Jacob's old age.

"Old age," translated into spiritual language and applied to God, signifies "eternity."

Jesus Christ was the Son of God's eternity.

From all eternity He was God's Son.

He was never derived, he was eternally begotten; he is God of God, very God of very God, equal with, and of the same substance as, the Father. The term "sonship" can never be applied to him in the divine sense, as it is applied in the human.

In the divine sense he is the eternal expression of the Fatherhood of God, the eternal and essential expression. He is his Son, and the Son of his love.

On the human side he is derived.

His humanity is of the seed of the woman.

Mary is his mother.

God is his Father.

In his humanity he is the express image of God's person.

He is the engraving of God in flesh.

Joseph, the son of Jacob's old age sets him forth as the eternally begotten Son who was "made flesh, and dwelt among us."

Joseph was Jacob's beloved son.

"Now Israel loved Joseph, more than all his children." Genesis xxxvii: 3.

Jesus Christ was the "beloved Son" of God.

"This is my beloved Son in whom I am well pleased." Matthew iii: 17.

Jacob made Joseph a coat of many colors.

"He made him a coat of many colors." Genesis xxxvii: 3.

a. This coat was such as was worn only by a son or heir. By one who held the place of headship and Lordship.

Our Lord Jesus is continually set forth as the heir.

In the parable of the wicked husbandmen. Matthew xxi: 38.

In Romans iv: 13. "The heir of the world."

Hebrews i: 2. "His Son, whom he hath appointed heir of all things."

b. The coat, or robe, signifies exalted dignity, Lordship.

In giving this splendid robe to his son, Jacob publicly exalted him and declared his coming Lordship.

Concerning our Lord Jesus Christ it is written:

"Wherefore God also hath highly exalted him, * * * that every tongue should confess that Jesus Christ is Lord to the glory of God the Father." Philippians ii: 10, 11.

c. This robe was of many colors.

Color in Scripture stands for quality, function, title.

Blue sets forth heavenly things: for, it is the color of heaven.

Scarlet is the color of earth, the color of kings, of royalty, and sets forth these things.

The *many* colors give us the many offices and, therefore, the many titles of the Son of God.

"On his head were many crowns." Revelation xix: 12.

The titles are many indeed.

Note some of them:

Son of Mary.

Son of Abraham.

Son of David.

Son of Man.

Son of God.

The Son of the Father.

God the Son.

The Messiah.

The Christ.

The Word of God.

King of the Jews.

King of Israel.

King of Nations.

King of Kings.

The Prince of the Kings of the Earth.

The Prince of Peace.

The Branch.

The Plant of Renown.

The Lily of the Valley.

The Rose of Sharon.

Alpha and Omega.

Beginning and Ending.

The Image of God.

The First and the Last.

The Amen.

The Express Image of God's Person.

The Brightness of his Glory.

The Faithful and True Witness.

The Wonderful.

The Counsellor.

The Advocate.

The Mighty God.

The Everlasting Father.

The robe of many colors then fittingly sets forth the manifold glories of Christ, the Father's well beloved.

Joseph had visions of future sovereignty over his brethren.

"And he said unto them, Hear, I pray you, this dream which I have dreamed:

For, behold, we were binding sheaves in the field, and, lo, my sheaf arose, and also stood upright; and, behold, your sheaves stood round about, and made obeisance to my sheaf.

And his brethren said unto him, Shalt thou indeed reign over us? * * * And they hated him yet the more."   Genesis xxxvii: 5-11.

The central chord of prophecy is the declaration that Jesus Christ shall rule and reign over his brethren according to the flesh, the Jews.

"He shall reign over the house of Jacob forever." Luke i: 33.

Joseph responded willingly when his father called him to go forth to do his will.

"And Israel said unto Joseph, Do not thy brethren feed the flock in Shechem? Come, and I will send thee unto them. And he said to him, Here am I." Genesis xxxvii: 13.

So the eternal Son of God came to do the will of the Father.

"Then said I, Lo, I come (in the volume of the book it is written of me) to do thy will, O God."   Hebrews x: 7.

"For I came down from heaven, not to do mine own will, but the will of him that sent me."   John vi: 38.

Joseph's Father sent him to seek his brethren.

"* * * Come, and I will send thee unto them." Verse 13.

The correspondence is absolute.

Our Lord Jesus Christ according to the will of the Father came into this world to seek his brethren of the house of Israel.

"He answered and said, I am not sent but unto the lost sheep of the house of Israel."   Matthew xv: 24.

Joseph's first announcement of his mission was made to his brethren as to shepherds.

"Thy brethren feed the flock in Schechem."   Verse 13.

It is certainly far from accident, or mere coincidence, that the first announcement of the mission of the beloved Son to the people in the land of Israel should be made to shepherds.

But there is the fact: When Joseph was first announced to his brethren they were as "shepherds keeping their flock."

There is the other fact to match it: When Jesus Christ was first announced as the Sent of the Father, that announcement was made to those who kept their flocks.

To the spiritual mind there is no more "happy chance" in this coincidence than in the movement of the stars on high.

After Joseph went forth on his mission to seek his brethren he became for a time a wanderer in the field.

"And, behold, he was wandering in the field." Verse 15.

In spiritual nomenclature, "the field is the world." Matthew xiii: 38. And no more truthful designation can be found for the Son of God as he sought to fulfill his earthly mission than that of "Wanderer."

"And Jesus said unto him, Foxes have holes, and birds of the air have nests; but the Son of man hath not where to lay his head." Luke ix: 58.

Joseph found his brethren in Dothan.

"And Joseph went after his brethren, and found them in Dothan." Verse 17.

Dothan signifies, "Law, or Custom."

And it was there that Jesus found his brethren, dwelling under the bondage of the law, and slaves to mere religious formalism.

"And the Lord said unto him, Now do ye Pharisees make clean the outside of the cup and the platter; but your inward part is full of ravening and wickedness." Luke xi: 39.

"For laying aside the commandment of God, ye hold the tradition of men." Mark vii: 8.

Joseph's brethren mocked and refused to receive him.

"And they said one to another, Behold, this dreamer cometh." Verse 19.

Of our Lord it is written:

"He came unto his own, and his own received him not." John i: 11.

Joseph's brethren took counsel how they might slay him.

"Come now, therefore, and let us slay him, and cast him into some pit." Genesis xxxvii: 20.

In the same guilty spirit the Jews took counsel to slay the Son of God.

"When the morning was come, all the chief priests and elders of the people took counsel against Jesus to put him to death." Matthew xxvii: 1.

And like their ancestors of old in Dothan, they hated him.

Joseph's brethren mocked him and set him at naught.

"They conspired against him. * * * And they said one to another, Behold this dreamer." Verses 18, 19.

"And Herod with his men of war set him at naught, and mocked him." Luke xxiii: 11. Mark xxv: 11-19. Isaiah liii: 3.

Judah counselled his brethren to sell him to the Ishmaelites.

"Come let us sell him to the Ishmaelites." Verse 27.

Not only is the selling of the Son of God thus typically announced, it is also foretold by the prophet.

"So they weighed for my price thirty pieces of silver." Zechariah xi: 12, 13.

Both type and prophecy were fulfilled to the letter.

"And said unto them (Judas said), What will ye give, me, and I will deliver him unto you? And they covenanted with him for thirty pieces of silver." Matthew xxvi: 15.

Joseph was sold to the Ishmaelites, and Christ after his sale was turned over to the Ishmaelites of history, the Romans.

Joseph's brethren cast him into a pit.

"And they took him, and cast him into a pit; and the pit was empty, there was no water in it." Verse 24.

The Pit wherein is no water is another name for Hades, the underworld, the abode of the disembodied dead: of all the dead before the resurrection of Christ.

"The pit wherein is no water."　Zechariah ix: 11.

"For as Jonah was three days and three nights in the whale's belly, so shall the Son of man be three days and three nights in the *heart* of the earth."　Matthew xii: 40.

It was here our Lord, as to his soul, abode between death and resurrection.

Joseph was taken out of the pit alive, in his body.

"And they lifted up Joseph out of the pit."　verse 28.

The actual order of the occurrence is that Joseph was first cast into the pit and then sold; but the moral order of the type is not deranged by that fact; it is in the light of the Antitypical history that we make the type to be verified, as well as to verify it.

The lifting out of the pit, is one of those divine anticipations of the resurrection scattered all through the Old Testament from Genesis to Malachi.

Reuben came to the pit and found him gone, and went away believing him dead.

"And Reuben returned unto the pit; and, behold, JOSEPH WAS NOT IN THE PIT; and he rent his clothes.

And he returned unto his brethren and said, The child is not; and I, whither shall I go?"　verses 29, 30.

Reuben practically represents the Jew of to-day.

To-day the Jew is ignorant of the fact that Christ is alive.

He knows nothing of resurrection.

Joseph's coat was taken and dipped in the blood of a victim and then presented to the father.

"And they took Joseph's coat, and killed a kid of the goats, and dipped the coat in the blood * * * and they brought it to their father."　Verses 31, 32.

The application of the type is self-evident.

The blood of Jesus Christ as the blood of a scape-goat, a sin offering, was presented to the Father.

After Joseph had been rejected by his brethren he was taken down into Egypt, a far country, in order that he might become a saviour unto the Gentile world as such.

"And they (the Ishmaelites) brought Joseph into Egypt." Verse 28.

After Christ was rejected by the Jews and had been raised and taken up to the throne of God, the Apostle Peter preached Christ unto the Jews, and declared that if they would confess the sin of which they had been guilty in rejecting him, God the Father would send him back again.

They rejected him in resurrection, even as they had rejected him before the cross.

God then called Paul, gave him the full revelation, and sent him to preach the Christ, the Messiah, to the Jews, as the Son of God risen from the dead; offering them no longer the kingdom, but a participation in the Church, the body of Christ.

They refused Jesus of Nazareth as the Son of God, even as they had refused him on the offering of the prophets and the Apostle Peter as the Christ; then, this now doubly rejected Christ was presented by the Apostle Paul to the Gentiles, as the Risen Son of God.

After Joseph was rejected by his brethren and taken to Egypt he was exalted to the throne of Pharaoh.

In Joseph therefore we have the REJECTED MAN, THE REJECTED JEW, ON THE THRONE OF POWER.

"And Pharaoh said unto Joseph * * * Thou shalt be over my house, and according to thy word shall all my people be ruled; only in the throne will I be greater than thou." Genesis xli: 39, 40.

Now read: Revelation iii: 21.

"To him that overcometh will I grant to sit with me

in my throne even as I also overcame, and am set down with my Father in his throne."

To-day our Lord Jesus Christ shares the throne of the Father as Joseph shared the throne of Pharaoh.

As Joseph ruled over Pharaoh's house with his word, so to-day our Lord Jesus Christ rules over the Father's household, the household of faith, the Church, by and through his word.

And let it be clearly kept in mind that while Joseph was on the throne of Pharoah he was not on his own throne; that is to say, he was not in the place of rule over his brethren.

And to-day, while our Lord Jesus Christ is on the throne of His Father, He is not on His own throne. Read the passage just quoted in Revelation again and it will be seen that our Lord Jesus Christ himself makes a distinction between his throne and the Father's throne, and promises reward to the overcomer, not on the Father's throne, but on his own; and we know, according to the promise of the angel made to Mary, and the covenant made to David, and the title he wears as the king of Israel, the Son of David, and the Son of Abraham, that his throne is at Jerusalem, the "city of the Great King." On his Father's throne he sits to-day as the Rejected Man, the Rejected Jew.

While on the throne of Pharaoh, Joseph, the Rejected Hebrew, gets a Gentile Wife.

"And he (Pharaoh) gave him (Joseph) to wife Asenath, the daughter of Potipherah, priest of On." Genesis xli: 45.

And here we find the suggestion of the great truth about Christ to-day. Read Acts xv: 14.

"God at the first did visit (is visiting now) the Gentiles, to TAKE OUT OF THEM A PEOPLE FOR HIS NAME"

Now when a man seeks to marry a woman he loves

he seeks her in order that HE MAY PUT HIS NAME UPON HER. When his name is upon her she is his Wife.

The fact that Christ is now calling out a people from among the Gentiles in order that He may put His name upon them, is the declaration that He is calling out this body of Gentiles in order that they may be brought into living union with Himself, be His mystical Bride, His Wife.

Joseph's rejection by his brethren meant the getting of a Gentile Bride.

That is the meaning of Christ's rejection by His brethren after the flesh in this hour, *He is getting a Gentile Bride.*

While seated on the throne Joseph became the giver of the bread of Life to the starving world.

"And when all the land of Egypt was famished, the people cried to Pharaoh for bread: and Pharaoh said unto all the Egyptians, Go unto Joseph." Genesis xli: 55.

It was a wonderful thing that the despised and rejected Jew should be the passport to the favor of Pharaoh; a wonderful thing that the rejected Jew should be exalted into the place of a Saviour for a famine-smitten world; it was a wonderful thing that this rejected Jew should be the only Saviour for that starving world.

Equally true and wonderful is it to-day that Jesus the rejected Jew is the passport to the favor of God; that he is "the way, the truth, and the life," and that "no man cometh unto the Father" but by him; wonderful that this rejected Christ should be exalted into a Saviour for a famine-smitten world; wonderful that this rejected Christ is the alone Saviour for a starving world.

Joseph was sent by his Father to his brethren that

he might be a blessing unto them, and they refused; then God turned their sin so that while it should remain as a judgment to them, it might become a blessing to others.

In sending His Son to fulfill the promises made to the Fathers, God would have brought covenant and numberless blessings to Israel; they refused, and God has made use of their blindness and sin to turn salvation to others.

He has made the very sin and blindness of the people, to be the occasion of grace and mercy to the whole world.

"Through their fall salvation is come unto the Gentiles." Romans xi: 11.

Joseph became the saviour of all peoples and tongues.

"And all countries came to Joseph." Genesis xli: 57.

Listen to the fulfillment of the type in Revelation v: 9.

"Thou wast slain, and hast redeemed us to God by thy blood, out of every kindred, and tongue, and people, and nation."

When the famine-stricken people came to Pharaoh he caused a proclamation to be sent forth in these terms:

"Go to Joseph."

"And when all the land of Egypt was famished the people cried to Pharaoh for bread: and Pharaoh said unto all the Egyptians, Go unto Joseph; what he saith unto you, do." Genesis xli: 55.

This was the Gospel in Egypt, the good news of salvation in Joseph, and the good news that whosoever was hungry might go to Joseph.

It was the good news that Joseph could meet the case.

The Gospel, the good news to-day is, that there is salvation in Jesus, that whosoever will may go to him: the word is: "Go to Jesus."

The good news is, that he meets the case of every one; the good news is, that the rejected Hebrew has been taken from the pit and the dungeon and has been exalted to the throne of God with power to meet the soul's need, whatever it may be.

Without Joseph presented as a saviour to Egypt there would have been no hope for Egypt.

Without Christ for the world there would be no hope for the world.

Take Joseph from Egypt and all would have been famine in Egypt.

Egypt would have been turned into a desert waste.

Take Christ out of the world as he is in it to-day; take him out of art and literature, out of society and government, and you would have a famine.

You would destroy the best paintings in the world's galleries, the best statues, the noblest poetry, the most exalted prose; society would have no salt to preserve it from corruption; government would have no bridle to hold in check the wild beast tendencies in man; hope would stand paralyzed in the path of life, and despair with tortured face and silent lips would stand on guard above the graves of our dead. Everywhere there would be soul famine, not for bread, but for the hearing of the word of God.

When the Church at the "Rapture" has been removed from the world and the Gospel is silent, such a time will come.

"Behold, the days come saith the Lord God, that I will send a famine in the land; not a famine of bread, nor a thirst for water, but of hearing of the words of the Lord.

And they shall wander from sea to sea, and from the north even to the east; they shall run to and fro to seek the word of the Lord, and shall not find it." Amos viii: 11, 12.

Joseph had resources without limit to meet the hunger of the Egyptian world.

"And Joseph gathered corn as the sand of the sea, very much, until he left numbering; for it was without number." Genesis xli: 49.

So are the riches of grace in Christ, without number, without limit.

"The riches of his grace." Ephesians i: 7.

"Exceeding riches of his grace." Ephesians ii: 7.

"The unsearchable riches of Christ." Ephesians iii: 8.

"The same Lord over all is rich unto all that call upon him." Romans x: 12.

"Rich in mercy." Ephesians ii: 4.

"The grace of our Lord exceeding abundant." I Timothy i: 14.

"Abundant mercy." I Peter i: 3.

"The things that are freely given to us." I Corinthians ii: 12.

"I will give unto him that is athirst of the fountain of the water of life freely." Revelation xxi: 6.

"Whosoever will, let him take the water of life freely." Revelation xxii: 17.

"In him dwelleth all the fulness of the godhead bodily." Colossians ii: 9.

Our exalted Joseph has indeed riches of salvation to meet all the needs of the world.

After Joseph's rejection his brethren suffer famine and are forced to go forth of their own land into Egypt, become, in fact, wanderers.

As soon as Christ is rejected his brethren after the flesh, the Jews, begin to endure suffering.

They suffered in the siege of Jerusalem under Titus. More than a million are said to have perished in that siege, the horrors of which have never been fully told. Thousands were carried away captive and sold into abject slavery, while the rest were driven before their conquerors like the chaff before the wind of the summer's threshing floor. For two thousand years they have been the people of the trembling heart and the restless foot. They have wandered in all lands seeking their life, until their sufferings and sorrows have been such as no other nation ever knew.

If Jesus Christ is known as a man of sorrows and acquainted with grief, it may be said that the Jews are the one nation whose fitting title might be, a nation of sorrows and acquainted with grief.

Read Deuteronomy xxviii: 58-67, and you have this blood-written history prophetically anticipated, and told with such perfectness of detail that it would seem almost as if penned to-day.

Although Joseph's brethren ao not know him when they come into Egypt, he knows them and has his eye constantly upon them.

"And Joseph knew his brethren, but they knew not him." Genesis xlii: 8.

Although the Jews do not know their own Messiah to-day, yet through all these ages of anguish he has had his eye on them, and has followed them with profound grief along every path of pain.

"For mine eyes are upon all their ways; they are not hid from my face." Jeremiah xvi: 17.

"I know Ephraim, and Israel is not hid from me." Hosea v: 3.

Joseph spoke roughly to his brethren and caused them to be put in prison.

Joseph punished them.

"Spake roughly unto them." Genesis xlii: 7.

"And he put them all together into ward (prison) three days." Genesis xlii: 17.

Joseph was the cause of their trouble now.

Joseph was punishing them for their past dealing with himself.

The secret of all Judah's suffering during the past centuries is to be found in the fact that the rejected Messiah has been dealing "roughly" with them. He has been punishing them, making use of their wilfulness and the cupidity of the nations, but, all the same, punishing them.

"My God will cast them away, because they did not hearken unto him: and they shall be wanderers among the nations." Hosea ix: 17.

"He that scattered Israel." Jeremiah xxxi: 10.

"All countries whither I have driven them." Jeremiah xxxii: 37.

"Behold your house is left unto you desolate.

For I say unto you, Ye shall not see me henceforth, till ye shall say, Blessed is he that cometh in the name of the Lord." Matthew xxiii: 38, 39.

"That upon you may come all the righteous blood shed upon the earth, from the blood of righteous Abel unto the blood of Zecharias son of Barachias whom ye slew between the temple and the altar.

Verily I say unto you, All these things shall come upon this generation" (nation). Matthew xxiii: 35, 36.

Nothing can account for the unparalleled suffering of this people, but the judgment and discipline of the Lord. He has spoken roughly unto them.

In spite of his rough dealing with them, Joseph at heart was full of love towards his brethren.

"And he turned himself about from them, and wept." Genesis xlii: 24.

Behold the Antitype:

And when he (Jesus) was come near, he beheld the city, and wept over it. Luke xix: 41.

"O Jerusalem, Jerusalem, thou that killest the prophets, and stonest them which are sent unto thee, HOW OFTEN WOULD I HAVE GATHERED THY CHILDREN." Matthew xxiii: 37.

On the third day Joseph's brethren found him presented to them as one who was willing to be a saviour through the way of substitution. Verses 18-24.

On the third day he caused Simeon to be bound in the place of his brethren, and declared that by this means they might all be delivered.

In the third day era, that is to say on the resurrection side of the grave, on the day of Pentecost, the Apostle Peter presented our Lord Jesus Christ as the risen one whom God had exalted to be a prince and a saviour unto Israel, declaring that if the latter should repent of their evil and sin towards him whom he had sent to be Messiah and King, he would accept his death as the substitution for the judgment due them; that he would save them and send his Son again to be both Messiah and Saviour.

He commanded them to make this confession through baptism, and by this act testify that he who had died, had indeed been raised from the dead.

For the first seven chapters of the book of Acts, this Gospel of death and resurrection is preached unto the Jews.

And this is God's order in respect to the Gospel: "the Jew first, and then the Gentile."

Note the deep significance of Joseph's word:

"This do, and live." Verse 18.

Do what?

Put a substitute in your place and you shall live.

And this is the Gospel we are to preach to the sinner to-day.

Put Christ in your place of judgment, present him by faith to God as the substitute ready to answer for, and meet the claims of judgment against you.

Claim Christ as your personal substitute.

The substitution of the man dead on the cross, is made effective by faith in the man alive from the dead on the third day.

Let it be repeated: the man dead on the cross is made effective as a substitute to all who believe in him as the man alive from the dead on the third day; thus the substitution presented by Joseph on the third day, as the way of salvation from condemnation and prison, when typically welded together, unmistakably gives the Gospel of the crucified substitute made available by the third day to our Lord's brethren in the flesh, and the whole world, for faith.

Joseph gave orders to fill his brethrens' sacks, return their money, and provide for them by the way.

"Then Joseph commanded to fill their sacks with corn, and to restore every man's money into his sack, and to give them provision for the way." Verse 25.

By this action Joseph became a sanctuary and refuge unto them in a strange land.

In spite of all the judgment which he allows to fall upon them, the Holy One of Israel has been as a sanctuary and a refuge unto the Jew in every land whither he has come.

This is his promise in Ezekiel xi: 16.

If the suffering and the sorrow of the Jews be evidence that God has judicially dealt with them, equally true is it that their marvellous preservation in the face of these sufferings, demonstrates that God is behind history on their behalf, and has provided for them through all the way.

"For I am with thee, saith the Lord, to save thee; though I make a full end of all nations whither I have scattered thee, yet will I not make a full end of thee." Jeremiah xxx: 11.

In spite of all his dealings with them Joseph's brethren failed to recognize him.

"And Joseph knew his brethren, BUT THEY KNEW NOT HIM." Genesis xlii: 8.

What a type this is!

How accurate! How prophetic!

For two thousand years, in the face of the exaltation of Christ and the adoration of the whole world; in face of their own miraculous preservation through the ages, the Jews do not know that this rejected Hebrew on the throne of God is their own brother after the flesh, and their very Messiah and King.

They are blinded.

"Blindness in part is happened to Israel." Romans
xi : 25.

2. Corinthians iii : 13-16.

John xii : 35-41.

No sadder spectacle can be conceived than that of this
homeless people, linked by ties of nationality, race, and
eternal covenant to the Christ of God, and yet utterly
ignorant of him as brother and Lord.

No more startling spectacle can be conceived than this :

*A Jew on the throne of the universe with unlimited
power of blessing for Jews, and these same Jews on earth
wanderers and sufferers before the face of men.*

The three chapters, from forty-two to forty-four inclusive, may properly be said to be an account of the tribulation of Jacob's Children : and as his name is Israel,
then we have in this sojourn and experience in Egypt,
*a Time of Tribulation for the Children of Israel before
they know and own Joseph.*

What the type indicates, prophecy in unmistakable
utterance declares :

There is a time of unparalleled suffering in store for
the children of Israel, specially for the Jews, before they
know and own the Lord.

This time of suffering and sore trial is called
definitely, "the time of Jacob's Trouble."

"Alas ! for that day is great, so that none is like it : it
is even THE TIME OF JACOB'S TROUBLE." Jeremiah
xxx : 7.

"For then shall be great tribulation, such as was not
since the beginning of the world to this time, no, nor
ever shall be." Matthew xxiv : 21.

This time of tribulation to Joseph's brethren, this time
of Jacob's trouble, took place AFTER JOSEPH HAD TAKEN
A GENTILE WIFE AND PLACED HER ON THE THRONE.

The type is absolutely accurate; for, we learn from Revelation fourth and fifth chapters, that the church, the Bride, the wife of Christ is taken up to the throne in the heavens before the tribulation bursts forth.

In the fourth chapter twenty-four elders are seen on thrones in association with the Lord of Glory.

These twenty-four, as to number, set up the idea of the priesthood, for such was the number of the priestly courses in the temple; as to eldership, they set forth administration and rule; the symbol is that of the church, considered individually, as kings and priests, corporately, as the bride of Christ, exalted to the throne.

In the fifth chapter these enthroned and crowned elders break forth into rapturous praise, anticipatively celebrating the coming of the king and kingdom; they cry out: "we shall reign on (over) the earth." Revelation v: 10.

In the fourth and fifth chapters then you have indisputably the Church of Christ in heaven, on the throne with Christ.

It is only after the church is seen seated in the heavens with Christ on the throne, that we get an account of that tribulation, which is none other than the time of Jacob's trouble.

There is no warrant, outside the imagination of men, for the thought that the Church will go through a tribulation particularly intended as sifting time for Israel, and furnace blast for the world.

If we get wrong in our doctrine, the moment we go back to our type we are made right.

Remember it:

Joseph's brethren do not get into trouble and suffering till AFTER JOSEPH TAKES A GENTILE BRIDE TO THE THRONE OF POWER.

THE TRIBULATION COMES IN AFTER THE WIFE HAS BEEN
SEPARATED FROM ALL OTHERS AND EXALTED TO THE
THRONE.

Precisely so does the Spirit of God paint the actual
facts in the New Testament.

There, we see THE CHURCH CAUGHT UP INTO THE
HEAVENS AND THE THRONE OF GOD, BEFORE A SINGLE
WORD IS SAID OF THE TRIBULATION; THEN, AFTER THE
CHURCH IS SEEN SEATED AND SHELTERED ON THE THRONE,
THE SPIRIT GIVES A DESCRIPTION OF THE TRIBULATION,
THE GREAT ONE, RUNNING THROUGH THIRTEEN CHAP-
TERS; AND NOT ONCE IS THE WORD CHURCH MENTIONED;
OR, THE THOUGHT OF IT SUGGESTED.

Joseph was made known to his brethren THE SECOND
TIME.

"And at the second time Joseph was made known to
his brethren." Acts vii: 13.

The application is self evident.

Only when our Lord comes the second time will his
people, the Jews, know and own him.

"And they shall look upon me whom they have
pierced." Zechariah xii: 10. Revelation i: 7.

The conversion of the Apostle Paul is a typical verification of the Joseph type and a vivid illustration of the
actual fact.

Listen to what he says in I Timothy i: 15, 16:

"I obtained mercy, that in me first Jesus Christ might
shew forth all long suffering, for a pattern to them
which should hereafter believe on him to life everlasting."

Paul WAS NOT CONVERTED BY THE PREACHING OF THE
GOSPEL but by THE APPEARING OF OUR LORD JESUS
CHRIST FROM HEAVEN, IN GLORY, above the gates of
Damascus. Acts ix: 1-5.

"At midday, O king, I saw in the way a light from heaven, above the brightness of the sun, shining round about me." Acts xxvi: 13.

Paul was converted by the appearing of Christ in glory; not since Paul's day has a single soul been converted by the appearing of Christ in glory.

It has been, and is, by the Gospel alone that conversion takes place.

It is never by the personal visible appearing of Christ to individuals.

Yet Paul draws attenion to this manner of his conversion.

He draws particular attention to it.

Let us read it:

"And last of all he was seen of me also, as of one born out of due time." I Corinthians xv: 8.

Born out of due time is ahead of the time.

Now let it be remembered that when our Lord appeared to Paul he spoke to him not in Greek but in the Hebrew tongue; more than that, he addressed him by his Hebrew name, Saul.

Thus Paul was converted AS A HEBREW.

Paul takes particular pains after his conversion to identify himself as a Hebrew, an Israelite.

"For I also am an Israelite, of the seed of Abraham, of the tribe of Benjamin." Romans xi: 1.

Paul was converted as a Hebrew, an Israelite.

He was converted as a Hebrew, as an Israelite, by the Appearing of Christ.

His conversion is a witness that others will be converted as he was; even, by the Appearing of the Lord.

But Gentiles are not to be converted that way in this age.

In this age the Gentiles are to be converted only through the preaching of the Gospel.

If the Gentiles are not to be converted by the appearing of Christ in this age, then it must be the Hebrews, and, particularly, the Jews.

But this is not the age for the conversion of the Hebrews, as such, by the personal, visible appearing of Christ.

This is the time for the "taking out" of the Church through the faith of the Gospel; and particularly, the taking of it out from among the *Gentiles.*

The time for the conversion of the Hebrews as Hebrews therefore, is still future.

THIS IS NOT THEIR TIME.

Paul says that AS A HEBREW he was born out of the due time, AHEAD OF TIME.

Paul's conversion as a Hebrew was ahead of Hebrew time.

If then Paul was converted as a Hebrew ahead of the time; if he was, so to speak, set out in the front line where all the world might see how as a Hebrew he was converted, then surely he is a pattern, a model of the way the rest of the Hebrews will be converted in the "due time."

As Paul was converted not by the Gospel but by the personal, visible appearing of Christ, so must the Hebrews as such, as a people, a nation, be converted.

As a nation they will never be converted by the Gospel; we are specifically told that "as concerning the gospel they are enemies for our (the Gentiles') sakes."

Among the Jews to-day it is an "election, beloved for the Father's sake," who believe the Gospel and are received into the body of Christ.

But the Jews as a people must be converted as Paul, the pattern, not by believing the testimony of the Gospel concerning the Messiah, but by *seeing* Him whom they pierced, as it is written:

"Behold, he cometh with clouds; and every eye shall see him, and they also which pierced him." Revelation i: 7.

This appearing of Christ is a *Second* Coming.

At the Second Coming the Lord Jesus Christ will be revealed to his people the Jews, and accepted by them.

Thus we get back to the type in Joseph.

Joseph was revealed in his true glory to his brethren the second time.

When Joseph was made known to his brethren the second time he had a close and tender interview with them.

There is nothing more tender and beautiful than the story of that interview as the Spirit records it for us:

"Then Joseph could not refrain himself before all them that stood by him; and he cried, Cause every man to go out from me. And there stood no man with him, while Joseph made himself known unto his brethren.

And he wept aloud: and the Egyptians and the house of Pharaoh heard.

And Joseph said unto his brethren, I am Joseph: doth my father yet live?

And his brethren could not answer him; for they were troubled at his presence.

And Joseph said unto his brethren, Come near to me, I pray you. And they came near. And he said, I am Joseph your brother, whom ye sold into Egypt.

Now, therefore, be not grieved, nor angry with yourselves, that ye sold me hither; for God did send me before you, to preserve life.

For these two years hath the famine been in the land; and yet there are five years, in the which there shall neither be earing nor harvest.

And God sent me before you, to preserve you a posterity in the earth, and to save your lives by a great deliverance.

So now it was not you that sent me hither, but God: and he hath made me a father to Pharaoh, and lord of all his house, and a ruler throughout all the land of Egypt.

Haste ye, and go up to my father, and say unto him, Thus saith thy son Joseph, God hath made me lord of all Egypt: come down unto me, tarry not.

And thou shalt dwell in the land of Goshen, and thou shalt be near unto me, thou, and thy children, and thy children's children, and thy flocks, and thy herds, and all that thou hast:

And there will I nourish thee, for yet there are five years of famine, lest thou, and thy household, and all that thou hast, come to poverty.

And, behold, your eyes see, and the eyes of my brother Benjamin, that it is my mouth that speaketh unto you. (What a wonderful double type is here: Joseph to them has been dead, and now he is endeavoring to convince them that he, Joseph, is alive; that it is he, himself, and not another: how beautifully anticipative of that other scene where the true Joseph seeks to convince his brethren that he is alive from the dead; that it is he, himself, and not another.)

And ye shall tell my father of all my glory in Egypt, and of all that ye have seen; and ye shall haste, and bring down my father hither.

And he fell upon his brother Benjamin's neck, and wept; and Benjamin wept upon his neck.

Moreover, he kissed all his brethren, and wept upon them: and after that, his brethren talked with him." Genesis xlv: 1-15.

Not a word can be added to the simplicity and beauty

of that description. Yet beautiful and deeply touching as it is, it is but a shadow of that other moment when the real Joseph shall be made known to his brethren.

Read what the prophet says in anticipating that moment:

"And they shall look upon me whom they have pierced, and they shall mourn for him, as one mourneth for his only son, and shall be in bitterness for him as one that is in bitterness for his first son." Zechariah xii: 10-12.

"And one shall say unto him, What are these wounds in thine hands? Then he shall answer, Those with which I was wounded in the house of my friends." Zechariah xiii: 6.

Then will that wonderful chapter, the Fifty-third of Isaiah, be understood in all its depths of meaning.

For then will repentant Judah take up the chapter and make its sublime language the language of their sorrowful, yet believing confession.

Then will they cry:

"We hid as it were our faces from him; he was despised, and we esteemed him not.

Surely he hath borne our griefs and carried our sorrows (yes, through all these ages their sorrow has been a deep burden on his soul) : yet we did esteem him stricken, smitten of God, and afflicted.

But he was wounded for our transgressions, he was bruised for our iniquities; the chastisement of our peace was upon him; and with his stripes we are healed.

All we, like sheep, have gone astray; we have turned every one to his own way; and the Lord hath laid on him the iniquity of us all."

It will be an interview the like of which the world has never seen; that moment when repentant Judah shall bow down with tear-wet cheeks before him who was, the crucified.

In that hour they will bemoan the crime of the cross.

And the loving and tender Joseph will seek to comfort them, showing them that God in his eternal purpose was behind their fall; showing them that terrible and inexcusable as it was, God has made that great hour of darkness and blindness on their part to turn to the enlightenment and enrichment of the Gentile world.

What words of comfort he will give them, what assurance of his love.

Then the prophecy of Zechariah will be fiulfilled:

"In that day there shall be a fountain opened to the house of David, and to the inhabitants of Jerusalem, for sin and uncleanness." Zechariah xiii: 1.

Judah and his brethren were brought to know Joseph before the rest of the household of Jacob.

The prophecy is that Judah shall be saved first.

"The Lord also shall save the tents of Judah first." Zechariah xii: 7.

Joseph sends for Jacob after he has revealed himself to Judah and his brethren.

In Scripture, Judah stands for Judah and Benjamin considered together.

You will note that it is Judah and Benjamin who are made prominent in the revelation of Joseph.

Jacob in prophetic language signifies the Ten Tribes.

Sending for Jacob and his household, in typical language, is sending for the Ten Tribes of Israel.

Precisely as the type brings Judah before the self-disclosed Joseph and then Jacob or Israel is brought into the land into the presence of Joseph, so the Scriptures clearly teach us that after the Lord comes to repentant Judah and is received by them at Jerusalem, he will send for the remaining household of Jacob, for the lost and wandering tribes of Israel, to come into the land to own and greet him.

"And they shall bring all your brethren for an offering unto the Lord, out of all nations." Isaiah lxvi: 20.

In passing it may be said that the account of the journey of these lost tribes as they seek to return to their own land to greet the manifested Joseph, is given in Ezekiel xx: 34-38.

Also, Isaiah 35th chapter.

After the revelation of Joseph, his brethren go forth to proclaim in the land of Canaan that he is alive and is the ruler in the land of Egypt.

"And they went up out of Egypt, and came into the land of Canaan unto Jacob their father;

And told him, saying, Joseph is yet alive, and he is governor over all the land of Egypt." Genesis xlv: 25, 26.

They went forth preaching good news.

That good news had two parts:

Joseph was alive.

Joseph was a king.

Joseph who had been reported dead, and believed to be so through all these years by his brethren, was alive and reigning in power in the great Egyptian world.

After our Lord returns and has gathered all Israel unto him according to covenant in the promised land, he will send them forth to be the missionaries of the world; they will go forth and preach the Gospel of resurrection, the Gospel of the man alive from the dead; they will proclaim that this man alive from the dead is returned unto the world from whence he had been rejected, and is reigning in power in the land of promise; they will invite all nations to come up to worship the true Joseph, the king, in his glory at Jerusalem.

"Ye shall be named the priests of the Lord; men shall call you the MINISTERS of our God." Isaiah lxi: 6.

"Yea, many people and strong nations shall come to seek the Lord of hosts in Jerusalem, and to pray before the Lord.

Thus saith the Lord of hosts, in those days it shall come to pass, that ten men shall take hold, out of all languages of the nations, even shall take hold of the skirt of him that is a Jew, saying, We will go with you; for we have heard that God is with you." Zechariah viii: 22, 23.

What wonderful facility they will have.

The people of the polyglot tongue!

Speaking all the languages of earth, they will go forth and tell that he whom they denied and nailed on a cross, is alive; he whom they rejected as the king of the Jews, is on the throne of all Israel; he is the King of Kings, and Lord of Lords.

His name in that day shall be Emmanuel, God with us; the land shall be Emmanuel's land, the land of the God who is with us.

Joseph makes ready his chariots and goes forth to meet Jacob (Israel) in the land of Goshen.

This is really the epiphany of Joseph.

He reveals himself in splendor and kingliness to his people.

He meets Judah in Goshen first, and then meets his father, the household of Jacob.

This is a representation of the truth as we have already seen it.

It is the coming of Christ in his glory to meet Judah first, and then all Israel.

Our attention is specially drawn to his appearing to the people in chariots of glory.

So of the greater Joseph we read:

"For, behold, the Lord will come with fire, and with his chariots like a whirlwind." Israel lxvi: 15.

Joseph settles and establishes his brethren and the household of Jacob in the land of Goshen.

"And they came into the land of Goshen." Genesis xlvi: 28.

"And thou shalt dwell in the land of Goshen." Genesis xlv: 10.

"And Israel dwelt in the land of Egypt, in the country of Goshen." Genesis xlvii: 27.

Goshen was the best part of the land of Egypt.

This is the declaration of Pharaoh.

"The land of Egypt is before thee: in the best of the land make thy father and brethren to dwell; in the land of Goshen let them dwell." Genesis xlvii: 6.

Egypt is a type of the world.

Goshen as the best part of Egypt is typically the best part of the world.

It is, typically speaking, the most favored land.

The most favored land in fact must, logically, be the land which the Lord shall select for the true Joseph and his people.

That land therefore must be Palestine.

And it is.

It is the land that is always under the eyes of the Lord.

"But the land whither ye go to possess it, is a land of hills and valleys, and drinketh water of the rain of heaven;

A land which the Lord thy God careth for: the eyes of the Lord thy God are ALWAYS UPON IT, FROM THE BEGINNING OF THE YEAR EVEN UNTO THE END OF THE YEAR."

Characteristically, Palestine is called Joseph's land.

This may be seen in the blessing which Jacob before dying gives to Joseph.

"And of Joseph he said, Blessed of the Lord be his land." Deuteronomy xxxiii: 11-15.

In this land God will indeed settle them that they may no more be plucked up forever. Ezekiel xxxvii: 21-28. Jeremiah xxxi: 31, 40. Jeremiah xxxii: 40, 41. Jeremiah xxxiii: 7-26. Amos ix: 14, 15.

After Joseph and his brethren are settled in the land of Goshen, the Egyptians (that is to say, the Gentiles) on account of the famine, offer to sell themselves to him for bread, and through him become the bondmen of Pharaoh. Genesis xlvii: 13-25.

Joseph buys their lands and themselves in exchange of corn and bread.

Joseph buys them for Pharaoh, but they really belong to Joseph as the "lord of all Egypt."

In belonging to Joseph they belong to Joseph's kindred.

Thus the Gentiles in Egypt were practically the bondmen of the Jews. The word of God foretells that this will be the condition of the Gentile world, when the Jew has been exalted to the place of power under the coming Messiah of Israel, the Christ.

"And the house of Israel shall possess them (the Gentiles) in the land of the Lord for servants and handmaids; and they shall take them captives, whose captives they were; and they shall rule over their oppressors." Isaiah xiv: 1, 2.

"For the nation and kingdom that will not serve thee (Israel) shall perish; yea, those nations shall be utterly wasted." Isaiah lx: 12.

All Egypt at the last owns Joseph as the Saviour-Lord.

"And they said, thou hast saved our lives." Genesis xlvii: 25.

So the day is coming when the knowledge of the Lord shall cover the earth as the waters cover the face of the deep; he will be owned and acknowledged by all the world as the alone Saviour and Lord. Ps. lxxii: 10. Ps. ii: 8. Philippians ii: 9-11.

At the close of this story Jacob is seen giving forth his blessing to all. Genesis, 49th chapter.

Scripture teaches that when the wanderings of Jacob are over; when the children of Israel are finally settled in their inheritance under their king, they will become the fruitful source of blessing to the whole earth; and then will be fully justified that saying of our Lord:

"SALVATION IS OF THE JEWS." John iv: 22.

"And the remnant of Jacob shall be in the midst of many people, as a dew from the Lord, as the showers upon the grass." Micah v: 7.

"And the Gentiles shall come to thy light, and kings to the brightness of thy rising." Isaiah: 1-3.

Joseph's brethren at the last put him in the place of God, as the representative of God.

And his brethren also went and fell down before his face; and they said, Behold, we be thy servants.

And Joseph said unto them, Fear not: for am I in the place of God?" Genesis l: 18, 19.

Yes, the time is coming when like Joseph's brethren all Israel will fall down before the Lord Jesus Christ in his glory and say:

"Lo, this is our God; we have waited for him, and he will save us; this is the Lord, we have waited for him, we will be glad and rejoice in his salvation." Isaiah xxv: 6-9.

Like Thomas they will cry:

"My Lord, and My God."

The name of Joseph signifies Addition.

Addition is Increase.

And "Increase" is the very word which describes the unfolding kingdom and glory of the infinite Joseph.

"Of the increase of his government and peace there shall be no end, upon the throne of David, and upon his kingdom, to order it, and to establish it with judgment and with justice, from henceforth even forever." Isaiah ix : 7.

——————

THE STORY OF JOSEPH IN THE CONCRETE.

1. He is the son of Jacob's old age.

2. He is the well-beloved of the Father.

3. He wears a coat of many colors.

4. He has visions of coming rulership and walks in the light of it.

5. He is the called and sent of the Father.

6. He responds to the Father as one who delights to do his will.

7. He is sent by the Father to seek his wandering brethren.

8. His first manifestation is made to the shepherds.

9. He finds his brethren in the land of law and cere- mony, in Dothan.

10. He becomes a wanderer in the "field."

11. His brethren hate him and take counsel to kill him.

12. They mock and despise him.

13. They reject him and sell him to the Ishmaelites.

14. He is cast into the pit without water.

15. He is taken out of the place of death alive.

16. He is taken into a "far country."

17. Judah finds his grave empty but does not know that he has risen from the place of death, that he has been raised.

18. In the far country he is exalted to the throne of power.

19. While rejected by his brethren and an outcast from his native land, he gets a Gentile Bride.

20. While he is the despised and rejected one of his brethren, he becomes a Saviour unto the Gentile world.

21. He takes his Gentile Bride to the throne before the tribulation falls on his brethren.

22. The tribulation, the day of Jacob's trouble, comes in after Joseph has put his Gentile Bride on the throne.

23. When his brethren are in the midst of their affliction, and at the hour when Jacob says all these things are against him, Joseph makes himself known in delivering power to his brethren.

24. Joseph is only recognized and owned by his brethren "the second time."

25. He goes forth with the chariots of glory to meet Judah in the chosen land.

26. After Joseph appears in glory Jacob comes with all his remaining household into the land.

27. Joseph establishes his brethren in the chosen land.

28. After Joseph and his brethren are established in the chosen land the Gentiles become subject unto the Jew.

29. After he is established in the land, Jacob (Israel) becomes a fruitful centre of blessing to all.

30. Joseph at the end is owned of his brethren as in the place of God, as God manifest in the flesh unto them.

31. The bowing down of Joseph's brethren is the climacteric fulfillment of all the dreams and visions that had gone before on Joseph.

32. His name signifies an endless increase in glory.

To him who studies this "concrete" reverently, on bended knees, and with open Bible before him, each line will become a volume of prophetic revelation, and make manifest an Antitypical verification.

19. While rejected by his brethren and an outcast from his native land, he gains a Gentile bride.

20. While he is the despised and rejected one of his brethren, he becomes a Saviour unto the Gentile world.

21. He takes his Gentile Bride to the throne before the tribulation falls on his brethren.

22. The tribulation, the day of Jacob's trouble comes on after Joseph has put his Gentile Bride on the throne.

23. When his brethren are in the midst of their affliction, and at the hour when Jacob says all these things are against him, Joseph makes himself known to deliver ing power to his brethren.

24. Joseph is only recognized and owned by his brethren "the second time".

25. He goes forth with the chariots of glory to meet Judah in the chosen land.

26. After Joseph appears in glory, Jacob comes with all his remaining household into the land.

27. Joseph establishes his brethren in the chosen land.

28. After Joseph and his brethren are established in the chosen land the Gentiles become subject unto the Jew.

29. After he is established in the land, Jacob (Israel) becomes a fruitful source of blessing to all.

30. Joseph at the end is owned of his brethren as in the place of God, as God ministed to the flesh unto them.

31. The bowing down of Joseph's brethren is the climacteric fulfillment of all the dreams and visions that had gone before on Joseph.

32. His name signifies an endless increase in glory.

To him who studies this "Figure", reverently, on bended knee, and with open Bible before him, each line will become a volume of prophetic revelation, and make manifest an Antitypical verification.

THE UNRENT VEIL.

The Unrent Veil.

The Apostle Paul tells us in Hebrews x: 20, that the veil which hung before the most holy place in the Tabernacle was a type of the flesh, that is to say, of the humanity of Christ.

It was known as the "Beautiful" veil.

It hung as a covering before the typical presence of God in the most holy place.

Symbolically, God dwelt behind the veil.

As the veil sets forth the humanity of Christ, it specifically teaches that the humanity of Christ was the veil of Godhead.

God was enveiled in Christ.

So long as this veil hung down it shut men out from God.

So long as Christ walked the earth in his beautiful and perfect humanity he shut men out from God.

And this is self evident.

For, if the humanity of Christ is the standard humanity; if the humanity of Christ is the humanity alone in which God will consent to dwell; if the humanity of Christ is the only kind of humanity that can approach God, then the humanity of Christ is a barrier to the ordinary sons of men.

The perfect humanity of Christ is a witness to the separation of the natural man from God.

The Incarnation of Christ while it proclaims God in his humanity, acts as a barrier to all who do not possess that humanity.

You may admire the beautiful veil.

You may draw near and find it perfect.

But the more beautiful, the more perfect, the clearer it will be that it shuts out God.

Admire Jesus Christ as he walked on earth.

Find him perfect, as you will.

The more perfect, the more evident that your humanity and his are distinct: that there is nothing in common.

The perfect humanity of Jesus Christ is an infallible witness to the separation between the natural man and God.

The beautiful veil then teaches the startling truth that the Incarnation does not bring man to God; it does not bring God to man.

Incarnation neither brings man into union with God, nor God into union with man.

The life of Christ as he lived it on the earth was a barrier to men, shutting them out from God.

With all the beauty and perfection of his life he is constantly saying by it:

"Except ye be as holy, sinless, and perfect as I am, ye cannot even see God."

As long as the veil hung down it shut man out from the presence of God.

Jesus Christ as long as he walked the earth in his perfect humanity shut men out from God.

Only when the beautiful veil was stained with the blood of sacrifice could it be put aside and entrance be made into the presence of God.

It was not the beauty of the veil that made entrance into the presence of God possible.

No! Not until that veil was stained with the blood of a victim could it be put aside, and the worshipper enter the shekinal presence.

A man might stand before it and admire it; he might even copy it, and produce a symphony of similar colors, but there was only one way in which he could put it aside, find it a doorway, and enter the presence of the God of Israel, and that was by staining the veil with blood.

Let it hang down in shining beauty; let it be unstained by blood; let its very stainlessness attract; yet, by that very stainlessness and beauty it would say in inexorable language:

"Ye cannot enter here."

It is not by the beautiful life of Christ that we may enter the presence of God.

It is not by an attempt to copy the sweet perfections of that life.

Nay. It is only when the perfect humanity of Christ is stained with crimson of his blood, that it becomes a doorway into the presence of God.

Only by putting the blood of sacrifice on the veil could it be put aside, and turned into a doorway of entrance into the presence of God.

Not by the life he lived in spotless humanity does Jesus Christ give liberty and boldness to enter the presence of God.

Only when his humanity is covered by the blood of sacrifice; only when his flesh is stained with his own blood of atonement, can the way into the presence of God be opened.

Listen to holy Scripture:

"Boldness (liberty) to enter into the holiest by the BLOOD OF JESUS.

By a new and living way,

Which he hath consecrated (OPENED) for us,

THROUGH THE VEIL, THAT IS TO SAY, HIS FLESH."
Hebrews x: 19, 20.

Mark it well;

IT IS THROUGH THE VEIL BY THE BLOOD OF JESUS.

Not by the *earthly life* of Christ then do we enter into the presence of God, but by the SACRIFICIAL DEATH OF Christ.

It was only when that veil was stained with the blood of atonement, that the way into the holiest of all was made open.

It is only when the humanity of Christ is stained with the blood of his own atonement, that the way into the holiest of all on high was made open.

Not till the veil of the temple was rent in twain, was the way into the presence of God made open before all the world.

The veil of the temple was not rent in twain till Jesus died.

It was rent in twain at the very hour when he died.

He died at the very hour when the sacrificial lamb, which was a type of himself, died on the altar.

At the hour when the lamb died, Jesus the Christ of God died.

At the hour when Jesus died, the veil, which was a type of his flesh, was rent in twain.

At the very hour when it was rent in twain, it was covered with the blood of a lamb.

Jesus Christ is the lamb of God.

Jesus Christ was the veil of God.

Jesus Christ as the veil of God was rent by nail and spear, and covered with his own atoning blood.

When Jesus the veil of God was thus rent and stained with blood, the way into the presence of God was opened for all who could come unto God by him.

Not by the unstained, unrent veil, do we enter into the presence of God.

We enter in only, by the blood of the RENT VEIL.

THE RENT VEIL.

THE RENT VEIL.

The Rent Veil.

The account of the rending of the veil of the temple is given by three of the evangelists.

"And, behold, the veil of the temple was rent in twain, from the top to the bottom."   Matthew xxvii: 46-52.

"And the veil of the temple was rent in twain, from the top to the bottom."   Mark xv: 38.

"The veil of the temple was rent in the midst."   Luke xxiii: 45.

The veil was rent while hanging up between heaven and earth.

Like that veil, the Son of God was hung up between the heaven and the earth.

He was hung on the accursed tree.

"Being made a curse for us: for it is written, Cursed is every one that hangeth on a tree."   Galatians iii: 13.

The veil of the temple was rent in twain from top to bottom at the time of Christ's death.

According to tradition, that veil was so strong that two pairs of oxen attached to either edge and driven in opposite directions could not pull it apart.

Hanging down loosely, therefore, it would require something above nature to have rent it in the manner described.

The fact that it was rent from the top to the bottom, and not from the bottom to the top, is a declaraion that it was not only above nature, but by the hand of God.

The death of Christ was not, in the last analysis, according to nature or by the hand of man; it was from above, and by the hand of God.

"THOU hast brought me into the dust of death." Psalm xxii: 15.

"FOR THINE arrows stick fast in me, and THY hand presseth me sore."   Psalm xxxviii: 2.

"ALL THY waves and THY billows are gone over me." Psalm xlii: 7.

"THY wrath lieth hard upon me."   Psalm lxxxviii: 7.

"It pleased the Lord to bruise him."   Isaiah liii: 10.

"Awake, O sword, against my shepherd."   Zechariah xiii: 7.

"Is it nothing to you, all ye that pass by? Behold, and see if there be any sorrow like unto my sorrow, which is done unto me, wherewith the Lord hath afflicted me in the day of his fierce anger.

From ABOVE hath he sent fire into my bones. * * * The yoke of my transgressions is bound by his hand." Lamentations i: 12-14.

The veil was rent in twain at the hour of the evening sacrifice: 3 o'clock.

At that hour the lamb was on the altar, Christ was on the cross.

All three, the hour, the lamb, the Christ, were in perfect conjunction.

The veil was actually rent at the moment when Christ cried, "It is finished."

"When he had cried again with a loud voice, yielded up the ghost.

And, behold, the veil of the temple was rent in twain." Matthew xxvii: 50, 51.

"He said, It is finished; and he bowed his head and gave up the ghost."   John xix: 30.

As he hung on the cross he could see the smoke from the altar, and knew he was the fulfillment of that sacrifice; wherefore he cried, "It is finished."

As soon as the veil was rent it was changed from a barrier into a gateway.

While Christ walked on the earth his perfect life was a barrier between God and men.

Listen to the solemn statement in John xii: 23, 24: "Except a corn of wheat fall into the ground and die, it abideth alone; but if it die, it bringeth forth much fruit."

Take note of that word, "Abideth alone."

Yes, in his unsacrificed humanity Christ abideth alone.

But the moment he dies, then the way is open for relation to God, for union with Christ in resurrection, and for participation in his life; hence, for multiplication of sons in his likeness.

When the veil was rent, the way into the holiest of all was opened.

Because of the perfect sacrifice of Christ, the way into the presence of God is now opened for all; but as of old the high priest must needs present the blood of an accomplished sacrifice, as his only plea to enter the most holy place, so he who would enter before God and worship to-day, must come with the blood of the cross as his only plea.

And because the blood of the cross is the blood of an accomplished and accepted sacrifice, and has been shed so freely for all, he is invited to come with perfect assurance, and even boldness, in the name of that blood.

"Having, therefore, brethren, BOLDNESS to enter into the holiest by the BLOOD OF JESUS, * * * let us draw near * * * in FULL ASSURANCE OF FAITH." Hebrews x: 19-22.

A GOLDEN BELL AND A POME-
GRANATE.

A GOLDEN BELL AND A POME-
GRANATE.

A Golden Bell and a Pomegranate.

"A golden bell and a pomegranate, a golden bell and a pomegranate, upon the hem of the robe round about." Exodus xxviii: 34.

Among the many articles of dress which the high priest wore was a blue robe called the robe of the ephod.

Aaron the high priest was a type of the Lord Jesus Christ, our high priest.

Robe is a symbol of character.

Blue is the color of heaven, a symbol of grace and the infinite.

Taken in its unity the blue robe of the ephod sets forth the character of our Lord Jesus Christ.

It sets him forth in his character of the heavenly man, full of grace, and like the blue infinite and eternal.

That he was a heavenly man, is seen by contrast with other men.

It is seen in the contrast of birth.

Other men are conceived in sin and shapen in iniquity.

He was conceived by the Holy Ghost.

It is seen by contrasting his motives with those of other men.

The radii of human motives are earth and earthly things.

The final motive is *self*.

But with him self never came into view.

In Incarnation it is said that "he emptied himself."

He said as a constant refrain: "I came not to do mine own will, but the will of him that sent me."

The radius of his life was not earth, but heaven.

He came to testify of heaven and the Father.

From heaven he came, of heaven he spoke, towards heaven he lifted his eyes, and towards heaven he daily walked.

Each day his life was a witness that grace was poured out on his lips and flowing from his touch.

Find such a man born of woman anywhere and you have found a miracle.

Such a man can alone come from the infinite.

Thus the blue robe of the ephod sets forth Jesus Christ as the Infinite, the Heavenly man full of grace.

On the hem of this blue robe was a string of golden bells; and wherever the high priest walked when he walked back and forth, these golden bells gave out their sound.

A bell has a tongue; a bell therefore is the symbol of speech, of testimony.

The golden bells then tells us of the perfect speech, the testimony, and the doctrine of the Son of God.

Perfect was his speech in tone.

He never lifted up his voice nor cried aloud; when he said peace to the wild storm in Galilee, he spake as softly as a mother to her child; when he commanded the demons to come out of men, it was with the quiet accents of infinite, measureless power; once only did he cry out aloud, and that was on the cross; and that was not his own cry but the concentrated agony of every soul for whom he endured the forsaking of the Father.

How perfect was the tone of that caressing word: "Come unto me, all ye that labor and are heavy laden, and I will give you rest."

His speech was perfect in wisdom.

Again and again, when men came to him, and sought to entangle him in his speech, his wisdom triumphed over them as the morning rises above the night.

His speech was perfect in its intellectual power.

The intellectuality of his simplest words have never been measured.

To-day the mightiest intellects of the world on bended knee, and with reverent gaze, seek to fathom to some degree the crystal depths, and partially rise to the power, of his more than mortal thought.

His speech was perfect in Doctrine.

His doctrine was immense; he taught that the God of the universe loved men; that among fallen and rebel men he sought sons; that so great was his love for men and his desire for sons, that he had sent his only begotten Son into the world to meet the demand of his righteousness against them; he had sent him to die, and in his death to swallow up all the claims of justice against them; he had sent him to die, in order that he might rise as the eternal head and giver of life to men for simple faith in his name; he had sent him into the world to die and rise again, that whosoever should believe in him might not perish, but have eternal life and heavenly sonship.

He declared that the cross towards which he journeyed should be the pledge of divinest love through all ages, and the empty grave, and the risen man, the seals, the witnesses, of its triumphant power.

His speech was perfect in its prophetic forecast.

The growth, the development of his church, the condition and the circumstances in it to-day, are simply the actual fulfillment of his prophetic word; while the world is moving on in its unbelief, its lawlessness, and appeal to arms, even, as he said.

Those who heard him speak in those far Judean days declared:

"Never man spake like this man."

Every succeeding age has verified and justified their wonder.

Ah! the golden bells! the perfect speech!

Between each of the golden bells was a pomegranate.

A pomegranate is the one perfect fruit in nature.

Fruit in symbolic language stands for deeds.

The perfect fruit then, reveals the perfect deeds of the perfect man.

Listen to what they said concerning his every deed:

"He hath done all things well."

It may seem startling to say, but it is an indisputable fact, that our Lord Jesus Christ was not a genius.

No!

A genius is one who has great ability in some one particular direction; that one ability rises above all his other equipment as the mountain above the plain; it dwarfs all other powers which he may possess; not infrequently, this very exaltation of power, capacity or gift, serves only to draw attention to deficiency in some other direction.

But Jesus Christ did one thing just as well as another; if he did one thing well, he did the next thing just as well; he did *all* things well; his deeds were the perfect fruit of a perfect life.

Golden bell and pomegranate.

Perfect words! perfect deeds!

But pomegranate as perfect fruit signifies perfect life.

There can be no perfect fruit without perfect life.

The perfect life of the pomegranate could be seen and known only when you took a knife and cut it open.

Then you saw with amaze that it was filled with crimson fluid, and in this crimson fluid floated pure white seeds.

And lo! the perfect life of Jesus of Nazareth was never revealed till the sharp point of a Roman spear pierced his side, opened his heart, and the crimson blood flowed forth.

Then were revealed the pure white seeds of a germinal life.

He himself anticipating that Roman spear had said: "Except a corn of wheat fall into the ground and die, it abideth alone; but if it die, it bringeth forth much fruit."

By that death upon the cross he satisfied the claims of righteousness against the sinner, and in resurrection took his place as one filled with the seeds of life for men.

For two thousand years on the throne of God he has been the germinal life of the world.

Whatever has been spiritual, pure, sweet, and god-like through the years of human history since he left us, has been due to his white, fair, germinal life on yonder throne.

The seed life revealed through the crimson of his blood.

When the high priest went into the sanctuary and ministered before God on behalf of the people, though out of sight, they knew he was alive, and in the divine presence for them.

And our high priest is out of sight; he is within the veil in the upper sanctuary; he ministers for us in the divine presence; he ever liveth to make intercession.

And how may we know that he is alive and ministering for us as we keep our pilgrim way?

How may we know that his nail-marked body did not fall into the dust of Palestine long ago, and that he himself is but a translucent spirit shining afar and helpless, as he hears us cry and name his name?

We may know by the golden bells.

Each time the high priest moved in the sanctuary here below, the golden bells gave forth their sound; those sounding bells were witnesses that he died not, that he lived before the Lord.

Each golden bell had a tongue; many golden bells make many golden tongues.

When Aaron was out of sight the many tongues told that Aaron was alive.

Well! we got the sound of those golden bells, we heard the sound of those many tongues, on the day of Pentecost.

On the day of Pentecost came tongues of fire and sat on each of the disciples.

The disciples spake, and the people heard in many tongues the wonderful works of God.

There are your golden bells.

Aye! the Holy Ghost on the day of Pentecost, is the fulfillment of the golden bells ringing on the hem of the high priest's robe.

His many tongues rang out sweet golden music to the listening ears, from within the upper Holies.

What music they rang!

And what speech they uttered!

They said:

"I am alive and in Heaven."

"I am alive forevermore, and in Heaven for you."

Ah! so many fail to reach the meaning of Pentecost.

It is the enduement of power for that Church which must take the Risen Man's place.

It is all that.

But it is far more.

It is the supreme witness that he is alive, in yonder heaven, on the throne of God for us; *for it ought to be known and kept clearly in mind, that while the disciples were the witnesses of the resurrection, the Holy Ghost is the alone witness that he who arose from the dead and ascended to heaven, entered within the veil, and is now alive on the throne of God, in the Most Holy Place.*

Ah! the golden bells! the golden bells!

The golden bells and the pomegranates were never separated.

Wherever there was a bell there was a pomegranate.

That is to say:

With the testimony of the Spirit there must be Fruit of the Spirit.

So was it from that Pentecostal hour.

From that hour there was a startling new testimony in the world: the story of a man who had triumphed over death, and now lived at the right hand of God for men.

And side by side with this testimony of the Spirit, there was startling new fruit in the world: the pomegranates were seen.

This was the new fruit seen blooming in the earth·

Love.

Joy.

Peace.

Longsuffering.

Gentleness.

Goodness.

Faith.

Meekness.

Temperance.

These constituted the perfect fruit, the divine pomegranate.

The bells and the pomegranates, the testimony and the fruit, these bore indisputable evidence that in the sanctuary of God, the man who had walked on earth among men, was alive and acting for men.

As the robe sets forth the character of Christ, and those who are truly Christians are partakers of Christ, of his life and of his nature; as the robe sets forth heavenly mindedness and grace, then, as Christians, we ought to walk this earth as a heavenly people filled with grace.

Heavenly!

That is what we are who wear his name.

He has said: "Ye are not of this world."

An apostle has declared that our citizenship is in heaven, not here.

Our interests are in heaven.

Our Father is there.

Our Saviour is there.

Our friends, many of them, are there.

Our abiding, unfailing home is there.

Our source of life and light for this world. even, are there.

The full attainment and realization of immortality will be there.

We ought to walk as a heavenly people.

We ought not to be afraid of the walk, the end is sure, its glory certain.

We ought to be full of grace.

Gracious, gentle, tender.

Full of blessedness and peace.

That is the blue robe.

As spiritual priests are we wearing the blue robe?

Are we wearing the blue robe of heavenly mindedness and grace?

As the golden bells and the pomegranates were on the hem of this robe, and bells and pomegranates set forth perfect speech, perfect deeds, then our life as Christians, ought to be full of perfect speech, perfect deeds.

Is it so with us, we who call ourselves by that "worthy" name, "Christian?"

As we walk, do we give forth the sound of the golden bells?

The golden bells of perfect speech, perfect words?

What kind of speech do we use?

Are our words clean, sane, pure?

Are our words, golden words of purity, chastity?

As we walk, do we give forth the sound of a perfect testimony?

Are we testifying of heaven, of the grace of God, of our Lord and Master?

Are we speaking golden words in the ears of lost and dying men, golden words of grace?

As we walk, do we reveal the pomegranates with the bells?

The perfect fruit.

The perfect deeds.

The perfect life.

Are we doing good, doing good in his name?

Do our words and our deeds go together?

As we walk in the professed Christian life, do men hear the sound of our golden bells?

Do men see the beauty and perfection of our pomegranates, golden bells and pomegranates, perfect words and perfect deeds, proclaiming a heavenly life and a gracious character?

As we walk, do we give forth the sound of the golden
bells?

The golden bells of perfect speech, perfect words;
What kind of speech do we use?

Are our words clean, pure, pure;

Are our words, golden words of purity, chastity?
As we walk, do we give forth the sound of a period
testimony?

Are we testifying of heaven, of the grace of God, of
our Lord and Master?

Are we speaking golden words in the ears of lost and
dying men, golden words of grace?

As we walk, do we reveal the pomegranates with the
bells?

The perfect fruit,
The perfect deeds,
The perfect life.

Are we doing good, doing good in his name?

Do our words and our deeds go together?

As we walk in the professed Christian life, do men
hear the sound of our golden bells?

Do men see the beauty and perfection of our pomegranates, golden bells, and pomegranates, perfect words
and perfect deeds, proclaiming a heavenly life and a
gracious character?

THE STORY OF TWO BIRDS.

The Story of Two Birds.

"And the Lord spake unto Moses, saying,

This shall be the law of the leper in the day of his cleansing: He shall be brought unto the priest.

And the priest shall go forth out of the camp; and the priest shall look, and, behold, if the plague of the leprosy be healed in the leper,

Then shall the priest command to take for him that is to be cleansed two birds alive and clean, and cedar wood, and scarlet, and hyssop:

And the priest shall command that one of the birds be killed in an earthen vessel over running water;

As for the living bird, he shall take it, and the cedar wood, and the scarlet, and the hyssop, and shall dip them and the living bird in the blood of the bird that was killed over the running water;

And he shall sprinkle upon him that is to be cleansed from the leprosy seven times, and shall pronounce him clean, and shall let the living bird loose into the open field." Leviticus xiv: 1-7.

The bird was a sparrow. (So verse 4, on the margin, reads.)

It was to these sparrows undoubtedly that our Lord had reference in Matthew x: 29. "Are not two sparrows sold for a farthing?"

He speaks of himself, anticipatively through the Spirit, as a sparrow.

"I watch, and am as a sparrow alone upon the housetop." Ps. cii: 7.

A sparrow was a small and insignificant thing.

317

Equally insignificant and unattractive did the Son of God appear to those for whose sake he came.

"He was despised, and we esteemed him not." Isaiah liii : 3.

There were two birds.

These set forth, primarily, the two-foldedness of Christ.

He was from heaven.

"He that came down from heaven." John iii : 13.

He was of earth.

"The man Christ Jesus." I Timothy ii : 5.

The sparrows must be clean.

Clean and sinless was the Son of God.

"Without sin." Hebrews iv : 15.

The wood was cedar.

Cedar is fragrant.

The wooden Roman cross became an altar from whence ascended to the throne of God the fragrance of an unparalleled devotion, the perfect and pleasing sacrifice of his eternal Son.

"Christ also hath loved us, and hath given himself for us, an offering and a sacrifice to God for a sweet-smelling savor." Ephesians v : 2.

There must be scarlet in the offering.

There is one scarlet that God sees, one scarlet alone; without that color in it no offering can be acceptable to God.

"Without shedding of blood is no remission." Hebrews ix : 22.

There must be hyssop.

This was bound with scarlet twine to the cedar wood, and used to apply the blood.

It was the weakest thing in nature.

It took hold for life and sustenance on the rock.

And this is faith.

Faith in itself is nothing, faith is the nexus between need and supply, the link between weakness and strength; as the hyssop was the instrumentality for applying the blood, so is faith. Without faith it is impossible to please God or approach him; for God wants the blood, the blood of his Son, and without faith it is impossible to make the blood of avail.

"Without faith it is impossible to please him." Hebrews xi: 6.

"Saved through faith." Ephesians ii: 8.

The priest went outside the camp to slay the birds.

He went outside the gate.

"Wherefore Jesus also, that he might sanctify the people with his own blood, suffered without the gate." Hebrews xiii: 12.

The priest did everything, the leper did nothing.

"Not by works of righteousness which we have done." Titus iii: 5.

"By grace are ye saved through faith, * * * not of works." Ephesians ii: 8-10.

"A man is justified by faith without the deeds of the law." Romans iii: 28.

"Neither is there salvation in any other." Acts iv: 12.

One bird was killed in an earthen vessel.

The earthen vessel is a type of the body?

"We have this treasure in earthen vessels." II Corinthians iv: 7.

Thus, typically, we have a view of our Lord Jesus Christ, slain in his mortal body.

The bird was slain by command of God.

It was by the will and command of God that our Lord Jesus Christ went to the cross and suffered its ignominious death.

"Became obedient unto death, even the death of the cross." Philippians ii : 8.

"He spared not his own Son." Romans viii : 32.

"He gave his only begotten Son." John iii : 16.

"God sent his Son to be the propitiation for our sins." I John iv : 10.

The bird was killed over running water.

Running water is a symbol of the word and the spirit in operation; or, of the word made living and active by the operation of the Spirit.

"Except a man be born of water (out of the water) and of the Spirit (out of the Spirit), he cannot enter the kingdom of God." John iii : 5.

"Ye are clean through the word which I have spoken unto you." John xv : 3.

"The washing of water BY THE WORD." Ephesians v : 26.

"Out of his belly shall flow rivers of LIVING WATER." (But this spake he of the Spirit.) John vii : 38, 39.

From these Scriptures it is evident that water is a symbol of the word; living water, or running water, the word and the Spirit in operation.

We learn therefore that Jesus Christ offered himself to God according to the word, and through the eternal Spirit.

"Christ, who through the eternal Spirit offered himself without spot to God." Hebrews ix : 14.

The living bird was dipped in the blood of the dead bird.

The living bird was thus identified with the dead bird; or, to put it in another way: the *living bird bore the marks and stains of the dead bird.*

No more vital moving picture of the resurrection of the Son of God could be given.

In resurrection he bears the marks of the death of the cross; he rises in the body in which he died; it is in this body bearing all the marks of the death through which it passed, that he showed himself to his disciples.

"And when he had thus spoken, he showed them his hands and his feet." Luke xxiv: 40.

"Thomas * * * said unto them, Except I shall see in his hands the print of the nails, and put my finger into the print of the nails, and thrust my hand into his side, I will not believe.

"Then came Jesus * * * . Then saith he to Thomas, Reach hither thy finger, and behold my hands; and reach hither thy hand, and thrust into my side." John xx: 27.

"Every eye shall see him, and they also which pierced him." Revelation i: 7.

"And one shall say unto him, What are these wounds in thine hands? Then shall he answer, Those with which I was wounded in the house of my friends." Zechariah xiii: 6.

The living bird was let loose.

Our Lord Jesus Christ died once for all; the one offering was perfect; in resurrection he was freed forevermore from judgment and death.

"Knowing that Christ being raised from the dead, dieth no more; death hath no more dominion over him." Romans vi: 9.

The living bird after being loosed rose up into the air towards heaven.

If the living bird be a type of the resurrection of the Lord, then that bird ascending to the upper sky, is the silent, but eloquent prophecy, that he would also ascend as the living and immortal man to heaven.

"He was taken up; and a cloud received him out of their sight." Acts i: 9.

The living bird when it rose up into the air towards heaven carried with it the blood of the offered sacrifice.

When our Lord Jesus Christ ascended to heaven and sat down on the throne of God, he took with him the blood of his own sacrifice, and placed it there as a precious and eternal memorial.

"By his own blood, he entered in once into the holy place." Hebrews ix: 12.

The leper who would be cleansed by the blood of the bird must come to the priest.

He must come to the priest and own his need of cleansing.

The constant admonition and invitation of the Son of God is: "Come unto me."

And in response to a question of the Master, Simon Peter once responded: "Lord to whom shall we go? thou hast the words of eternal life." John vi: 68.

He himself has said: "No man cometh unto the Father, but by me." John xiv: 6.

The priest must apply the blood of the dead bird seven times to the leper.

It is the Lord Jesus Christ the great high priest who must apply his own blood in the case of each individual sinner who applies to him for cleansing.

"Unto him that loved us, and WASHED US FROM OUR SINS IN HIS OWN BLOOD." Revelation i: 5.

Seven signifies completeness.

When the great high priest applies the blood, the application is complete, perfect.

"The blood of Jesus Christ cleanseth us from ALL sin." I John i: 7.

The blood was finally applied by means of the hyssop.

Great as is the power of the high priest, willing and anxious as he is to apply his cleansing blood to the condemned sinner, he can do so only when that sinner believes. Once in his own country, here on earth, he could not do many mighty works because of unbelief; so, even now in yonder heaven, with the fulness of the blood at his command, he is powerless to make that blood of avail to those who will not believe.

When the blood was at last applied, the leper had a living and beautiful witness that he was clean in God's sight.

That living witness was the live bird flying in the upper heaven, stained with blood of the dead bird.

If anyone should say unto him:

"Where is the evidence of your ceremonial cleansing; where is the witness that you are satisfactorily clean in God's sight?"

He could point to that bird flying upward and say:

"Behold, there is the witness of my cleansing; that red spot yonder in the blue heavens is my witness; that is my record on high; I do not point you to myself, but to that blood in yonder heaven."

So to-day, we may point to that man who in heaven bears the marks of the cross; to that throne on which he sits, stained with his sacrificial blood, and say:

"Behold, my evidence, my witness on high."

Beautiful as was that bird with its stain of blood against the skies of blue, beautiful to that leper who saw in it his right and title to enter the camp, and share the blessings of the people of God, from whom he had been so long excluded, more beautiful, and in a comparative not possible to utter, is that blood stain in the heart of the deepest blue of the universe of God, the blood stain of him who died for us; and who, through all the ages of eternity, will bear the stigmata of the cross in his immortal body, while his throne high and lifted up will gleam with its crimson glory.

This is the witness and the evidence that shall never fade.

"My witness is in heaven, and my record is on high." Job xvi: 19.

"Who is he that condemneth? It is Christ that died, yea, rather, that is risen again, who is even at the right hand of God, who also maketh intercession for us." Romans viii: 34.

THE PRESENT OR HOLY GHOST AGE.

The Present or Holy Ghost Age.

In order to study it intelligently, consider it under seven heads:

1. Beginning.
2. Ending.
3. Characteristics.
4. Purpose of God.
5. Relation of Christ to this age.
6. Relation of this age to Christ.
7. The signs of the end.

THE BEGINNING.

The beginning of this age is two-fold:

1. *Secret.* "He breathed on them, and saith unto them, Receive ye the Holy Ghost." John xx: 22.

This tremendous act was known only to the disciples. It was a coming of the Holy Ghost weeks before Pentecost; so far as the world was concerned it was wholly secret.

2. *Public.* "And suddenly there came a sound from heaven, as of a rushing mighty wind, * * * and there appeared unto them cloven tongues, like fire." Acts ii: 2, 3.

The rushing sound and fiery tongues stand in marked contrast to the unseen and silent breath. While the latter has all the characteristics of the unseen and secret, the former is set before us in terms which indicate the reverse; sound, rushing wind, and fire in the shape of flaming tongues, as strongly as language can indicate, assure us that the later coming of the Holy Ghost was open and public.

This was the day of Pentecost.

THE ENDING.

The ending of this age is two-fold:

1. *Secret.* "The Day of the Lord so cometh as a thief in the night." I Thessalonians v: 2.

The Day of the Lord is an age following this; it begins with the action of a thief, the snatching away of something coveted and precious; that something is the Church; the departure of the Church from the world is the beginning of the ending of the age; the departure of the Church is secret, just as secret as the disappearance of the treasure that the thief "snatches" away; the ending of this age therefore is on one side of it, secret.

2. *Public.* Revelation xix: 11; xx: 1, 2.

In these passages the Lord is represented coming in public state and splendor from heaven to overthrow Anti-Christ and his armies, and openly bind Satan. This dispensation therefore has an open and a secret ending; in relation to the presence and mission of the Church, it ends secretly at the Coming of the Lord to take the Church out of the earth; in relation to the time limit for the Gentile rule and the blindness of Israel, it ends publicly at the Coming of Christ with his church to inaugurate the new age of the "times of Restitution."

CHARACTERISTICS.

1. *The Presence of the Holy Spirit.*

The Holy Spirit has always been present in the earth moving men, descending upon them, operating in them; but never, as now, taking up his abode and dwelling permanently in men.

He dwells in Believers as the Comforter.

"And I will pray the Father, and he shall give you another Comforter, that he may abide with you forever:

Even the Spirit of Truth; * * * he shall be in you." John xiv: 16, 17.

He dwells in the Believer as the power and energy of God.

"Now unto him that is able to do exceeding abundantly above all that we ask or think, according to THE POWER THAT WORKETH IN US." Ephesians iii: 20.

In the Church corporately.

He is the Giver of Spiritual gifts. I Corinthians xii: 4-11.

He is the true Administrator in the Church, the true Vice-gerent of the Lord.

"As they ministered to the Lord and fasted, the Holy Ghost said, Separate me Barnabas and Saul for the work whereunto I HAVE CALLED THEM, * * * so they, being sent forth BY THE HOLY GHOST." Acts xiii: 2, 4.

2. *The preaching of the Gospel of Death and Resurrection is a characteristic of this age.*

"Moreover, brethren, I declare unto you THE GOSPEL; * * * how that Christ died for our sins according to the Scriptures;

And that he was buried, and that he rose again the third day according to the scriptures." I Corinthians xv: 1-4.

The Gospel of the Death of Christ, is the Good News of Reconciliation.

"When we were enemies, we were reconciled to God by the death of his Son." Romans v: 10.

The Gospel of his Resurrection, is the good news that we may be saved by his life, that life which rose superior to death. Romans v: 10.

"We shall be saved by his life."

3. *The reign of Grace characterizes this age.*

This is the age in which God is dealing in absolute grace with a sinful and rebellious world.

"THE DISPENSATION OF THE GRACE OF GOD." Ephesians iii: 2.

"For by grace are ye saved." Ephesians ii: 8, 9.

4. *This is an age of Regeneration; that is to say, Regeneration is a fundamental characteristic of this age of the Holy Ghost.*

"Except a man be born of the Spirit he cannot enter into the kingdom of God." John iii: 5.

5. *The presence of the Church is a marked and peculiar characteristic of this age.*

The Church is constituted of all persons who truly believe on the Lord Jesus Christ.

"Ye are all the children of God by faith in Christ Jesus." Galatians iii: 26.

The Church is the Body of Christ through whom he is reincarnated on the earth, and becomes the Omnipresent Man.

"Now ye are the body of Christ and members in particular." I Corinthians xii: 27.

6. *This age is characterized by the existence of a class of persons called Christians.*

"And the disciples were called Christians first in Antioch." Acts xi: 26.

A Christian is an UNMANIFESTED *Son of God.*

"Now are we the sons of God; and it doth not yet appear (it is not yet made manifest to the world) what we shall be; but we know that, when he shall appear we shall be like him." I John iii: 2.

7. *The building up of a new humanity is a peculiar characteristic of this age.*

"One New Man." Ephesians iv: 13. Ephesians iv: 21-24.

8. *Faith. Faith in this age is the channel of Grace.*
"For by grace are ye saved THROUGH faith."
Ephesians ii: 8.

9. *The Test Question of the age is one of its strik-ing characteristics.*

That test question is: "What think ye of Christ?"

"What think ye of Christ? Whose son is he?" Mat-thew xxii: 42.

10. *The separation of Christians from the natural side and principles of this age, called "the world."*

"Ye are not of the world, but I have chosen you OUT OF THE WORLD." John xv: 19.

"Who gave himself for our sins that he might deliver us from this present evil world." Galatians i: 4.

"Whosoever therefore will be a friend of the world, IS THE ENEMY OF GOD." James iv: 4.

"If any man love the world, the love of the Father is not in him." I John ii: 15.

"The cross of our Lord Jesus Christ, by whom the world is crucified unto me, and I unto the world." Galatians vi: 14.

"Be ye not unequally yoked together with unbelievers * * * . Wherefore come out from among them." II Corinthians vi: 14-17.

"Be not CONFORMED TO THIS WORLD." Romans xii: 2.

These are the ten-fold characteristics of this age.

THE PURPOSE OF GOD.

The purpose of God in this age is not the salvation of the whole world, but a taking out of the whole world a people for his name, a selection, an election.

"God at the first did visit the Gentiles, to take out of them a people for his name." Acts xv: 14.

RELATION OF CHRIST TO THIS AGE.

He is a Bridegroom seeking a Bride.

"He that hath the bride is the bridegroom." John iii: 29. Matthew xxv: 1. Ephesians v: 29-33.

RELATION OF THIS AGE TO CHRIST.

1. The Jew. BLIND. "Blindness in part is happened to Israel until the fulness of the Gentiles be come in." Romans xi: 25.

2. The Gentile. DEAD. "And you who were dead in trespasses and sins." Ephesians ii: 1.

3. The Church. SLEEPING. "Wherefore he saith, Awake thou that sleepest." Ephesians v: 14.

THE SIGNS OF THE END.

1. *Scoffers, who will mock at the doctrine of the Second Coming of Christ.*

"Knowing this first, that there shall come in the last day scoffers, walking after their own lusts.

And saying, Where is the promise of his coming? For since the fathers fell asleep, all things continue as they were from the beginning of the creation?" II Peter iii: 3, 4.

2. *Conflict between Capital and Labor.*

TESTIMONY OF SAINT JAMES.

1. Great wealth in the hands of the few.
2. Wealth hoarded up.
3. Reduction of wages.
4. Conflict between Capital and Labor.
5. Suffering of the rich at the hands of the poor.

"Go to now, ye rich men, weep and howl for your miseries that shall come upon you.

Your riches are corrupted, and your garments are motheaten.

Your gold and silver is cankered; and the rust of them shall be a witness against you, and shall eat your flesh as it were fire. Ye have heaped treasure together for the last days.

Behold, the hire of the labourers who have reaped down your fields, which of you is kept back by fraud, crieth; and the cries of them which have reaped are entered into the ears of the Lord of Sabaoth.

Ye have lived in pleasure on the earth, and been wanton; ye have nourished your hearts, as in a day of slaughter.

Ye have condemned and killed the just; and he doth not resist you.

Be patient, therefore, brethren, unto the coming of the Lord. Behold, the husbandman waiteth for the precious fruit of the earth, and hath long patience for it, until he receive the early and latter rain.

Be ye also patient; stablish your hearts: for THE COMING OF THE LORD DRAWETH NIGH." James v: 1-8.

TESTIMONY OF SAINT JOHN.

3. *The Coming of Antichrist.*

"Little children, it is the last time; and as ye have heard that Antichrist shall come, even now are there many Antichrists; WHEREBY WE KNOW THAT IT IS THE LAST TIME." I John ii: 18.

4. *The whole world Under Arms.*

"For they are the spirits of devils (demons), working miracles, which go forth unto the kings of the earth and of the WHOLE WORLD, to gather them to the battle." Revelation xvi: 14.

"Ye shall hear of wars and rumors of wars * * * for nation shall rise against nation, and kingdom against kingdom." Matthew xxiv: 6, 7.

5. *The world instead of being in spiritual submission to Christ will be in organized rebellion against him.*

"And I saw the beast, and the kings of the earth, and their armies, gathered together to MAKE WAR AGAINST HIM THAT SAT ON THE HORSE." Revelation xix: 19.

THE TESTIMONY OF SAINT PAUL.

Departure from the faith.
Wandering Spirits.
Spiritualism.
Religious hypocrisy.
The doctrine of celibacy.
Fastings.

"Now the Spirit speaketh expressly, that in the latter times some shall depart from the faith, giving heed to seducing spirits, and doctrines of devils (demons); Speaking lies in hypocrisy; having their conscience seared with a hot iron; Forbidding to marry, and commanding to abstain from meats, which God hath created to be received with thanksgiving of them which believe and know the truth.

For every creature of God is good, and nothing to be refused, if it be received with thanksgiving:

For it is sanctified by the word of God and prayer." I Timothy iv: 1-5.

Perilous times.
Religious formalism.
Inordinate love of pleasure among professed Christians.

Godliness persecuted.

Evil waxing WORSE AND WORSE.

"This know also, that in the last days perilous times shall come.

For men shall be lovers of their ownselves, covetous, boasters, proud, blasphemous, disobedient to parents, unthankful, unholy.

Without natural affection, truce breakers, false accusers, incontinent, fierce, despisers of those that are good,

Traitors, heady, high minded, LOVERS OF PLEASURES MORE THAN LOVERS OF GOD;

Having a form of Godliness, but denying the power thereof. * * *

These also RESIST THE TRUTH:

Yea, and all that will live godly in Christ Jesus shall suffer persecution.

But evil men and seducers shall wax WORSE AND WORSE." II Timothy iii: 1-13.

The Church will reject Doctrinal preaching.

Christians will seek teachers who will please them.

Christians will be turned from the truth.

Christians will be turned to fables.

"For the time will come when they will not endure sound doctrine; but after their own lusts shall they heap to themselves teachers, having itching ears;

And they shall turn away their ears from the truth, and shall be turned unto fables." II Timothy iv: 1-4.

A great Apostacy.

Setting up of Antichrist.

Deification of a sinful man.

Revelation of Satan's power.

Strong delusion.

Universal acceptance of the Devil's great lie.

"Let no man deceive you by any means: for that day shall not come (the millennium), except there come a falling away, first, and that man of sin be revealed, the son of perdition;

Who opposeth and exalteth himself above all that is called God, or that is worshipped; so that he, as God, sitteth in the temple of God, showing himself that he is God. * * *

For the mystery of iniquity doth already work; only he who now letteth (hindereth), will let, until he be taken out of the way.

And then shall that wicked be revealed, whom the Lord shall consume with the Spirit of his mouth (see Isaiah xi: 4), and shall destroy with the brightness of his coming (the epiphany of his *parousia, i. e.:* the brightness, the revelation of his bodily presence).

Even him whose coming is after the working of Satan, with all power and signs and lying wonders,

And with all deceivableness of unrighteousness in them that perish; because they received not the love of the truth, that they might be saved.

And for this cause God shall send them STRONG DE-LUSION, that they should believe a (THE) LIE:

That they might ALL BE DAMNED who believed not THE truth, but had pleasure in unrighteousness." II Thessalonians ii: 1-12.

THE TESTIMONY OF OUR LORD.

Wars and rumors of wars.
Famines.
Pestilences.
Earthquakes.

Persecutions.

False Teachers.

Abounding lawlessness.

Utter defection in Christianity.

False Christs.

Great Sorrows.

The unparalleled Tribulation.

Existence on earth impossible, even to the Elect, unless God shall shorten the days of trial.

Signs and portents in Heaven.   Matthew xxiv: 5-30.

Distress of Nations.

Perplexity of Nations.

Universal heart failure.

"And there shall be signs in the sun, and in the moon, and in the stars; and upon the earth distress of nations, with perplexity; the sea and the waves roaring;

Men's hearts failing them for fear, and for looking after those things which are coming on the earth; for the powers of heaven shall be shaken.

And THEN shall THEY see the Son of man coming in a cloud with power and great glory.

And when these things BEGIN to come to pass, then LOOK UP lift up YOUR heads; for your redemption draweth nigh."   Luke xxi: 25-28.

The old faith will disappear.

"When the Son of man cometh, shall he find (THE) faith on the earth?"   Luke xviii: 8.

HOW THE END WILL COME TO THE CHURCH.

1. *The Church will be taken away before the evil culminates.*

"I also will keep thee from the hour of temptation, which shall come upon all the WORLD."   Revelation iii: 10.

"And she brought forth a man child who was to rule all nations with a rod of iron: and her child was *caught up* unto God and to his throne." Revelation xii: 5.

The man child is the Christ; the Christ is constituted of head and body, as making the perfect man; as the Head has been caught up, the Body, the Church, must be also.

2. *The Church will be "caught up."*

"Then we which are alive and remain, will be caught up together." I Thessalonians iv: 17.

The Greek word for "caught up" is *harpagasómetha,* from *harpázo,* to "snatch away."

3. *The Church will be caught up in distinct order.*

a. The dead in Christ will be raised first.

b. Then the living will be changed. I Thessalonians iv: 16, 17.

The Scriptures give some striking examples of translation.

"And Enoch walked with God; and he was not, for GOD TOOK HIM." Genesis v: 24.

Elijah was translated. II Kings ii: 11.

Our Lord Jesus Christ was taken up.

"And when he had spoken these things, while they beheld, he was taken up." Acts i: 9.

The Apostle Paul was caught up.

"I knew a man in Christ above fourteen years ago * * * such an one caught up to the third heaven." II Corinthians xii: 2.

4. *The Church will be caught up at the sound of the trump.*

We have here a Roman military figure.

The Imperator, or General, gave the command, the next in authority took it up and passed it on to the trumpeters, who sounded the order.

Just so, Christ as the mighty Imperator will give the word of command to the Archangel; he will command the angel trumpeter to sound; then the great army, those who have been sleeping so to speak on their arms, and the living who have remained in the ranks and on guard, will respond; the dead, and then the living.

The dead will come forth in rank and order as perfectly as an army on parade; there will be no confusion; no one will find himself in a rank belonging to another.

"Every man in his own order." I Corinthians xv: 23.

The word "order" is *tágmati;* succession, rank, division, band.

5. *The Church will be caught up in clouds as was the Lord.*

"Caught up in the clouds." I Thessalonians iv: 17.

6. *We shall be caught up together.*

7. *The Church will be caught up to meet him.*

"To MEET THE LORD IN THE AIR." I Thessalonians iv: 17.

The word "meet" signifies to go forth in order to return with.

The word is *apántasin;* the same word in Matthew xxv: i, 6.

"Went forth to *meet* the bridegroom." Evidently with the intention of returning with him.

"And from thence, when the brethren heard of us, they came to *meet* us as far as Appii forum."

The brethren came out to meet Paul in order that they might return in his company to the city.

8. *The event will be secret to the world. I Thessalonians v: 2.*

9. *The effect on the world of this Translation.*
Surprise, confusion.

The Holy Spirit as the possible blessing to the world will be taken away.

"He who now letteth (hindereth, hindereth the revelation of Antichrist), will let (hinder) until he (the Holy Spirit) BE TAKEN OUT OF THE WAY." II Thessalonians ii: 7.

Restraint of evil will be gone, Antichrist will rapidly be made manifest as the head of all evil.

HOW THE END WILL COME TO THE WORLD.

By the Appearing of Christ in Flaming Fire, and Vengeance Judgment.

"In flaming fire taking vengeance on them that know not God, and that obey not the Gospel of our Lord Jesus Christ." II Thessalonians i: 7-9.

It will be a time of terror.

"Sudden destruction cometh upon them * * * they shall not escape." I Thessalonians v: 3.

"Howl ye; for the day of the Lord is at hand; it shall come as a destruction from the Almighty." Isaiah xiii: 6.

OUR ATTITUDE.

Not looking for *signs*, but *waiting* for the Son,

A beautiful key word and picture in Luke viii: 40.

"AND IT CAME TO PASS, THAT, WHEN JESUS WAS RETURNED, THE PEOPLE GLADLY RECEIVED HIM; FOR THEY WERE ALL WAITING FOR HIM."

THE TIMES OF THE RESTITUTION
OF ALL THINGS.

The Times of the Restitution of all Things.

Acts iii: 21.

There are three other subordinate or relative titles for this dispensation:

The Last Day.

The Day of the Lord.

The Regeneration.

It is evident that they refer to the same period because each begins with the same event: The Coming of Christ.

Times of the Restitution.

"And he shall send Jesus Christ, which before was preached unto you;

Whom the heavens must receive until (that is till the time arrives) the times of restitution." Acts iii: 20, 21.

When the moment for the restitution period arrives he will come; thus the Restitution is introduced by the Coming of Christ.

Last Day.

"And this is the Father's will which hath sent me, that of all which he hath given me I should lose nothing, but should raise it up again at the last day."

"I will raise him up at the last day." John vi: 39, 40, 44.

Resurrection of those who are Christ's takes place at his coming. "They that are Christ's at his Coming." I Corinthians xv: 23.

Thus the Last Day begins with the Coming of Christ.

The Day of the Lord.

343

"The day of the Lord so cometh as a thief in the night." I Thessalonians v: 2.

Matthew 25, tells us that the Lord is coming as a Bridegroom for his Church in the night; Hebrew time begins in the night; the day begins in the evening.

The Coming of the Lord therefore begins the day of the Lord.

The Regeneration.

"And Jesus said unto them, Verily I say unto you, That ye which have followed me, in the regeneration, when the Son of man shall sit in the throne of his glory." Matthew xix: 28.

Matthew xxv: 31, tells us when Christ shall sit in the throne of his glory.

"When the Son of man *shall come* in his glory; and all the holy angels with him, *then* shall he sit upon the throne of his glory."

As the regeneration is to be when Christ shall sit upon the throne of his glory, and He will sit upon the throne of His glory when he comes, then the Regeneration will begin at the Coming of Christ the second time.

These several days end with the same event, *i. e.:* the end of time and the bringing in of the New Heavens and the New Earth.

TEACHING VALUE OF EACH NAME.

Last Day.

The day of the Last Man, the Son of Man; used particularly in respect to beginning, to emphasize the period when the Second Man will bring in Resurrection.

Day of the Lord.

The day in which the whole universe shall confess that Jesus Christ is Lord, to the glory of God the Father.

It is applied particularly to the moment of Christ's appearing in glory.

It is Vengeance judgment; it is wrath and anger against the world.

"Howl ye for the day of the Lord is at hand; it shall come as a destruction from the Almighty." Isaiah xiii: 6.

"For, behold, the Lord will come with fire, and with his chariots like a whirlwind, to render his anger with fury, and his rebuke with flames of fire." Isaiah lxvi: 15.

"The day of the Lord's anger." Zephaniah ii: 2.

"The day of wrath, and revelation of the righteous judgment of God." Romans ii: 5.

"The Lord Jesus shall be revealed from heaven with his mighty angels;

In flaming fire taking vengeance on them that know not God, and that obey not the gospel of our Lord Jesus Christ." II Thessalonians i: 7, 8.

The Day of the Lord is not to be confounded with the *Coming of the Lord*.

The Day of the Lord has special reference to the public appearing of Christ with his Church, to inaugurate the period of judgments that are to follow.

The *Coming* of the Lord particularly signifies that moment, when he shall descend into the air secretly for his Church, to take her out of the way of the judgments that are to fall on the earth.

The *Day* of the Lord as a title is applied to the whole period because it is the period of the Lord's controversy with the world.

The Regeneration.

The day when the New Creation, the New Generation, all who are Regenerated in Christ, shall obtain sway over the earth.

The day whose culmination is the Regeneration of Heaven and Earth.

Times of Restitution.

The Greek is *apokatastáseōs,* the restoration of a thing to its former estate.

The day in which Jesus Christ as the *Last Man* shall *put down* all rule and authority and restore all things to the rule, the authority, and the glory of God, the Father.

The whole day is a *Day of Judgment;* a day in which all things are judged from God's point of view.

The key words are: "Putting down," "Subduing."

Thus while the Last Day, Day of the Lord and Regeneration, each apply to this dispensation of Restitution, the true, supreme, generic title is:

TIMES OF RESTITUTION.

The opening key to this dispensation is found in the word, "times."

The Greek word is *chrónōn;* it is plural and signifies epochs, eras or ages. More than one epoch is thus indicated. Revelation 20th shows that there are two epochs or parts: The Thousand years and After the Thousand years. In order that the Dispensation may be properly studied as a whole, it is necessary to divide the subject into three parts.

The Thousand years.

After the Thousand years.

The Things Restored.

THE THOUSAND YEARS.

The study of the Thousand years may be divided under seven heads.

The Beginning.

The Official Title.

Definition of Title.

Characteristics.

God's Attitude.

Purpose of God.

The Ending.

1. *The Beginning.* The Appearing of Christ and the Binding of Satan. Revelation xix: 11-21.

"And he laid hold on the dragon, that old serpent, which is the Devil, and Satan, and bound him a THOUSAND YEARS." Revelation xx: 2.

2. *The Title.* The Day of Christ.

"Being confident of this very thing, that he which hath begun a good work in you, will perform it until the Day of Jesus Christ."

"Till the Day of Christ." Philippians i: 6, 10.

"The Day of Christ." Philippians ii: 16.

3. *Definition of the Title.* The day in which Christ, the once rejected Messiah, will be owned by repentant Israel, and the subdued nations, as the Jewish king, and Jewish and Israelitish Lord of the whole earth; it is the day of the Christ, the day of the MESSIAH.

Characteristics. These are twenty-one in number. They may be separated into three sets of seven each.

The seven-fold manifestation of the Christ.

The seven-fold glory of Israel.

The seven-fold manner of rule.

THE SEVEN-FOLD MANIFESTATION OF CHRIST.

1. *At Jerusalem, as the man who was once crucified there.*

"This same Jesus, which is taken up from you into heaven, shall so come in like manner." Acts i: 11.

From Jerusalem he ascended, it is to Jerusalem he will return.

"Every eye shall see him, and they also which pierced him: and all kindreds of the earth (all the tribes of the land; the people of Israel in their own land) shall wail (*kópsontai,* a beating of the breasts, a wailing lamentation) because of him." Revelation i: 7.

"In that day shall there be a great mourning IN JERUSALEM * * * and the land shall mourn." Zechariah xii: 11, 12.

"They shall mourn for him (because of him), as one mourneth for his only son." Zechariah xii: 10.

"Sing and rejoice, O daughter of Zion: for, lo, I come, AND I WILL DWELL IN THE MIDST OF THEE." Zechariah ii: 10.

"Thus saith the Lord, *I am returned to Zion,* AND WILL DWELL IN THE MIDST OF JERUSALEM." Zechariah viii: 3.

"And he said unto me, Son of man, *the place of my throne,* AND THE PLACE OF THE SOLES OF MY FEET, WHERE I WILL DWELL IN THE MIDST OF THE CHILDREN OF ISRAEL FOREVER." Ezekiel xliii: 7.

"The name of the city from that day shall be THE LORD IS THERE." Ezekiel xlviii: 35.

After his return and the deliverance and gathering of Judah it is said:

"The Lord dwelleth in Zion." Joel iii: 21.

"The king of Israel, even the Lord, IS IN THE MIDST OF THEE." Zephaniah iii: 15.

"And his feet shall stand in that day upon the mount of OLIVES, WHICH IS BEFORE JERUSALEM ON THE EAST." Zechariah xiv: 4.

2. *As Son of Abraham. Inheritor of the Land of Palestine.*

"Jesus Christ, the Son of Abraham." Matthew i: 1.

To Abraham God said:

"I will give unto thee, and to *thy seed* after thee * * * all the land of Canaan, for an everlasting possession." Genesis xvii: 8.

"Now to Abraham and his seed were the promises made. He saith not, And to *seeds,* as of many; but as of one, And to thy *seed,* WHICH IS CHRIST." Galatians iii: 16.

3. *As Son of David, heir of the Throne.*

"Jesus Christ, the Son of David." Matthew i: 1.

"And the Lord God shall give unto him the throne of his FATHER DAVID:

AND HE SHALL REIGN OVER THE HOUSE OF JACOB FOREVER." Luke i: 32, 33.

"Upon the THRONE OF DAVID." Isaiah ix: 7.

4. *As Son of Man, executing judgment.*

"And hath given him authority to execute judgment also, BECAUSE HE IS THE SON OF MAN." John v: 27.

5. *As four-fold King.*

KING OF RIGHTEOUSNESS.

"Behold, a king shall reign in righteousness." Isaiah xxxii: 1.

KING OF ISRAEL.

"On the next day much people that were come to the feast, when they heard that Jesus was coming to Jerusalem,

Took branches of palm trees, and went forth to meet him, and cried, Hosanna! Blessed is THE KING OF ISRAEL." John xii: 13.

———————

KING OF KINGS.

"And on his thigh a name written, KING OF KINGS." Revelation xix: 16.

———————

KING OVER ALL THE EARTH.

"And the Lord shall be King over all the earth; in that day shall there be one Lord, and his name one." Zechariah xiv: 9. (his name one) : that is, Jesus; in proof read Philippians ii: 10, "At the *name of Jesus* every knee should bow, of things in heaven, and things in earth, and things under earth."

6. *As the mighty God, and God the Son.*

"For unto us (Israel) a child is born, unto us a son is given, and the government shall be upon his shoulder; and his name shall be called Wonderful, Counsellor, THE MIGHTY GOD." Isaiah ix: 6.

"The Lord, that made heaven and earth, bless thee OUT OF ZION."

The Lord who will be IN Zion at that time is the Lord Jesus Christ; he is here affirmed to be, as John in the first chapter of his gospel declares, the maker of heaven and earth; and therefore, indeed, the Mighty God.

"Unto the Son he saith * * * And, Thou, Lord, in the beginning hast laid the foundation of the earth; and the heavens are the works of thine hands." Hebrews i: 8, 10.

7. *As the Supreme Teacher of all the earth.*

"He will teach us of his ways; for out of Zion shall go forth the law, and the word of the Lord FROM JERUSALEM." Isaiah ii: 3.

"Yea, many people and strong nations shall come to seek the Lord of hosts IN JERUSALEM, and to pray BEFORE THE LORD." Zechariah viii: 22.

THE SEVEN FOLD GLORY OF ISRAEL.

1. *Israel and Judah restored to the land under their king.*

"Thus saith the Lord God, When I shall have gathered the house of Israel from the people among whom they are scattered, and shall be sanctified in them in the sight of the heathen (Gentiles), then shall they dwell in their land that I have given to my servant Jacob." Ezekiel xxviii: 25, 26.

"Thus saith the Lord God, Behold, I will take the children of Israel from among the heathen * * * and bring them into their own land:

And I will make them one nation in the land upon the mountains of Israel; and one king shall be king to them all; AND THEY SHALL BE NO MORE TWO NATIONS, neither shall they be divided into two kingdoms any more at all * * *

And David (The Beloved, The Christ), shall be king over them." Ezekiel xxxvii: 21-28.

"For I will take you from among the heathen and gather you out of all countries, and will bring you into your own land." Ezekiel xxxvi: 24.

Amos ix: 14, 15.

"Hear the word of the Lord, O ye nations, and declare it in the isles afar off, and say, He that scattered Israel will gather him, and keep him, as a shepherd doth his flock." Jeremiah xxxi: 10.

2. *Jerusalem will be rebuilt to the Lord.*

"Behold, the days come, saith the Lord, that the city shall be built to the Lord * * * it shall not be plucked up, nor thrown down, ANY MORE FOREVER." Jeremiah xxxi: 38, 40.

"And the city shall be builded upon her *own heap.*" Jeremiah xxx: 17-22.

"Then shall Jerusalem be holy." Joel iii: 17-21.

"In that day it shall be said to Jerusalem, Fear thou not * * * the Lord God in the midst of thee is mighty * * * I will make you a name and a praise among all people of the earth." Zephaniah iii: 14-20.

3. *The Temple will be rebuilt in splendor.*

For an account of this great work read Ezekiel chapter xl-xliii inclusive.

4. *The Twelve Apostles will rule over the reunited Twelve Tribes.*

"That ye may eat and drink at my table in my kingdom, and sit on thrones, judging (ruling) THE TWELVE TRIBES OF ISRAEL." Luke xxii: 30.

"Behold, a king shall reign in righteousness, and PRINCES (The Apostles) shall rule in judgment." Isaiah xxxii: 1.

5. *Restored and converted Israel will be the missionaries to the nations.*

"But ye shall be named the priests of the Lord; men shall call you the MINISTERS OF OUR GOD." Isaiah lxi: 6.

6. *Israel will be the Chamberlains of the King.*

"And there were certain Greeks among them that came up to worship at the feast (the passover):

The same came therefore (on Palm Sunday, the day when Jesus was proclaimed as King of Israel) to Philip (a Jew) * * * and desired him, saying, Sir, we would see Jesus.

Philip cometh and telleth Andrew: and again Andrew and Philip tell Jesus." John xii: 20-23.

"In those days it shall come to pass, that ten men shall take hold out of all languages of the nations (the ten nations), even shall take hold of the skirt of him that is a Jew, saying, We will go with you; for we have heard that God is with you." Zechariah viii: 23.

7. *Israel will be head over all the nations of the earth.*

"The Lord shall make thee Head and *not* the Tail." Deuteronomy xxviii: 13.

"For the nation and kingdom that will not serve thee shall perish; yea, those nations shall be utterly wasted." Isaiah lx: 12.

"For the Lord will have mercy on Jacob, and will yet choose Israel, and set them in their own land; and the strangers (the Gentiles) shall be joined with them, and they shall cleave to the house of Jacob.

And the people shall take them and bring them to their place; and the house of Israel shall possess them (the people, the Gentiles) in the land of the Lord for servants and handmaids; and they shall take them captives, whose captives they were; and they shall RULE OVER THEIR OPPRESSORS." Isaiah xiv: 1, 2.

"Thy children, whom Thou mayest make Princes in all the earth." Ps. xlv : 16.

THE SEVEN-FOLD MANNER OF RULE.

1. *Christ will rule with a rod of Iron.*

"Thou shalt break them with a rod of iron; thou shalt dash them in pieces like a potter's vessel." Ps. ii : 7-12.

"He must reign, till he hath put all enemies under his feet." I Corinthians xv : 25.

2. *By means of his judgments, the world will learn righteousness.*

"For when thy judgments are in the earth, the inhabitants of the world will learn righteousness." Isaiah xxvi : 9.

"Who so privily slandereth his neighbor, him will I cut off; him that hath an high look and a proud heart will I not suffer.

He that worketh deceit shall not dwell in my house; he that telleth lies shall not tarry in my sight.

I will *early* (in the first part of his reign) destroy all the wicked of the land, that I may cut off all wicked doers from the City of the Lord." Ps. ci : 5-8.

"Verily he is a God that judgeth in the earth." Ps. lviii : 11.

The Thousand years will be a *reign* of Righteousness."

Righteousness will not *dwell* in the earth till after the New Heavens and the New Earth.

"New heavens and a new earth, wherein dwelleth righteousness." II Peter iii : 13.

3. *The Church will reign and rule with Christ.*

"We shall also reign with him." II Timothy ii : 12.

Hebrews ii : 5-10.

"When Christ, who is our life, shall appear, then shall ye also appear with him in glory." Colossians iii: 4.

"To him that overcometh will I grant to sit with me in my throne, even as I also overcame and am set down with my Father in his throne." Revelation iii: 21.

"And hast made us unto our God kings and priests; and we shall reign on the earth (over the earth)." Revelation v: 1-10.

"The saints shall judge (rule) the world. I Corinthians vi: 2.

Corporately, the Church will remain in, and rule from, the heavens.

"But the saints of the most high (high places) shall take the kingdom." Daniel vii: 18, 27.

"And made us sit together in heavenly places in Christ Jesus." Ephesians ii: 6.

"I go to prepare a place for you." John xiv: 2.

Individually, Christians may reign on the earth.

The twelve Apostles will reign on the earth with Christ.

"When the Son of Man shall sit in the throne of his glory, ye also shall sit upon twelve thrones judging the twelve tribes of Israel." Matthew xix: 28. Luke xxii: 30.

"Then came the first * * * And he said unto him, have thou authority over ten cities."

"And he said likewise to him (the second), Be thou also over five cities." Luke xix: 15-19.

Rulership on earth in the kingdom is a matter altogether of reward.

All Christians go to heaven, but only those Christians who are deserving of reward will be permitted to come from heaven and take part in the thousand years on earth.

This truth brings into view the doctrine of rewards as related to the days of the kingdom.

"Every man's work shall be made manifest; for the day (the day of Christ) shall declare it, because it shall be revealed by fire; and the fire shall try every man's work of what sort it is.

If any man's work abide which he hath built thereupon (on that foundation other than which no man can lay, Jesus Christ), he shall receive a reward. If any man's work shall be burned (any Christian man's, of course), he shall suffer loss; but he himself shall be saved; yet so as by fire (through the fire; just as Lot had all his work burned up in Sodom; yet because he was in the covenant of God was brought out alive while the fire was falling)." I Corinthians iii: 10-15.

"Let no man beguile you of your reward." Colossians ii: 18.

"Look to yourselves, that we lose not those things which we have wrought but that we receive a full reward." II John viii.

"For the Son of Man shall come in the glory of his Father, with his angels, and then he shall reward every man according to his works." Matthew xvi: 27.

"And behold, I come quickly; and my reward is with me, to give every man according as his work shall be." Revelation xxii: 12.

Four kinds of crowns are held out as reward.

An incorruptible crown.

"Now they do it (run in a race) to obtain a corruptible crown; but we an incorruptible." I Corinthians ix: 25.

A crown of righteousness.

"Henceforth there is laid up for me a crown of righteousness, which the Lord, the righteous judge, shall give me at that day (day of Christ) : and not to me only, but unto all them also THAT LOVE HIS APPEARING." II Timothy iv : 8.

A reward offered for a thing implies that the thing for which the reward is offered is not common; or, is attended with trial and difficulty. This is the meaning here : reward for so apparently simple a thing as loving and necessarily longing for the appearing of Christ, is offered, because it is now, and will be more and more as this age goes on, a rare thing to find Christians desiring the Coming of the Lord; it will be more and more attended with trial for any Christian to take that attitude.

A crown of life.

"Blessed is the man that endureth temptation: for when he is tried, he shall receive the crown of life, which the Lord hath promised to them that love him." James i: 12.

A crown of Glory.

"And when the chief shepherd shall appear, ye shall receive a crown of glory that fadeth not away." I Peter v: 4.

The Greek term used to describe this crown is *amarán-tinon,* Amaranthine. The Amaranthine crown is specifically for those in the Church of Christ who have faithfully set forth the word of Christ during his absence. To this list of titular rewards may be added:

The morning star.

"He that overcometh, and keepeth my works unto the end, to him will I give power over the nations :

And he shall rule them with a rod of iron; as the vessels of a potter shall they be broken to shivers: even as I received of my Father.

And I will give him the morning star." Revelation
ii: 25-28.

The morning star comes before the day, and is seen
only by the watchers; consequently, it is the symbol of
those who in the deep spiritual night of earth, between
the midnight and the morn, wait and watch for the secret
sudden descent of the Lord, as the Bridegroom, to his
Church.

As it is possible to gain a crown, so is it possible to
lose a crown.

"Behold, I come quickly; hold that fast which thou
hast, that no man take thy crown." Revelation iii: 11.

This is illustrated by Luke xix: 24-26.

"And he said unto them that stood by, Take from him
the pound, and give it to him that hath ten pounds."

The function of the Church, corporately, is seen in
Revelation xx: 6.

"As *priests* of God they reign with him a thousand
years."

Their place is in the heavens; for the first time the
doctrine of the "Intercession of the Saints" has its full
meaning.

The function of the Church, individually, is set forth
in Revelation i: 6.

"Hath made us kings and priests."

Not only priests, but kings; and this kingliness to be
exercised as a matter of individual reward in relation to,
and upon the earth.

The Church will reign throughout all ages.

"Glory in the Church, throughout all ages"—*pásas
tàs genéas.* Ephesians iii: 21.

4. *There will be universal peace during the thousand
years.*

"Neither shall they learn war any more." Isaiah ii: 4.

"They shall not hurt nor destroy in all my holy mountain: for the earth shall be full of the knowledge of the Lord, as the waters cover the sea." Isaiah xi: 5-9. Isaiah lxv: 25.

5. *The earth will be made fruitful.*

"Then the earth shall yield her increase." Psalm lxvii: 4-6.

"The desert shall rejoice, and blossom as the rose." Isaiah xxxv: 1. Isaiah li: 3.

"And I will multiply the fruit of the tree and the increase of the field." All this, of course, specially in Israel. Ezekiel xxxvi: 30.

"There shall be showers of blessing." Ezekiel xxxiv: 26. Ezekiel xlvii: 9-12.

"The plowman shall overtake the reaper, and the treader of grapes him that soweth seed." Amos ix: 13.

6. *Human life will be prolonged.*

"For the child shall die an hundred years old." Isaiah lxv: 20.

"And the inhabitant shall not say, I am sick." Isaiah xxxiii: 24.

Life is here found to depend not on grace and overwatching providence, but on righteousness; a man will live as long as he is righteous, and no longer; death will be judgment on the life. Satan being bound, and the regenerating Lord enthroned in power, there will be no excuse for sin.

7. *The heavens will be opened to the view of earth.* They were open at the beginning.

They were open to Enoch, Elijah, Jesus, Paul.

They were wondrously opened to Jacob. Genesis xxviii: 10-12.

They will be opened by the Coming of the Son of God. Revelation xix: 11.

"And I saw heaven opened."

"I will hear the heavens, and they shall hear the earth." Hosea ii: 21. That is to say, there will be communication between them.

"And he saith unto him (Jesus to Nathanael), Verily, verily, I say unto you, Hereafter ye shall see heaven open, and the angels of God ascending and descending upon the Son of Man." John i: 51.

It is through these opened heavens that the city of God will be seen shining in all its celestial splendor. Revelation xxi: 9-27.

Proof that the view of the city given in the preceding verses is during the thousand years: the fact that there are nations on the earth, nations that walk in the light of it. There are no nations during the Eternal state.

This heavenly city so wonderfully described, is the place which our Lord went "to prepare." It is the abode of the Church corporately.

These are the great characteristics of the Thousand years.

THE PURPOSE OF GOD.

Two-fold.

1. To put down authority and power by a world-rejected man.

"When he shall have put down all rule and all authority and power." I Corinthians xv: 24.

2. To test man in the flesh, in a kingdom ruled by a heavenly man, on principles of divine righteousness.

THE ATTITUDE OF GOD.

Looking upon the world as filled with the enemies of Christ. "For he must reign till he hath put 'all enemies' under his feet." I Corinthians xv: 25. Psalms ii: 4-8.

"The Lord said unto my Lord, Sit thou at my right hand, until I make thine enemies thy footstool."

"The Lord shall send the rod of thy strength out of Zion: rule thou in the midst of thine enemies." Psalm cx: 1, 2.

THE ENDING.

The end of the thousand years comes with the loosing of Satan.

"And when the thousand years are expired, Satan shall be loosed out of his prison." Revelation xx: 7.

AFTER THE THOUSAND YEARS.

The Beginning. Revelation xx: 7, the loosing of Satan.

The Motive. To make a final test of man in the flesh through the agency of Satan.

The Order of events.

This order is eleven-fold.

1. *The missionary tour of the Devil.*

"And (the Devil) shall go out to deceive the nations which are in the four quarters of the earth." Revelation xx: 8.

2. *The nations deceived.* Revelation xx: 8.

Why are they deceived? How is it possible for men to be deceived by the Devil, when for a thousand years the earth has been full of the glory of God, and the presence of the Christ?

The answer is, that all who dwell on the earth are not truly regenerated; they give only feigned submission to the King of Kings and Lord of Lords. They are held in subjection, not by love to the Lord, but by the fact that Satan, their ally, is a bound prisoner in the bottomless pit. *Feigned faith* is all that they possess.

"The strangers (the Gentiles, or the sons of the Gentiles) shall submit themselves unto me (*submit;* on the margin it reads; lie, or, yield feigned obedience)." Psalm xviii: 44. Psalm lxvi: 3 (the margin the same). Psalm lxxxi: 15.

3. *The Great Apostasy.*

The coming up of the deceived nations, Gog and Magog. Revelation xx: 8, 9.

4. *The Great Fire Deluge.*

"And fire came down from God out of heaven, and devoured them." Revelation xx: 9.

"Upon the wicked he shall rain snares (quick burning coals), fire and brimstone, and an horrible tempest." Psalm xi: 6.

5. *The End of the Devil.*

"And the Devil that deceived them was cast into the lake of fire, and shall be tormented forever and ever." Revelation xx: 10.

6. *The Great White Throne.*

"And I saw a great white throne, and him that sat on it." Revelation xx: 11.

7. *The Great Dissolution.*

"The earth and the heaven fled away." Revelation xx: 11.

The word "fled" from which we get our English word "fugitive."

The old creation can no longer abide in the presence

of the throne sitter; he can no longer abide it, and it flees away, becomes a fugitive. It is dissolved by fire.

"The heavens shall pass away with a great noise, and the elements shall melt with fervent heat; the earth also, and the works that are therein, shall be burned up, * * * the heavens, being on fire, shall be dissolved, and the elements shall melt with fervent heat." II Peter iii: 5-7, 10-12.

Verse 7 shows that this dissolution is coincident with the White throne judgment.

"Reserved unto fire against the day of judgment and perdition of ungodly men."

The heavens will pass away with a great noise.

The heavens, *hoi ouranoi,* the atmospheric heavens.

"Pass away." *Pareleúsontai.* To disappear, vanish away.

"With a great noise" *hroizeedòn,* a whizzing, rushing sound.

"The elements shall melt with fervent heat."

The elementary forces, the gases, will be in combustion. Here is an immense chemical transaction; the heavens will be a vast sheet of flame; the earth will be enveloped as in a robe of fire. The earth will be melted, turned into a liquid state.

"The hills shall melt and flow down at his presence." Psalm xcvii: 5.

"Behold, the Lord maketh the earth empty; and maketh it waste, and turneth it upside down, and scattereth abroad the inhabitants thereof." Isaiah xxiv: 1.

Every scientific reason for this.

Astronomy predicts such to be the end of the world.

The world, however, is not to be completely destroyed.

This is evident from the use of the word "perish" in
II Peter iii: 5, 6.

"By the word of God the heavens were of old, and
the earth standing out of the water and in the water;

Whereby the world that then was, being overflowed
with water, perished."

The contour of the original earth was entirely changed
but the earth as to its material construction was not actually destroyed.

The earth will be shaken as in a sieve by the tremendous cataclysm through which it will pass, but things
that cannot be shaken will abide.

"That those things which cannot be shaken may remain." Hebrews xii: 27. Haggai ii.

It is simply melting the earth down in order that it
may be moulded over again; it is getting rid of the old
order for the new.

God will know how in the midst of these terrors to
take care of those who are his.

Those who are righteous need have no fear of the
burnings.

"Who among us shall dwell with the devouring fire?"
Isaiah xxxii.: 14.

"He that walketh righteously." Isaiah xxxiii: 15.

He will provide shelter for his earthly people.

"Come, my people, enter thou into thy chambers, and
shut thy doors about thee: hide thyself, as it were, for a
little moment, until the indignation be overpast." Isaiah
xxvi: 20.

"For, behold, the day cometh, that shall BURN AS
AN OVEN; and all the proud, yea, and all that do wickedly,
shall be stubble: and the day that cometh shall burn
them up, saith the Lord of hosts, that it shall leave them
neither root nor branch.

And ye shall tread down the wicked; for they shall be as ashes under the soles of your feet in the day that I shall do this, saith the Lord of hosts." Malachi iv: 1-3.

8. *The Universal Confession.*

"Wherefore God also hath highly exalted him, and given him a name which is above every name:

That at the name of Jesus every knee should bow, of things in heaven, and things in earth, and things under the earth;

And that every tongue should confess that Jesus Christ is Lord, to the glory of God the Father." Philippians ii: 10, 11.

That this is the moment for the confession is evident; it cannot be after the judgment, because at that moment Hades the under world is empty: hence, here and now, is the supreme moment; it is a confession, not unto salvation, but similar to that in James ii: 19.

"Thou believest that there is one God; thou doest well: the devils (demons, disembodied souls in Hades) believe, and TREMBLE."

A confession that comes too late.

9. *The Second Resurrection.*

"And I saw the dead, small and great, stand before God; and the books were opened: and another book was opened, which is the book of life: and the dead were judged out of those things which were written in the books, according to their works." Revelation xx: 12, 13.

Proof that this is the *second* resurrection:

"The rest of the dead lived not again until the thousand years were finished. This is the *first* resurrection." Revelation xx: 5, 6.

There is a first resurrection; it begins with the resurrection of Christ, and closes with his Coming.

"Every man in his own order; Christ the first fruits; afterwards they that are Christ's AT HIS COMING." I Corinthians xv: 23.

As there is no resurrection during the thousand years: as the resurrection recorded in verses 12, 13, is the only one mentioned after the thousand years, it must be the *second*, as it is, the last.

And this resurrection is called:

a. The Resurrection of the REST OF THE DEAD. Revelation xx: 5.

The word for "the rest" is *loipoi;* it comes from a verb which signifies, "to be left," "to be deserted," "to be left over, forsaken," "to be destitute." It means to be deficient.

What a picture!

These are the left over from the First Resurrection.

These are the "Deficients." "The Degenerates."

Deficient of the life which is alone in Christ Jesus, these are as a consequence the degenerates of eternity.

And, oh! horror! the "deserted," the "forsaken" through eternity.

b. The Resurrection of Shame. Daniel xii: 2.

c. Resurrection of the Unjust.

"There shall be a resurrection of the dead, both of the just and the UNJUST." Acts xxiv: 15.

d. The Resurrection of Damnation." John v: 29.

The word "damnation" is "judgment;" it is really "condemnation." Those who appear at that judgment have already been in the "prison" of Hades, and come forth only to receive final and public sentence.

Those who will appear at the Judgment Resurrection:

1. The unjust, the Christless dead. Acts xxiv: 15.

The unjustified, those who have not been justified through faith in our Lord Jesus Christ.

2. The Apostate Angels.

"For if God spared not the angels that sinned, but cast them down to hell (the word used here is *tartaros,* signifying lowest abyss, the lowest part of Hades,) and delivered them into chains of darkness (the word rendered "chains" reads "dens," "caves," "cells") to be RESERVED UNTO JUDGMENT. * * * The Lord knoweth how to reserve the unjust unto the day of judgment to be punished." II Peter ii: 4-9.

"And **the** angels which kept not their first estate (these are the sons of God who in the sixth chapter of Genesis came down and took the daughters of men for their wives) but left their own habitation, he hath reserved in everlasting chains, under darkness, unto the judgment of the great day." Jude. vi.

The Church will be the associate judge with Christ in that hour.

"The saints shall judge the world * * * we shall judge angels." I Corinthians vi: 2, 3.

"To execute upon them the JUDGMENT WRITTEN: this honor have ALL HIS SAINTS." Psalm cxlix: 6-9.

The judgment will be a judgment of Books.

The Book of Creation. Romans i: 20.

The Book of Conscience. Romans ii: 14-16.

The Book of the Law. Romans ii: 12.

The Book of the Gospel. Romans ii: 16.

The Book of Works. Revelation xx: 12.

The Book of Words and Speeches. Matthew xii: 37. Jude. xv.

The Book of Thoughts. Luke ii: 35.

The Book of Life. Revelation xx: 12.

All Secrets will be revealed.

"There is nothing covered, that shall not be revealed; and hid, that shall not be known." Matthew x: 26.

"The Secrets of Men." Romans ii: 16.

The deed for which the apostate angels will be judged.

"The Sons of God saw the daughters of men that they were fair; and they took them wives of all which they chose. * * * The angels which kept not their *first estate* (the word "estate" is *archéen,* a province, a country), but left their own habitation." Jude. vi.

"They which shall be accounted worthy to obtain * * * the resurrection from the dead (the First Resurrection) NEITHER MARRY, NOR ARE GIVEN IN MARRIAGE * * * they are EQUAL TO THE ANGELS." Luke xx: 35, 36.

Equality with the angels here signifies immortality; these angels then were immortal; as immortals do not marry, marriage was the sin of the angels; they descended from the realm of the immortal to the mortal.

In the light of this deed of the angels we have an explanation of Saint Paul's admonition to Christian women.

"For this cause ought the women to have power (the word used for "power" signifies a covering—a veil,) on her head, because of the angels." I Corinthians xi: 10.

There will be no probation at this Judgment.

"Between us and you there is a great gulf fixed." Luke xvi: 26.

Although the Book of Life is opened there is not one of all that throng whose name is written therein.

The proof. All who are Christ's take part in the First Resurrection.

During the Thousand years only the sinner and the accursed die. Ps. ci: 8. "I will early destroy all the wicked."

The Book of Life is the Golden Register bearing the

names of those who are in the bond of the covenants and who have life in Christ; the names of these, and these alone, are written therein.

The angels will call the name of each one who shall stand at that solemn bar; the Recording Angel will look at the golden page of the Book of Life, but will fail to find these names written there.

In the following passages will be found mention of the Book of Life:

Exodus xxxii: 32, Ps. lxix: 28, Isaiah iv: 3, Daniel xii: 1.

The final doom of all who take part in the Second Resurrection.

"And whosoever was not found written in the Book of Life was cast into the lake of fire." Revelation xx: 15.

10. *The New Heavens and Earth.*

"And I saw a new heaven and a new earth." Revelation xxi: 1.

The heavens made pure, and the old earth after its purifying fires made over again.

11. *The delivering up of the kingdom to the Father.*

"Then cometh the end, when he shall have delivered up the kingdom to God, even the Father." I Corinthians xv: 24.

Having as the Second Man restored all things that the First man marred; having undone all his evil work, our Lord Jesus Christ will hand this delivered and restored earth back to the Father.

THINGS RESTORED.

1. *The Nation of Israel.*

To their own Land.

To their King.

Themselves made the Memorial Nation of Eternity.

"For as the new heavens and the new earth, which I will make, shall remain before me, saith the Lord, so shall your seed and your name remain." Isaiah lxvi: 22.

"Thus saith the Lord, if heaven above can be measured, and the foundations of the earth searched out beneath, I will also cast off the seed of Israel.

"If these ordinances (of the heavens) depart from before me, then the seed of Israel also shall cease from being a nation before me forever." Jeremiah xxxi: 37, 36.

2. *Man restored to the image and likeness of God.*

That is to say he will be the representative of God authoritatively and morally.

But he will get far more in the Restoration than he lost by the Fall.

He will be an Immortal, deathless Son of God; the enthronement and manifestation of God in the flesh. God Incarnate.

3. *The Earth restored to God.*

Not as it is found at the end of the six-days creation, but as it was in that primeval creation recorded in the first verse of Genesis; and before it fell into chaos.

It will go back to that undescribed hour when "In the Beginning, God created the heaven and the earth."

Thus God gets his world back again; that world whose pristine beauty was first marred by Satan; that world which after its first re-creation was again stolen from him by the great adversary.

But he gets it back with *Plus*.

Plus the Church of Christ.

That is to say, a race far above what Adam would have been, if he never had fallen.

A race far above Satan and his angels, to whom he first gave it.

A race superior to the fairest angels of his realm; for these we are told are to be the messengers and servants of the Church. Hebrews i: 14.

A race of God's own perfect Sons, each son a perfect God-man.

THE BOOK OF JEREMIAH.

The Book of Jeremiah.

The proper title for this book is: "The Day of Jacob's Trouble."

Characteristically, the book might be called "A Treatise on Verbal Inspiration." Out of fifty chapters, at least forty begin with a "thus saith the Lord," or its cognate terms.

Subjects of the book:

Israel's sins; Threatened judgment and final captivity of Judah in Babylon; Destruction of Jerusalem; Restoration of a part of all Israel; The Day of Jacob's Trouble under Antichrist; Restoration of the Ten Tribes; Rebuilding Jerusalem to the Lord ; Millennial glories; Christ in the land; Closes with the captivity of Judah.

Key words:

Chapter xxx: 7. "Jacob's Trouble."

Chapter xxx: 18. "The City shall be builded upon her own heap."

Chapter i: 9. "Behold I have put my words in thy mouth."

Chapter xv: 16. "Thy words were found, and I did eat them; and thy word was unto me the joy and rejoicing of mine heart."

Historic Periods. The reigns of Josiah, Jehoiakim, and Zedekiah.

Scriptures to read. II Kings. Chapters, 22, 23 and 25.

Contents of Chapters:

Chapter 1. Call and message of Jeremiah.

Chapter 2. Arraignment of Israel. They forsake the Fountain of Living waters and seek broken cisterns that can hold no water.

Chapter 3. The Ten Tribes are carried away because of idolatry. Judah repents not and is more sinful than the Ten. The Lord invites the Ten to come back. He promises to receive them in blessing. A view of the final restoration of both houses. Jerusalem seen to be the Throne of the Lord in the Last Days.

Chapter 4. The coming anguish and desolation of Jerusalem.

Chapter 5. Judah a rebellious and revolting heart.

Chapter 6. Reprobate Silver.

Chapter 7. The Temple of God become a den of thieves.

Chapter 8. The stork, the turtle, and the crane know their seasons as appointed of God, but Israel, the people of God, know not his judgments.

Chapter 9. The sin of Judah finds judgment in the tears of Jeremiah.

Chapter 10. A warning to the Ten Tribes wherever they may be.

Chapter 11. Judgment and woe gathering for Judah.

Chapter 12. Judah to be plucked out of the land.

Chapter 13. The nation of Judah as unable to change its ways as the Ethiopian his skin, or the leopard his spots.

Chapter 14. A testimony of sin.

Chapter 15. God's word precious to a faithful witness in an hour of sin.

Chapter 16. The Ten Tribes though lost to the view

of man, not lost to the eyes of God. He will find and
bring them back again.

Chapter 17. The cursed man: He who maketh flesh
his arm: The blessed man: He who trusteth in the Lord.

The character of the human heart. Deceitful above
all things, and desperately wicked. Unfathomable by
the science and wisdom of man it is, and can be, known
only to God. And this heart, in the heart of Judah, cul-
minated in a wickedness of which man himself has never
yet realized the enormity, the murder of God's Son; and
this wickedness God had seen and anticipated. And
therefore it is, that here he raises the question, "Who
can know it?"

Chapter 18. Helpless as the clay in the hands of the
potter, why should man, the vessel, rebel against God
his Maker?

Chapter 19. Like a potter's broken vessel, Jerusalem
is to be.

Chapter 20. Hatred of truth puts its witness in the
stocks.

The folly of the Devil, and the madness of man, to
attempt to arrest the truth by such a barricade on the
highway of God's plan and purpose.

Chapter 21. Doomed to go to Babylon.

Chapter 22. All the earth called to witness God's
uttered word against Judah; by this Judah is set before
all the earth as the living and historic seal on the truth
of the written word of God.

Chapter 23. The Coming of Christ, Restoration of
Israel, and the Millennial kingdom.

Judah ordained to stay in Babylon seventy years.

Chapter 26. The death of the speaker plotted, as
though the silence of human lips could silence the lips
of God.

Chapter 27. Rulership in the earth, as under the Providence and ordering of God, transferred from the Jew to the Gentile, in Nebuchadnezzar.

Chapter 28. A false prophet puts a lie against the truth of God and is slain by him in the shame of his lie; for God reiterates his will that the rule of the earth shall be in the hands of the Gentiles.

Chapter 29. After seventy years Judah shall return.

Chapter 30.

1. Judah and part of Israel to be brought back. Verses 2, 3.

2. Day of Jacob's Trouble; spoken of by our Lord in Matthew xxiv: 21.

3. Antichrist arises and is overthrown by the coming of the Christ. Verse 8.

4. Christ will be the blessed King. Verse 9.

5. The City will be rebuilt. Verse 18.

6. The people re-established. Verses 18-22.

7. The glory of the promised kingdom to be brought in by judgments at the Coming of the King. Verses 23-24.

Chapter 31. Restoration.

Chapter 32. The chapter of the Title Deeds.

Jerusalem is besieged. The prophet is in prison. He buys land of his cousin and takes title deeds of the purchase. All this witnesses that in spite of coming captivity, dispersion, and ages of wandering, the Lord holds the title to the land, and will bring his people back, and give it to them. Verses 6-44.

It is in the light of this Jeremiah chapter that we are to read the fifth chapter of the book of Revelation; singing, because of all it means, with the inspired and heavenly choristers, who fill that chapter with their triumphant praise.

In that fifth chapter, the Lord Jesus Christ, the Risen One in the courts of Glory, is seen to take out of the hands of the Father, a book sealed with seven seals within and without. The moment he takes this seal all the voices of the redeemed break forth in song, declaring that the Son of God shall take the kingdom and reign; and that they who have been redeemed by his blood shall reign with him over the earth. The breaking of the seals which follows, is the series of judgments by which the Lord enters into the possession of the land, and the kingdom of his purchase. In Jeremiah therefore we have typically and prophetically the indication, that in spite of all the conditions in Israel, the Lord would yet set up the covenanted kingdom; and that it would be restored and set up on the basis of a purchase price paid by the king; Revelation gives us in symbol the hour and the process by which the Lord will enter into the power and joy of that possession; as the scene in Revelation takes place after we get a picture of the Church raptured to heaven, then it is evident that the kingdom with all it means of restoration to Israel and glory to the Church, will not take place till after the Lord at his Parousia descends into the air *for* his church. Jeremiah xxii, and Revelation v explain each other; and because they do so, though written pages apart, bear witness that both were written by the same spirit; both are inspired of God.

Chapter 33. The Full Restoration chapter.

Chapter 34. All Judah shall be bondsmen in Assyria because they refused to proclaim liberty to the bondsmen in their own land.

Chapter 35. The Rechabite chapter.

The Rechabites promised their father never to drink wine, or to build houses.

They kept the word of their father, and by this became a living witness against Israel, who kept not the word of their God. Because of their faithfulness, God gives them a man to stand before him forever.

In this incident we have a resplendent fore-picture of the Church.

1. The Rechabite comes in after the Jew has been judicially set aside. Only after the Jew has been judged of God, and set aside because of his failure as to the Living Word, does the Church come into view.

2. The Rechabite drinks no wine.

Wine is a symbol of earthly joy. The church is not to find her joy in earthly sources.

3. The Rechabite lives in a tent, he is a pilgrim and a stranger during all his life. Concerning the Church the Apostle says in Philippians iii: 20, 21, that the Christian is the citizen of a country which is in heaven; and the Apostle Peter declares that the Christian is a "pilgrim and a stranger" in the earth.

4. The Rechabite was governed by the word of his father.

The Christian must be governed by the word of God; it is to be the rule of his faith and practice.

5. A man was in the presence of God for them continually.

The Church has a man in the presence of God who "ever liveth to make intercession."

Chapter 36. The Penknife chapter.

The king in Israel does not like God's written word. He takes a penknife, cuts out the leaves that are displeasing to him, and casts them into the fire. God commanded that the book should be rewritten, and the judgments reaffirmed.

The age in which we live is a penknife chapter in the book of time. The record of this age is, that men occupying the position of authority in the church of Christ, with the penknife of Rationalism and Higher Criticism, cut out of the word of God all those passages which, by virtue of their conflict with human reason or human judgment, fail to please them, and cast them into the fire, kindled by the human intellect. ·But just as the book in the days of Jeremiah came forth from the fire kindled on the hearth of the king's palace, so the word of the living God in our day or in any day of assault, will arise from the fires of human judgment, and be reaffirmed to the heart and conscience of men. The king who so easily served himself of the penknife in those far-away days, and imagined that he had completely nullified that which was written, has long ago passed out of the realm of time, and is only remembered as the weakling who endeavored to measure his little concept against the thought of God. He is gone, but the book remains, and over the fulfillment of the judgments of God against Israel as foretold by Jeremiah, we read the verified assurance that this word is settled in the heavens forever.

Chapter 37. Cast into prison the prophet comes forth to speak again the same message; whatever may be the variable experience of the ambassador of God, the word remains unchanged; and he who would speak it at all, is forced to speak it in its unchangeableness.

Chapter 39. Jerusalem taken.

Chapter 40. Jeremiah spared and allowed of God to remain in the land with a few.

Chapter 41. The remaining few add rebellion to rebellion.

Chapter 42. God will forgive, and make the few the beginning of the Restoration, if they will abide in the land, and not go down into Egypt. Otherwise he will punish.

Chapter 43. The "Sinful People" refuse the word of the Lord, and deliberately go down into Egypt.

Chapters 44 and 45. Threatened judgments on those who go down into Egypt.

Chapters 46-49. Judgments of God against Gentile nations whom he has used in the correction of his people. Verses 27-28.

Chapters 50 and 51. The kingdom of Antichrist. Babylon his capital. His capital destroyed to make way for the revelation of the kingdom from Heaven.

The words of Jeremiah end here with the overthrow of Babylon and the coming Exaltation of Jerusalem; and it is to be noticed that whenever the one is down, the other is always up.

Chapter 52. Appendix. Details of the plucking out and Captivity of Judah.

Thus this book of Jeremiah is the witness of Israel's sin, God's forbearance, his warnings, his grace, the terribleness of his judgments, and the accuracy of his word.

Israel is shown to be without excuse; every footstep witnesses to the grace and truth of God.

In reading Jeremiah we learn that the wages of sin is death. God keepeth faith with his word for evil as well as good; for wrath as well as grace. And as Israel stands convicted on the page of history, so will every unbelieving soul stand convicted at the bar of God; and of each it will be asked as the prophet asked of Judah, "What wilt thou say when he shall punish thee?"

Thus in sum, the book shows Israel indicted, convicted, condemned, and God justified in all his ways.

Concerning Jeremiah it may be said: His ministry began in, and ran through a period of absolute apostasy. The Ten Tribes had been carried away because of their idolatry; a few families remained. These united with Judah to plunge deeper into sin, into idolatry, and all shameful social practices.

Under Josiah there was a measure of reform, but under Jehoiakim and Zedekiah there was complete departure from God, and iniquity cried aloud for judgment.

On such a background the testimony of Jeremiah could be nothing less than an arraignment; no matter how promiseful might be at times his message, the burden of it must be that of denunciation and judgment.

So intense was his testimony in this direction, that his very name has passed into a sort of by-word to express denunciation and bitter lamentation; when we wish to indicate a railing, or utterance that is more than usually intense in pessimism and bitterness, we use the word, *jeremiad.*

Such a testimony could produce but one result upon a people who had so completely departed from the living God. It angered them, brought out in them a feeling of hatred for the prophet who dared to speak God's truth, and expose them.

They did what all guilty people do; they turned upon him, and denounced him as a scold, a discord, and a defamer; they endeavored to minimize his value, defamed him at every turn, sought to involve his speech against himself, find in him occasion to prove the dishonesty of his life, and finally resorted to violence against him.

Such a response to testimony carried with it two distinct tests for Jeremiah: it would test him not only in faithfulness to the word, but to the value of the word for himself. It would also test the exact ratio of interest he had in the people; how far their sins and their threatened future affected him.

He responded to both tests. Not only did he reaffirm under every trial the ministry committed to him, but he made manifest that he rejoiced in the word of God as one that findeth great spoil. He said: "Thy words were found, and I did eat them; and thy word was unto me the joy and rejoicing of my heart."

He met the test in regard to the people; not only did he measure their defaming by the distance in which they stood from God, and therefore, their blindness, spiritual arrogance and helplessness, but he entered into and became a very part of their condition; so that he felt their very sins and wickedness, and shivered in anticipation of their coming woes. So deeply did he enter in, that tears were his meat and his drink night and day. So deep, that he stood forth in the midst of his people a veritable man of sorrows and acquainted with grief.

He had courage.

No man could have stood alone as he stood with every finger pointed at him, without friends, the object of contempt and scorn, and his life hanging in the balance of some careless caprice, unless he had been endowed with courage. But his courage found its source in the unshaken faith that he was speaking the very truth, the actual words of God.

Such facts carry with them their own lessons; they teach us clearly enough the necessity for, and the reward of unfailing conviction in, the message of God. No more sublime evidence of that faith which acts against the evidence of sight has ever been given, than in the

real estate transaction between Jeremiah and his cousin.
Shut up in prison, the city besieged, knowing by the
warning of God that the enemy would be victorious, his
people led away captive for seventy years, and the land
to lie desolate and unoccupied, he nevertheless buys
the field in Anathoth, subscribes and takes evidences of
purchase. He does this easily in the face of all the re-
monstrances of common sense, because he believes the
promise of God that his people shall be restored. It is
a direct walking in the faith of coming to-morrows.

The subsequent history of the nation confirmed the
word of God, and justified the faith of his servant. The
history of the people in all the ages since, has been as
much a justification of the prophet, as of the Lord he
served. Time has shown the deeper and longer range
of his prophetic vision. The fires which burned his
writings have gone out, but the word he wrote is rewritten on every page of Judah's history. The events
that shall set up the platform on which the Day of
Jacob's Trouble is yet to be displayed in all its lurid magnificence, the overthrow of iniquity, the replacing of all
Israel, the exaltation of Jerusalem, and the song of a reunited and regenerated people in Immanuel's land, and in
Immanuel's presence, will yet proclaim, not only that the
word spoken by Jeremiah was the word of God, but that
this man, the man who wished that his head were waters,
and his eyes a fountain of tears; this man of the sorrowful countenance, mocked of men, denied of kings,
plunged in the mire of dungeons, and the deeper mire of
human contumely and scorn; that this man was indeed
a man of God, God's own prophet, telling him out in the
ears of men for truth, both in judgment and in grace;
and in that hour when the King cometh to his own again,

holding in his hands the Title Deeds of that Holy land, sealed with his blood as its purchase price, not among the least of those to whom he shall speak in gentleness, and to whom his hand shall give special and shining reward, will be this man, who shrank at first in fear and trembling from the exalted call, but rose up to the height of his immense privilege, the moment he realized he was called to speak and proclaim the very words that God himself had breathed; not the least among them all, shall be this man, the prophet Jeremiah.

As a deeply suggestive lesson of God's foreknowledge and definite ways, let it be remembered that before Jeremiah was conceived, or formed in time, God had foreseen and ordained him to this very hour and work.

Thus from beginning to end, Jeremiah was completely removed from the realm of accident, both in constitution and career, and stands forth as the concrete manifestation of the will, the wisdom, and the purpose of God. And it suggests to us how, if we will own God in this high relationship to ourselves; if we will see that our life from beginning to end has been as much planned as the whole creation of God; and that from the beginning, as in all the way, we have been, and are, as much in the thought of God as was Jeremiah, then we may walk continually in an atmosphere of Divine fellowship, Divine assurance, and unclouded peace, knowing that as we are in the changeless purpose of our God, so all things shall work together to our good, for our glory, and for his.

THE CHURCH.

The Church.

The word Church is the Greek word *Ecclesia,* "The called out."

Doctrinally, the Church is a body of persons called out by the power of God, to faith in a Crucified and Risen Christ, having had wrought in them by the Spirit and the Word, the nature of the Risen Christ, indwelt by the Spirit, made members one of another, and linked by that Spirit to the Risen Man in the Heavens.

This is the Church.

Note:

1. Historically, the Church had no existence before the resurrection of Christ.

"Which in other ages was not made known unto the sons of men, as it is now revealed unto his holy apostles and prophets by the Spirit." Ephesians iii: 1-5, 9-10.

The Patriarchs, such as Abraham, Isaac, Jacob, and Joseph, were not in the Church; they were quickened by the Spirit, but not united to a Risen Man in the Heavens; and this, from the simple fact, that at that time, such a person as a Risen Man was not yet manifested.

2. The Church had no existence when Christ was on the earth. The Church was yet future.

"I WILL build my church." Matthew xvi: 18.

The mission of Christ as the minister of the Circumcision was exclusively to the lost sheep of the house of Israe'

"Now I say that Jesus Christ was a minister of the Circumcision for the truth of God, to confirm the promises made unto the fathers." Romans xv: 8.

"But he answered and said, I am not sent but unto the lost sheep of the house of Israel." Matthew xv: 24.

"These twelve Jesus sent forth, and commanded them, saying, go not into the way of the Gentiles. * * * But go rather to the lost sheep of the house of Israel." Matthew x: 5, 6.

"And set up over his head, his accusation written, THIS IS JESUS THE KING OF THE JEWS." Matthew xxvii: 37.

3. The resurrection of Christ was the beginning of the Church.

On the day that Christ arose from the dead he breathed on his disciples, and by that act quickened them into vital union with himself as the Risen One, thus uniting them to one another in himself, and forming the living, mystic, and spiritual body, the Church; *this hour was the birth hour of the Church.*

"He breathed on them, and saith unto them, Receive ye the Holy Ghost." John xx: 22, 23.

On the day of Pentecost the Spirit was made manifest in the earth, as the witness of the risen Christ; and then, and there, the Lord baptized the disciples, in the Spirit, into the body in which, and through which, he was henceforth to manifest himself on the earth. On that day the Spirit deposited in this spiritual body all the gifts and powers required for service in the name of an ascended Lord.

"For by (IN) one Spirit are we all baptized into one body." I Corinthians xii: 13.

"There are diversities of gifts, but the same Spirit. But all these worketh that one, and the self-same spirit, dividing to every man severally as he will." I Corinthians xii: 4-11.

In Acts xi, you have the Church passing out of the confines of Judaism.

In Acts xiii: 42-44, you find the Church broadening to receive the Gentiles.

In Acts xv: 14-17, you have the purpose of God in this age to take out from among the Gentiles a people for his name.

"Simeon hath declared how God at the first did visit the Gentiles, to take OUT OF THEM a people for his name." Acts xv: 14.

God's name in this age is THE CHRIST; the name of his people therefore must be Christians. This age, consequently, is the Christian age, the age of the Calling Out, the Church age.

4. The Church, doctrinally, was alone fully revealed to Paul.

"For this cause I Paul, the prisoner of Jesus Christ for you Gentiles,

If ye have heard of the DISPENSATION OF THE GRACE OF GOD which is *given to me* to you-ward.

How that by REVELATION he made known unto me the MYSTERY (as I wrote afore in few words),

Whereby, when ye read, ye may understand my knowledge in the MYSTERY OF CHRIST:

Which in other ages was not made known. * * * Unto me, who am less than the least of all saints, is this grace given, that I should make known among the Gentiles the unsearchable riches of Christ." Ephesians iii: 1-8.

The Church is a mystery hidden from the beginning of the world in God, and known only to God.

"The MYSTERY which from the beginning of the world hath been HID IN GOD, who CREATED ALL THINGS BY JESUS CHRIST." Ephesians iii: 9.

5. The Church is the New Man.

"For to make in himself One New Man." Ephesians ii: 15.

A new, immortal, divine race of men; the answer to God's proposition in Genesis i: 26. "Let us make man in our image."

In Genesis we find that Adam and Eve were called by a common name: "He called *their* name Adam." Genesis v: 2.

Adam and Eve, typically, set forth Christ and his Church; therefore we find that Christ and his Church have a common name:

"For as the body is one, and hath many members, and all the members of that one body, being many, are one body; so also is Christ." I Corinthians xii: 12.

The word Christ is preceded by the article, "The Christ." And thus the name Christ is given to the Church, as the body of him who is called, also, the Christ.

6. The Church is the Body of Christ.

"The Church which is his body." Ephesians i: 22, 23.

"For his body's sake, which is the Church." Colossians i: 24.

"Now ye are the body of Christ." I Corinthians 12: 20.

"So we, being many, are one body in Christ." Romans 12: 5.

7. The Church is prospectively the Bride of Christ.

"For this cause shall a man leave his father and mother, and shall be joined unto his wife, and they two shall be one flesh.

This is a great mystery: but I speak concerning Christ and the Church." Ephesians v: 31, 32.

Christ "the man" left his father in Heaven, and Mary his mother on earth; cutting off all ties he was joined for death and life, unto the Church, as her husband; she is his affianced, and the marriage must necessarily be in the future.

"Let us be glad and rejoice: for the marriage of the Lamb is come, and his wife hath made herself ready." Revelation xix: 7.

"Come hither and I will show thee the bride, the Lamb's wife." Revelation xxi: 9.

8. Ministry in the Church is a gift from the ascended Lord to his Body on the earth.

Ephesians iv: 7-12.

"And GOD hath set some in the church; first, apostles; secondarily, prophets; thirdly, teachers; after that, miracles; then gifts of healings, helps, governments, diversities of tongues." I Corinthians xii: 28.

There is a vast difference between Ministry and Priesthood.

The priest reveals man to God; the minister reveals God to man.

Priesthood on earth is a witness that man is at a certain distance from God; ministry is a witness that God has entered into communion with man: that he is ready to reveal his mind, his thought, his intimate feelings.

In the Church of Christ there is no separate class of priests; all are spiritual priests.

"Ye also, as lively stones, are built up, a spiritual house, an holy priesthood, to offer up spiritual sacrifices, acceptable to God by Jesus Christ." I Peter ii: 5.

The attempt to set up a class of priests in the church who shall have rule and authority over their brethren, is repudiated and rebuked by the significant passage in Hebrews viii: 4. "For if HE were on earth, HE SHOULD

NOT BE A PRIEST, seeing that there are priests that offer gifts according to the law."

Note here:

1. If Christ were on earth he would not be a priest.

2. If he were on earth he would recognize priesthood alone in Israel, in the tribe of Levi, in the family of Aaron.

3. Israel is not the Church; on the contrary, something wholly different.

4. As priesthood on earth belongs exclusively to the people of Israel, then there is no priesthood on earth in the church, except that spiritual priesthood which belongs to all believers.

5. As Christ himself *was not,* and if he were on the earth to-day *would not* be a priest, then it becomes not only absurd but sinful, for any class of men in the Church, to exalt themselves into an office that the head of the church not only never occupied, but which by the express revelation of the spirit, he declares he *could not* occupy if he were *with* his church.

6. As Christ is priest in Heaven alone, and alone for those who are represented as seated in Heavenly places in Him, then the moment the Church accepts priesthood on earth, she not only sets aside and loses the Priesthood of Christ, but places herself on Jewish ground, under law, and outside of Grace; in short, priesthood in the Church, apart from that common to all Believers, is as much a senseless blunder as a spiritual crime. The Scriptures emphatically declare that there is no hierarchal class of men in the Church.

The common distinction between Clergy and Laity, growing out of this hierarchal idea, has no warrant in the word of God; on the contrary, the *whole Church* is called the *clergy* of God.

"Neither as being lords over God's heritage, but being ensamples to the flock." I Peter v: 3.

The word rendered heritage is *kleros;* from which we get our word, *Clergy.* It is spiritual arrogance for any member of the Church of Christ to call himself a CLERGY-man in distinction to, and as indicating an official superiority over, the rest of the Church.

Elders and Bishops are not mentioned among the gifts to the Church.

These were appointed by the Churches and approved or appointed by the Apostles.

"And when they had ordained them Elders in every Church." Acts xiv: 23.

Elders and Bishops are identical.

"For this cause left I thee in Crete, that thou shouldest set in order the things that are wanting, and *ordain Elders* in every city, as I had appointed thee:

For a Bishop must be blameless, &c." Titus i: 5, 7.

The Elders which are among you I exhort, who am also an Elder, and a witness of the sufferings of Christ, and also a partaker of the glory that shall be revealed:

Feed the flock of God which is among you, taking OVERSIGHT." I Peter v: 1, 2.

By these passages we learn that an Elder is an officer having oversight of the flock; one who has oversight is an OVERSEER, an overseer, in the Greek, is a Bishop; a Bishop and an Elder then, are one and the same.

The word Elder signifies the character of the *person* bearing office: according to Apostolic precedent he must be an elderly man. The word Bishop sets forth the character of the *office* which the Elder bears; it is oversight, overseeing the flock.

Bishop and Elder do not exist at all to-day. They do

not exist because there are no longer Apostles or Apostolic delegates to approve their election by the Church.

The Pastor is a Gift to the Church.

In the true sense, a Pastor cannot be ordained by any set of men, or called, or elected by any assembly; he is a Pastor by divine ordination, altogether superior to any mere human planning; and any Church which has a Pastor, has him by the Providence and "Call of God," exclusively.

A Pastor signifies a shepherd.

"And I will give you pastors according to mine heart, which shall feed you with knowledge and understanding." Jeremiah iii: 15.

His office is to feed, not with the bread and meat that sustain the flesh, but with the knowledge and understanding, that come alone through the ministration of the Word.

"He saith unto him, Feed my lambs.

He saith unto him, Feed my sheep." John xxi: 15, 16.

An Evangelist is one who publishes the Gospel, who points to the open door of God's grace, and invites the hungry to enter in that they *may* be fed.

A Teacher is one who sets forth the doctrine and the related truths of the Word, building up, and setting in order the Christian life.

The Pastor is one who *divides* the truth to the flock, or assembly, over whom God hath appointed him.

There may be, in the providence of God, more than one pastor sent to a Church.

Deacons are officers appointed by the Church.

They are never to be ordained.

A Deacon signifies a *servant*.

Let it be kept well in mind that *Office* in the Church is not a gift; office is a local matter concerning such and such an assembly.

9. The Church is to assemble for worship, and that worship, is to be in the Breaking of Bread.

"And upon the first day of the week, WHEN THE DISCIPLES CAME TOGETHER TO BREAK BREAD." Acts xx: 7.

The Church and the world are not to be mixed together in public assembly.

10. The Church meets officially on the first day of the week.

"And upon the FIRST DAY OF THE WEEK WHEN THE DISCIPLES CAME TOGETHER." Acts xx: 7.

11. The Church is a building.

"Ye are God's building." I Corinthians iii: 9.

A building in process of construction.

"In whom all the building, fitly framed together, groweth unt a holy temple in the Lord:

In whom ye also are builded (Greek, *being builded*) together for an habitation of God through the Spirit." Ephesians ii: 21, 22.

12. The Church, considered in assembly relations, is presented to Christ as a Virgin.

"For I have espoused you to one husband, that I may present you as a chaste virgin to Christ." II Corinthians xi: 2.

The characteristics of a Betrothed Virgin are: Chastity, separateness, and faithfulness to the one to whom betrothed.

13. Jesus is now the absent Bridegroom, preparing a place for the reception of the Bride.

"I go to prepare a place for you." John xiv: 2.

14. He will come again for the Church.

"And if I go and prepare a place for you, I will come again, and receive you unto myself; that where I am, there ye may be also." John xiv: 3.

"Then shall the kingdom of heaven be likened unto ten virgins, which took their lamps, and went forth to meet the Bridegroom. * * * The Bridegroom came; and they that were ready went in with him to the marriage." Matthew xxv: 1-10.

15. He will present her to himself.

"Christ also loved the Church, and gave himself for it;

That he might sanctify and cleanse it with the washing of water by the word,

That he might present it to himself a glorious Church, not having spot, or wrinkle, or any such thing; but that it should be holy and without blemish." Ephesians v: 25-27.

16. He will marry the Church as his wife; marriage signifies union; this marriage union is set forth in the declaration of Saint Paul in Ephesians v: 30: "For we are members of his body, of his flesh, and of his bones."

This union will be fully manifested in resurrection.

"And God hath both raised up the Lord, and will also raise up us by his own power.

Know ye not that your *bodies* are the members of Christ? * * * He that is joined unto the Lord is ONE SPIRIT." I Corinthians vi: 14-17.

"For the Lord himself shall descend from heaven with a shout, with the voice of the archangel, and with the trump of God; and the dead in Christ shall rise first;

Then we which are alive and remain, shall be caught up together with them in the clouds, to meet the Lord in the air." Thessalonians iv: 16, 17.

17. The Church will be taken away before the Tribulation.

"I also will keep thee from the hour of temptation, which shall come upon all the world, to try them that dwell upon the earth." Revelation iii: 10.

There are many evidences that the Church will not go through the Tribulation.

The Tribulation is distinctively Jewish.

"Alas! for that day is great, so that none is like it: it is even THE TIME OF JACOB'S TROUBLE." Jeremiah xxx: 7.

The location of this trouble is pre-eminently in Judea.

"Then let them which be in JUDEA flee into the mountains." Matthew xxiv: 16.

The legitimate division of the book of Revelation places the Tribulation after the "DOOR IN HEAVEN IS OPENED, AND JOHN, AS THE TYPE OF THE TRUE CHURCH, IS CAUGHT UP."

After this (after the repudiation of the professing Church in Laodicea) I looked and behold, a door was opened in heaven; and the first voice which I heard was as it were of a trumpet talking with me; which said, "Come up hither * * * and immediately I was in the Spirit." Revelation iv: 1, 2.

The twenty-four elders seen in the fourth and fifth chapters are the Church; The church is seen enthroned in the heavens with Christ in the fourth chapter; in the fifth she is heard breaking forth into songs of exultant praise concerning the kingdom yet to be established on the earth. Then you get the sorrow and anguish of the sixth chapter, the turmoil and tribulation on the earth; after this you have the seventh chapter; not a word is said there which by any possibility can be construed in relation to the Church; on the contrary, all the nomenclature denies the presence of the Church. The seventh chapter gives the picture of a sealed number among the Jews; the eighth chapter records a great multitude of Gentiles coming up out of the tribulation; all the time this is going on the Church, symbolized by the Twenty-four Elders in the fourth and fifth chapters, is seen in the heavens with Christ, above the storm, the torment, the darkness, and the tribulation going on below.

The very phraseology of Revelation iii: 10, ought to settle the matter; not only is the direct promise given by the Lord to the Church that he will keep her out of the hour of tribulation, but the characteristic which he gives to those who are to pass through it, as those "that DWELL ON THE EARTH," ought to be all sufficient to deliver any expositor from the ruinous blunder of putting the Church through such an uncalled-for trial. The Church of Christ, considered from God's point of view, does not "dwell on the earth."

As to the earth, the Church is a stranger and a pilgrim; "strangers and pilgrims." I Peter ii: 2. According to Saint Paul in Philippians iii: 20, 21, she is a "citizen of that country which is in Heaven; and in Ephesians we are told, in unmistakable language, that as a Church we "sit together in HEAVENLY PLACES in Christ Jesus." Ephesians ii: 6.

The Tribulation has to do with people on the earth, and whose habitation is to be on the earth. The Church is not earthly in any aspect. According to the mind of God, as Christians, we have been taken out of the world in the resurrection and ascension of our Lord, we have then been sent back into the earth in the name of the rejected and absent king, as his ambassadors, to represent him, to walk through the world as those who, being away from home and on their way home, are waiting the sound of the voice which John heard, the voice of a trumpet talking with them, and calling them up into heaven through the "opened door." To talk of the trial and sifting of a heavenly people by the measures ordained for an earthly people, is to destroy all laws of analogy, break in pieces type and symbol, and bring the Church down from the heights of the infinite glory, that she may camp between the Red Sea and Jordan.

It is confusion worse confounded.

But the Scriptures are full of illustrations and declarations which leave no room for mistakes.

Take the case of Enoch, a fair and beautiful type of the Church; he is caught away from the earth just before the Flood.

Lot, who is a type of the Church, of that side of the Church which has worldly tendencies, of those Christians who must be "burned out" before they will come out, is snatched from Sodom, before the fires fall on the doomed city.

And God takes pains to declare that he can do nothing till he comes out.

Joseph is a type of our Lord Jesus Christ. Joseph gets a Gentile Bride, and puts her on the throne, before the "trouble" overtakes Jacob, and his sons, in the famine hour.

The more the matter is studied in the light of the position which the Church holds to the world, and to an absent Christ, the more incongruous becomes the idea of a tribulation for the Church.

18. The Church will be taken out of the world secretly.

"For the day of the Lord so cometh as a thief in the night." I Thessalonians v: 2.

There are several significant things here.

The beginning of the day of the Lord, is in the night.

It begins with the symbolized activity of a thief; the object of a thief's coming is to steal the treasure. The antitypical treasure is the Church; the day of the Lord will begin IN THE NIGHT, the spiritual night of the world, with an act like that of a thief, that act will be the stealing away of the Church.

A thief not only comes in the darkness of the night, he comes secretly, unwarningly; and again and again we are told by the Son of God himself, that when he comes for his church, it will be at an hour when men are not thinking.

Now the action of a thief in taking a precious thing from its possessor, is to "snatch" it away. This is the very expression used by the Apostle when he declares in the previous chapter of the Epistle, the fourth, that the Church will be "caught away" to "meet" the Lord in the air.

19. The Church will come back from Heaven with Christ in Glory.

"When Christ, our life, shall appear, then shall ye also appear WITH HIM IN GLORY." Colossians iii: 4.

To appear from Heaven in glory, the Church must have first been caught up into Heaven, into glory.

20. The Church will be associated with Christ in the rule of the age to come.

"For unto the angels hath he not (he hath not) put in subjection the world to come." Hebrews ii: 5.

"And again when he bringeth in the first begotten into the world (when he bringeth the first begotten AGAIN into the world) he saith, And let all the angels of God worship him." Hebrews i: 6.

The world to come, that is, the age to come, will not be under the rule of angels, but under the rule of the Risen Man.

With him, in that rule, will be the "many sons of Glory." "For it became him, for whom are all things, and by whom are all things, in bringing many sons unto glory, to make the Captain of their salvation perfect through suffering." Hebrews ii: 10.

"And we shall REIGN ON (OVER) THE EARTH." Revelation v: 10.

"And shall reign WITH HIM a thousand years." Revelation xx: 6.

21. The Church will sit with Christ in the Judgment.

"Do ye not know that the saints shall judge the world? * * * Know ye not that we shall judge angels?" I Corinthians vi: 2, 3.

22. The Church will come down, in the Eternal state, into the new earth, to dwell in, and be the Tabernacle of God; so that the whole scheme of God in Christ will at last be revealed; and the manifestation as described in the Gospel according to Saint John, will be matched and completed by the declaration of Saint John in the Revelation.

In John i: 14, you read: "The word was made flesh and dwelt among us."

The Greek is *ekénosen,* "tabernacled."

Now read Revelation xxi: 3: "The Tabernacle of God is with men, and he will dwell with them."

The Tabernacle of God in the Gospel according to Saint John, is the One Man, the Son; the Tabernacle in the Revelation, is the countless men, the "many sons of glory."

And it is said, God will dwell or tabernacle with men; that is to say, God will be made manifest, not only in the person of the Christ, but in the Church.

Here then is the wondrous destiny of the Church, to be the Pavilion of splendor, the glorious body of perfect beings, through whom Godhead shall shine in a glory, on glory telling.

From the above exposition certain deductions follow:

1. The Church is not earthly, but Heavenly.

"And hath raised us up together, and made us sit together in HEAVENLY PLACES." Ephesians ii: 6.

"If ye then be risen with Christ (since ye are risen)." Colossians iii: 1.

2. Times and seasons are not for the Church.

"And to make all men see what is the fellowship of the mystery, which from the beginning of the world hath been hid in God, who created all things by Jesus Christ:

To the intent that now unto the principalities and powers in HEAVENLY PLACES might be known BY THE CHURCH, the manifold wisdom of God." Ephesians iii: 9, 10.

"But of the times and seasons, brethren, ye have no need that I write unto you." I Thessalonians v: 1.

"And he said unto them, it is not for you to know the times or the seasons." Acts i: 7.

3. The Church is not the kingdom but the mystery in the kingdom.

"THE MYSTERY OF (THE) CHRIST." Ephesians iii: 4.

The nomenclature of the Church shows that it is not the kingdom idea.

Pastors, Deacons, Elders, are not the officers of a kingdom; and Christians as Kings and Priests, are not to enter on that function till Christ the King comes, and sets up the kingdom. The Church is in the kingdom, as the Royal family and the court are in the kingdom, but the hour of the reign is yet distant; the Apostle speaks a settling word upon this attempt to transmit the Church idea into the kingdom idea.

"Now ye are full, now ye are rich, ye have reigned as kings WITHOUT US: I would to God ye *did* reign, that we also *might* reign with you." I Corinthians iv: 8.

4. The Church, like the Bride, is to be waiting for an absent and returning Bridegroom.

"Then shall the kingdom of heaven be likened unto ten virgins, which took their lamps, and went forth to meet the Bridegroom." Matthew xxv: 1.

"And to WAIT FOR HIS SON FROM HEAVEN." I Thessalonians i: 10.

5. Corporately, the glory of the Church is the highest glory.

That is to say: corporately, the glory of the weakest Christian in the Church is higher than the glory of the greatest of God's servants outside the Church. For example, the man who belonged to Cæsar's tenth legion had a higher glory than the soldier who belonged to the fourth or fifth. His glory came to him because of the legionary glory. Some individual soldier in the fourth legion might have been personally more glorious than any individual in the tenth legion, but because he was not attached to that famous legion, he was not so glorious in his standing in Rome.

There is no question that Abraham in his personal glory is at the very altitude, seeing that he is the Father of the faith-filled, and because of his faith, justified before God, and called his friend, the friend to whom God unfolded his plan, and from whom he would not hide that thing he was about to do; but it is not a matter for dispute that the glory of the Christian, even the weakest, is beyond the glory of Abraham; not because of what he is in himself, but because he is a member of the Church, the Body of Christ, that Body, that Church, which has the highest of all glories.

SOME STUDIES IN THE BOOK OF RUTH.

Some Studies in the Book of Ruth.

STUDY No. 1.

1. There was a famine in the land. Ruth, i: 1. See Judges xxi: 25.

The prophet Amos speaks of a famine which is neither a famine of bread, nor a thirst for water, but of *hearing the words of the Lord*. Amos viii: 11. Such a famine seems to be in Christian lands to-day. When ministers of the gospel turn their pulpits into platforms for the discussion of political questions; when the essay takes the place of the sermon, and audiences are treated to a geographical and horticultural analysis upon the islands of the sea, or a series of disquisitions upon Literature, upon Art and Science; when apologies are made for the Bible; when all miracles are explained upon rational grounds, or rejected as myths, or tolerated as poetry; when the study of Browning is exalted over Paul or John; when, in short, "Timely Topics" and matters of "modern and immediate interest" are considered superior to the old gospel, to doctrinal preaching, and to a thus saith the Lord, it is not hard to realize that a spiritual famine has indeed begun, nor difficult to understand the apathy, indifference, unspirituality, and downright unbelief in the Church to-day.

2. They went down into Moab, the enemy's country. Ruth, i: 1.

This is always the result of spiritual famine in the individual life. Just as soon as the soul ceases to feed on God and his word, it goes out into the stranger country, and seeks its resources in regions not owned of God, nor owning Him.

3.   Naomi's husband died.   Ruth i: 3.

The statement is sequential and logical, after spiritual famine comes, inevitably, spiritual death.

4.   Her sons took wives of the women of Moab.   Ruth i: 4.

The moment the spiritual life runs low, the demands of the flesh are roused.   The moment the joys of heaven are insufficient, the joys of earth grow intensely tempting.   Where there is no communion in the spirit, there is always, and immediately, union with the flesh.

5.   They sojourned in Moab.   Ruth i: 4.

We are called to be pilgrims and strangers on the earth: to own this world as a scene through which we are passing in the name of the King, to the hour of the Kingdom, and the coming of the King in his glory. When spiritual famine and death have set in, and the Christian gets married to the things of this life, completely taken up with them, he ceases to become either a pilgrim or a stranger, he goes into the purchase of real estate, he settles down to live in this world, he roots himself into all its ways and claims.   Dwellers on the earth, not citizens of heaven.

6.   There arose in Naomi's heart a desire to return to the land of God.   Ruth i: 6.

She wanted to go back because she was by birth an Israelite, and in the bond of the covenant people; when the root of the divine relationshp is in the heart; where regeneration, spiritual birth, has been a reality, sooner or later the heart tires of the unreality of the flesh, its deceptions and betrayals, and yearns as did the prodigal, for home, for the home-land of the soul.

7.   She complains that the Lord has dealt bitterly with her.   Ruth i: 20.

This seems to be the eternal refrain of those who fail by the way, charging God with folly, and putting on him the responsibility of sorrow, and the harvest of pain. It is not the truth: The truth is, we sow what we reap. He who sows to the flesh, will of the flesh reap corruption; he who sows to unbelief, will reap severance from God's mind and spirit, will be in a state of constant disunion and disorder, always running against the will of God instead of with it, and thus always provoking judgment instead of grace.

8. She went out full, but the Lord brought her back empty. Ruth i: 21.

She had had the sense of God's favor. She had her husband and sons, and the blessing of God's Providence, his watch-care and love. In face of all that, when the test came and it pinched her, she went out from him. But he determined to bring her back, and to do that he was forced to cut her loose from the things that held her in Moab. He cut her loose by cutting off the ties that held her. Again and again God finds it necessary to take away the things that bind his children in the land of Moab. Sometimes it is a husband, or a wife or child. Sometimes it is fortune or fame, or a good name; often it is health. He takes away all these things on which we boast and exalt ourselves. The things which come between us and his service. It is enough to make one tremble, to see a Christian bound up with the things of this life to such a degree, that his face is towards the world and his back to God. It makes one tremble, for if that man or that woman be really God's child, God will put in the knife and cut off the hindering thing, be it what it may, and he will bring back his blood-bought child, even, if he must bring him back empty.

STUDY No. 2.

1. Ruth takes the place of a dependant before Boaz.
Ruth ii: 2.

Gleaning was for beggars. The beggar's place is the
opportunity for grace in him who can give. As a Gentile, and not of Israel, Ruth must take the beggar's place,
and get what grace will give to faith.

2. Boaz met Ruth's dependence with abundant grace.
Ruth ii: 8.

This is the response which the Lord now makes to
every attitude of dependence on Him. He does not drive
away.

He says come: "Him that cometh I will in no wise cast
out."

3. Ruth is amazed at the grace of Boaz. ii: 10.

"Amazing grace" is still the song.

4. Ruth set aside the ties of nature and went out by
faith in another. Ruth ii: 11.

5. Boaz took the place of her losses and comforted
her. Ruth ii: 13.

6. He fed her with his own hand. Ruth ii: 16.

7. She found her place among the workers. Ruth
ii: 17.

No sooner was Paul awakened to the grace and fullness
of his Lord than he cried out, "Lord, what wilt thou have
me to do?"

8. He bade her not to be found in the field of another.
Ruth ii: 22.

How suggestive! Our service is unto the Lord, in his
work, and not unto another, not even unto self: "Ye are
bought with a price, ye are not your own."

9. She gleaned in the field to the end of the harvest.
This is the position of the Church. A gleaner in the

world till the end of the harvest, rather till the "time" of the harvest, which is the end of the world—*i. e.,* the end of this age.

STUDY No. 3.

1. Boaz as a kinsman of Ruth. Ruth ii: 1.

A greater than Boaz, "being in the form of God, * * * made himself of no reputation, and took upon him the form of a servant, and was made in the *likeness of men.* Phil. ii: 6-7. "As the children are partakers of flesh and blood, he also himself likewise took part of the same," Heb. ii: 14, and thus he became our kinsman, a "brother born for adversity."

2. There was a nearer kinsman than Boaz. Ruth iii: 12.

In spiritual language, that nearer kinsman is the law. Just as the nearer kinsman, according to the flesh, was under responsibility to raise up the name of the dead man and bring in life and sonship, so the law was ordained that it might give life. The law proposed as its end, life to all those who should submit themselves to it. The responsibility then of the law, speaking of it in the personal sense, was to stand in the kinsman's place, and give life in the name of the dead man, Adam.

3. The nearer kinsman failed to do his part. Ruth iv: 6.

Like the kinsman, the law failed to do its part. It failed, of course, through the weakness of the flesh, failed because the flesh could not respond to the demands of the law. Rom. viii: 3.

4. Boaz came in and took the place of the nearer kinsman. Ruth iv: 9.

"What the law could not do, in that it was weak through the flesh," God has done, in sending his Son "in the likeness of sinful flesh," Rom. viii : 3, wherefore it is written that we are "married unto Him, * * * that we should bring forth fruit—unto God." Rom. vii : 4.

5. Boaz purchased Ruth for his wife. Ruth iv : 10. Christ also loved the Church and gave Himself for it. Eph. v : 25.

6. He betrothed Ruth to himself. II Cor. xi : 21.

7. He advocated her claims in the gate. Ruth iv : 1. Christ is in the place of authority to-day. In the "Gate of Power." In that upper gate, he is the ceaseless advocate of his "bride," the Church.

8. He married her publicly.

Christ will own the Church as his "wife," in "the public" splendor of the coming glory.

STUDY No. 4.

Ruth was a Gentile brought into the place of blessing through the failure in Israel. Through Israel's failure as a people in responsibility to God, the Gentiles have been brought in, and the Church is now being called out from among them.

2. She took the place of dependent faith and got fullness of grace, new life.

3. The kinsman could not redeem the inheritance, nor raise up the name of the dead.

The law can neither redeem, nor give life.

4. Boaz took the place of Redeemer and life giver. Christ is the life giver, because He is the Redeemer.

5. Boaz made the woman his wife.

6. He raised up the name of the dead.

As the life giver, Christ has raised up the name of man, until, the "man in Christ," will stand in the inheritance.

BOAZ IN RUTH.

1. He is the Kinsman.
2. The Redeemer.
3. The Life Giver.
4. The Advocate.

} Christ. The Antitype of Boaz.

THE POSITION OF THE BOOK OF RUTH.

Ruth comes in after Judges, and is placed before Samuel. That is to say, after the failure in Israel, when, according to Judges, "every man did that which was right in his own eyes," and before the setting up of the kingdom, as recorded in Samuel. Now, as Ruth is a Gentile, and a type of the Church, the very position of the story teaches the whole general truth of the occasion of the Church, and her relation to Israel, and is at once not only a prophetic testimony as to dispensational truth, but an anticipative record of history. The fact of history is, that after the failure in Israel, more particularly after the failure in Judah, in the rejection of Christ as the King, God brought in the Church, a body and a bride for Christ, now being gathered out by the Gospel and the Spirit from among the Gentiles; and the prophecy is, that when the fullness of the Gentiles shall be come in, that is, when the Church member shall be complete, then Christ, like Boaz, will come for His Church, and the kingdom in Israel will be set up. Ruth, as a book placed between Judges and Samuel, testifies that the occasion of the Church is the failure in Israel, and the relation of the Church to the kingdom, is that of a bride who is sought for and found by the king, before he comes to sit on his throne.

The position of the book is another evidence of the divine superintendence, even, in its arrangement, and another witness that it is to be dealt with on higher ground than that of mere literature.

JOHN XI AND JOHN XII.

JOHN XI AND JOHN XII.

John XI and John XII.

THE GOSPEL IN LAZARUS.

1. The condition of Lazarus:

He was sick. Sin, a disease, a sickness. Isa. I.

He was dead. Sin progressive, spiritual death. Eph. ii: 1.

He was corrupt. This the end of sin, moral putrefaction. What a picture of a helpless, hopeless, ruined sinner.

Dead, corrupt in his grave. Rom. ii.

2. Manner in which Jesus dealt with Lazarus:

He called him. The Lord calls by Gospel, Spirit, Providences.

Called him to come forth. "Come out," this the generic idea of salvation.

Called him by name. The call is to individuals.

3. The manner in which Lazarus responded to Jesus:

He received his word.

He heard. Power came with the word. Rom. x: 17.

4. What Lazarus got by hearing the word:

He got life. John vi: 47.

He got a place at the supper table with Christ. John xii.

THE WORK OF THE CHURCH.

1. To take away the stone.

Every obstacle between a dead sinner and a life-giving Saviour.

We roll away the stone.

419

He calls forth the dead.

We preach the good news.

He makes it good.

2. To loose those who are alive but bound with grave clothes.

To teach, this the function of the church.

Truth only can make free.   John viii: 32.

3. To walk the path of separation with a denied Saviour.

He withdrew with his disciples.   John xi: 54.

This is not the time of our manifestation.

We wait for the manifestation of the sons of God Rom. viii: 19.

COMFORT BY THE WAY.

1. Our sickness may be to the glory of God.

2. Jesus may seem not to answer our prayers.

His very delay works for good.

By this delay Lazarus got to know resurrection life.

3. The Christian does not die, he falls asleep.

4. Jesus weeps with those who weep—our sorrow is his.

DISPENSATIONAL ORDER.

1. Jesus is coming to wake his friends out of sleep.

"I go that I may wake him out of sleep."

What a moment it will be.

2. Those who are living shall not die.

"We shall not all sleep."   I Cor. xv: 51.

3. Those who are living when he comes, like Martha, will go forth to meet him, secretly.

4. His coming will be, at first, only for his friends; known only to the "family that Jesus loves," the Church.

5. After the resurrection of his friend, Jesus sits down to supper with him.

The Bridal supper after the Rapture.

Each gets his or her place here.

Lazarus gets his—at the table.

Martha, serving.

Mary, at his feet.

6. After the supper, the "next day," Jesus goes forth openly with his disciples, as King of Israel, to Jerusalem.

Thus will Christ appear *with* his Church after he comes *for* her.

7. The people—the Jews, receive him with acclamation as their King.

This they will do when he comes a second time. Zech. xii: 10.

8. After he enters Jerusalem as King, the Greeks, the Gentiles, come, saying they would see him also. John xii: 21. After the throne in Israel is set up, all the nations of the earth shall seek unto Jerusalem, saying, we would see the King; and ten men out of the nations shall take hold of the skirt of him, that is a Jew, saying, "We will go with you; for we have heard that God is with you." Zech. viii: 23.

THE "IMMINENT" COMING OF CHRIST.

I. THE IMMINENT COMING OF
CHRIST

The "Imminent" Coming of Christ

Is the Second Coming of our Lord Jesus Christ imminent?

Do the Scriptures teach that the Church is to be in a constant state of readiness for such an event?

Benjamin Wills Newton, an English writer of some force, a professed believer in the Pre-Millennial Coming, and author of a pamphlet entitled, "Five Letters on Events Predicted in Scripture as Antecedent to the Coming of the Lord," denies it.

He bases his denial, among other things, upon our Lord's statement that Peter should live to an old age, then die a violent death, and Peter's own statement in his second Epistle that he was himself preparing for death.

Newton's followers in this country add to the catalogue which he cites other events predicted before our Lord's return, such as the coming of the "wolves" anticipated by Paul after his departure from the Ephesian midst, the prophecies concerning the "last times," the rise of Antichrist, Paul's vision of the Lord, and the Lord's announcement that the Apostle must go to Rome, the statement of the Apostle James that the husbandman has "long" waiting for the fruit of the earth, a statement made in connection with his exhortation concerning the coming of the Lord as evidence that neither he nor the Church expected the Lord in their day, the fact that Peter not only knew he was to die before the Lord could come, but that he says nothing about the coming in the first sermon he preached to the Gentiles in the house of Cornelius, the fact that on the day of Pentecost the disciples were not waiting for the Lord, but the descent of the Holy Ghost, the antecedent fact that the Lord did not tell them to wait at Jerusalem for his coming but the coming of the Spirit, the impossibility that the "two men in white" could have taught that the coming of the Lord was imminent in the face of his immediate ascent from Olivet, and his command to wait for the Spirit, together with the supreme fact that our Lord had commanded the disciples to preach the Gospel to the whole world, and that such commission would require a long time to fulfill. In addition to all this it is held that the disciples could not have received a command to wait and watch for the Lord's Second Coming before he had yet passed out of the region of his First Coming.

As all these events and conditions must be fulfilled before the Lord could return, it is self-evident that neither Christ, nor any of his Apostles believed, or taught, that the Coming was an imminent event; and that, therefore, the doctrine that the Church is to "wait for the Son of God from heaven," as a possible event in any age of her history, is not a part of the faith "once delivered to the saints." Indeed, so it is said, in A. D. 59, seven years after Paul had written to the Thessalonians that the Lord was coming, in order that the Church might not longer be in error, and that no man henceforth should have any excuse, even, to quote Paul in favor of the imminency, *the Lord told Paul that his Coming was not impending.*

Before our Lord Jesus Christ could possibly come there were those who must fall on sleep, there were tasks to be done, there was the whole reach of the Gospel age which must be traversed.

The Second Coming of Christ, as an event, therefore, most be placed in the nimbus of a "long," a remote future.

Although this argument is set forth by a Pre-Millennialist, it is, substantially, the position held by all Post-Millenarians; that is, the Coming of Christ is not to be expected in our day, and is not a working doctrine for this hour. But the Newtonians have not learned to be as logical as the Post-Millenarians; for they teach that in exact proportion as it may be proved that the Coming of Christ does not belong to the domain of the present, in that exact proportion it is to be held in the consciousness of the Church of the present age as a particularly vivid and inspiring hope; that instead of watching and waiting for the Lord in our day, we are to transfer this actual attitude to a far-distant generation of the Church, and then, by some intense exercise of the mind, retransfer the actual expectancy of that Church to our own consciousness, so that it will be just as vivid and inspiring as though we stood in the generation to whom the Lord at last will come.

It ought to go without saying, that if the Coming of Christ is not possible in our day, nor for many days, or years, or it may be for centuries, to talk about it as a pre-eminently present, vivid, and inspiring hope is pure nonsense.

That the Church will triumph at some time and fulfill all the purpose for which God ordained this age, all Christians believe, and in one way or another according to their light are working for it; but it is an amazing process of thinking that enables any mind to lug in the doctrine of the Second Coming, and stand for it particularly, if it is not imminent in any age of the Church.

We are, therefore, forced back upon this question: Was the Coming of Christ ever held out to the Church at any time in her history as an imminent event? I answer, it was; and in a fashion so plain that he who runs never so fast, whether he run over the words of Christ, the Church, or the Pastoral Epistles, unless he be wilfully blind, may see and read.

It was delivered as a hope to the Church by Christ our Lord, and all his Apostles; and the aggregate teaching of the Word is that between us and the Coming of Christ *for* his Church there is not a single predicted event that *must* be fulfilled; that all events predicted between us and the Lord's descent into the air for his Church are contingent on that one event, and are to be so understood; that while the Christian is doing what his hand finds to do, is fulfilling the commission that is laid out for him in time, he is to be ready for that event which is not in the sequences of time, nor bound by its laws. He is to be ready for the "unknown" hour in which our Lord may come.

This teaching is a part of the faith "once delivered to the saints."

It *was* delivered by our Lord Jesus Christ to his disciples before the crucifixion.

He taught them that he would be rejected of the Scribes and Pharisees, be put to death, on the third day rise again, and "ascend up where he was before." (John vi: 62.)

He taught that after he had ascended they were to wait and watch, and be ready for his return in an "unknown" hour.

Listen to his own words in Mark xiii: 32-37.

"But of that day and that hour knoweth no man, no, not the angels which are in heaven, neither the Son, but the Father.

"Take ye heed, watch and pray; for ye know not *when* the time is.

"For the Son of man is as a man taking a far journey, who left his house, and gave authority to his servants, and to every man his work, and commanded the porter to watch.

"Watch ye therefore; for ye know not *when* the master of the house cometh, at even or at midnight, or at the cock-crowing, or in the morning;

"Lest, coming suddenly, he find you sleeping.

"And what I say unto you, I say unto all, 'Watch.'"

In this passage our Lord says:

(1). He is a householder.

(2). He is going away.

(3). While he is away his disciples will form a "house."

(4). In this house he appoints servants with authority.

(5). He gives to every one his work.

(6). The porter is to "watch."

(7). They of the house do not know when the Master will return, whether at "even," or at "midnight," or at the "cockcrowing," or in the "morning."

(8). The angels of heaven do not know.

(9). He himself does not know.

(10). Only the Father knows.

(11). What he says to them he says to *all* the house, "Watch."

What he says in Mark he emphasizes in Matthew.

There he says his Coming will be as sudden as the flood that drowned the world, as the fire that flamed on Sodom.

He not only exhorts them to watch but he says: "Be ye also ready" (Matthew xxiv: 44).

He warns them that the servant who teaches that the Lord for any cause delayeth "his Coming" is an "evil" servant; not because he smites his fellow-servants in "authority" and drinks with the drunken is he called an evil servant, but because he *first* says that the Lord is not at hand, that he delayeth, and thus teaches that there *is* something between the household and the Master of the house (Matthew xxv: 48).

He warns that kind of teachers that they shall be "cut off."

If this language was not an exhortation to those living disciples to be ready and watching for the Lord in their day, then language is a juggle, and the Son of God is under a condemnation that would be hard enough even for an ordinary teacher to bear, to say nothing of him who calls himself "The Truth."

2. It *was* believed by Christ and his disciples when he gave the great commission to evangelize the world. They believed it necessarily because he had said that neither he nor they knew at what hour he might be ordered of the Father to return. To say that he and they did not believe, specially, that he did not believe what he himself had said, is to make a charge so grave that it falls on the head of him who makes it.

3. It *was* given by the "two men in white;" for they said that this same Jesus who had just been taken up should come again "in like manner" as he was taken away.

When he went away there was no flash of glory, no disturbance of the ordinary course of the world. It was unseen, unknown to the world, and from the midst of his disciples.

To come back in like manner, he must come to the midst of his disciples, unknown to the world, and outside of its ordinary course of events. This is what the Lord himself had taught, and what the disciples believed. The angels came to seal the Lord's testimony and confirm the faith of his disciples.

4. They believed it, *even* on the day of Pentecost while waiting for the descent of the Spirit; as those taught in the Scriptures of Israel they had a special right to believe it; for, according to Saint Peter, this sublime event was the begun fulfilment of the prophecy of Joel, who declares that that out-pouring was to be in connection with the Coming of the Lord.

5. It was taught by *Peter himself* immediately upon the border of Pentecost. He declared to a great crowd of Jews in Solomon's porch that, if the nation would repent and convert, the times of refreshing would come from the *presence of the Lord;* and he would "send Jesus Christ" again to them; and he would do this in fulfilment of what "all the prophets from Samuel" had spoken and foretold of "these days."

6. There is no *sane reason* to doubt that Peter preached it to the Gentiles in the house of Cornelius.

Because no mention is made of it in the report of the sermon is not evidence that he did not refer to it.

In the history of Philip and the Eunuch, it is not said that when Philip "preached Jesus" unto him that he also preached baptism; yet the fact that the Eunuch breaks out so suddenly at sight of the water with the exclamation, "Here is water; what doth hinder me to be baptized?" is evidence enough that Philip had preached it; the fact that **Peter** had so recently preached it to the Jews would be in evidence that it was a part of his homiletics in the house of Cornelius to the Gentiles.

But if it were just possible that Peter did not preach it in that sermon he simply "lapsed," or was "unmindful" of his commission as a "servant in authority," just as preachers and teachers have been all through the ages since.

7. Paul did *not* unfold any "chronological imminency" from the very fact that our Lord had taught that the imminency was *unchronological,* "unknown," not down in any of the calendars of time.

8. It has been asserted that if the imminency of Christ is taught by any of the Apostles, it must have been by a revelation that made it distinct from any revelation of the Coming in the Old Testament.

It *was* so taught. Paul puts it on record in the first Epistle ever written to the Church, the Epistle to the Thessalonians.

In the Old Testament we are told the Lord will come *with* all his saints to the Mount of Olives, and that his feet shall stand in that day upon that mount which is "before Jerusalem on the east" (Zechariah xiv: 4).

Not a word is said in the prophet concerning any resurrection of the dead, or any resurrection "from among" the dead.

But by this special word to the Thessalonians the Apostle informs them that the Lord before he comes to the Mount of Olives *with* his saints, will descend into the air, and halt there long enough, he does not say how long, long enough to raise the dead in Christ, change the living, and receive them "in the air;" it is after this resurrection and transfiguration into the air that he continues on his way *with* his saints that he may once more place his "feet" on that Olivet from which he ascended.

There is certainly quite a difference between the statement of the Coming of Christ in Zechariah and that in the Thessalonians; there is a notable difference between coming *for* the dead and the living saints into the *air,* and the coming to the *earth with* all his saints glorified; a vast difference between a coming in which there is no resurrection, and a coming in which the resurrection is made the specific occasion of the Coming

And so imminent does Paul regard this particular phase of the Coming which he affirms to the Thessalonians that he exhorts them to comfort themselves concerning their dead in the light and hope of it.

That they may make no mistake he says: "We who are *alive* and *remain unto the coming* of the Lord."

If this language does not mean imminency, then language has no certain meaning, and the particular use of it here is concrete puerility.

To say that the "we" is inclusive of the whole Church through all the ages does not change its force, because it is in the present that it is used, and means the "we" who are alive at any age in which it is spoken.

But that there may be no misunderstanding of the matter the Apostle actually prays that the Thessalonians may not die, that they may continue alive till the Lord's return.

Listen to the prayer:

"And I pray God your whole spirit and soul and body be preserved blameless unto the coming of our Lord Jesus Christ" (I Thessalonians v: 23).

The word to "preserve" signifies among other things to "maintain." Let it be assumed that the Apostle is praying that the spirit, soul and body may be watched over, kept in "custody," so that the entire man "in" the Coming may be manifested "blamelessly," in view of verse 16 of the previous chapter, where it is specifically announced that those who are dead shall come forth in the Coming, it is evident that, as he is writing to those who are "alive," so he is praying concerning them that they may be preserved entire, that there may not be a separation between spirit, soul and body, and in that hour to which they may be conserved, they may stand forth blamelessly, having known how to "possess their vessel in sanctification and honor."

To say he is praying that after death, and between that hour and the resurrection of which he had just spoken, the body may be preserved in one place, soul and spirit in another, weakens the assurance already given concerning the dead, and in final analysis makes meaningless the prayer.

If he was praying exclusively that at the Coming of Christ they should, whether dead or alive, be found blameless, the request for the preservation of the entire man has no place; that preservation was, and that preservation is, in the very nature of the case, assured to all the dead in Christ now. The Apostle was not only praying that the Thessalonians to whom he wrote might be blameless in the Coming of the Lord Jesus Christ, he was praying that they all might be preserved alive to that Coming, and thus take part among the "we who are alive and remain."

The Apostle does more than this. He sets the Thessalonian assembly before all others as the model assembly of the whole Church of Christ. He draws special attention to their attitude, and commends them for it.

And what was that model attitude for the whole Church?

Hear his own language!

"To wait for his Son from Heaven, whom he raised from the dead, even Jesus."

That is what the Thessalonian Church was doing in A.D. 52, nearly twenty years after our Lord had given the original command to "wait;" not only the Church corporately, but that which goes to make up the corporate church, each individual member of it. Each individual member under the authoritative teaching of the Apostle was "waiting for the Son of God from heaven."

8. What Paul taught the Thessalonians in A.D. 52, he taught the Romans in A.D. 58, or six years later.

He says: "The God of peace shall bruise Satan under your feet shortly" (Romans xvi: 20).

The word here used with the dative and translated "shortly," signifies "speedily," "soon," "immediately."

According to Revelation 20th, the bruising of Satan under the feet of the Lord is consequent on the Coming of the Lord; thus the Apostle teaches the Romans that "speedily," "soon," "immediately," they might expect the Coming of the Lord and all its triumphant consequence. That in giving this assurance the Apostle was holding out with it the same thought of resurrection and transfiguration that he had taught in Thessalonica is evident from the declaration in the eighth chapter, that he with them was "waiting for the adoption, to wit, the *redemption* of the body;" a redemption which he had taught the Thessalonians was to occur by resurrection and transformation.

9. It is absolutely *unscriptural* to say that any event "must come to pass first" before the Lord comes for his Church. To say so is to say positively that the hour when the Lord will *not* come is known. But the Lord says he is coming in an hour "unknown," and that hour unknown might be the very hour when "ye think *not.*"

10. To *exclude* Peter's Epistle as a witness to the imminent Coming is to be guilty of the sin of using Jehudi's pen-knife; for, side by side with the declaration that he is preparing for death even as the Lord showed him, he writes an exhortation to the same people, and in the same Epistle, to be looking for the Coming of the Day of the Lord.

"Looking for and hasting the *coming* of the day" (II Peter iii: 12).

An examination of the fifteenth verse will show that Peter is in accord with Paul.

Peter says the day of the Lord will come as a "thief in the night."

Paul says the same thing.

A thief comes in the night, that is, *before* the day is manifested. The Coming of Christ in glory is to begin, it is to be preceded, by a tremendous event which is compared to the coming of a thief. Say nothing about what the thief does, what he steals, and on whom the loss falls, the fact set forth by this illustration is, that before the manifestation of Christ openly, his day is introduced by an event that comes just as secretly, stealthily, and unexpectedly, as the coming of a thief. The "arrival" of the day is as the arrival of a thief in the night. Paul tells us what that event is. It is the descent of the Lord into the air before he comes to the Mount of Olives in judgment. Peter tells the people to whom he is writing about his death, even while he is writing about it, to look, to be in readiness for that thief-like act that shall begin the day; and, therefore, he is telling them to be ready for a coming that may take place, even, *while he is preparing for death.*

11. Nor *do* we look in vain in the Pastoral Epistles for this teaching concerning the imminent Coming.

We find it in Paul's Epistle to Titus.

To him he writes: "Looking for that blessed hope, and the glorious appearing of our great God and Saviour Jesus Christ" (Titus ii: 13).

Of course the Greek word for "looking" is "expecting." Thus Paul exhorts Titus to be looking for, expecting the Lord in his day.

And when did Paul write this exhortation?

I answer, in A.D. 66.

That is, fourteen years after he had commended the Thessalonians for waiting for the Son of God from heaven, twelve years after he had written to the Philippians that he with others was "looking" for the Saviour, the Lord Jesus Christ, to change his living but "vile" body, and six years after the Lord, in vision, had ordered him to Rome; that is to say, *six years later than the time in which certain writers declare that it was impossible for Paul, under the circumstances, to believe in the imminent Coming.*

Thus the Holy Ghost *did* affirm precisely to Paul in A.D. 52 what the Lord had announced in the beginning in respect to the imminent Coming. The Lord Jesus Christ did *not* in A.D. 59, by anything he said, deny to Paul what the Holy Ghost had said in 52, but, on the contrary, six years later than the "order to Rome," he led Paul by the same Spirit to exhort another preacher, while he preached, to be looking, waiting, for the Coming of the Lord; and any assertion that at any time the "Lord told Paul that his Coming was not imminent," is not only extra-scriptural, but so amazingly a *denial* of Scripture, so flagrantly a denial of the Master's word, "in an hour when ye think *not*," that one is forced to ask himself whether he has read aright; whether such statements, *to say the least,* are possible from the pen or lips of one who professes to hold in his consciousness a "vivid" hope of the Coming of his Lord.

12. We *dare not* eliminate James from those who taught and lived in the power of the imminent Coming.

James tells those to whom he writes that the husbandman has "long" waiting for the fruit of the earth, but he comforts them with the thought that the "Coming of the Lord *draweth nigh:* that he standeth *before the door."* To say that James did not mean that the Coming was "nigh," but a "long" way off; that he was not "before" the door, not even in sight of it; that he thought of a Coming that might be hundreds or thousands of years after the poor troubled souls whom he had exhorted to be patient in the view of it had passed into the realm of death, is to put on record the most monumental piece of spiritual bluff, of unsanctified deception, and, at the same time, in the most marked manner, to bear witness to the non-inspiration of an Apostle. Even Higher Critics and Rationalistic Analysts could not do worse.

13. What our Lord, and Peter, and Paul, and James testify, John, the beloved disciple, who lay on the Master's heart and heard its most intimate pulse-beat, also teaches. In his general Epistle he declares that the Christian who is alive and hangs his hope on a Coming Lord purifies himself by that hope, **purifies himself by living in** view of its imminency.

14. When we read the last page of Holy Scripture we hear the voice of the Spirit saying "Come;" and he who hears that the Lord is surely coming is exhorted by that Spirit to "say come."

The last exhortation is intensely striking. It is the prayer commanded not to the Church corporately, but to the individual member of the Church. To say that this prayer is to be made operative only in a fixed hour in a far future long after the individual has offered it and fallen on death, is to say that the exhortation has no special meaning; if it is fixed his prayer cannot hasten it. But precisely as those who love Jerusalem are exhorted by the prophet to give the Lord "no rest" till he make that city a praise in the earth, and just as Peter exhorts his hearers to hasten the *Coming* of the day, so the Apostle John, under the inspiration of the Spirit, exhorts the individual Christian to pray for the Coming of the Lord, in the firm belief that his prayer will contribute in some measure to the quickening of the Lord's returning footsteps.

The last words the ascended Lord speaks in the ear of his church are these: "Behold, I come quickly; surely I come quickly."

The last recorded prayer of the Bible is: "Even so, come Lord Jesus."

And when the Bible is closed, and the silence grows round him, he who has read that Bible for the first time will feel quivering in his soul the inevitable, inexorable conclusion that the next thing is the Coming of the Lord.

I assert, then, without the fear of any sane contradiction, that the imminent Coming of our Lord is taught in Scripture.

It is taught in the New Testament.

It is illustrated in the Old Testament. It is illustrated by the sudden translation of Enoch, who was "snatched" away without dying to meet the Lord; by the taking of Lot out of Sodom before the judgment fell, and that by the "voice" of an angel.

I repeat that between us and the Coming of the Lord for his Church there is not a single predicted event that *must* be fulfilled.

And all this in the very nature of the case.

The Church is not a time thing at all. The church occupies a parenthesis in time as a consequence of the displacement temporarily of the time people, Israel.

Times and seasons belong unto Israel, not to the Church. Israel is to be looking for "signs;" the Church is to be waiting for a "sound," the all-compelling sound of a voice and a trump.

The Coming of our Lord, therefore, as it relates to the Church, is non-chronological. It is not bound up with the sequences of time nor the calendar of events.

It takes precedence and right of way over all things that are predicted in respect of the Church this side of the appearing and kingdom.

It takes the right of way over all such predicted events as the death of Peter, as already shown.

It takes precedence over all such events, even as the mercy of the Lord took precedence over his formal and explicit prediction that Nineveh should be destroyed in forty days; and was not because of that mercy.

The death of Peter as a predicted "certainty" was contingent on the "uncertainty" of the Lord's Coming. If the Lord did not come, Peter, moving along the ordinary sequences of time, would reach old age, and according to the Lord's prophetic vision at that point would die, and in the manner indicated. The Lord foresaw that point in time so far as it coincided with Peter's history, and could announce the culmination in Peter's death, but he did not know (and why and how, does not enter into the question here), he did not know, according to his own positive statement, *when* his own advent, known only to the Father, might anticipate that hour.

Peter's death was altogether contingent on the Lord's Coming.

The Lord's Coming for his Church is a contingency with which all predicted events have to settle their accounts.

In grammatical construction some things are understood even when not expressed. When, therefore, we meet such statements as those concerning Peter's death, it is to be understood that the event will take place if the Lord does not come.

What would have taken place if the Lord had come before the Gospel was preached and the Church fully formed, may be put in the category with the question: How would the Church have come into view at all if the Jews had accepted the supposedly "sincere" offer of the Lord Jesus as their King? All these questions are met by the answer that "known unto the Lord are all his ways;" and that just as on the rejection of the Lord by the Jews, he brought into view this larger age, so his unrevealed resources are equal to all developments or eccentricities of time.

With that in this issue we have nothing to do.

The sufficient fact for every reverent mind that bows to the Word of the Lord is that he has said it was possible, that it is possible now, that the "unknown" is still dominant in the imminency of his Coming.

It is a poor piece of work to attempt to rob the Church of the hope bequeathed it; to attempt to stop the chariot wheels of the dominant truth by piling up the pebbles from secondary truths in its way; it is a poor piece of work to help those who deny the coming of the Lord at all, by building up between the Church and the imminent person of her Lord all the debris, all the baggage of times and seasons and events; it is a poor thing to help those who spiritualize all the promised realities of the Word, to shut the Church out from that "man in glory" who in some sudden "unknown" hour might make all his glory hers.

It must be a thankless task to contribute in any manner to that condition of doubt and perplexity that will lead the Church to abandon the attitude of waiting for him, who in the infinite pathos of a measureless simplicity and sincerity, said to her in the first pure days of their betrothal: "Watch therefore; for ye know not what hour your Lord doth come."

It must be a sad task, even though the pen be facile that achieves it, to take the eye off of him who is the imminent resurrection and the life, and listen with strained ears for the thud of the grave-digger's pick, and the clods on the coffin lid.

Nay, rather, let us go back to the days of the Apostolic Church, the Model Church, and "wait for his Son from heaven, even Jesus who delivered us from the wrath to come."

Let us accept the admonition of the angels, not to be "gazing up into heaven," as though Christ had gone out of the region of our world with all its woes and heartaches, forever; but let us accept the promise that he will come in "like manner," and, while we wait, do what our hands find to do along the commissioned and planned sequences of time, working with all our might in his name, lest coming suddenly he find us sleeping.

THE SYROPHENICIAN WOMAN.

The Syrophenician Woman.

Matthew xv: 22-28.

Mark tells us that the woman was a Greek, a Gentile, a Syrophenician. Her daughter was sick, grievously vexed with a devil (demon).

As soon as Jesus came into the coasts of Tyre and Sidon she met him and besought him to have mercy on her child.

But Jesus apparently paid her no attention, he preserved a strict silence; he preserved that silence in the face of her most insistent entreaties.

His irresponsiveness was so marked, his silence so obtrusive, so suggestive, that the disciples begged him to send her away, saying that her noise and lamentations were offensive.

To them he at once replied, declaring that he was not sent but to the lost sheep of the house of Israel.

No sooner did the woman hear this than she fell at his feet and worshipped him, saying: "Lord, help me."

He now spoke to her, telling her that he could not take the children's bread and cast it to the dogs.

Instantly, she cried out: "Truth, Lord! yet the dogs eat the crumbs which fall from the Master's table."

Then Jesus answered that her faith was indeed a great faith; and it should be done as she wished.

The record adds: "And her daughter was made whole from that very hour."

Three things are to be noted here:

1. This woman appealed to our Lord as the Son of David.

447

In doing so she took Israel's ground; for, as the Son of David he came to that people, and to that people only.

He himself says:

"I am not sent but unto the lost sheep of the house of Israel."

She was not of the house of Israel, she was a Gentile; as a Gentile she had no claim on the Son of David; as the Son of David he could make no response to her. Hence, he answered her not a word, he was silent; not because indifferent; not because he was trying her faith, but because she claimed blessing through a relationship that was not hers. She appealed to a title that had no operative meaning to one not in the bond and covenant of the chosen people.

2. She saw her error, owned him as Lord, fell down at his feet, worshipped him as Jehovah, and asked him to help her.

But neither as Lord could he respond; for, as Lord of the whole earth he had called but one nation to be his people; and for this people alone had he provided a typical ground of approach in the Levitical sacrifices.

This woman being a Gentile had no ground of approach; as a Gentile her place was that of a dog, not that of a child.

And without sparing her the Lord puts her in the dog's place.

He says, you are a Gentile dog, I cannot take the bread, I cannot take the blessings, which in covenant, belong to my people, and give them to you who are the dogs.

3. The woman rises at once to the occasion. She does not dispute. She says: "Truth, Lord."

In saying this, she owns herself as a Gentile, a dog.

She takes without controversy the place assigned her; and then goes further; she takes the attitude of a beggar, of one who has no claim, no ground whatever except in the over-abounding grace of the Lord. She says: "Lord, there are crumbs which fall from the Master's table. I believe that thou art not only the Lord of Israel, but the God of the whole earth, and the God of all grace; and that thou hast sufficient in thy grace, thy mercy, to meet my case."

The Lord owns a faith which rises above his silence; a faith which is willing to take the lowest place, even that of a despised Gentile dog, and in that lowly place worship, praise, and adore him.

The dispensational and moral value of the incident is immense.

Dispensationally, we are taught that the Lord abides by the distinctive obligations of the respective ages; that is to say, he owns that there are distinctive ages or dispensations; and that these are not to be confounded, neither the restrictions of one, nor the liberty of another.

He sets before us the truth that there is to be no confusion in divine matters; that we are not to take the things that belong to one class and give them to another. We are not to take, as is so commonly done by modern theologians, promises which belong to one class, and give them to another; we are not, for example, to take the promises which belong to Israel and give them to the Gentiles; we are not to mix up the age of Law and Grace, to confound the Church with the kingdom; nor to insist that the rule which holds good for Israel must hold good for the Gentile.

Morally, we learn the priceless value of that faith which in spite of all obstacles rises up straight-away to the heart of infinite grace and love and casts itself there in measureless abandon: the faith that trusts where it cannot trace, and will not take a "no" as the final answer from God.

THE LEAVEN.

The Leaven.

According to Dr. Adam Clarke, "Leaven is a species of corruption produced by fermentation and tends to putrefaction."

The Children of Israel were commanded to put away leaven during the observance of the Passover. "Even the first day ye shall put away leaven out of your houses: for whosoever eateth leavened bread from the first day until the seventh day, that soul shall be cut off from Israel." Ex. xii: 15.

Leaven must not come in contact with the offering of blood. "Thou shalt not offer the blood of my sacrifice with leaven." Ex. xxxiv: 25.

Leaven must be excluded from the meat offering. "No meat offering which ye shall bring unto the Lord shall be made with leaven." Lev. ii: 11.

Leaven is to be put away because the meat offering is holy. "Eat it without leaven beside the altar, for it is most holy." Lev. x: 12.

The Son of God says: "Take heed and beware of the leaven of the Pharisees and of the Sadducees." Matt. xvi: 6.

He warns the disciples against the "leaven of Herod." Mark viii: 15.

Paul writes the Corinthian Church: "Purge out the old leaven." I Cor. v: 7.

Gathering up this testimony and examining it in order, we discover that:

First. Leaven is in its nature corrupt, and corrupting that with which it is mixed.

453

Second. It is recognized as so corrupt and corrupting that it is required of God to be put away from everything which was intended to typify Christ, his sacrifice, or divine and holy things.

Third. Our Lord stamps it as the symbol of corrupt and corrupting doctrine. After his warning against the leaven of the Pharisees and Sadducees the disciples reasoned among themselves and supposed he meant bread; he corrected their error, and then it is added, "Then understood they how that he bade them not beware of the leaven of bread, but of the *doctrine* of the Pharisees and Sadducees." Matt. xvi: 12.

Leaven symbolizes the doctrine of the Pharisees.

The Pharisees had a *form* of godliness but denied the power. This formalism without power made them hypocrites, and Jesus testifies, "Beware of the leaven of the Pharisees, which is hypocrisy." Luke xii: 1. A form of godliness denying the power is ritualism.

The leaven of the Pharisees is *Ritualism*.

But leaven symbolizes the doctrine of the Sadducees. The Sadducees believed neither in angel nor spirit. They denied the resurrection. This is materialism.

The leaven of the Sadducees is *Materialism*.

Fourth. The apostle Paul uses leaven to set forth corrupt doctrine. "This persuasion cometh not of him that calleth you. A little leaven leaveneth the whole lump." Gal. v: 8—9.

"Persuasion," and its influence, is compared to the work of leaven. This persuasion was the doctrine of Judaizing teachers who taught that the Gentiles must needs be circumcised, and walk under the law as a rule of life. This is *Legalism*.

The "little leaven" among the Galatians is *Legalism*.

Ritualism! Materialism! Legalism! Each of them corrupt and corrupting doctrines, and indicated by leaven.

Fifth. Leaven is used by the Son of God to warn against the *character* of Herod: "Beware of the leaven of Herod." Mark viii: 15.

The leaven of Herod was manifested the day that Christ was crucified. "The same day Pilate and Herod were made friends." Luke xxiii: 12.

Pilate stands for the world, Herod represents the professed follower of God. Herod making friends with Pilate is the follower of God becoming a friend of the world.

The leaven of Herod is *Worldliness.*

Sixth. The apostle uses leaven to portray the vain boasting of the flesh. "Your glorying is *not good.* Know ye not that a little leaven leaveneth the whole lump?" I Cor. v: 6.

Glorying is compared to the working of leaven. He uses a word which describes its effect in dough: "Ye are *puffed up.*" Verse 2.

The leaven among the Corinthians is *Vain-glorying.*

Seventh. He makes use of the leaven to emphasize his warning against the *works of the flesh.* "The leaven of malice and wickedness." I Cor. v: 8.

Worldliness! Vainglory! Malice! Wickedness! Evidences, each one of them, of fleshly energy and lust, and symbolized according to the Spirit of God, by leaven.

Summing up, it is manifest that leaven is used uniformly to signify either *corrupt doctrine or the energy and lust of the flesh.*

Two exceptions are to be found in Scripture to the exhortation against leaven. The first occurs in Leviticus xxiii: 17: "Ye shall bring out of your habitations two wave loaves of two-tenth deals: they shall be of fine flour; they shall be baken *with* leaven; they are the first-fruits unto the Lord."

The first fruits was the first sheaf of the harvest. It was *lifted up* before the Lord on the morrow after the sabbath, viz., *the first day of the week*. Lev. xxiii: 10, 11. "Christ is the first fruits." I Cor. xv: 23. The first to arise from among the dead. The sheaf of the first fruits, therefore, represents the resurrection of Christ. Fifty days after the first sheaf was presented it was made into flour and baked in these two loaves. "And ye shall count unto you from the morrow after the sabbath, from the day that ye brought the sheaf of the wave offering; seven sabbaths shall be complete: even unto the morrow after the seventh sabbath shall ye number fifty days; and ye shall offer a new meat offering unto the Lord. Ye shall bring out of your habitations two wave loaves of two tenth deals; they shall be of fine flour; they shall be baken with leaven; they are the first fruits unto the Lord." Lev. xxiii: 15—17.

Fifty days after the resurrection of Christ, on the day of Pentecost (*penteekostos,* fiftieth), the disciples "were all with one accord in one place. And suddenly there came a sound from heaven, as of a rushing mighty wind, and it filled all the house where they were sitting. And there appeared unto them cloven tongues, like as of *fire,* and it sat upon each of them. And they were all filled with the Holy Ghost." Acts ii: 1—4.

Thus endued with power from on high they were baptized *in* the Holy Ghost into one body. All this as the result of Christ's resurrection and ascension. *They* were the result of Christ's resurrection in this new relationship, just as *the loaves were the result of the coming forth and the lifting up of the first sheaf. The flour of that first sheaf was in the loaves and the life and power of the risen Son of God were in these disciples through the Holy Ghost which he shed forth.* The loaves, therefore, typify the Church, one leaf formed out of the Jewish assemblies, another out of the Gentile assemblies, constituting one body united to the *Man in the Glory.*

As believers we are before God in the character of the Risen One, with no sin on us (that is, against us), but as those who still walk on earth and in bodies of mortality there is sin *in* us. Leaven is a type of sin in the flesh, therefore leaven is introduced into these loaves to show that while before God we are clean in Christ, yet in us, in our flesh, there dwelleth the nature of corruption and sin. Thus leaven in the offering is not only in accord with the uniform teaching of the Word about it, but is another evidence of the divine accuracy of the types.

The other exception is in Amos iv: 4, 5: "Come to Bethel, and transgress; at Gilgal multiply transgression * * * and offer a sacrifice of thanksgiving *with* leaven." Leaven is here set over against transgression, while the context shows conclusively that the Lord is speaking in judgment and rebuke concerning the corruption and hypocrisy in Israel.

In the light of God's unvarying testimony about leaven let us examine two remarkable passages:

"Your glorying is not good. Know ye not that a little leaven leaveneth the whole lump? Purge out, therefore, the old leaven that ye may be a new lump, as ye are unleavened. For even Christ our passover is

sacrificed for us. Therefore let us keep the feast, not
with old leaven, neither with the leaven of malice and
wickedness; but with the unleavened bread of sincerity
and truth." I Cor. v: 6—8.

Three things are mentioned: the old leaven, a new
lump, ye are unleavened.

First. THE OLD LEAVEN. The old leaven is that
which corrupts man and manifests itself in the evil tendencies already described. It is his fallen fleshly nature.

Second. THE NEW LUMP. Primarily the Corinthian
assembly, afterwards the individual member of Christ in
that assembly, looked at as without leaven. A new nature in which is no sinful flesh. The new nature received
in union with a risen Christ.

Third. YE ARE UNLEAVENED. In this we have the
standing and character of the Church of Christ even
down here and now. "As he is, so are we in this world."
I John iv: 17. "Faultless before the presence of his
glory." Jude xxiv.

And just because these Corinthians stood before God
in Christ's perfection, the apostle urges them to purge
out the old leaven, cast off the works of the flesh, cease
their glorying, and put away from their midst the
unclean man, the fornicator, whom they had tolerated
and not judged. As leaven was rigorously excluded
from the typical passover, there must be no toleration
of the working of leaven, or the flesh, in connection with
the Antitype.

As Israel kept the feast, so must the Church. Keeping the feast is owning the judgment of death and appro-
priating its benefits. The Christian is to own the judgment of God against the flesh and reckon it put to death,
judicially, in the death of Christ. He is to cast it out like

old leaven as corrupt and corrupting, nor ever seek to purify it, lead it to God, or change it, but *purge it out*.

He is to appropriate the deliverance of that judgment, own that it has delivered him from dependence on the flesh, that he is no longer a debtor to the flesh to live after the flesh, even for righteousness; but that he has been made free by the dead body of Christ, in order that he might be married to another, even to him who is raised from the dead (see Rom. 7), and recognizing himself in the risen Christ, allow that risen one to walk in him and manifest continually that he is a *new lump*.

The other passage to be considered is Matt. xiii: 33: "Another parable spake he unto them: The kingdom of heaven is like unto leaven, which a woman took, and hid in three measures of meal, till the whole was leavened." By many expositors, this parable is used to illustrate the final triumph of the Gospel in this age. The leaven is made to serve as a symbol of the Gospel, the woman who hides it as the Church, and the three measures of meal the world, into which the Church is to introduce the Gospel until the world itself shall be permeated by, and brought under subjection to it.

This parable stands fourth in order of the seven recorded, and sustains a relationship, both intimate and logical, to the preceding ones.

In the sower we are shown how the Gospel would be received during the absence of the Lord. Of the four parts of ground over which the sower went forth, only a fourth brought fruit to perfection, and that in varying degree. No hint is here given that at any one time, during the preaching of the Word, would it be universally received. History, so far, has not justified any such confidence, or warranted us in reading into the parable any other conclusion than that of *limited recep-tion.*

In the second parable an enemy secretly introduces tares, *hides* them among the good seed; that is, an en-deavor is made to *corrupt* the seed already sown. When the wheat comes forth the tares appear also, and so closely resemble the wheat that orders are given not to root them up till the harvest. The harvest is explained to be the end of the world, or age (*aion,* the preceding word rendered world is *kosmos*) ; and whatever else is taught, and much else is taught, we are shown unmis-takably that the field, which is the world, *not* the Church, is a *mixed field till the very end of the age.*

Now, if the Lord intended us to believe that the whole world would be permeated by the Gospel he could have illustrated that fact by pointing us to an *unmixed* field, a field *all wheat.* On the contrary he uses a figure which, in strongest terms, declares that the children of the kingdom and the children of the devil will dwell side by side, in this world, till the end of the age.

In the parable of the mustard tree there is pictured the growth of the professing church from small begin-nings. But this tree gives shelter to the birds of the air, and the birds are used in the parable of the sower to indicate the presence and power of the "wicked one." We have no authority for pressing a parable to interpretation in all its details; but as the birds have already been used as factors in interpretation, it ought not to seem a strained application to learn through this use of them, that the professing church in proportion as it becomes *rooted in the earth* will afford a nesting-place and shelter for Satan. And, as in the preceding parable he introduces himself among the good seed of the kingdom in the shape of tares, the interpretation would appear to fall in the line of direct analogy; but without claiming this, and more which seems plainly taught, it is at least demonstrable that nothing in the symbolry hints at the undivided triumph of the Gospel in this dispensation.

The parable of the leaven follows immediately that of the mustard tree, and forces us to a retrospection in order to see the "drift" from which we approach it.

Beginning with the parable of the sower, indicating, as it does, a not universal reception of the Gospel, going on with the story of the tares, presenting to us the introduction of a false and corrupt profession of Christianity, and a world divided between God and Satan till the end, and closing with the mustard tree, showing us the birds which our Lord uses as a symbol of evil and uncleanness nesting in and finding shelter in the professed kingdom of heaven in this age, are we warranted to expect— would we have any legitimate ground on which to base our expectation—that the next parable would reverse the whole course of the previous teaching, and announce to us the universal reception of the Gospel? The answer to such a question must be in the negative. No such expectation is or could be warranted. And when it is added that the symbol on which such an interpretation relies is the known and confessed symbol in every other scripture to set forth corruption and sin, such an exegesis of the parable is ruled out of court.

But apart from all that has been said, the evidence against such a rendering lies in the parable itself.

First. The woman *hides* the leaven in the lump, but the Gospel is to be made *known* openly: "What I tell you in darkness speak ye *in the light;* and what ye hear

in the ear, that preach ye on the house-tops." Matt.
x: 27.

Second. The three measures of meal constitute a
lump which is leavened. But in Leviticus ii: 15, we
read: "A meat offering shall be of fine flour; * * *
it shall be of fine flour unleavened." The meat offering sets forth the perfect man Christ Jesus, the Head of
the Church, in glory; it sets forth also, the Church, the
body of Christ, on earth, as we have already seen, and
as the apostle conclusively proves: "Purge out therefore the old leaven, that YE *may be a* NEW LUMP, as YE
are UNLEAVENED." I Cor. v: 7. The three measures
of meal, or the lump which is leavened, therefore, does
not set forth the world, but the Church—at first the true
Church in Christ, and then mixed with it the outward
profession of Christ. And it may be mentioned here
as highly suggestive, that at this present moment Christendom is divided into three great religious measures or
parts: The Greek Church, the Roman Church, the
Protestant Church. As the lump is not the world, the
teaching which makes leavening the lump, the leavening
of the world, falls to the ground, and with it the figure
of the Gospel leavening the world.

Now reading leaven in the light of the divine definition as corrupt doctrine and fleshly practice, and the
three measures of meal as the profession of Christ in this
age, it is evident that we have in this parable a prophecy
that the time is coming when Christendom will be filled
with the evils of corrupt doctrine and fleshly energy, and
that so far from overcoming the world by means of her
unleavened bread of sincerity and truth, the Church will
herself, if not watchful, be overcome of error, and worldliness, and fleshly lust. Nor does examination into the

"present state of religion" seem in any wise to contradict the prophecy.

To all spiritually minded believers there is in this revelation of the truth an exhortation to own the indwelling leaven, cast off and cast out the works of the flesh, and walk before God in the new and divine life of the risen and coming Man. And all the more as we see "the Day approaching."

SEVEN THINGS ABOUT LOT.

Seven Things about Lot.

Lot is a representative character. He is a saved man, elected and called, with Abraham, to the same country, with this difference, that while Abraham types out the faithful, Lot sets forth the unfaithful, Christian.

There are seven clearly marked stages in this man's career.

I. Lot chose his inheritance after the sight of his eyes. Gen. xiii: 10-11.

He left God out of the matter and chose his portion according to his best interest; not so Abraham; he was willing to abide in faith that God would fulfill unto him the promises of good.

Unlike Abraham, but just like Lot, many Christians are to-day seeking their own interest first, and the cause of Christ last; unwilling to trust all to him who has said, "Seek ye first the kingdom of God, and his righteousness; and all these things shall be added unto you." Matt. vi: 33. This choice of Lot was the beginning of all his subsequent disasters.

II. Lot pitched his tent *toward* Sodom. Gen. xiii: 12.

Sodom is a type of this world. Lot began with a worldly choice; no wonder that he gravitated toward the world.

Many Christians are in the second stage; they are not exactly *in* the world, but they are pitching their tents *toward* Sodom.

III. Lot took up his dwelling place *in* Sodom. Gen. xiv: 12. "Whatsoever a man soweth, that shall he also reap." Gal. vi: 7.

He started with a worldly choice, and he reaped worldly sympathies, and wordly desires, and, by the law of continuance, was driven to gratify them; once tamper with the unclean thing, and you will soon lose all power to resist its influence; and by and by, you will even dare to justify in act, that from which you once shrank back in thought.

Alas! how many who wear the name of Christ are to-day living not in heavenly places with him, but dwelling in Sodom, subject to its sin.

IV. Lot took office in Sodom. He sat in the gate. Gen. xix: 1. He become identified with its interests, a sustainer of its policy.

Behold Christians to-day, seeking office and power at the hands of a world that killed their Lord, a world of whom he has said, its friendship is enmity with God; and, "whosoever, therefore, will be a friend of the world, is the enemy of God." James iv: 4.

Instead of testifying against this evil and untoward generation, the church is supporting it.

V. By entering into Sodom, Lot lost his testimony. Gen. xix: 14. The world despised him. How keenly the world despises a worldly Christian, one who does all that they do, and yet professes to be elect of God and an heir of glory. What a subject for contempt is that man, be he layman or minister, who plunges into the world and its economies, who digs deep the foundation of his interest, in the soil of earth; and then seeks to warn men of the judgments that are coming.

The very angels who came to warn Lot thought him so unworthy that, at first, they refused the shelter of his house; preferring all night in the streets to the companionship of a man who had betrayed his Lord.

VI. When the city was destroyed, Lot lost all his works.

The city that he tried to improve became a waste.

There are many men, honest no doubt, who are seeking to moralize or reform the world. But their efforts must be fruitless, for judgment has been pronounced upon it.

At the coming of Christ, all Christians who are dwelling in it, whether from pure worldly motives and sympathies, or from honest desires to improve it, shall alike have their works destroyed. The command of God to his people is, "Come out from among them, and be ye separate, saith the Lord, and touch not the unclean thing; and I will receive you." II Cor. vi: 17. Or again, he exhorts the child of God, "to keep himself unspotted from the world." James i: 27.

VII. Lot escaped only with his life. Read I Cor. iii: 13-15.

At the judgment seat of Christ, where only the saved shall appear, many a saved person will receive no reward. Their works will be burned up. They will be saved, yet, so as through the fire; saved, because salvation is by grace, and not by merit. And, because, their works were wood, hay and stubble; because they did not improve their opportunities, and dealt in work that was only rubbish; because they were downright disobedient to the will of God in their work; because, in short, they built wrong material into the temple of God, they will suffer loss; hence, the solemn admonition, "Behold, I come quickly; hold that fast which thou hast, that no man take thy crown." Rev. iii: 11.

Behold the record and the end of a worldly Christian, *saved, but not crowned.* Having life, but not authority in the kingdom.

Whose example will you follow, Lot or Abraham?

FOUR JUDGMENTS.

Four Judgments.

The scriptures teach that there are four judgments.

1. *The judgment of the cross.*

The cross revealed the judgment of God against sin. "For he hath made him to be sin for us, who knew no sin; that we might be made the righteousness of God in him." II Cor. v: 21. "Who his own self bare our sins in his own body on the tree." I Pet. ii: 24. "For Christ also hath once suffered for sins, the just for the unjust." I Pet. iii: 18.

In that terrible hour he appeared as the substitute in behalf of his people to receive the judgment due to them, and therefore, concerning every one that believeth in him, it is written, "He hath everlasting life, and shall not come into condemnation" (judgment). John v: 24.

2. *The judgment seat of Christ.*

"For we (Christians) must all appear before the judgment seat of Christ; that every one may receive the things done in his body, according to that he hath done, whether it be good or bad." II Cor. v: 10.

The apostle is addressing Christians: he is speaking only of Christians; and as all will be in glorified resurrection-bodies when they do appear at the judgment seat, it is evidently not a question of salvation, but of reward according to service. Those who have been faithful shall receive a reward: those who have not been faithful shall suffer loss. "The fire shall try every man's (every Christian man's) work, of what sort it is. If any man's work abide, which he hath built thereupon, (on Christ), he shall receive a reward. If any man's *work* shall be burned, he shall suffer loss: *but he him-*

self shall be saved: yet so as by (through) fire." I Cor. iii : 13-15.

3. *The judgment of the nations.*

This takes place at the coming of Christ from heaven with his Church to the Mount of Olives. "Then shall the Lord go forth and fight against those nations, as when he fought in the day of battle. And his feet shall stand in that day upon the Mount of Olives." Zech. xiv: 3, 4. "Let the heathen be wakened, and come up to the valley of Jehoshaphat : for there will I sit to judge all the heathen round about." Joel iii : 12. "For I will gather all nations (that is the nations of the restored Roman Empire) against Jerusalem." Zech. xiv: 2. "When the son of man shall come in his glory, and all the holy angels with him, then shall he sit upon the throne of his glory; and before him shall be gathered all nations." Matt. xxv: 31, 32.

In this judgment the living and not the dead appear. There is no thought of resurrection in the scene : it is smiting the nations with a rod of iron just previous to the establishment of the kingdom.

4. *The judgment of the Great White Throne.*

This occurs at the close of the thousand years. This is the second resurrection : the coming forth of the Christless dead to receive final retribution. "The rest of the dead lived not again till the thousand years were finished. * * * And I saw a great white throne. * * * And I saw the dead, small and great stand before God. * * * and the dead were judged. * * * and whosoever was not found written in the book of life was cast into the lake of fire." Rev. xx: 5-15.

THE TWO-FOLD COMING.

The Two-Fold Coming.

The second coming of our Lord Jesus Christ, while spoken of as one great event, has two separate parts. It is of the utmost importance to distinguish, and never to confound them.

In the first part he comes as a *thief*. Rev. xvi: 15.

In the second part he comes as *lightning*. Luke xvii: 24.

In the first, The *morning star*. Rev. xxii: 16.

In the second, Sun of *righteousness*. Mal. iv: 1, 2.

In the first, As a *bridegroom*. Matt. xxv: 1—6.

In the second, As a *king*. Matt. xxv: 31—34.

In the first, To the *marriage*. Matt. xxv: 10.

In the second, To the *throne of his glory*. Matt. xxv: 31.

In the first, To the *virgins*. Matt. xxv: 1.

In the second, To the *nations*. Matt. xxv: 32.

In the first, *Before* the marriage. Matt. xxv: 1.

In the second, *After* the marriage. Luke xii: 36.

In the first, *For* his bride. John xvi: 3.

In the second, *With* his bride. Col. iii: 4.

In the first, Into the *air*. I Thess. iv: 17.

In the second, descends to the *Mount of Olives*. Zech. xiv: 3, 4.

In the first, comes to *receive* his *bride* to himself. John xiv: 3.

In the second, comes to be received by repentant Israel. Zech. xi: 10.

In the first, comes to take his bride into the heavenly city. John xiv: 1—5. Cant. iv: Eph. v: 27.

In the second, comes to enter as king into the earthly Jerusalem. Matt. xxv: 31. Jer. iii: 17. Zech. viii: 3. Luke i: 32, 33.

The first stage is called "Our gathering together unto him." II Thess. ii: 1.

The second stage is called "The revelation of Jesus Christ from heaven." II Thess. i: 7.

The first stage, "The Blessed Hope." Titus ii: 13.

The second stage, "The Glorious Appearing." Titus ii: 13.

The first stage or part is called the *Coming*, from the Greek word *parousia*, and signifies *presence*.

The second stage is called the *"Brightness* of his coming," and is from the Greek word *epiphantea*, meaning brightness or glory: thus the *epiphaniea* of his *parousia* is the glory of his presence. In other words, when he first descends into the air to receive his church, he will be invisible to the world; after an interval during which the kingdom of Antichrist is running its course on earth, he will manifest himself to the gaze of all the nations gathered at Jerusalem, and descend in visible glory and power to overthrow them.

A BIBLE READING ON CHRISTIANS.

A Bible Reading on Christians.

1. What we were.

"Dead in trespasses and sins." "We were dead in sins." Eph. ii: 1, 5.—"And were by nature children of wrath, even as others." Eph. ii: 3. "So death passed upon all men for that all have sinned." Rom. v: 12. "Being in time past, Gentiles in the flesh, * * * at that time ye were without Christ, being aliens from the commonwealth of Israel and strangers from the covenant of promise, having no hope, and without God in world: * * * ye were far off." Eph. ii: 11-13.

2. Where we were.

"The men which thou gavest me *out of the world.*" John xvii: 6. "In time past ye walked according to the course of this world, according to the prince of the power of the air, the spirit that now worketh in the children of disobedience: among whom also we all had our conversation in times past in the lusts of our flesh, fulfilling the desires of the flesh and of the mind." Eph. ii: 2, 3.

3. What we are now.

a. In relation to God.

"For ye are all the children of God by faith in Christ Jesus." Gal. iii: 26. "Beloved, now are we the Sons of God." I John iii: 2. "Whosoever believeth that Jesus is the Christ, is born of God." I John v: 1. "As he is, so are we in this world." I John iv: 17. "We are the children of God, and if children, then heirs; heirs of God, and joint heirs with Christ." Rom. viii: 16, 17.

b. In relation to the world.

"Ye are my witnesses," saith the Lord. Isa. xliii: 10. "And ye shall be witnesses unto me, * * * unto the uttermost part of the earth." Acts i: 8. "Ye are the light of the world." Math. v: 14. "Ye shine as lights in the world." Phil. ii: 15. "We are ambassadors for Christ." II Cor. v: xx.

4. Where we are.

"Raised up together and made to sit together in Heavenly places in Christ Jesus." Eph. ii: 6. "Risen with Christ." Col. iii: 1. "Your life is hid with Christ in God." Col. iii: 3.

5. What we have.

"God for Christ's sake hath forgiven you." Eph. iv: 32. "Your sins are forgiven you for his name's sake." I John ii: 12.

"Verily, verily, I say unto you, he that believeth on me hath everlasting life." John vi: 47. "We have the mind of Christ." I Cor. ii: 16. "All things are yours: * * * the world, or life, or death, or things present, or things to come; all are yours." I Cor. iii: 21, 22.

6. What we shall be.

"We know that when He shall appear, we shall be like him; for we shall see Him as He is." I John iii: 2. "And hast made us kings and priests: and we shall reign on the Earth." Rev. v: 10.

"They shall be priests of God and of Christ, and shall reign with Him a thousand years." Rev. xx: 6.

7. Where we shall be.

a. If we die.

"Absent from the body, present with the Lord." II Cor. v: 8.

b. If Jesus comes.

"We which are alive and remain shall be caught up together with them in the clouds, to meet the Lord in the air: and so shall we ever be with the Lord." I Thes. iv: 17. "Then shall ye also appear with Him in glory." Col. iii: 4.

"And his feet shall stand in that day upon the mount of Olives, * * * and the Lord my God shall come, and all the saints with him." Zech. xiv: 4, 5.

"Those that wait upon the Lord * * * shall inherit the earth." "For such as be blessed of him shall inherit the earth. The righteous shall inherit the land and dwell therein forever." Ps. xxxvii: 9, 22, 23.

"Blessed are the meek: for they shall inherit the earth." Math. v: 5. "And I saw a new heaven and a new earth. * * * and he that sat upon the throne said behold I make all things new." Rev. xxi: 1-5.

8. What is our duty now—

a. In relation to God.

"I beseech you therefore, brethren, by the mercies of God, that ye present your bodies, a living sacrifice, holy, acceptable unto God, which is your reasonable service. And be not conformed to this world: but be ye transformed by the renewing of your mind, that ye may prove what is that good, and acceptable, and perfect will of God." Rom. xii: 1, 2. "For ye are bought with a price: therefore glorify God in your body, and in your spirit, which are God's." I Cor. vi: 20.

b. In relation to one another.

"First gave their own selves unto the Lord, and unto us by the will of God." II Cor. viii: 5. "Bear ye one another's burdens." Gal. vi: 2. "We then that are strong ought to bear the infirmities of the weak, and not to please ourselves." Rom. xv: 1.

c. In relation to the world.

"Shine as lights in the world; holding forth the word of life." Phil. ii: 15, 16.

"Let your light so shine before men that they may see your good works and glorify your Father which is in heaven." Math. v: 16. "Be ye therefore followers of

God, as dear children; And walk in love. * * * But fornication, and all uncleaness, or covetousness, let it not be once named among you, as becometh saints; neither filthiness, nor foolish talking, nor jesting, * * * walk circumspectly, * * * Redeeming the time, because the days are evil. * * * And be not drunk with wine, wherein is excess; but be filled with the spirit; speaking to yourselves in psalms, and hymns, and spiritual songs, singing and making melody in your heart to the Lord, giving thanks always for all things unto God and the Father, in the name of our Lord Jesus Christ: Submitting yourselves one to another in the fear of the Lord." Eph. v. "Whether therefore ye eat, or drink, or whatsoever ye do, do all to the glory of God." I Cor. x: 31.

9. Our attitude in relation to his coming.

"Ye turned to God from idols to serve the living and true God, and to wait for His Son from heaven." I Thes. i: 9, 10.

"Let your loins be girded about, and your lights burning." Luke xii: 35.

"Therefore be ye also ready: for in such an hour as ye think not, the Son of man cometh." Math. xxvii: 44.

ONENESS OF CHRIST AND HIS PEOPLE.

Oneness of Christ and His People.

1. The Scriptures declare that Christ and his people are one. "For both he that sanctifieth, and they who are sanctified, are all of one." Heb. ii: 11. "He that is joined unto the Lord is one spirit." I Cor. vi: 17. "Ye were called unto the fellowship (partnership) of his Son Jesus Christ our Lord." I Cor. i: 9. "As he is, so are we in this world." I John iv: 17. "And we are in him." I John v: 20.

2. This oneness has existed from all eternity. "He hath chosen us in him before the foundation of the world." Eph. i: 4. "The mystery which from the beginning hath been hid in God." Eph. iii: 9.

3. We were given to Christ that we might be one with him. "The men which thou gavest me out of the world, thine they were, and thou gavest them me." John xvii: 6. "Behold, I and the children which God hath given me." Heb. ii: 13.

4. The Son of God came down and took our nature in order to be one with us. "Forasmuch then as the children are partakers of flesh and blood, he also himself likewise took part of the same." Heb. ii: 14.

5. He became one with us in our sins — that is, he took our sins and confessed them as his own. "Mine iniquities have taken hold upon me. They are more than the hairs of mine head." Ps. xl: 12. "He hath borne our griefs and carried our sorrows." Isa. liii: 4. "Himself took our infirmities and bare our sicknesses." Matt. viii: 17.

6. He manifested this oneness on the cross. "Our old man is (was) crucified with him." Rom. vi: 6.

7. We are one with him in death and burial. "Therefore we are buried with him by baptism into death." Rom. vi: 4. "We have been planted together in the likeness of his death." Rom. vi: 5.

8. We were made one with him in life, or made alive together. "God * * * when we were dead in sin hath quickened us (made us alive) together with Christ." Eph. ii: 4, 5.

9. One with him in resurrection. "And hath raised us up together and made us to sit together in heavenly places in Christ Jesus." Eph. ii: 6.

10. We are one with him in his acceptance before God. "He hath made us accepted in the Beloved." Eph. i: 6.

11. We are now one with him in God. "Your life is hid with Christ in God." Col. iii: 3. "And ye are complete in him." Col. ii: 10.

12. We shall be one with him in the appearing and glory, "When Christ, who is our life, shall appear, then shall ye also appear with him in glory." Col. iii: 4.

13. We shall be one with him in his reign. "We shall also reign with him." II Tim. ii: 12.

14. God with him has given us all things. "He that spared not his own Son, but delivered him up for us all, how shall he not with him also freely give us all things?" Rom. viii: 32.

15. Finally, we shall be like him. "We shall be like him, for we shall see him as he is." I John iii: 2.

MAN'S RUIN—GOD'S REMEDY.

Man's Ruin—God's Remedy.

I. Man is a sinner by transgression. Rom. iii: 10-18. Isa. lxiv: 6.

II. By nature. Rom. viii: 7. Rom. vii: 18. Rom. v: 12.

III. He is spiritually dead. Eph. ii: 1. I Cor. ii: 14.

IV. There is no difference as to guilt. Rom. iii: 22, 23. God requires perfect holiness. Are you short in *one* requirement, you are guilty of sin. Are you short in two requirements, you are guilty of sin. The moralist who just fails to be holy, is guilty of sin. The out-breaking transgressor is guilty of sin. There is, then, no difference on the count of sin; both are guilty.

V. God cannot clear the guilty. Ex. xxxiv: 7. Numb. xiv: 18. Ezk. xviii: 4.

VI. God sent his son Jesus Christ into the world to take the sinner's place, and suffer his doom. Rom. viii: 3. Gal. iv: 4, 5. Gal. iii: 13, I Pet. ii: 24. I Pet. iii: 18.

VII. The question of sin is now settled. John xix: 30. Heb. ix: 26.

VIII. Grace finds a righteous channel in the death of Christ. Rom. iii: 24.

IX. Jesus Christ is now presented as a Saviour to sinners. Acts v: 31. Acts xiii: 38.

X. Salvation is received by receiving Jesus Christ through faith. John i: 12. John iii: 16, 18, 36. John v: 24. John vi: 47. Rom. x: 9. I John v: 1. I John v: 13.

The philosophy of this faith.

1. It claims Jesus as substitute, and Saviour.
2. It takes God at his word.

> "Believe on Him, who died for thee,
> And sure as He has died,
> Thy debt is paid, thy soul is free
> And thou art justified."

LAW AND GOSPEL.

Law and Gospel.

The law and the gospel do not go in company. They are by nature as far apart as life and death. The one is the ministry of death, the other of life.

The law is the whip-lash of judgment.

The gospel is the silver bell ringing the anthem of love. The law brings a work to *do*. The gospel brings a word to *believe*.

The law is the reflex of one side of God's nature; the reflex of his terrible holiness, his exact justice. It reveals what man is not. He is not holy. He is not righteous. He is not accepted before God. It reveals what man is. He is a sinner, a hopeless sinner, a hopelessly lost sinner.

The gospel is the good news that the law has been honored, the claims met, and God satisfied: the good news that Jesus honored the law in life, met the penalty in death, and at God's right hand, a risen man, is witness of God's eternal satisfaction. The gospel brings the good news that there is forgiveness with God, and that life eternal is his gift. It brings a new life, in which and by which, we may live above the law, so binding us to the heart of God in vital union with his Son, that we need no thunder of judgment to keep us right, but filling us so full of Christ, if we will it, that we may love one another as brethren and neighbors in the Lord, even, as we love ourselves, while we love the God, in Jesus the Christ, with all the mind and strength.

The truest way to bring men under law to God, so that his will shall be righteously obeyed, is to preach the gospel, the good news of his love, and then shall it become true, that "we love him *because* he first loved us."

THE ROD AND THE ROCK.

The Rod and the Rock.

Numbers xx.

There are two scenes in which the rod and the rock are brought before us. The one, at Rephidim, in the wilderness of Sin. The other, at Kadesh, in the desert of Zin. The account of the first is given in Ex. xvii: 4-6. The people thirsted for water and murmured against Moses, "and Moses cried unto the Lord, saying, what shall I do unto this people, they be almost ready to stone me? And the Lord said unto Moses, go on before the people, and take with thee of the elders of Israel; and thy rod, wherewith thou smotest the river, take in thine hand, and go. Behold, I will stand before thee there upon the rock, in Horeb; and thou shalt smite the rock, and there shall come water out of it, that the people may drink. And Moses did so in the sight of the elders of Israel." The rock typifies Christ, "for they drank of that spiritual rock that followed them, and that rock was Christ." I Cor. x: 4. Smiting the rock is smiting Christ; "we did esteem him stricken, smitten of God." Isa. liii: 4. The rod was the instrument used in smiting, and as the smiting sets forth judgment, therefore the rod of Moses is the rod of judgment. That this is the character of the rod may be seen from other scripture. In Ex. vii: 14—17, he uses the rod to smite the river with blood. In Ex. ix: 23, he uses it to bring down the judgment of fire and hail. Now the fact that God commands Moses to take this rod and use it upon the rock in his presence, sets forth clearly that God would shew unto the people the way of salvation through the judgment of the cross.

But what God does is done forever. What, then, are we to understand by the apparent repetition of the scene, and the second smiting of the rock; smiting too with this very rod of judgment? Either we are to understand that Christ is crucified a second time, or else Moses was disobedient. Moses *was* disobedient. The Lord did not tell him to smite the rock at all, but *speak* to it. "And the Lord said unto Moses, take the rod and gather thou the assembly together, thou and Aaron, thy brother, and speak ye unto the rock before their eyes, and it shall give forth his water." Num. xx: 8. It will be noticed that Aaron is introduced into this scene, and not in the first. Aaron sets forth priest-hood, and priest-hood is intercessory, but intercession is based, only, on sacrifice. If then the first smiting of the rock sets forth the one sacrifice of Christ, once for all, the second scene in which Moses with Aaron is commanded to speak to or supplicate the rock, sets forth the priestly relation of Christ on the basis of that sacrifice to his people. Having been crucified, he dies no more. He now liveth at the right hand of God to make intercession for his people and unfold the blessings they need. Passing through the wilderness we contract defilement by the way. How shall it be removed? By *speaking* to him, telling it all out before him, and he will cleanse us from all unrighteousness. We want blessings and grace. What shall we do? *Speak* to him, and the streams of mercy will flow forth as from an endless fountain.

THE ROD THAT BUDDED.

The Rod that Budded.

In Numbers xvi. we get an account of Korah's con-spiracy against the priest-hood, the test to which Moses invited them, and the consuming wrath of God, which destroyed them and swallowed up the rebels, Dathan and Abiram. We learn, also, in Numbers xvii. that, in order to set an open seal of his favor upon the priest-hood of Aaron, God required each tribe to bring a stick with the name of their family upon it, and lay them up before the Lord in his sanctuary, saying unto them that the rod which blossomed and budded and brought forth almonds, should be the rod of him whom he recognized as Priest. On the morrow it was found that Aaron's rod had so blossomed and budded and brought forth almonds. Now, this testified not only of the divine ordination upon the house of Aaron, but it sets forth precious truth concerning the priest-hood of Christ. The budding of the rod is the coming forth of life out of death; for it was a dead or, at least, rootless stick. So, the life which is given of God, is made manifest out of death. Out of his dying, came forth the resurrection.

Again, as this rod set forth the priest-hood and took place after or on the other side of death, so we learn that the priest-hood of Christ is on the other side of the grave. Not on the earth. "For if he were on earth, he should not be a Priest." Heb. viii: 4. "For it is evident that our Lord sprang out of Judah, of which tribe Moses spake nothing concerning priest-hood." Heb. vii: 14. We learn that the Priest-hood of Christ is heavenly, so, also, is that of his Church; that, therefore, there is

no warrant for earthly priest-hood in the Church of
God; that the priest-hood on earth belongs now, as it
did then, to the family of Aaron, of the tribe of Levi.
That, in short, priest-hood on earth is recognized only
in Israel; and that as he is not now dealing with Israel
and will not do so till the Church is received into glory;
therefore, any priest-hood on earth, to-day, is unscriptural; and that, therefore, we are to consider him who is
the "Apostle and High Priest of our profession, Christ
Jesus." Heb. iii: 1.

OUTLINES OF PROPHESY.

Outlines of Prophesy.

1. Jesus Christ is coming to this world again.

"I will come again." John xiv: 3. "And when he had spoken these things, while they beheld, he was taken up; and a cloud received him out of their sight: and while they looked steadfastly toward heaven, as he went up, behold, two men stood by them in white apparel; which also said, ye men of Galilee, why stand ye gazing up into heaven? This same Jesus, which is taken up from you into heaven, shall so come in like manner as ye have seen him go into heaven." Acts i: 9—11. I Cor. i: 7. I Cor. xi: 26. I Cor. xvi: 22. Phil. iii: 20, 21. Phil. iv: 5. Col. iii: 4. I Thess. i: 9, 10. I Thess. ii: 19. I Thess. iii: 12, 13. I Thess. iv: 15—18. I Thess. v: 23. II Thess. i: 7—10. II Thess. ii: 1—8. II Thess. iii: 5. II Tim. iv: 1. Titus ii: 13. Heb. ix: 28. Heb. x: 37. James v: 7, 8, 9. I Peter i: 7. I Peter v: 4. II Peter i: 16. II Peter iii: 4. I John ii: 28. I John iii: 2. II John vii. Jude xiv. Rev. i: 7. Rev. ii: 25. Rev. iii: 11—20. Rev. 4th Chapter. Rev. xix: 11—21. Rev. xxii: 7, 12. 17—20. Job xix: 25—27. Isa. xxvi: 21. Isa. xl: 10. Isa. lxii: 11. Jer. xxiii: 5, 6. Dan. vii: 13. Hosea v: 15. Joel iii: 9—11. Hag. ii: 7. Zech. xiv: 1—5. Mal. iii: 1—5.

2. His coming will be unexpected.

"For in such an hour as ye think not, the son of man cometh." Matt. xxiv: 44. Mark xiii: 34—37.

3. He will come as a bridegroom for his bride.

"And at midnight there was a cry made, Behold, the bridegroom cometh." Matt. xxv: 6.

4. He will raise the dead, and change the living saints, and gather them to himself in the air.

"For the Lord himself shall descend from heaven with a shout, with the voice of the archangel, and with the trump of God: and the dead in Christ shall rise first: Then we which are alive and remain, shall be caught up together with them in the clouds, to meet the Lord in the air; and so shall we ever be with the Lord." I Thess. iv: 16, 17.

5. He will reward his people in the air.

"We (that is, christians) must all appear before the judgment seat of Christ; that every one may receive the things done in his body, according to that he hath done, whether it be good or bad." II Cor. v: 10. "Every man's (every christian man's) *work* shall be made manifest; for the day shall declare it, because it shall be revealed by fire; and the fire shall try every man's work of what sort it is. If any man's (any christian man's) work abide which he hath built thereupon, he shall receive a reward. If any man's work shall be burned, he shall suffer loss: but he himself shall be saved; yet so as by fire." I Cor. iii: 13—15.

6. The world will know nothing of this stage of Christ's coming till after the departure of the church. "For yourselves know perfectly, that the day of the Lord so cometh as a thief in the night." I Thess. v: 2. Luke xvii: 26—30.

7. The first resurrection takes place at the coming of Christ for his Church.

"The Lord himself shall descend from heaven with a shout, with the voice of the archangel, and with the trump of God: and *the dead in Christ shall rise first.*" I Thess. iv: 16. "The REST OF THE DEAD LIVED NOT

AGAIN UNTIL THE THOUSAND YEARS WERE FINISHED. *This is the first resurrection."* Rev. xx. 5.

8. With the departure of the church, the hindrance to Antichrist will be removed.

"For the mystery of iniquity doth already work: only he who now letteth (hindereth) will let, until he be *taken out of the way.* And *then* shall that Wicked be revealed." II Thess. ii: 7, 8.

The hinderance to Antichrist is the Holy Ghost. As a restraining power he will be taken away with the church.

9. Before Antichrist is revealed and just after the church departs, there will be a falling away, or apostasy.

Let no man deceive you by any means: for that day (the thousand years, the millennium) shall not come, except there come a falling away first, and that man of sin be revealed, the son of perdition." II Thess. ii: 3. That is to say, as the man of sin cannot be revealed till there is first a falling away, and as there cannot be an absolute lapse until the withdrawal of the Holy Ghost as a restraining power, and this can take place only with the departure of the church, the order of events is clearly defined: that is, the church is translated, iniquity comes to a head and Antichrist is revealed.

10. During this period of apostasy, there are wars and commotions, as a result of which, the old Roman Empire emerges into political, governmental, and geographical unity once more, as in the days of the Cæsars. A Prince arises to rule, and brings Israel into prominence in their own land, making a covenant with them for seven years.

"And *he* shall confirm the (a) covenant with many for one week." Dan. ix: 27.

"Many" refers to Israel. Week is heptade, and signifies a period of seven, as decade signifies ten, and here stands for seven years.

Who is the Prince? Verse 26 says, "The *people* of the *Prince that shall come*"—shewing that this Prince who is to come is to arise out of a certain people. Who are the people? The 26th verse indicates the people who destroyed Jerusalem. The people who destroyed Jerusalem were Romans: the people of this Prince, then, are Romans: and this Prince shall arise to be ruler over that nation, and make a league for seven years with many in Israel; for the many are Daniel's people, the Jews. The Romans did not make a league with the Jews after the destruction of Jerusalem. The Romans are not in existence now as a nation. The Jews are not in their own land, hence this prophecy of Daniel goes into the future; and as God's dealings cannot take place with Israel until the church is corporately complete, or taken out of the world, therefore this Prince and his people must arise after the departure of the church, and as Antichrist, the man of sin, has just been shewn to arise after the rapture of the church, we identify this Prince of the Romans with him. Besides, this prince is readily identified with the little horn of Daniel's vision, and the little horn is in all its characteristics the same as the wicked of Paul, the man of sin.

11. In the midst of the week or seven years, Satan is cast out of Heaven to the earth.

"The Devil which deceiveth the whole world was cast out (of heaven) into the earth. Woe to the inhabiters of the earth and of the sea! for the Devil is come down unto you, having great wrath, because he knoweth that he hath but a short time." Rev. xii: 7-12.

12. The Roman Prince is now energized by Satan, and revealed as the man of sin, or Antichrist. "And I stood upon the sand of the sea, and saw a beast rise up out of the sea, having seven heads and ten horns, and upon his horns ten crowns, and upon his heads the name of blasphemy. And the dragon (the Devil) gave him his power, and his seat, and great authority. And there was given unto him a mouth speaking great things and blasphemies: and power was given unto him to continue forty and two months. (Three years and a half, shewing this casting out of Satan as the energizing power, takes place in the midst of the seven years). And he opened his mouth in blasphemy against God, to blaspheme his name, and his tabernacle, and (even) them that dwell, (are dwelling), in heaven." (The tabernacle is the church and thus the church is seen to be dwelling in heaven while Antichrist rages: proving that the church is taken out of the world before this point is reached). Rev. xiii: 1—6.

"That man of sin, the son of perdition, who opposeth and exalteth himself above all that is called God, or that is worshipped: so that he, as God, sitteth in the temple of God, shewing himself that he is God." II Thess. ii: 3, 4.

13. He persecutes those on the earth called the "saints," those who turn unto the Lord after the church has been taken hence.

"And it was given unto him to make war with the saints, and to overcome them: and power was given him over all kindreds, and tongues, and nations." Rev. xiii: 7.

14. In the midst of the seven years, he breaks his covenant with Israel, and sets up his image in Jerusalem.

"In the midst of the week (heptade, the seven years) he shall cause the sacrifice and the oblation to cease (Israel will, at the first return to their own land, go back, in a measure, to the mosaic ritual), and for the overspreading of abominations, he shall make it desolate (or as the margin reads, "Upon the battlements, shall be the idols of the desolator." (the image spoken of in the 13th chapter of Revelation). Dan. ix: 27.

This corresponds with the testimony of Paul in II Thess. ii: 3, 4, where the man of sin sitteth in the temple of God, that is, of course, at Jerusalem, demanding to be worshipped as God.

15. At this sign, many who are loyal to Christ, flee away, as forewarned by the Lord. "When ye, therefore, shall see the abomination of desolation, spoken of by Daniel the prophet, stand in the holy place (whoso readeth, let him understand), then let them which be in Judea, flee into the mountains." Matt. xxiv: 15.

16. At this time two witnesses will appear in Jerusalem, testifying of Jesus unto Israel.

"And I will give power unto my two witnesses, and they shall prophesy a thousand, two hundred and three score days (that is three years and a half), clothed in sackcloth. These have power to shut Heaven, that it rain not in the days of their prophecy; (reminding us in this respect of Elijah's power) : and have power over waters to turn them to blood, and to smite the earth with all plagues (reminding us of Moses in Egypt), as often as they will." Rev. xi: 3, 6.

In the transfiguration scene, Moses and Elijah appear on the mount with Jesus. Peter, who was an eyewitness, tells us in an epistle, that this scene represented the coming and Kingdom of Christ as in panorama. It is evident, therefore, that when Christ comes to establish the Kingdom in Israel, Moses and Elias will occupy pre-eminent positions; and as in this very chapter we have the prelude to the coming of Christ, and the triumph of the Kingdom, and these two witnesses possess all the characteristics of Moses and Elias, and as Moses and Elias can have no imitators; and as the prophet Malachi declares absolutely that Elias will come before the great and notable day of the Lord, "Behold, I will send you Elijah (Elias) the prophet before the coming of the great and dreadful day of the Lord," Mal. iv: 5, then these two witnesses are none other than Moses and Elias, and thus we understand why the Devil was not permitted to have the body of Moses to corrupt it with the corruption of death, as we read in Jude 9; was not permitted to have it, in order that he might appear in it again; and thus, also, we understand why Elijah was translated without seeing death.

17. Through the testimony of these witnesses, an elect remnant is brought out who refuse to worship the beast, and instead, give glory to Christ, as the true God.

"And the remnant * * * gave glory to the God of heaven." Rev. xi: 13.

18. Antichrist, or the beast, puts the two witnesses to death; and God gives them resurrection.

"And when they shall have finished their testimony, the beast that ascendeth out of the bottomless pit shall make war against them, and shall overcome them, and kill them. And after three days and a half, the Spirit of life from God entered into them, and they stood upon their feet; * * * and they heard a great voice from heaven, saying unto them, Come up hither. And they ascended up to heaven in a cloud." Rev. xi: 7-12.

19. Antichrist becomes enraged at the rebellion in Israel, and gathers an army and comes against Jerusalem to destroy it and the people.

"For I will gather *all nations* against Jerusalem to battle; and the city shall be taken, and the houses rifled, and half of the city shall go forth into captivity." Zech. xiv: 2. "And I saw the beast, and the kings of the earth, and their armies, gathered together to make war against him that sat on the horse" (Christ). Rev. xix: 19.

20. At this moment the Lord will descend from heaven to the Mount of Olives in mighty power.

"Then shall the Lord go forth, and fight against those nations, and his feet shall stand in that day upon the mount of Olives, which is before Jerusalem on the east." Zech. xiv: 3, 4. That this does not refer to the first coming of Christ must be clear. He did not go forth at that time to fight against the nations. When he went to the mount of Olives it was as one despised and rejected of men. He has not stood upon the mount of Olives and fought against the nations since the resurrection. The great act is yet to take place.

21. The saints, or, the church, will descend from heaven, whither they had been previously caught up, with Christ in great glory.

"The Lord, my God, shall come and all the saints with *thee*" (him). Zech. xiv: 5. "When Christ, who is our life, shall appear, then shall ye also appear with him in glory." Col. iii: 4. Rev. xix: 11—15.

22. He will cast the beast and the false prophet into the lake of fire.

"And the beast was taken, and with him the false prophet that wrought miracles before him. These both were cast alive into a lake of fire burning with brimstone." Rev. xix: 20.

23. Satan will be bound a thousand years.

"And I saw an angel come down from heaven, having the key of the bottomless pit and a great chain in his hand. And he laid hold on the dragon, that old serpent, which is the Devil, and Satan, and bound him a thousand years, and cast him into the bottomless pit." Rev. xx: 1—3.

24. The kingdom of Christ will now be established for a thousand years.

"And they (those who sat on thrones, the Church who come with Christ, and the martyrs who had suffered after the departure of the church), lived and reigned with Christ a thousand years." Rev. xx: 4. "And they sung a new song, saying, * * * *we shall reign on the earth.*" Rev. v: 9, 10.

25. At the close of the thousand years, Satan will be loosed to deceive the nations, and organizing a rebellion, shall have his host destroyed by fire from heaven, and be cast, himself, into the lake of fire.

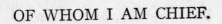

OF WHOM I AM CHIEF.

Of Whom I am Chief.

In I Tim. i: 15, we read that "Christ Jesus came into the world to save sinners of whom I am chief."

So Paul wrote, and for centuries, people have been accustomed to look upon the Apostle of the Gentiles as the head centre of earthly sin, as an example of profound and total depravity. Good inquiry room workers have not failed to seize the strategic value of the utterance in their dealings with the outcast, and have not omitted to comfort the black sheep and the unpromising with the thought, that if the chief of sinners could be saved, how readily hopeful was their case.

But Paul has suffered too long already under a misapprehension; as the result of a failure to read Paul in all the full Pauline light. It is only necessary to turn over to the letter which he wrote to the Philippians to see that the popular view of him as a pre-eminent sinner, an accentuatedly bad man, is not justified, and is, even, contradicted in his own full testimony. Listen to this: "circumcised the eighth day of the stock of Israel, of the tribe of Benjamin, an Hebrew of the Hebrews, as touching the law, a Pharisee * * * " Touching the righteousness which is in the law *blameless*. Phil. iii: 5—6. Read his defense in Acts xxiv: 14. "So worship I the God of my Fathers, *believing all things which are written in the law and in the Prophets.* Read again in Acts xxvi: 4—6. "My manner of life from my youth, which was at the first among mine own nation at Jerusalem, know all the Jews; which knew me from the beginning, if they would testify, that after the *most straitest sect of our religion.* I lived a Pharisee."

This is Paul's biography. There is no thought here—in the general acceptance of the term—of such a thing as the chief of sinners; on the contrary, here is a man absolutely religious—even his persecution of the church was done in the name of religion and God, and as he believed, for the upbuilding of the cause of truth and righteousness: living a life so absolutely blameless, so thoroughly without the fear of reproach as to conduct, as to personal morality, that he challenges those who have known him from childhood up, to come forward and testify against him if they can.

What then are we to understand by the word chief, in connection with this thought of sinners saved by grace? The rendering of the word chief by the actual Greek word "first" would throw light at once: "of whom I am the first." The following verse broadens the light; here we have the same word rendered properly: "Howbeit for this cause I obtained mercy," because what he did against the church, he did ignorantly and in unbelief, "that in me *first* Jesus Christ might show forth all long suffering, for a pattern of them which should hereafter believe on him to life everlasting." The word pattern completes the idea of chief. That is to say: Paul declares himself to be the first one of sinners brought to the knowledge of Christ, and a pattern of the long suffering and grace of God in his case. Evidently, Paul was not the first sinner to be turned to the Lord, he must therefore stand as the first one in a class of sinners, and not only as a pattern of the long suffering and grace of God, but as a pattern of the way in which that grace was manifested in the bringing of him to serve the Lord. If we turn to his first epistle to the Corinthians we will find him confirming this suggestion and enunciating it.

He says: "Last of all, he was seen of me also, as one born out of due time." I Cor. xv: 8. *One born ahead of the time.*

Let us enquire how Paul saw the Lord Jesus and we shall have the whole truth. We know how he saw him. He saw him appearing in glory above the Damascus gate, and smitten to earth with that glory, he cried out, and owned Jesus of Nazareth as the Messiah, and the Lord God of Israel. The truth is, Paul was never converted by the preaching of the Gospel, but by the appearing of our Lord Jesus Christ; and as the nation of Israel is never to be converted by the preaching of the Gospel, but by the appearing of God in glory to the Mount of Olives, where they shall look upon him whom they have pierced, it is evident that Paul as a Hebrew of the Hebrews, standing forth as the incarnate blindness bigotry and persecution of that people against the Son of God, is thrown forward ahead of Israel's time dispensationally; and as one born out of due time—that is out of Israel's time—becomes the *protos,* the first one of Israel converted by the appearing of Christ in glory; and is thus the witness, of the long suffering and grace of God towards that people, and the pattern, the sample of the way, in which, at the last, they shall be brought to know and own him; like Thomas, believing only when they shall see him, and thrust in their hands into the print of the nails; believing in him and owning him only, as Paul did, when he shall flash down out of Heaven earthward, in the glory of his appearing.

EARTHLY THINGS.

Earthly Things.

"If I have told you earthly things, and ye believe not, how shall ye believe if I tell you of heavenly things?"

The Kingdom of God and the doctrine of the second birth do not seem, on the surface at least, like earthly things; yet, since these are the things of which Jesus had been speaking to Nicodemus, the Kingdom of God and the doctrine of the second birth, *must* be classed among the earthly things. Our Lord's declaration that Nicodemus, as a teacher, ought to have known and understood them as such, makes it evident that the explanation and justification for so startling an appellation, are to be found in the very scriptures which the learned Rabbi professed to teach. An examination of these scriptures will show that this is the truth.

One of the scriptures with which Nicodemus ought to have been exceedingly familiar was that of the prophet Ezekiel. Read carefully Ezekiel xxxvii: 21-28. "Thus saith the Lord God, Behold I will take the children of Israel from among the heathen, whither they be gone, and will gather them on every side, and bring them into their own land; and I will make them one nation in the land upon the mountains of Israel; and one king shall be king to them all; and they shall be no more two nations, neither shall they be divided into two kingdoms any more at all; neither shall they defile themselves any more. * * * David my servant *shall be* king over them; * * * and *they shall dwell therein forever;* and my servant David *shall be their prince forever.* My tabernacle shall be with them; yea, I will be their God, and they shall be my people."

Note here:—

1. The children of Israel are to be brought back into their own land.

2. The two kingdoms, Judah and Israel, are to be united in one indissoluble kingdom in the land.

3. One king is to reign over them all.

4. This king is "David my servant." The word David would be better rendered, "The Beloved," hence, "The Beloved my servant." This king is none other than our Lord Jesus Christ.

That Christ is to be king on the throne of David is evident by the statement of the Apostle Peter on the day of Pentecost. Speaking of David in the Psalms, the apostle says, God swore unto him with an oath that "of the fruit of his loins, according to the flesh, he would raise up Christ to sit on his throne." Acts ii: 30. The prophet Isaiah foretold it; "unto us," (that is unto Israel,) "a child is born, unto us a son is given * * * and his name shall be called, the Mighty God * * * upon the throne of David, and upon his kingdom." Isaiah ix: 6, 7. When he was born, he was called the "King of the Jews;" when he rode into Jerusalem, he was saluted as the "King of Israel," "the Son of David;" above his cross was written, "This is the King of the Jews."

5. God will be, in a special and covenant way, in the person of His Son, the God of this Kingdom.

This is the kingdom of God.

It is a kingdom in Israel set up on the earth.

It is an "earthly thing," not because it is of the earth, but because it is displayed in the sphere of the earth.

Now turn to Ezekiel xxxvi: 26, 27. "A new heart also will I give you, and a new spirit will I put within you; and I will take away the stony heart out of your flesh, and I will give you a heart of flesh." This is regeneration pure and simple.

When this regeneration is to be accomplished is set forth in verse 24. "I will take you from among the heathen, and gather you out of all countries, and will bring you into your own land." Evidently the reference is to the setting up of the unfailing kingdom in Israel, and *when* the King shall have come. That regeneration opens the door to literal earthly blessings, may be seen by reading verses 28-30: 33-38. "Ye shall dwell in the land, * * * I will call for the corn, and will increase it * * * and I will multiply the fruit of the tree, and the increase of the field * * * the desolate land shall be tilled * * * so shall the waste cities be filled with flocks of men; and they shall know that I am the Lord."

Thus regeneration is one of the earthly things, not because it is of the earth, but because it is one of the characteristics in the Kingdom of God in Israel, as seen in its display in the sphere of earth.

In fulfilment of covenant promise, the Son of God came as the Beloved of the Father, as the king over Israel. Nicodemus, one of the rulers in the Sanhedrin, one who ought to have known all about regeneration, seeks an interview. He never rises to the idea that this Jesus is the Holy one of Israel, his King. He sees him only as a teacher sent from God. The Lord comes down to his level. He takes the part of a teacher, he says to him: "You come to learn truth, you want doctrine; very well, I say to you that the fundamental thing to know is regeneration—without a second birth, no man can enter, no man can even see the coming kingdom in Israel. Nicodemus is all in darkness. Then Jesus seeks to remind him of the Prophet Ezekiel, he says, "Marvel not that I said unto thee, ye must be born again." He tells him that this new birth must be of the spirit, and in saying so, quotes the very thought and, almost, the very words of Ezekiel; but no ray of light flashes through the darkened mind of this teacher in Israel. His manifest ignorance here is the ground of our Lord's seemingly singular rebuke, "Art thou a master in Israel, and knowest not *these* things."

He does not understand these "earthly things."

How could he understand "heavenly things?"

By heavenly things our Lord meant the Church.

The Church is a body of persons called out of all nations to faith in a crucified and risen Christ, exalted to be the second Adam, and the new head, in whom all things in heaven and earth are to be united. Each one of this body is born from above, receives new life from the risen man, is linked up with him in vital union forever, and forever is indwelt by his Spirit. This body of persons is not called to dwell on earth, as Israel, but to walk *through* it as pilgrims and strangers, testifying *against* it. In the new era which will dawn at the coming of Christ, they will dwell with him in heaven, and reign with him in associated glory over the kingdom of God in Israel, the bride, the queen consort of the king; as it is written: "Thou hast made us kings and priests and we shall reign on (over) the earth." Rev. v: 10; as again it is written in Daniel vii: 27: "And the kingdom and dominion * * * *under the whole* heaven, shall be given to the people of the SAINTS of the most High (to the holy ones in the high places, to the Church in the heavenly places) whose kingdom is an everlasting kingdom."

These are the heavenly things, not because they are more divine or spiritual than the earthly things, but because heaven, and not earth, is the sphere in which the Church is to be displayed to the glory of God's grace.

This distinction between the heavenly and the earthly things is made constantly in scripture in Ephesians iii: 15, the apostle speaks of "the family in heaven and the family in earth," that is to say, of the Church and Israel; the one above, the other below, in the final order of the kingdom.

Our Lord was absolutely precise in the use of his terms. He told the exact truth about Nicodemus; if the latter did not comprehend the Master when he spoke of earthly things, how much less could he have understood him if he had spoken of heavenly things?

This interview not only shows the wisdom of the Lord, it clearly manifests the inexcusable blindness of Israel, and justifies God in bringing in the new dispensation of the Church; this hour of the heavenly calling and measureless grace, not to Jews only, but also to the Gentiles; while, at the same time, it teach : us the necessity of rightly dividing the word and the times of God, and seeing to it that we do not confound the earthly and the heavenly things.

These are the heavenly things not, because they are
more divine or spiritual than the earthly things, but because heaven, and not earth, is the sphere in which the
Church is to be displayed to the glory of God's grace.
This distinction between the heavenly and the earthly
things is made constantly in scripture; in Ephesians iii:
15, the apostle speaks of "the family in heaven and the
family in earth," that is to say, of the Church and Israel;
the one above, the other below, in the final order of the
kingdom.

Our Lord was absolutely precise in the use of his
terms. He told the exact truth about Nicodemus: if
the latter did not comprehend the Master when he spoke
of earthly things, how much less could he have understood him if he had spoken of heavenly things?

This interview not only shows the wisdom of the Lord;
it clearly manifests the inscrutable blindness of Israel,
and justifies God in bringing in the new dispensation
of the Church; this hour of the heavenly calling and
measureless grace, not to Jews only but also to the
Gentiles; while at the same time, it teaches us the necessity of rightly dividing the word and the times of God,
and seeing to it that we do not confound the earthly and
the heavenly things.

MOSES.

Moses.

Moses the man of God.
—Deut. xxxiii: 1.

The life of Moses presents a series of striking antitheses.

He was the child of a slave, and the son of a queen. He was born in a hut, and lived in a palace. He inherited poverty, and enjoyed unlimited wealth. He was the leader of armies, and the keeper of flocks. He was the mightiest of warriors, and the meekest of men. He was educated in the court, and dwelt in the desert. He had the wisdom of Egypt, and the faith of a child. He was fitted for the city, and wandered in the wilderness. He was tempted with the pleasures of sin, and endured the hardships of virtue. He was backward in speech, and talked with God. He had the rod of a shepherd, and the power of the Infinite. He was a fugitive from Pharaoh, and an ambassador from Heaven. He was the giver of the Law, and the forerunner of Grace. He died alone on Mount Moab, and appeared with Christ in Judea. No man assisted at his funeral, yet God buried him. The fire has gone out of Mount Sinai, but the lightning is still in his Law. His lips are silent, but his voice yet speaks.

The history of such a life is well worth attention, and the principles which underlie its antitheses, the closest study.

He was born in Egypt, the most mysterious land of Antiquity.

He was born in an era when human science, and human wisdom, had made some of their mightiest advances. He was born at a time when the keenest persecution was directed against his race. Providence presided at his birth, a Providence which not only caused him to be hidden from the hands of those who would have destroyed him, but caused him to fall into the only hands which could have safely rescued him. A Providence which took him out of the cabin of the slave, where he could never have been aught but a slave, and placed him where alone in all the wide world he could be best fitted and trained to be just the reverse of a slave, a leader and manager of men.

He had forty years in which to cultivate his human vanity, amid the splendors of mortal power. He had forty years in which to reflect upon the folly of human vanity, amid the solitudes of the desert. And he had forty years in which to walk in the wilderness with God, and know the joy of that infinite communion.

He goes back from the silence of the solitude, to the tumult of the town, and in the name of the ever-abiding Jehovah confronts Pharaoh, and demands the freedom of his people.

He takes these people, three millions in number, men, women and children, and leads them forth from the land which had been occupied by them and their ancestors four hundred years.

He conducts them into the wilderness and organizes an army of more than half a million fighting men.

Having given them freedom, he endows them with a religion, a religion which is absolutely new and original; a religion whose laws in relation to God and man touch the profoundest elements of life, both natural and spiritual.

He maintains this multitude in a savage land, without cities, without commerce, without manufactures, with-

out agriculture, for forty years. He endures their mur-
murings, quenches their rebellion, meets their necessi-
ties, defeats their enemies, solidifies their character, accentuates their nationality, and waits till the old generation, with their limitations of birth, previous habits and
traditions are all dead, and the new generation have become entirely alienated from and grow up without obligation to the past; and then, under a new leader trained
under his own hand, filled with his spirit, and moulded
by his words, he sends them a compact, concrete nation,
into a new land, to form an empire whose latest page in
history has not yet been written; and then when his work
is done, goes silently, thoughtfully and alone into the
solemn stillness of the mountain heights; and there, unseen by mortal eye, unheard by mortal ken, passes out
of the land of the heart-ache and the dying into the
blessedness of the years of God.

The history is unique, the events have in them the
echo of age on ages telling. His figure stands out
strong and simple against the passing eras; and lo, there
is none like unto him amid the merely natural sons of
men.

In endeavoring to study more closely and more anal-
ytically his marvellous character, we are forced to consider him in the many and varied rôles he filled.

He was a scholar. He was learned in all the wisdom
of the Egyptians. There was a time not far distant
when that little phrase did not mean so much, but to-
day when the pick and the spade of the Egyptologist are
turning up the soil of the land of Mizraim, and the eye
looks with wonder on temple and tomb, with all the evidences of a Science and Civilization in some respects
equal to, if not superior to our own, the phrase gathers

immense force; and we repeat, with added emphasis, the words of the martyr Stephen, "Moses was learned in all the wisdom of the Egyptians."

He knew the esoteric as well as the exoteric wisdom of the Egyptians. He knew all that the common people knew, and he knew what alone the priests of the temple knew. He understood cosmogony, he was learned in astronomy, he was an adept in geology, he knew medicine, he taught the circulation of the blood, and comprehended the life of the soul.

He had seen the wonders of Bubastis, knew the riddle of the Sphynx, and possessed the secret of that mighty Pyramid, that Pillar of the Lord, whose story shall yet be told to a startled world.

He was a patriot, a lover of his people, a lover of his nation.

He saw them bend their backs beneath the taskmasters' burdens, he heard the cry of the oppressed, and his soul stirred within him; and when the moment came to express his sympathy and lend his aid, he did not hesitate at any cost to himself, but struck the blow which made one slave driver less, and one freeman more.

Surrounded by the influence of forty years of magnificence, of lawless luxury and unlimited power with every possibility of self-pleasing at his hand, and before him the alternatives of ignominy and shame, it was a sublime patriotism, an unspeakable devotion which led him at last to exchange the mosaics of the palace for the sands of the desert, the fountains of wine for the brooks by the way, the sceptre of a king for the crook of a herdsman.

He was a great organizer of men and forces. Consider what a task it was to take a people which stood at the end of four hundred years of the most abject slavery and denationalization; to take this vast multitude amounting to millions, and so organize them that there should be unity of feeling, unity of movement, and the sense of obedience, compatible with liberty and self-respect. There must have been something profoundly majestic and royal in the bearing as well as the life of such a man.

He was a great general. The Egyptians had been driven back by the Red Sea, but they could easily have pursued and overtaken the Israelites by another route, the short and direct route to the Promised Land; but this was just the route that Moses did not take. The course he did follow was not only through the Wilderness, but among wild and hostile tribes, among men born to the back of a horse and the use of arms, jealous, fierce, and against the intruder in the land.

And yet he so led them that they became a terror to their foes, their very name a sound of alarm.

He was the founder of a religion. The primary article of this new religion was the unity of God. And when you consider that polytheism was universal, that Egypt was the hotbed, the cradle and the nursery of idolatry, his conceptions of God, and his regulations against idolatry are something more than remarkable, they are astounding. This religion commanded righteousness of life, purity of motive towards man, and devotion to God, godliness and exalted humanity. His sanitary enactments kept the nation alive, and in themselves form the alphabet of all practical morality.

He was a great Prophet. He not only saw the Future, he saw the Past. His vision of the Past is given to us in the story of Creation, and in the history of the Patriarchs. His story of Creation stands without a rival for simplicity of style, for concentration of statement, for depths of knowledge, and anticipations of Science; and as human Science freeing itself from its limitations and prejudices comes into possession of actual facts, each discovery serves only to confirm the truth, and establish the exactitude of his declarations.

But Moses saw the Future. He saw Christ and drew his portrait.

He saw him as the Only Begotten of the Father, the First Born, the Pure, the Sinless, the Holy, the Sacrifice for sin, the Substitute for sinners, the Resurrection, the Life, and the Coming King; and he drew this portrait in the sacrifices and the ceremonials which he established, the Tabernacle which he built, and the priesthood he ordained.

And he who will sit down and study his writings will understand what the Son of God meant when he said: "Moses wrote of me; if ye believe not his writings, how shall ye believe my words?"

Nay, he who studies these writings of Moses, he who examines the ordinances and the ceremonies, will find that in every lamb to slaughter led, in every garment the priesthood wore, in every board and bar, in every curtain, cord and vessel of the Tabernacle, Moses was writing of Christ the Crucified, and setting forth the Great Salvation.

Moses himself was the figure and type of Christ. Like Christ he was the son of a virgin. Like Christ his life as a babe, was in mortal danger. Like Christ he left the court of glory.

Like Christ he was a teacher of men, a man of sorrows and acquainted with grief.

Like Christ, on account of the sin of the people, he was shut out for a season from the favor of God.

But not only is he in himself a type and figure of Christ, he is also a witness of the coming grace of Christ; for Moses is the incarnation of the Law; and Moses dying there on the Mount, Moses unable to enter into the Promised Land is a picture of pictures, telling us that the Law cannot take us into the kingdom of God; that this Law must be met, satisfied, and set aside in death, before the people can go over Jordan, the river of Judgment; and thus prophesies of the Coming of him who should take the Law, make it honorable in his life, meet its demands in his death, and then by grace divine, lead the people safely through the Judgment into the Covenant Realm.

The very last act and attitude of the man, therefore, is the proclamation of a needed and coming Saviour, of a needed and coming hour of Grace.

And from beginning to end as we look at his career we must say he was great. Beside him the greatest of earth are pigmies. There is only one who stands in stature above him, he of whom he was the type, the Christ, the Lord and Master of us all.

And when you come to analyze his greatness, to lay hold of the one quality that made him all he was, you will find that it was neither his wisdom, nor learning, nor genius, but his unfaltering faith in God. By that faith he endured as seeing him that is invisible, turned his back on the pleasures of sin for a season, on the glories of Egypt, on the advantages of time, and looking across the intervening ages, saw the Christ of God, the Judgment Seat, and the recompense of the reward. It was a faith that confronted a world, smiled at death, and laid hold on God. A faith that above all the din of time got the surge of the great waves of eternity, and beyond them, saw the shores of the infinite peace and rest.

Yes, his greatness was his faith.

It brought him the hand of God to lay him down to rest in Moab's lonely vale. It brought him into the Promised Land at last, and gave him fellowship in the glory of the Transfiguration Mount. And by and by it will bring him that great day and hour of triumph for his soul when the redeemed of all ages standing on the crystal sea shall lift up the song of Moses and the Lamb, and thus join his name in hallelujahs of interlacing praise with the name of him whose face shone out from amid the burning bush, and whose voice spake to him on the Holy Mount. An hour of triumph indeed for him, the one-time fugitive from Pharaoh's court, standing in the court of God, hearing on every breeze, from every voice in angelic choir, and from the lips of the redeemed out of every nation, people, kindred, and tongue, now the name of Jesus the Lamb of God, and anon his own name, mingling and ringing in the rhythm of the eternal antiphonal song of Moses and the Lamb.

* * * * * * * * * * * * *

Reading the story of his life and catching glimpses of his coming glory, what shall we say, what can we say, but that of all the riches of heaven or of earth, of all the gifts and dowers possible to mortal man, nothing is so precious, nothing is so infinite, nothing has in it such endless recompense, both subjective and objective, as that faith which believes in, and lays hold on God.

PAUL.

PAUL.

Paul.

Paul, a servant of Jesus Christ.
—*Rom. i: 1.*

If Moses is the central figure amid the witnesses for God in the Old Testament, Paul is the central figure amid the witnesses for Christ in the New Testament.

If the life of Moses presents a series of startling antitheses, the life of Paul is equally antithetical.

He was a Roman and lived a Jew. He was a Pharisee and preached to the Gentiles. He was born a freeman and became a slave. He was born a freeman under the most tyrannical of masters, and became a slave under the most liberal of Redeemers. He was a rigid ritualist and an enemy of ceremonies. He lived under law and taught only Grace.

He was blamelessly righteous and the chief of sinners.

He set aside the ordinances and placed himself under a vow. He would not allow Titus to be circumcised, but, himself, offered as a sacrifice in the Temple. He claimed citizenship with Christ and appealed to Nero. He preached peace and stirred up riots. He persecuted Christians and built churches. He was Saul the Destroyer and became Paul the Worker.

He died in Rome and lives in Heaven. His pen is silent, but his epistles still speak.

Not only is his life antithetical, but he, himself, stands in antithetical contrast to the Moses whom he supersedes.

Moses enfranchised a nation. Paul liberates a soul. Moses stamps the name of *Jew* on the world, Paul stamps the name of *Christian* on the world. Moses reveals God as Lawgiver, Paul reveals God as Grace-giver. Moses points to the kingdom, Paul points to the church. Moses points to the land that is full of fountains and brooks of water, and highest hills, Paul points to him who is the Fountain of *living* waters, and to the land that is higher than the hills.

Moses talks about going into the land, Paul talks about going into the Glory. Moses has to do with that which is local and transitory, Paul has to do with that which is infinite and eternal. If he supersedes Moses, he outranks the disciples. Peter may represent the Christian in the flesh, James the Christian under the Law, John the Christian walking in love, but Paul represents the Christian as risen and seated at the Right Hand of God. Paul is the Imperial apostle. The apostle of conflict, but victory; of restless energy, but eternal hope. Paul gives us the Christianity of the head as well as the heart; intellectuality as well as spirituality; reason as well as faith, and faith both the base and apex of true reason.

To Paul is committed the doctrine of the church, from Paul come the epistles to the church. If Christ is the incarnation of the Doctrine of God, then Paul is the incarnate definition of the Doctrine of God.

Whatever may have been his physical stature, his moral elevation casts its shadow across our times, and his head and shoulders can be seen above the tallest mountains.

He was born in Tarsus, a no mean city of Cilicia. He was born under Roman sway at the hour of her apogee; at the hour when she was seeking architecture from Greece, commerce from the islands, and science from Egypt. He was born at an hour when the tramp of returning legions could be heard coming back from the fields of conquest; and when Roman arches, telling the power of Roman prowess and Roman civilization were being erected on every square.

He spoke Greek, Latin and Hebrew, and knew the Aramaic and Syriac vernacular. He was at home in the Greek Anthology, and was versed in all the legends of the Talmud. He breathed the atmosphere of Grecian and Eastern metaphysics; came to Jerusalem; sat at the feet of Gamaliel, and drank in deep draughts of Hebrew history, Law and Tradition, and to the predisposition of seeker after truth added the terrific conditions of religious bigot and national partizan.

He was a member of the Jewish Sanhedrin, and, therefore, once married. He sat in the Council which tried the martyr Stephen, assisted as a witness at his death, and inflamed with hatred against Christ and Christianity, went to Damascus with authority to extirpate "this heresy."

Jesus met him above the Damascus gates; he fell down, and amid the dust of repentance owned the Christ of God, and straightway, went forth to preach him, showing to his countrymen that this Jesus is the Christ, openly alleging that the Jews had fulfilled their prophets in condemning him.

But he saw a wider field than Judea, and heard a louder call than the voice of his own people. He saw in the night the vision of a man in Macedonia who stretched out his arms and said: "Come over and help us."

And then, *straightway* he took the mightiest journey, and crossed the widest distance, ever accomplished by mortal man: he passed over the distance between Jewish exclusiveness and pagan liberalism. He passed out of the realm of narrow provincialism, and entered the broad realm of a dying and needy world.

To him, Corinth appealed as well as Jerusalem, the Greek as well as the Jew. Under the phylacteries of the one, and the curled locks of the other, he knew there was a human soul, needing a Saviour. His doctrine was unique. He taught that Jesus of Nazareth was the Son of God, crucified for sin, dead, buried, raised the third day, ascended to Heaven and seated at the right hand of God; from whence he should come to establish a kingdom *in* Israel and *over* Israel, a kingdom of God as well as man.

He taught that the church is the Temple of God, the Body of Christ, his Bride; that the church is *not* the kingdom, but the *reigning* family *in* the *coming* kingdom. He taught that Christ is the *second* Adam, the Head and beginning of a new creation, and that the work of God in this age is to create a new race in the moral image of Christ, and at His Second Coming, to clothe this new race in him with his outward image and glory.

In dealing with the world's evil he relied wholly on the Gospel.

He did not stand on the public corners and arraign the municipal corruption of Athens, Corinth, Ephesus, or Rome. He did not organize investigating committees against moral and political iniquity. He did not take the field for clearer and more popular government. He neither acted the part of a secret detective nor a political partizan.

He saw the whole world given over to sin. He saw **vice** in its most tempting form; he saw it in statues, sculptured in marble, and painted on canvas. Aye, he saw it in flesh more beautiful than marble, more beautiful than rarest canvas, and exposed to common view. He heard it in siren voices, and caught it in the breath of the very flowers. He knew that virtue was the exception and vice the rule. Lasciviousness and wantonness touched him on every side, he touched them on every side, and yet he never thought of lifting a crusade against them.

Whether it was corruption in office, the squandering of the people's money, or the shameless, open sin in temples of Venus, he did one thing, and one thing only: he preached the Gospel of Christ, declared that it was the power of God unto salvation, and by it ploughed the furrows of truth so deep that the temples of sin fell into them, were buried, and forgotten.

He dealt in wisdom with the church at large. He never placed it under law, but always under love; he unfolded truth, wrote letters that touched every secret wrong, gave place to the Spirit of God in every assembly, and allowed that assembly in the Spirit to work order out of chaos, harmony out of discord.

The ministry which he had begun with such "straightwayness," he continued till his voice had been heard in Antioch, in Athens, in Ephesus, in Corinth, in Macedonia, along the Adriatic coast, in Spain, and in Imperial Rome.

He climbed mountains, threaded valleys, crossed rivers, passed through towns and villages, hamlets and deserts, and sailed the seas till he had placed to his credit thousands of miles as a traveller, and thousands of lives as a winner of souls.

And in fulfilling this ministry he passed continually through the gateway of suffering.

He was put in prison at Philippi, stoned out of Thessalonica and Berea, arrested in Ephesus, left for dead in Galatia, nearly torn to pieces in Jerusalem, shut up in a dungeon at Cæsarea, shipwrecked on the Mediterranean, tied to a soldier's arm at Rome, sealed up in the Mamertine prison, and at last, according to tradition, beheaded on the Appian Way.

To read the story of his ministry, is to read the story of persecution, affliction, misrepresentation, and lack of appreciation.

Let me repeat what he says in one of his letters:

"We are fools for Christ's sake; we are despised; we hunger and thirst, and have no certain dwelling place; we work with our own hands; we are reviled; we are persecuted; we are defamed; we are made the filth of the world, the offscouring of all things."

Listen to what he says in another letter:

"Of the Jews, five times received I forty stripes save one; thrice was I beaten with rods; once was I stoned; thrice I suffered shipwreck; a night and a day have I been in the deep; in journeyings often, in perils of water, in perils of robbers, in perils of mine own countrymen; in perils by the heathen, in perils in the city, in perils in the wilderness; in weariness and painfulness; in watchings often; in hunger and in thirst; in fastings often; in cold and nakedness. Beside those things that are without, that which cometh upon me daily, the care of all the churches."

Of all the sufferings which he endured, the keenest, the bitterest, were from those who professed to be Christians.

The first church at Jerusalem looked on him with jealousy and suspicion, discounted his doctrine, minimized the value of his labors, and sought to compromise him before the Elders of the people. But his keenest sufferings from Christians were produced by those whom he had blessed. They criticized him and found fault with him.

To be sure, like the Galatians at first, they could not do enough for him, could not exalt his praises high enough, were willing to take out their own eyes and give them to him.

But the moment he commenced to probe them with the truth they resented it, and referring to it he says: "The more I love you the less I be loved." They stabbed him with that weapon with which pastors in our day are stabbed, "They say."

They used this keen and cowardly instrument against him in every direction, against his private life, his eccentricities, his social life, or his lack of it, and his doctrinal concepts, until at times his heart was almost broken; almost broken with the heartless thoughtlessness of those who called themselves the Disciples of Christ.

No preacher ever had greater professions of friendship made to him, and no preacher, perhaps, was ever more thoroughly betrayed by men, until at the last he wrote: "All men forsook me."

It is easy to meet the assaults of infidelity, to overcome the errors of unbelief, and by the grace of God resist the wiles of the devil, but the preacher who can come into contact with the fault-finding and rasping judgments, the merciless misunderstanding and unreasonable demands of those who profess to be the sons of God, and still keep his faith, still continue to minister, and seek to help unselfishly, reveals the existence of a faith and Christly manhood superbly great.

And Paul did all this, and when he stood on the threshold of eternity cried, so all heaven and earth might hear: "I have fought the fight, I have kept the faith."

In analyzing his history we are led to consider the rôles he filled.

Like Moses he was a great patriot. He was a Jew, an Israelite, a Hebrew of the Hebrews, a Pharisee of the Pharisees.

He never set aside his national or ancestral pride; and he was so devoted to that nation and to that people that not only did he claim that the Jew had the first right to the Gospel, but declared his own willingness to be accursed from Christ for their sakes in order that they might be saved.

He was the greatest of missionaries.

Without aid from societies, without support of wealth, without modern means of communication, without railroads, or steamboats, without telegraphs to send his messages, with no reporters to serve up his sermons, or make them known to the general public, and advertise him as the greatest and most wonderful of preachers, he travelled thousands of miles, addressed multitudes among all nations, peoples, kindreds and tongues, and made the name of Christ known from the pillars of Hercules to the waters of Damascus, from the hills of Rome to the deserts of Arabia.

He was a great preacher.

He stirred the council at Jerusalem, swayed the multitude on the steps of Antonia, held in silence the audience in the Acropolis, moved the mixed multitudes at Corinth, and was as earnest with the little company of Lydia's household, and the startled jailer at Philippi, as when he wept over the crowds in Ephesus.

He was a great builder of churches.

He filled the cities and dotted the plains with them.

Wherever he came he led men and women to Christ, and then organized them into worshipping and working assemblies.

He was a great theologian.

He dealt with the high themes of God and Satan, Sin and Holiness, Life and Death, Time and Eternity.

His Epistle to the Romans is a masterpiece of legal reasoning and divine defining.

His Epistle to the Ephesians is a series of faultless deductions, spiritual revelations, and heavenly exaltations.

All his theology is Christo-centric, and every phrase is a volume of infinite suggestions.

He was a tireless worker.

No sooner had he finished one journey than he began another.

He was a great pastor.

He sought out the weak, he yearned after the erring, he restored the fallen, he encouraged the downcast, and gave his time to all who claimed it, not only of one church, but of all, not only of a province, but of a world.

He was a great hero.

He did not hesitate to face the anger, the mockery and the menace of a whole nation, and that his own, in behalf of the truth.

He did not hesitate to stand up against the whole church and rebuke its Chiefest Apostle.

And on that dark and terrible night when the wild winds broke from the black clouds and the blacker sea became white with the rage of the storm, and the ship moaned and careened, and broke, plank by plank, and sailors and soldiers shivered with fear, and cried with terror, he stood forth calm and unmoved, and in a voice which rang across the sea, and has rung across the ages to us, cried: "Sirs, I believe God, that it shall be *even as it was told* me."

But in analyzing his character more profoundly we must examine the elements or forces which moved him, not only as a man, but as a Christian worker. And they are easily found, and give the secret of his mighty continuance and unparalleled success.

He believed that the souls of men were in danger.

And so terrible was this danger to him that he was willing, if needs be, to act the part of another Christ, and like him become a curse for men. He believed that Christ alone could save them, and to preach any other Gospel, in his eyes, was soul-murder; and he rang anathema upon all such preachers.

He believed that Christ had so completely bought him with his precious blood that he had no longer any personal rights in himself; and therefore without hesitation called himself the SLAVE OF JESUS CHRIST.

He believed that Christ loved even him, Paul; that on the cross Christ saw Paul and died for Paul; that from heaven he saw Paul, and wielded his Providence for Paul.

And this contemplation of Christ's love for him constrained him until he cried: "The love of Christ constraineth me."

He believed that Christ was a real and living person, and he made that personal and actual Christ the objective of his life. He said: "For me to live is Christ."

The Christ who is real and personal, the man who is

living in yonder glory is the magnet, he says: "which draws me on; to him, for him I live, my life is for him, he only is my life."

And he believed that this personal and living Christ was coming back to the world, and he lived each day in the hope of that coming. He lived as though he might meet him at any moment in the bend of the road, any instant hear his voice, or feel the touch of his loving hand.

One word alone can give the secret of his Christian life and that word is "CONSECRATION;" an absolute surrender of all he had, and was, to Christ.

One watchword alone was in his life, that mightiest phrase which a human lip can utter and a human heart can feel, FOR CHRIST'S SAKE.

For Christ's sake, he broke with Tradition, for Christ's sake he became an outcast from his nation, for Christ's sake he lived yonder in Corinth, and ate black bread, and was naked, and cold and hungry.

When foes assailed him; when friends betrayed him; when his heart broke because of human meanness; when the night grew dark and he was alone and the clammy ooze of the deep dungeon was about him, there was one magic whispered watchword which stirred through his soul and held him, and that magic watchword was, "FOR CHRIST'S SAKE."

Nor can any man say that this surrender was fanatic and futile.

Fanatic and futile!

Let the millions, yea, the millions who have found their way to God through some word of his refute the charge.

Let the multitude to-day who read his words, and follow his testimonies, and seek to follow out the problem of the divine life in the soul through some brave suggestion of his, refute the charge.

And the day is coming when this consecration, this devotion, this self-immolation, shall find its full reward.

Some bits and glimpses of it came to him when he was caught up into the third heaven and heard unspeakable words, and caught visions which forever made him blind to the attractions of earth. He has been getting some installments of that coveted "with Christ" in which he has been resting these eighteen hundred years. And he will find it to the full in that hour when he shall come with Christ and all the world shall see that the SLAVE OF EARTH has become the KING OF HEAVEN.

But the reward that will most fill his soul will be to see the multitudes who have been brought to Christ directly and indirectly through his labors; to him it will be a joy of joys to greet those to whom he preached, and over whom he watched with fatherly love and care; to hear their happy voices amid the intoning of the angelic choirs, and know that he has been the instrument of their delight. For he himself has said: "What is our hope, or joy, or crown of rejoicing? Are not even ye in the presence of our Lord Jesus Christ AT HIS COMING?"

But above and beyond all that, his reward of rewards will be to see the joy that shall fill the heart of God's own Christ as he gathers his Blood-bought jewels about him; joy for Paul to know that he has been the mighty means through grace to fill his Master's life and make him glad; to him this shall be the kingly crown, the recompense and compensation for all the sorrows by the way.

And from that far hour of splendor he cries down to

us to-day with a voice of inspiration for our lives: "FOR ME TO LIVE IS CHRIST."

This was the secret of his life then; this was his peace here; this is his "far-better" now, and shall be his GLORY SURE TO COME.

THE DELICATE SEAL AND THE DAY OF REDEMPTION.

The Delicate Seal and the Day of Redemption.

*Ye were sealed with that
Holy Spirit of Promise.*
—Eph. i : 13.

In Ephesians iv: 30, it is written: "Grieve not the Holy Spirit of God, whereby ye are sealed unto the day of redemption."

Three things are to be observed here:

1. A day of redemption is coming to all those who are Christians.

2. We who are Christians are sealed unto the day of redemption.

3. We are exhorted as Christians not to grieve the Holy Spirit whereby we are sealed unto the day of redemption.

The word "redemption" signifies deliverance, and the root idea is a deliverance brought about by purchase, a ransom paid.

Redemption is three-fold: *For* us, *in* us, *upon* us.

For us by the blood of the cross. The blood was a ransom paid to justice, and by that we have been redeemed, delivered from judgment and death.

Redemption is *in* us by regeneration. We who have believed have been regenerated: that is to say, a new nature has been given us,—the nature of Christ: and this nature delivers us from the power of sin.

Then we have redemption *upon* us. Redemption upon us is upon our bodies. Our bodies are to be redeemed by resurrection and transfiguration. They are to be redeemed from the bondage of death and corruption. They will be made immortal, and like unto the body of the Son of God.

This is the redemption spoken of in the text.

There is a definite day or period set for that redemption. It will take place at the Coming of our Lord Jesus Christ. It will be a supreme moment.

The description of it is given by the Apostle in his First Epistle to the Thessalonians, fourth chapter, fifteenth, sixteenth and seventeenth verses.

"For this we say unto you by the word of the Lord, that we which are alive and remain unto the Coming of the Lord, shall not prevent (or go before) them which are asleep. For the Lord Himself shall descend from heaven with a shout, with the voice of the arch-angel, and with the trump of God; and the dead in Christ shall rise first: Then we which are alive and remain, shall be caught up together with them in the clouds, to meet the Lord in the air; and so shall we ever be with the Lord."

The figure is a military one. An army has been marching all day, and as the day wanes and the night draws on, the marching column halts and enters into bivouac. In a brief period those living hosts are lying stretched amid the dust of earth, wrapped in deepest slumber. Once moving, throbbing, alert with all the forces of life; now motionless, inert, no longer a part of the activities around, or beyond them. About the hour of the morning star the commanding general comes forward and speaks to one of his officers, and orders the advance of the sleeping army. The officer speaks to the trumpeter and bids him sound the *reveille*. In a moment is heard the wailing notes of the trumpet. Instantly the army is awake and risen. Men take their places in company, regiment, brigade, and division. Another trumpet sounds and those who have been standing on the picket line on guard come in and join the main body. And then begins the march before the commanding general.

This is the figure, and herein is the truth. There is an army in our midst at bivouac, a great army asleep upon their arms; they toiled and marched through a long and weary day, and then at the end of that day of toil and marching lay down to sleep, and are sleeping now, sleeping in the dust of earth. It is a sleep from which as it is said, "none ever wake to weep."

Go and look at this bivouac, this army of sleeping soldiers—you will find them all about you in the silent cemeteries (sleeping-places) *keeping the bivouac of the dead.*

They are sleeping there, they are resting there in the dust of old mother earth at last. Through the long, long day of life they bore, some of them, heavy and grievous burdens, and were footsore and weary through many a mile of their toilsome march. Not infrequently the stain of tears was upon their faces, and some of them bore marks of wounds received by the way. But the longest day and the most painful march must end at last. So was it with them: The sun went down, the shadows began to fall, and a voice, they heard, cried "Halt;" they obeyed, they laid them down to sleep. They are sleeping now.

Prophets, priests, apostles, a long and shining muster roll that gleams upon the page of history, and is all-sufficient to fill our hearts with memories of days that are past and gone—with memories of father, mother, loved one of our home, sleeping to-day.

They are asleep in Jesus.

They believed in him, they confessed his name, and when the hour of halting in the midst of life's busy ways came to them, they smiled, bade us good-bye, and lay down to rest in that name they wore, in him whom they had believed.

And he has not forgotten them; some day, as the Commanding General, he will come and gaze upon this bivouac of the dead who died, in him. It will be about the time of the morning star.

He will call to the Archangel and give the word for the army to awake, arise, and march. The Archangel will speak to God's trumpeter. He will stand forth and blow a blast, and lo, the sleepers in the dust of earth will awake, and arise, each in his own company and division —Patriarchs, Prophets, Priests, the Faithful in Israel, and the Church of the Living God.

Another trumpet will sound, and the living who are on guard, those who have been doing picket duty on the outposts of life—for, "some must watch while others sleep, thus runs the world away"—will go forth to join the rising ranks of those who are advancing upward to meet their descending Lord; and with shining faces and smiles of recognition to one another, will march in the grand review before the Living Christ.

It will be the day of redemption, the day of the redemption of our bodies, their deliverance from death and corruption. And this day of redemption is coming sooner than we dream, at an hour when we think not.

Just as Israel stood on the margin of the Jordan waiting for the trump to sound that they might go over and take possession of the Promised Land, so there is nothing between us and this Promised Land of immortality

and likeness unto his image and glory, but the sudden
sound of a trumpet at his second, and imminent coming.
This then is my first point; a day of redemption is coming to those of us who are Christians.

I note in the second place that we who are Christians
have been sealed unto that day of redemption. The
word "sealed" means stamped, branded, marked, warranted, guaranteed. A seal, a stamp, a mark has been
put on us; and that mark warrants us, guarantees us unto
the day of redemption. That is to say, the seal or mark
is a pledge that our bodies, dead or living, shall be delivered from mortality and made immortal.

A seal may be the witness, the pledge, the guaranty,
of purchase, ownership, and destination. I once saw a
splendid vase nearly covered with outer coverings. A
great seal was on it, and an inscription which said that
this vase has been purchased by an Oriental prince, and
was to be delivered to him in his palace in his native city.
Now we as Christians bear a stamp, a mark, a seal, and
an inscription which declares that we too, have been purchased by an Oriental Prince, even our God and Saviour,
Jesus Christ.

This seal is the pledge of that solemn purchase, the
witness that we are his, and the guaranty that we shall
be transported to his capital city in heaven, into his palace, into the throne room, and there shine as the vessels of glory. This seal is the declaration that we shall
be transported there on that great and wonderful day
called "the day of redemption." Like the prince's vase,
we are still surrounded, wrapped about with the outer
covering of mortality, but, in that Great Day, the covering will be taken off, and we shall shine in all the beauty
of his immortality. And we bear in our bodies the stamp,
the mark, the seal of that glorious hour.

This seal is indeed the most marvellous of seals. Some seals are made of clay, some of wax, some of lead, or iron, or brass, some of silver and of gold.

But this seal is beyond all this. This seal is a person. Yes, a real, a living person, dwelling in us. That person is none other than the Holy Spirit, the Third Person of the Most Blessed Trinity.

He is in us *the moment we believe.* He is both the sealer and the sealed. His very presence in us marks us, stamps us, puts a seal upon us, sets us apart, makes us different from all other beings in the universe.

He is in us a seal, a manifold witness and guaranty. The witness and guaranty that Christ died for us, that we are his by right of purchase, that we are accepted in him, and by him, that we are one in spirit with him. All this he is, but he is besides, the witness and the guaranty definitely of the redemption of our bodies, either by resurrection or by transfiguration.

He is so because he is himself the essential power of resurrection. By and through him Jesus Christ was raised from the dead. Hence, if he is in us, he is in us as the power by which our bodies are to be raised or changed, as it is written: "He shall quicken your mortal bodies by his spirit that dwelleth in you."

Here then is the immense fact: As Christians we carry in us the power that can raise our bodies from the dead, just as the seed carries in itself the power that will enable it to burst forth into bloom and beauty.

Here is the answer to every Nicodemus' question, "How can these things be?"—"How are the dead raised up, and with what body do they come?" We lay our hands upon our breasts and say: *"By the spirit who dwelleth in us."*

And is not this enough? Cannot he who paints the morning and the evening sky, cannot he, the Eternal Spirit of the Living God, cannot he raise the dead?

All men admit that resurrection is simply a question of God's power. Well, if God by his Holy Spirit is dwelling in us, that suffices. Behold then the comfort and the consolation of the indwelling of the Spirit.

He is in us the advance agent of the resurrection and the transfiguration, the guaranty and pledge of the great day of redemption and glory.

Think of it Christian, you carry about in you the seal and mark of that coming Mightiest of Days.

This leads me to note third and finally, that as Christians who have thus been so solemnly sealed to that Day of Days, we ought not to grieve this Holy Spirit who dwelling within, has sealed us.

The word "grieve" means to distress, to worry, to trouble. Do you think you can take in the full meaning of the idea that the Holy Ghost can be worried, distressed, and troubled, and that, too, by us? But it is true. The Holy Spirit in us is the most sensitive thing in the universe of God. Not a sensitive plant, not the hair-spring of a watch, is so delicate, so sensitive, as he.

It is true he is himself Power, and Power in the concrete, the Essential Power of the universe, the Power that gilds the sun, paints the lily, shatters the mountain; the Power that produces in us the Son of God, Christ in us the hope of glory, the Power that shall raise the dead and change the living, and carry us up bodily as on eagles' wings to the very throne of God. And yet with all this, he is in us more tender, more delicate than a breath of the evening breeze. He is in us *love divine,* and he will do nothing to force us. And just because of this tenderness and love we may most easily grieve, worry and distress him.

We may do all this by the places into which we go. There are places into which you could not take your wife without bringing a blush to her cheek and distressing her greatly. There are places into which you cannot take the Holy Ghost without bringing a blush to his cheek and distressing him. You cannot take him to the wine-glass, the dance, or the card table without making him blush, distressing and grieving him sorely.

We can grieve him by our deeds, by our actions in business, and pleasure. We can grieve him by the company we keep, by the conversation in which we engage, by its lightness and frivolity, by its utter lack of salt. We can grieve him by our thoughts, by their unkindness, their injustice, their bitterness, their impurity.

Oh, by a thought we may grieve this Blessed Spirit in us. We may grieve him by our relation to the house of God, by our attitude within it, or by absenting ourselves from it. We may grieve him by withholding testimony and restraining prayer, and by keeping back our gifts, whether of time, talent, or substance.

And this grieving and distressing may go on till the Spirit will no longer manifest himself, not only so that the world will not know that he is in us, but so that we ourselves may no longer know it.

He will not leave us, oh, no: He is here, in us, *to see us through to the end.* He will be with us in the hour of death in order that death may not possess our souls, and that between death and resurrection we may be surely with the Lord. He will be with us in the great Day of Redemption that we may not miss its mighty roll-call of the blood-purchased saints, but he will no longer manifest Himself to us here in our daily life.

Like a friend who is grieved he will no longer force himself on our attention. He will be silent and inactive in us.

The Holy Spirit silent and inactive in a son of God! And who can tell the loss that all this may mean? We lose him as Comforter and Consolation, as Power, as Communion with God, as the very essence of the Christian life.

Grieve not the Holy Spirit. Nay, let us own him, submit to him, make him the Regent in our lives, the Ruler and the Power. Own him and make him happy.

And, oh, my soul, when the Holy Ghost in thee is glad and happy, when thou dost deal tenderly and delicately with him, then thou shalt be free and happy and glad also.

"Grieve not the Holy Spirit of God, whereby ye are sealed unto the day of redemption."

MEET FOR THE MASTER'S USE.

Meet for the Master's Use.

*Then he said, Go, borrow thee vessels
abroad of all thy neighbors, even empty
vessels; borrow not a few.*

—2 Kings iv : 3.

"If a man therefore purge himself from these, he shall be a vessel unto honor, sanctified, and meet for the master's use." II Timothy ii: 21.

We have to consider here:

1. The relation which Christ sustains to the believer. He is the master. That word "master" is our English word "despot." He is the believer's despot. Whatever else he may be, back of all other things he is the believer's despot. His wish is law, his will is supreme, his authority incontestable; in short, his authority over a believer is the authority of a master over a slave. He has right unlimited to his body, his soul, his spirit, his time, his talent, his substance.

He occupies this position as Creator.

Consider him as a man if you will, see all his humanity as you may, he who with a word smoothed the billows of Gennesaret, with a word brought the dead to life, and with a look turned water into wine, by that same word framed the heavens of old, by that look flashed light through yonder sun, and by that power unspeakable created man.

He occupies this position as Redeemer.

Call the cross by what name you please, define his death after what fashion you desire, he who hung upon that cross, whom death could not touch till he bowed his head and bade it come, and who with the voice of authority and power commanded his Spirit to go, died under contract of his own will, died under contract of his own power, and made each drop of his blood the current coin of a measureless purchase; so that the earth, the cattle on the hills, and the souls of men are his, his by the right of merchandise transferred.

He occupies this position as Regenerator.

No stone was ever more voiceless of praise to God, no body embalmed in spice and shut within the portals of the tomb, was ever more dead in relationship to God, than each believer before Jesus Christ the glorified touched him with his power; and if to-day the believer can say, even with feeblest voice, "I believe, help thou mine unbelief," his voice of praise, his life of the Spirit, all date from that moment of contact with the Son of God. By the law of life and union then he is his; and this Master has the same authority and dominion over him that the vine has over the branches, that the tree has over its fruit.

In whatever direction you may analyze it, the relationship of Christ to the believer is the relationship of uncompromising absolutism. He is the Lord, he is the Tyrant, he is the Despot, he is the Master.

Consider in the second place:

2. The relationship which the believer ought to sustain to Christ.

He ought to sustain the relation of usefulness to the Master.

"Meet for the Master's use."

That word "use" signifies profit, advantage. He ought to be of profit, he ought to be of advantage to the Master.

Advantage, profit, use to him?

And why to him?

Consider him purely as a man. Did he not as a man seem to have all resources in himself? When he came to a wide sea did he use a bridge or a boat? When he wanted bread was it necessary to build bakeries, or to make fire in ovens to turn out loaves for five thousand hungry men? He who could tell men's thoughts had no need of telephones nor printing presses, nor bureaus of private information. He who could ascend to the gates of Glory as easily as you can mount your own stairway, and who sat down on the throne of God with the same ease and fitness with which you would enter your home and sit down in the fellowship of your family, can surely have no needs that any mortal being may supply, even though that mortal were the most devoted of believers.

Of what possible use then can these men and women of the earthly life be to him, even though they call themselves Christians and follow in his steps? Can they add to his righteousness, can they add to his power, will their failure in any direction affect him in any of these things? Consider these Christians: perplexed, troubled, tempted, doubting, despairing, dying, they fill the earth every day with their lamentations and weaknesses. Of what possible use can these be to him except to develop more intensely his pity; what effect can they have upon him except to deepen his conviction of their helplessness?

Come with me yonder into that old cathedral pile. The foundation stone was sunken in a far forgotten century. The dust upon its floor is the dust of the buried kings and queens beneath it. The very atmosphere is full of the lingering breath of priest and poet,

warrior and statesman of the long ago; old days and
old times with high deeds and plaintive cryings, with
tears of penitents and pomp of ritual have trodden
through these foot-worn aisles. Yonder from that
western window the light of a dying day streams through
the transfigured faces of the painted saints, burns crimson and gold through their illuminated garments, and
falls in slanting lines upon the dust-covered organ, flings
its gleams into the deep recesses behind the reedy
trumpets, and mingles its amber with the dark yellow of
the untouched keys. But all is silent in that instrument
once consecrated to noblest harmonies.

Two men enter.

They have journeyed together for a day along the
white winding roads of the vine-clad country. One is
strong, vigorous, full of the joy and brutality of unbroken life. The other is neither young nor old, neither
strong nor weak, not a phantom it is true, yet as soft
and noiseless as the waning light about him; to his companion, nevertheless, he is but a dim and shadowy figure,
a man of years and growing weakness. They have been
companions since the morning, and the stronger of the
two has looked with a feeling of pity half akin to contempt upon the other. No sooner are they across the
threshold of the building than the shadowy traveller
passes straight up the time-worn aisle and without a
moment's hesitation sits him down before the ancient
key-board. He touches it. There is a low, sweet mur-
mur, like a shiver of anticipated harmony. The notes
mingle, multiply, expand. The tone rises, the deeper
notes swell underneath as if to bear it up, and as it rises
and accentuates itself into ten thousand shades of expression, each more exquisite than the other, all the

vocabulary of sound seems to utter itself in rhythm and cry out encouragement to every hesitating harmony; the profounder billows of the organ hear the invitation and roll wave on wave of answering sound beneath, as when the sea breaks on a rock-bound shore and every rock multiplies the thunderous swell. On sweeps the refrain till the listener feels his heart torn out of him. The tears are on his face, joy and anguish commingled are in his soul. The sunlight seems to turn to deeper gold on the faces of the painted saints, every atom of dust rises and gathers into a cloud of glory, while arch, transept and nave, seem to float in a flood of light, of song, and of infinite gladness.

The organ had waited through the ages for its master; the master had waited for his organ.

Oh, this strange human soul, was there ever an organ like it? Did organ, century built, ever have such stops, such chords, such keys: laughter and tears, hope and despair, joy and sorrow?

And none could play it; and the day was dying, the day of time. But in the fading light God's Son bent down from Heaven and touched it. There at Pentecost, there at Damascus, there at Patmos, and on through the ages has continued to touch it till he has evoked from this human soul the wondrous notes of faith, of hope, of love and all glad things divine; by these human lives has so poured forth the pent-up floods, the unspeakable dialects and accents of divine harmony, that earth has looked on and listened in amaze. Man was built for Christ and needs him. Christ was built for man and needs him, needs him as the means by which to utter himself in life's noblest harmonies.

But now I would have you contemplate another scene.

It is under a hot eastern sky. In the narrow streets of the city men are dying of thirst. In the madness of that thirst they see the shining of the dew-drops on far-away stretches of meadow land. They hear the gurgle of mountain streams, the plash of falling fountains, and the rush of rivers between their full fed banks. The vision and the sounds mock them as they die.

But behold again.

Down the long street one of gentle mien and steady step moves on, and following him scores of willing ones bearing aloft upon their turbaned heads simple earthern jars. These jars are filled with water from the mountain heights where streams break forth in freshness. As the bearers of these jars follow the master, in obedience to his commands they cry, "Water of life, water of life, who will have it?" And now they press the earthern jars to the lips of the dying thirsty ones, and these drink and live, and are glad.

Only earthen vessels filled with sparkling waters for dying thirsty ones.

But everywhere it is true that men are dying of thirst. You may find them on the mountain, by the sea shore, in the town, in the palace, in the hovel, thirsty, unsatisfied, unhappy, heavy hearted, soul burdened, mad with dreams and hopes deferred that make the heart sick.

The Master would take the earthen vessels whom he calls his disciples, fill them with the water of life, send them to the dying, and in his name bid them give the thirsty ones to drink. Yes, through these vessels weak and frail, he would communicate himself. By their tears and sympathies, by all their common humanity, he would touch a dying world and bless it everywhere.

Once more an illustration.

In the olden time a worker in gold consecrated his days to the chasing and beautifying of a golden vase. He gave his days and years to the work. On this vase in rare and wondrous letters was written deep the name of God; around that name were woven all fair fruits and flowers and gentle forms of life, until it became a wonder in the land. Still he wrought, wrought patiently till the name of God seemed to be the one strange expanded thing beneath foliage, fruit and flowers.

One day they found him dead beside his work. Then was the truth revealed; he had wrought it for the king. The king ordered the body buried with great and splendid rites, but commanded his heart to be preserved and placed in the vessel fashioned with his life, that henceforth that golden vessel bearing in beauty the name of God, might also bear the heart that had loved and wrought it.

Is it too much to say that the Christian is that golden vessel? That the name of God has been written deeply in him? That out of that name unfold the fruit, the flowers, the beauty, and the potentiality of a life of sonship with God? Is it too much to say that the Master has wrought this Christian vessel, that it has cost him everything: Incarnation, earthly sorrow, and yonder cross?

Do you wonder that the King Eternal has commanded that each golden vessel shall evermore bear the heart of him who through life unto death wrought this name upon it? Oh, apart from all symbol, or figure, or fancy, is it hard to see that the Master can use those who call his Father's name upon them? Is it hard to see how he can speak through their lips, weep through their tears, bless by their hands, and with their feet walk the way that leadeth to homes of pain and woe? Is it hard to see that here is the highest, mightiest, and noblest end of a Christian life: to be used of the Master, to be of profit to him, to be to his advantage, to bear him forth in heart beat, to pour him forth in life tide, to translate him in all noblest harmonies?

This then is the relation which the believer should sustain to the Master.

Note finally:

3. The condition upon which the believer may sustain this relationship.

The condition is very simple but strong. He must be "meet." That is worthy, fit, prepared.

Many Christians are not used of the Master. They know it themselves with sad hearts. They are Christians. They believe the Word, they know that Jesus loves them, they pray and testify in his name, but they know, and others know that they are not used by him. The Master has not found them fit for use.

And what is that fitness? No fitness, no preparedness were required to receive the divine name and holy life. What then is the fitness, or the preparation demanded here?

I answer:

First of all if he would be used, the Christian must take *the vessel's place*. And what is that? Is it the place of an activity and energy of its own? I answer no, it is the place of quietness and nothingness, the place of submission to the Master's hand so that he may lift it, put it here and there, high or low, as it may suit him.

Oh, the hard, bitter battle! What piteous lessons to be learned! How again and again have many tried to serve the Master by some native power within and not by his hand without, and have learned at last, through anguish and keenest mortification of human pride, that the power was in the Master's hand and not in the vessel's merit at all.

But more, the vessel must be empty.

Behold, the Master comes to pour into His purchased vessel the ointment of His name. But the vessel is full, the Master turns away and the Christian is left to wonder why he is not used, why the Master does not make him the fragrant bearer of his name. Can you pour into that which is already full? Nay. And this Christian is full, full of cares, full of self's pleasing, self's plans and ways. There is no room in this Christian vessel. Christ is ready, but he cannot pour within; he cannot pour within because the Christian is not ready to receive; he is not fit for the Master's use.

But this is not all. *The vessel must be sanctified.*

Sanctified signifies to set apart, and necessarily in relation to divine things, set apart and devoted to the divine use. The Christian has been set apart and devoted to the use of God by the purchase and the cleansing of the Master's blood, but he must also purge himself, if you want the Master to use you, from persons, things that claim his use apart from the Master's use, and from every vessel as well as thing of dishonor.

Why should we hide it, or deny it, or fight it? There it is. The Cross, the Red Blood, Regeneration. That is what all these mean. They mean that we are called to live a life separate from the worldly throng, from its dusty ways and tracks of sin. You must separate yourself, if you want the Master to use you, from persons, places, and things, that in the slightest degre shut him out, weaken the touch of his hand upon you, or loosen your grasp in his; anything that hinders you even for a moment is being used of him.

Devoted to Christ. That is the fitness. That is the preparation. Not being learned in all things, not having genius, or wealth, or power. Oh no, strange, wonderful, paradox of paradoxes, your fitness, your preparedness for every good work in the Master's name, is just giving yourself up to him and saying:

"Lord, behold me as I am. Just as I am, I place myself in thy hand to use."

That is all. Empty and in his hand.

Repeat that, I pray you, far and wide, as the *sine qua non* of Christian life, as the secret of meetness for the Master's use.

"Empty and in His hand."

Is He using you?

No.

You can answer why.

The answer is: "I am filled with something beside Christ."

Are you satisfied? Can you be content? Do you not want him to use you, to pour sweet music through you, through you to quench the thirsty lip and inward fire, through you to flash forth in beauty and in fragrant fruitage the glory of the Father's name?

Will you let him use you? Will you sing in your soul to-day in glad and happy strain:

"Sanctified and meet for the Master's use."

And shall the upper gladness let fall its rhythmic welcome and echo back:

"Behold, a vessel sanctified and meet for the Master's use."

REV. D. H. DOLMAN, M.A.

Simple Talks on the Holy Spirit

With Introduction by James M. Gray, D.D., President, Moody Bible Institute, Chicago. $1.50

Plain, interpretive and evangelistic talks on the effect and work of the Holy Spirit as a gift offered to every Christian, with a stirring appeal for everyone's acceptance of the gift. So elementary as to be easily understood by the youngest Christian, yet so profound and comprehensive as to prove satisfying to doubt, and inspiring to faith.

ORRIN P. GIFFORD, D.D.

The Shadow of the Rock

And Other Addresses. $1.25

Evangelical, evangelistic and attuned both to the spirit of to-day and to the heart of the Scripture. The sermons abound in vivid illustrations fresh from daily experience. Significant titles are these: "The Great Adventure," "Seeking and Saving," "Having and Giving," "God's Good Will" and "Till He Comes."

NEAL L. ANDERSON, D.D.

*Minister, Independent Presbyterian Church,
Savannah, Ga.*

God's World and Word

Addresses for To-day. $1.25

"A new book of unusual timeliness and interest. The messages are by one whose convictions are immovably anchored in the truth of God's Word, but whose mind is open to the changes through which humanity is passing."
—*Christian Observer*.

WILLIAM CARTER, Ph.D., D.D.

The Other Side of the Door

With Introduction by S. Parkes Cadman, D.D., President, Federal Council of Churches. $1.50

A distinctly novel note is struck by Dr. Carter. Here are addresses on youth, maturity, womanhood, and specifically on redemption of the soul and the life in Christ Jesus. Such striking titles as "Milestones on the Way to God," "Tadmar in the Wilderness," "The Pillars of the Earth."—*Watchman Examiner*.

JOHN L. BRANDT, LL.D.

Great Bible Questions

A Score of Sermons on Interrogatory Texts.
$2.00

"The method employs illustration, biographical reference and a division of the subject in such measure as to make the messages grippingly interesting and not difficult to retain in thought. Fervor and earnestness mark each of them."—*Moody Bible Institute Monthly*.

G. CAMPBELL MORGAN, D.D.

The Gospel According to Mark

$2.50

Dr. Morgan's latest work is designed as a handbook for the reader who desires a true understanding of the earliest extant record of the earthly life of Jesus, the Gospel of Mark. Like Dr. Morgan's great book on "The Acts of the Apostles," this new volume is at the same time an exposition and an exegesis; it throws an abundance of light on the outward expression and the inner meaning of Mark's words. The International Sunday School lessons for the first half of 1928 being on Mark's Gospel, this is an extremely timely volume.

HENRY T. SELL, D.D.

Studies of Great Bible Cities

With Diagram. Paper, net, 50; cloth, net, 75c

The new volume in Sell's *Bible Study Textbooks* deals with the great cities around which flowed strong currents of Bible life and history portrayed here as they were at the height of their glory. A leading feature of the book is an illuminating chapter on "City Life in Olden Times." Real light is shed on the problem of urban life, a great problem both in olden times and to-day. Thus, to students of home missions, foreign missions, sociology and the Bible, this new book by Dr. Sell has decided significance.

CLARENCE E. MACARTNEY, D.D.

Parables of the Old Testament

Revised and enlarged, $1.50

A new revised and enlarged edition of Dr. Macartney's helpful work of which the *Baptist Standard* said: "This is a unique and splendid little volume. It leaves the beaten track and gives the reader 'something different.' If the preacher's energies are wearing down, let him read it. So of the Sunday School teacher and the B. Y. P. U., and B. W. M. W.

WILLIAM EVANS, D.D.

The Book of Genesis

The first section from *"The Pentateuch"* in the series *Through the Bible, Book by Book.*   75c

"Whether for individual study or for use in class-work the direction and suggestion afforded here, if used Bible in hand, will tend to a thorough mastery of Genesis."—*Sunday School Times.*

JAMES I. VANCE, D.D.
Author of "God's Open," "Being a Preacher," Etc.

Love Trails of the Long Ago
Love Stories of Bible Men and Women. $1.50

Some of the subjects introduced are Vashti, Eve, Zipporah, Jephthæ, Rebekah, David, Delilah and Mary of Bethlehem, and the supreme love between Jesus and all mankind. Here is an exceedingly attractive gift book, and it is also full of suggestive value to preachers, as well as to Bible readers generally.

WILLIAM P. MERRILL, D.D.
Pastor, Brick Presbyterian Church, New York

Prophets of the Dawn
Amos, Hosea, Isaiah, Micah. The Beginnings of the Religion of the Spirit. $1.50

A thoughtful and illuminating interpretation. Dr. Merrill has succeeded in making the critical Eighth Century B. C. real and full of suggestions to the crucial Twentieth Century A. D. Here is an unusually appealing volume for layman and minister alike. It is not mere history nor yet exegesis; it is rather an interpretation, invigorated by a vivid but restrained imagination that puts new vitality into the present-day understanding of Old Testament times.

ELMER E. HELMS, D.D.

Men Who Made and Marred History
Studies in Biblical Biography. $1.25

Dr. Helms' wide experience of life, of human nature and of the Bible gained during this long, varied and vigorous ministry, is abundantly reflected in these essays and addresses on great men of Bible days. "The Man Who Gave Us a Start" is Adam, of course, but who is "The Incorruptible Man," or "The Man of Iron," or "A Crooked Man Made Straight"? The series closes appropriately and glowingly with "The Man Pre-Eminent" —Jesus of Nazareth. The volume is one of power and inspiration for every Bible reader and student—minister or layman.

A NEW EDITION
AGNES SLIGH TURNBULL

Far Above Rubies
Heart Stories of Bible Women.
Second Edition. Illustrated, $2.00

Chicago Evening Post: "Here at last are Bible women revealed through the sympathetic, creative imagination of a woman, who with great dramatic sense lifts one out of the present into Bethsaida and Capernaum."